# Consumer Reports®

# Best Baby Products

## EIGHTH EDITION

by Sandra Gordon
& the Editors of CONSUMER REPORTS

CONSUMERS UNION, YONKERS, NEW YORK

## A Special Publication from Consumer Reports

| | |
|---|---|
| **Acting Editor, Special Publications** | Michael Urban |
| **Group Managing Editor** | Nancy Crowfoot |
| **Project Editor** | Greg Daugherty |
| **Coordinating Editors** | Sue Byrne, Merideth Mergel |
| **Design Manager** | Rosemary Simmons |
| **Contributing Art Directors** | Trish Gogarty, Antonio Mora |
| **Medical Editor** | Marvin Lipman, M.D. |
| **Health Research Manager** | Chris Hendel |
| **Contributing Copy Editor** | Tom Dixon |
| **Production** | Charlene Bianculli |
| **Technology Specialist** | Jennifer Dixon |
| **Special Publications Staff** | Joan Daviet |

## Consumer Reports

| | |
|---|---|
| **Editor/Senior Director** | Margot Slade |
| **Acting Director, Editorial Operations/ Director, Publishing Operations** | David Fox |
| **Design Director** | George Arthur |
| **Managing Art Director** | Tim LaPalme |
| **Product Manager** | Carol Lappin |
| **Manufacturing & Distribution** | Ann Urban |
| **Vice President and Technical Director** | Jeffrey A. Asher |
| **Director, Consumer Sciences** | Geoffrey Martin |
| **Senior Project Leader** | Joan Muratore |
| **Project Leader** | Werner Freitag |

## Consumers Union

| | |
|---|---|
| **President** | James A. Guest |
| **Executive Vice President** | Joel Gurin |
| **Senior Vice President, Technical Policy** | R. David Pittle |

Pediatric drug information © 2004 Thomson MICROMEDEX. All rights reserved.

First printing, February 2004
Copyright © 2004 by Consumers Union of United States, Inc., Yonkers, N.Y. 10703.
Published by Consumers Union of United States, Inc., Yonkers, N.Y. 10703.
All rights reserved, including the right of reproduction in whole or in
part in any form.
ISBN: 0-89043-986-9
Manufactured in the United States of America.

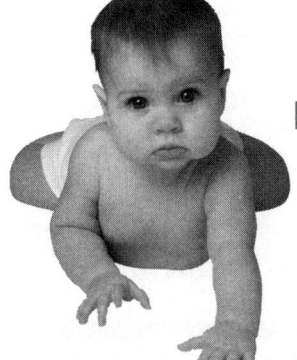

# ABC

# Contents

## Introduction

Welcome! Here's how to use this book
to get the best values and safest products
for your new baby ..................................................9

## A-to-Z Guide

# ABC

# Contents

## Special Reference Section

# About the Author

**Sandra Gordon** is the author of several books, including *The Shy Single* (Rodale Press), *The Aging Eye* (Simon & Schuster), and *The 30 Secrets of the World's Healthiest Cuisines* (John Wiley & Sons).

In addition, Sandra frequently writes for consumer magazines, including *Child, Parents, Parents Expecting, American Baby, More, Self, Redbook, Shape, Family Circle, Fitness, Cooking Light, Woman's Day, Parenting,* and *Fit Pregnancy.* Sandra also provides content for health-related Web sites and is a feature writer for the monthly corporate health magazine *Vitality.*

Formerly, Sandra was a health writer for the HIP Health Plan of New York, a New York City-based health maintenance organization. She started her career as an assistant food editor at *Glamour.*

A member of the American Society of Journalists and Authors, the Authors Guild, the International Association of Business Communicators, and the American Medical Writers Association, Sandra earned a B.A. in English from the University of Nebraska. She lives in Connecticut with her husband and daughters.

# Welcome!

## How to use this book to get the best values and safest products

Congratulations. You've got a new baby (or babies!) on the way. Of course, you'll want to welcome your offspring into the world not just with joy and love, but with a secure and nurturing environment. You've come to the right place. *Consumer Reports Best Baby Products* can help you do just that.

One of the first things you'll discover as a new parent is that this stage of life comes with many trappings: pacifiers, bottles, breast pumps, strollers, car seats, bouncers, cribs, swings, infant carriers, play yards, and baby gates—not to mention diapers, diapers, and more diapers. Step into any baby product store in the U.S. and you're apt to be overwhelmed. Indeed, baby products are a multibillion-dollar industry, with hundreds of products introduced each year. Does your baby really need all that "stuff?" The answer is no. Some things are necessary; others, as cute as they may be, are purely optional. In

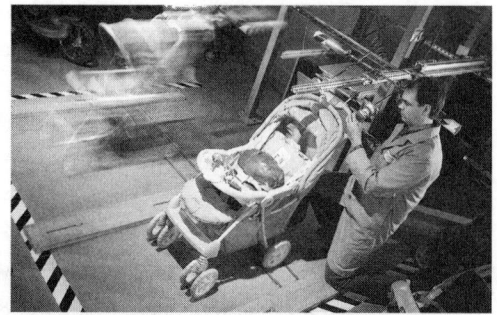

To test for durability, we put a 40-pound weight in each stroller then used a machine to walk it over the equivalent of 50 miles of bumpy pavement.

*Best Baby Products* we'll help you determine which is which and also advise you on brands and models.

*Best Baby Products* comes to you from CONSUMER REPORTS, the comprehensive source of unbiased advice about products and services, health, and personal finance, published by the nonprofit Consumers Union. Since 1936, the mission of Consumers Union has been to test products, inform the public, and protect consumers. We accept no advertising and buy all the products we test.

Our engineers, market analysts, and editors attend trade shows, read industry publications, and visit stores to spot the latest products and trends. The market analysts query manufacturers about their product lines and update databases of model information. Then staff shoppers anonymously visit dozens of stores or go online to buy the selected models, just as you would. While shopping for a baby can certainly be fun, we take it very seriously because, let's face it, there's nothing more precious than your newborn.

The products we purchase are put to the test in CONSUMER REPORTS' own labs in Yonkers, N.Y., or at a specialized outside laboratory under the direction of our engineers (as is the case with the crash testing of car seats). With baby gear, safety is always a key consideration, followed by convenience and usability. The knowledge of our baby-products experts—based on unbiased, side-by-side testing—can guide you in your search for safe products. *Best Baby Products* can also help you find the best value and tell you when a bigger price tag means greater quality—and when it doesn't. We'll even help you decide when you need to buy new, and when used (or hand-me down) is OK.

Although we're a research-based organization, we recognize that baby shopping isn't all science. Throughout this book we'll also offer comments from subscribers to our Web site, *www.Consumer Reports.org,* about what baby products worked for them, based on their lifestyles and other circumstances. While those comments may not be backed up by the same rigorous testing as the products we rate, you may find them useful in making your own decisions.

## How This Book Can Help

Organized in a handy A-to-Z format, *Best Baby Products* covers a wide range of essential baby (and parent) gear. Toward the back of the book, you'll find a special reference section with our Brand Locator for many major baby-products manufacturers. You'll also find a list of recent product recalls, a guide to the most commonly prescribed medications for babies, and a special bonus chapter on smart money moves for new parents.

The baby products marketplace is always changing, of course. New models are frequently introduced and old ones

**Stroller brakes are tested on this special ramp.**

discontinued. We've tried to make sure the products listed throughout this book will be available at the time of publication and that the prices reflect what you'll pay. But for the most recent product and pricing information available, be sure to also take advantage of your free 30-day subscription to Consumer Reports Online. If you haven't already registered for your free month, go to *www.ConsumerReports .org/babyOffer* and enter code 22726. With this book and the Web, you'll be set to go.

## Tuning In to the Trends

Several key trends are influencing the kinds of baby products you'll see in stores, in catalogs, and on the Web right now. Here's a quick peek:

**More functional designs.** Studying the preferences of parents, many manufacturers have decided that functionality is essential to sales success. And they're right. For the most part, the best products are not only safe, they're durable, user-friendly, and tailored to today's new-parent lifestyle. Consider strollers, for instance. Now that parents tote their children practically everywhere, there are strollers for all occasions, tastes, and budgets—from $20 umbrella strollers to models that steer more like a Porsche than a pram and are priced upward of $700. Many of the higher-ticket strollers have comfort features such as cup holders for both baby and parent, and outdoorsy or high-tech looks with rugged, fat tires, and suspension frames that supposedly allow your child to ride in bump-free bliss.

High chairs have also gotten in on the functionality act. Many have a height-adjustable seat as well as trays that can be removed and put back with one hand. Some recline so that baby can enjoy a post-meal snooze without having to be moved. Others are designed to grow with your baby, converting through the months and years from an infant high chair to a toddler chair to a computer chair for a teen. It may seem strange to picture your baby using the same chair more than a decade later, but manufacturers say it can happen.

You'll also find bassinets that convert to a crib, then to a toddler bed, then to a junior bed, and finally to two kids' chairs. Are these extended-life products the best long-term value or should you buy single-use products that meet your needs now? This book will help you decide.

**More stylish choices.** Functionality aside, manufacturers have also upped the style ante. From cutesy to sophisticated, you'll find products inspired by popular children's characters and television programs (such as *Dragon Tales* and *Blues Clues)* as well as chic lines that nod more to parents, such as designer diaper carriers that can pose as a handbag or briefcase and strollers whose look mimics SUVs, inviting a phenomenon known as "stroller envy."

What kind of "style statement" do you want to make? What "look" can you live with for several months or even years? Or does any of that even matter to you? These aesthetic questions are something to consider before and during your shopping trips because they can play a big role in the price of many products.

**Greater attention to safety.** Safety is a major concern among product manufacturers today, and safer designs continue to evolve.

## WHAT'S THAT SEAL MEAN?

The Juvenile Products Manufacturers Association (JPMA), which includes more than 400 companies that make and/or import baby products, administers a program that certifies manufacturers whose products meet voluntary safety standards. This certification means the company designed and built the product with the safety standards in mind and had it tested by an independent laboratory. The JPMA Certification program currently covers bath seats, carriages and strollers, full-size and non-full-size cribs, gates and enclosures, hand-held infant carriers, handles on infant car seats, high chairs, infant bouncers, infant swings, play yards, portable hook-on chairs, stationary activity centers, toddler beds, and walkers. For more information about products with the JPMA Certification Seal, visit *www.jpma.org*.

Other children's products may be certified by an independent laboratory to meet safety standards, or a company may self-certify that its product meets the safety standards. Those products may not be less safe than products certified under the JPMA program, but for consumers to have some guidance, the JPMA seal is of great help.

Products marketed specifically for babies are generally safe, partly because of government safety regulations. Agencies involved in ensuring safe products include:

• The Consumer Product Safety Commission *(www.cpsc.gov)*. It regulates baby equipment and oversees recalls. It enforces general rules that apply to most product categories as well as mandatory standards for a few specific categories, such as cribs and clothing.

• The U.S. Department of Transportation's National Highway Traffic Safety Administration *(www.nhtsa.gov)*. It oversees mandatory safety standards related to the crash performance of cars seats.

• The U.S. Food and Drug Administration *(www.fda.gov)*. It is responsible for the safety of baby formula and most baby food, while the U.S. Department of Agriculture *(www.usda.gov)* monitors baby food containing meat.

Products are approved for safety or certified to meet certain requirements through a system of standards, some mandated by federal regulation, some followed voluntarily by manufacturers. Federal agencies, industry groups, and consumer organizations such as Consumers Union, publisher of CONSUMER REPORTS, work to refine those standards on a regular basis.

CONSUMER REPORTS regularly tests key items of baby equipment, including cribs, crib mattresses, strollers, car seats, infant carriers, play yards, gates, toys, and baby monitors. We often hold them to more rigorous standards than the government requires or that they need to be certified to the voluntary standards. You'll find results of our safety tests in specific chapters throughout *Best Baby Products*.

## Money-Saving Strategies

A new baby can take a surprisingly big bite out of your budget. Here are some ways to save:

**Take advantage of freebies and coupons.** If you don't mind getting your name on mailing lists, call the toll-free customer-service lines or register at the Web sites of formula, baby-food, and disposable-diaper companies for their parenting newsletters and new-parent programs, including coupons and free samples. Even if you don't register, you may get them anyway. Somehow, when you have a new baby, word gets out.

**Consider a discount club membership.** At places like Costco or Sam's Club, you'll reap decent discounts on everyday items you'll

# New Baby Basics

## A master list for new moms and dads

Here's a checklist of what you should have on hand before your baby arrives. Many of these products have their own chapters in this book. For others covered in this book, we've indicated the chapters where the relevant advice can be found.

### Tooling Around
_____**Car seat.**
_____**Stroller.**

### Beds and Linens
_____**Crib.**
_____**Crib mattress.**
_____**Bassinet/cradle** (if you don't want to put your baby in a crib right away).
_____**Two to three fitted crib sheets.** See Crib Bedding chapter.
_____**Four or more waffle-weave cotton receiving blankets** for swaddling baby. See Crib Bedding chapter.
_____**Two mattress pads.**
_____**One to two waterproof liners** (for crib or bassinet).

### Diaper Duty
_____**Diapers.** Disposable or cloth.
_____**Diaper pail.** (Optional with disposables.)
_____**Diaper bag.**

### Dressing Baby
For advice on the following, see Clothing chapter.
_____**Four sleeping outfits or onesies** (one-piece sleepers), preferably with attached feet.
_____**Six side-snap T-shirts.**
_____**Four to six one-piece undershirts** that snap around the crotch.
_____**A small baby cap** (although the hospital will probably give you one).
_____**Six pairs socks/booties.**

_____**Two to three soft, comfortable daytime outfits.** Get only a few items in newborn size. Then, go for clothing in the 6-month size–your baby will grow into it quickly. But don't buy baby sleepwear that's too big; it's a fire hazard.

_____**Cotton sweater or light jacket.**

## Summer Babies:

_____**Brimmed hat.**

## Winter Babies:

_____**Snowsuit or heavy bunting.**

_____**Heavy stroller blanket.**

_____**Warm knit hat.**

## Feeding Time

If you're planning to breast-feed:

_____**Two or three nursing bras.**

_____**A box of washable or disposable breast pads.**

_____**Breast pump** if you expect to use one.

_____**Four small baby bottles** with newborn nipples for expressed breast milk.

_____**Bottle drying tree.**

_____**Bottle brush.**

_____**Insulated bottle holder for diaper bag** (the hospital may give you one).

_____**Three packs of cloth diapers** or burp cloths.

If you're planning to bottle-feed:

_____**Six 4- to 5-ounce bottles**, plus nipples, rings, and a dishwasher basket if you use a dishwasher.

## Bathing/Grooming

_____**Three soft hooded towels.**

_____**Two packs of baby washcloths.**

_____ **Baby body wash that doubles as shampoo.**

_____**Pair of blunt-tip scissors** or baby-sized nail clippers.

_____**Zinc-oxide-based diaper rash ointment.**

_____**Infant bathtub.**

_____**Soft brush and comb.**

_____**Mild laundry detergent.**

## Medicine Chest Essentials

_____**A pain-and-fever reducer** recommended by your baby's doctor, such as Infant's Tylenol.

_____**Cotton pads/swabs.**

_____**Nasal aspirator.**

_____**Digital thermometer.**

_____**Rubbing alcohol.**

_____**Petroleum jelly.**

## Keeping Baby Happy

_____**Pacifiers.**

## Extras: Nice But Optional

_____**Monitor.**

_____**Changing table.**

_____**A rocker or glider.**

_____**Soft carrier.**

_____**Swing.**

## THINK BIG

**W**hen you're buying baby gear (or making your wish list for a gift registry or baby shower), focus first on major items such as a crib, car seat, or stroller. They require the most time and effort. Then work your way down to smaller things like bottles, pacifiers, diaper pails, and the like. Or, if your energy's zapped, come back another day to tackle those items.

soon be using a lot of such as disposable diapers, baby wipes, and laundry detergent.

**Buy as baby grows.** Aside from the basics listed earlier in this chapter, hold off on buying baby products until you're sure you'll need a particular item. The wait-and-see approach can save you money. "We've found that we don't need to buy everything," says Beth Klingner of Pleasantville, N.Y., mother of 1-year-old Ben. "Some items have been loaned to us by generous friends and other items just don't seem that necessary now that we see what our baby's needs are."

**Shop around.** Prices can vary from one shopping venue to another, sometimes dramatically. Megastores and discount chains such as Baby Superstore, Babies "R" Us, Buy Buy Baby, Kmart, Sears, Target, Toys "R" Us, and Wal-Mart often have the lowest prices, although not always the largest selection. For personal attention and more informed sales help, smaller stores are a better bet, although keep in mind that salespeople may have an incentive to push their most expensive wares. And beware the emotional pull of lines like "But it's for your baby" or "It's not every day that you have a baby." Unless you're on your guard, it's easy to be persuaded to unwittingly spend, spend, spend.

**Watch for sales.** Toys "R" Us, Babies "R" Us, and Buy Buy Baby stores, for example, routinely put out newspaper inserts with savings of up to 20 percent or more for brand-name baby items.

**Go online.** Web shopping can be a convenient way to find the information you need about baby products and services and to make purchases—all without having to pack up your baby and the rest of your family and troop from store to store. Many baby and parent Web sites have online stores that offer good savings, especially at sale time, and periodically throw in free shipping.

**But watch your shipping costs when buying online.** They can sometimes negate any savings—and then some.

**Consider buying used.** Baby clothes, bedding, and toys can sometimes be found in thrift stores, online, and at yard sales at a small fraction of their original retail prices. "Since babies grow so fast, I bought a lot of inexpensive baby clothes on eBay *(www.ebay.com)* and other online stores, all new or in gently used condition," says Joyce Medina of Bakersfield, Calif., mother of 7-year-old Zerick. But some items such as car seats should always be purchased new to make sure they comply with the latest safety requirements and have no hidden flaws.

**Ask about return policies.** A store's return policies can make the difference between being a satisfied customer and finding yourself stuck with something you don't want or can't use. So be sure to inquire. It's not unusual for a store to allow returns only 30 days after a purchase, which won't help if you're shopping well before your baby arrives.

**Weigh warranties.** Manufacturers and retailers will often replace returned goods that have clear design or manufacturing defects. Hold on to warranty information so you can refer to it if there's a problem. You may also find a warranty being used as a sales tool. Some less expensive but adequately firm baby mattresses, for example, offer no warranties, while top-of-the-line models may have a "lifetime guarantee." That may be protection you don't need to pay for, considering that the typical use of a baby mattress is about two years per baby.

## Registering

Especially if you're a first-time parent, you may receive many baby

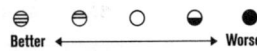

# RATING THE WEB SITES

*ConsumerReports.org* regularly evaluates Web sites to see how well they deliver the goods. Here's our latest e-Ratings of several major baby product sites:

**Babiesrus.com**
(at Amazon.com)
This easy-to-use site offers a wide selection of baby products. Lots of extras, including a gift registry, gift finder, checklists, and more make this site stand out. ◒

**babystyle.com**
There's a wide range of information and advice on this site, with much of it oriented toward keeping a new mom feeling stylish. The search feature is good. Unlike other sites in this category, we didn't find any product recalls information. ○

**buybuyBABY.com**
The privacy policy is satisfactory, but the customer service is less than adequate. Further, the product selection is limited, and browsing is inefficient. ◐

**RightStart.com**
A less-than-satisfactory privacy policy. There is, however, a live help feature and a large selection of baby products. ○

## OFFBEAT GIFTS FOR NEW PARENTS

**I**f you're the lucky person who already has everything—maybe this isn't your first child or you've already had more than one shower—here are several gift ideas to toss out there for well-meaning friends and relatives. Also keep them in mind when you're on the giving end again.

* Diaper service (where available) for the first month. For cloth-diaper users, this will be a big and welcome help.
* Cloth-diapering system. Again, for parents taking the cloth route, these diaper-and-cover combos are convenient.
* A personal chef for a day or a week. Having someone else do the cooking can give new parents a much-needed break. For more information contact the American Personal Chef Association at *www.personalchef.com*.
* A post-partum doula. Doulas are trained to provide emotional, physical, and educational support for women and their families soon after childbirth. For more information and to locate a doula in your area, log onto the Web site for Doulas of North America at *www.dona.org*.
* A gift certificate from a local day spa. It will let the new parent enjoy some pampering for a change.

items as gifts. To take the guesswork out of giving for your friends and family, consider registering at baby specialty shops and chain stores, online or in person. If you're having a baby shower, let your shower hostess know so she can pass the information along to guests.

Signing up with a registry can help you avoid duplicate or unwanted gifts and may get you coupons and other money-saving offers. Still, be aware that the information you provide when you register may be sold to other companies for marketing purposes.

When registering, our advice is to request practical items from the New Baby Basics checklist, earlier in this chapter. Be as specific as possible, including model numbers and colors. If you get things you didn't ask for and are not sure you'll use, don't be afraid to take them back. You can always use the store credit later, when the need for specific items arises (and it will).

**CHAPTER**

# 1

# Autos
## Kid-Friendly Vehicles

Whether you're in the market for a new car or your baby's birth leads you to re-evaluate your auto options, here's good news. With more than 200 models currently on sale in the U.S., there's no shortage of vehicles that can serve as a family car.

But choosing the best one for your needs depends on a number of variables, including the size of your family, the age of all your kids, and the types of activ-

**Honda Accord**

ities in which you participate. "Finding the right family vehicle doesn't have to be a difficult or long process if you invest some time to research your options before you go out shopping," says David Champion, the director of CONSUMER REPORTS' Auto Test Facility.

Can you get by with a sedan, or do you need the extra passenger space of a minivan or a sport-utility vehicle? That, of course, is the $18,000 to $40,000 question. "Parents need to think about how they'll be using the vehicle, what type of cargo they intend to carry, and how their needs may change during the years they own the vehicle," Champion says.

## Shopping Secrets

In general, focus on vehicles with a roomy and versatile interior, plenty of cargo space, ease of access, and windows that make it easy for kids to look outside. "If they can see what's going on, kids are much happier," Champion says. "If they can't look out the window, that can trigger boredom and bickering among siblings." Four-door sedans and wagons are fine for families with one or two children. Bigger families, or those using the vehicle for long trips, should consider a minivan or SUV with a larger cargo area and greater seating capacity. All minivans and a growing number of SUVs can seat seven passengers, and some accommodate eight.

Minivans provide convenient entry through sliding side doors, easy-to-access cargo areas, and good outward views, making them an excellent choice for families.

SUVs offer roomy interiors and four- or all-wheel-drive systems to better handle bad weather and unpaved roads. But young children may have a tough time getting into larger SUVs because these vehicles sit high off the ground. Loading groceries, strollers, and other items into the cargo area of a large SUV may be difficult for the same reason. Remember, too, that taller SUVs have a higher center of gravity, which makes them more top-heavy and more susceptible to rolling over than lower vehicles.

The trend toward car-based SUVs has provided a greater range of choices, including models that are more family-appropriate such as the Honda Pilot and the Subaru Forester.

## What Kind of Car Should You Buy?

To zero in on a vehicle that's right for your family, consider these questions:

**How many people will you be carrying?** If you have one or two children, a small or midsized sedan should do, while saving you money and offering better fuel economy than a larger vehicle. A roomier choice is a minivan or a seven-passenger wagon or SUV. All seven-passenger vehicles include a third-row seat that can be removed or folded down when not in use. Third seats in wagons typically face rearward and are best suited for children.

**How old are your children?** Plan ahead. Young children may not need much room now, but if you plan to keep your vehicle for a number of years, bear in mind that they'll grow. If you have older children, consider getting a car that will be easy to handle and control as they learn to drive. Small and midsized sedans and wagons are usually good choices; larger vehicles are harder to maneuver, and taller ones can be difficult to handle.

**How much cargo space do you need?** The trunk of a sedan may provide enough cargo room for smaller families. A vehicle with more cargo space may be a better choice for larger families or those who travel frequently, are involved in outdoor activities requiring lots of gear, or who need extra room for carrying supplies. Depending on your cargo needs, your choices will range from small wagons to extended-length minivans to large SUVs.

**How adaptable is the vehicle?** Does the rear seat fold down? If so, is it a split design that lets one side fold separately from the other? Can the front passenger seat fold down to accommodate long items? If you're considering a seven-passenger vehicle, check to see if the third-row seat folds flat or has to be removed from the vehicle to enlarge cargo capacity, which can be an inconvenience. Remember that vehicles that sit lower to the ground are easier to load and unload.

**What conditions will you be driving in?** If you'll be driving in rain and very light snow, a two-wheel drive vehicle will work fine. Front-wheel drive with traction control is the optimal 2WD configuration for driving in slippery conditions. All-wheel drive (AWD) provides an additional margin of safety and is a plus for most normal snow conditions or for traveling on dirt roads without high rocks, deep sand, or steep inclines. If you're likely to be driving in places where you'll encounter more severe conditions, you should opt for a four-wheel-drive vehicle with low-range gearing. If you drive on a lot of snow and ice, switching to a set of winter tires will provide additional grip and safety no matter what type of vehicle you have.

**How important is fuel economy?** As a general rule, the larger the vehicle, the lower the fuel economy. Small, lightweight sedans typically get the best mileage, while heavy SUVs get the worst. If you need more cargo room than a sedan can provide, consider a wagon. Some provide as much usable cargo space as an SUV, but they usually get better fuel economy.

**What safety equipment is included?** By law, every new passenger vehicle comes equipped with dual front air bags. But some sophisticated systems have occupant sensors to determine if the air bag should deploy and at what strength. An increasing number of vehicles have head-protection air bags that deploy to protect occupants in both the front and rear seats. In general, the safest place to put an infant car seat is in the center rear seat of the automobile, regardless of whether your car is equipped with air bags. For information on using an infant car seat in a car with air bags, see Chapter 11.

A feature called stability control is highly recommended by our auto experts, particularly on SUVs. It's designed to help keep the vehicle under control and on its path during cornering and prevent it from sliding or skidding. On SUVs, stability control can help prevent the vehicle from getting into a situation that could lead to a rollover.

In models with power windows, pay particular attention to the type of switch. Children leaning out of a window have choked themselves by accidentally kneeling or stepping on the window switch, causing the glass to move up forcefully. Windows operated by a toggle (which is pushed forward and rearward to operate the window) or a rocker switch (which is pushed down in the front and rear to raise and lower the glass) are easier for a child to inadvertently activate. Lever switches (which must be pulled up to raise the glass) and those mounted vertically or on an upswept armrest are harder to activate by accident.

## Vehicle Picks

In choosing the best family vehicles, CONSUMER REPORTS looks at a range of factors, including performance, comfort, ease of access, safety, reliability, roominess, and fuel economy. Here are our picks in several categories. (Reminder: For more info on kid-friendly cars and other topics, register for your 30-day subscription to CONSUMER REPORTS Online at *www.ConsumerReports.org/babyOffer* and enter code 22726.)

### Best Family Sedan: Honda Accord

An excellent sedan choice for families is the Honda Accord. Handling is more agile and the ride is steadier and more compliant than the previous model. The cabin is roomy and controls are intuitive. It's quieter, though less so than the Toyota Camry and Volkswagen Passat. Antilock brakes (ABS) are standard. The new five-speed automatic transmission shifts very smoothly and responsively. The base four-cylinder engine is smoother than many V6s. Head-protection air bags come only on the top-line EX V6. The V6 model is very quick and relatively fuel efficient. Touches such as the ability to open all windows through the key fob are nice. Crash-test results are impressive.

### Best Small Sedan: **Honda Civic**

Good performance, fuel economy, and interior space help make the Civic one of our top picks. The standard engine is a sprightly 1.7-liter, 115-hp Four, while the EX has a 127-hp version, and the HX has a fuel-efficient lean-burn engine. The automatic works very well. Handling is fairly nimble, though not quite as agile as that of the Ford Focus. The ride is a bit too firm, and road noise is pronounced. The control layout is a model of clarity with excellent fit and finish. Good crash-test results are another plus. The 160-hp Si drives similarly. The gasoline/electric Hybrid also performs like a regular Civic, though slower, and averaged 36 mpg in CR tests with a CVT.

### Best SUV: **Honda Pilot**

The Honda Pilot manages to combine the best of a wagon, SUV, and minivan at an affordable price. It's a car-based SUV that's similar to the upscale Acura MDX. The Pilot is a bit roomier, though, and less costly. It shares the MDX's smooth, powerful V6, five-speed automatic transmission, and full-time all-wheel-drive system. The Pilot delivers spirited performance yet respectable fuel economy, a comfortable ride, and secure, responsive handling. Pronounced road noise was our only qualm. The standard 50/50 split third-row seat folds neatly into the floor, creating ample cargo space. Access is easy, and fit and finish are impeccable. Crash-test results are impressive.

### Best Minivan: **Toyota Sienna**

The Toyota Sienna is our top-rated minivan and shows how far minivans have progressed. It's roomier than the previous model, with a new, powerful and fuel-efficient 3.3-liter V6 engine, a smooth five-speed automatic transmission, and optional all-wheel drive. The flexible interior features a 60/40-split rear seat that folds flat into the floor and incorporates many convenient features from other vehicles, such as a wide-angle rear-view mirror for the interior and sliding doors with retractable

windows. It has the most comfortable and quiet ride of any minivan and possesses responsive, secure, and predictable handling, though the steering is a bit light.

### Best Small Wagon: Pontiac Vibe

The Pontiac Vibe is a stylish small wagon that's virtually the same as the Toyota Matrix. It's available with either front- or all-wheel drive, both based on the Toyota Corolla. The base 1.8-liter four-cylinder engine drones loudly and performs modestly. GT models use a stronger version of this engine and come only with a six-speed manual transmission. Handling is fairly nimble, and the ride is compliant if a little jittery. Access is very easy, and the rear seat is quite roomy. The driving position is only so-so. The optional all-wheel-drive system (available only with the automatic transmission) works well but hurts acceleration and fuel economy. Folding the rear seats creates a large, flat load floor. Overall, this is a sensible alternative to a small SUV.

### Best Small SUV: Subaru Forester

The Subaru Forester is our top-rated small SUV. This car-based model is essentially a tall, all-wheel-drive wagon. It rides compliantly and handles well, with good steering feel. Braking is excellent. The engine provides adequate acceleration, and the optional automatic transmission shifts responsively. Standard all-wheel drive helps in all weather conditions and on the occasional dirt trail. Inside, you'll find lots of useful compartments. The front seats are firm and well shaped, and the rear has been improved slightly. The square cargo space is very usable. The 2.5 X version is an excellent value. Crash-test results are impressive. A new turbo model with 210 hp is also available.

CHAPTER

# 2

# Baby Bottles & Nipples

A-B-C

**E**ven if you breast-feed your baby, you'll likely need bottles—for pumped breast milk or perhaps a supplementary bottle of formula. After your baby turns 1 and is weaned from formula, whole cow's milk—usually delivered by bottle—will be a diet staple (in addition to breast milk, if you like), although you may decide to graduate your baby to a training cup at that point.

Different styles and colors of bottles abound, but your priority should be to find bottles that don't cause excessive spit-up, burping, and gas—and that are easy for your baby to hold and for you to clean.

## What's Available

Your main choices in bottle types are: standard, angle-neck, disposable, and "natural- flow." Both bottles and nipples are constantly being improved to reduce the bane of baby's existence: ingesting air bubbles, which may contribute to colic, spitting up, burping, gas, and the negative effect of suction—fluid in the ear. Bottles are made of clear or semitransparent plastic or glass. You may also see novelty shapes, such as animals or footballs.

The main makers of baby bottles are, in alphabetical order: Ansa, Avent, Dr. Brown's, Evenflo, Gerber, Munchkin, and Playtex. Here's what you have to choose from:

**Angle-neck bottles.** These bottles are bent at the neck, making them easier for you to hold at the correct position. Their shape also causes formula or breast milk to collect at the bottle's nipple end, so your baby is less likely to swallow air. Some have straws inside for getting formula from the base of the bottle, which is supposed to reduce air intake. But the straws can be hard to clean. (You'll need a tiny wire brush, available where baby bottles are sold.) One other downside: Angle-neck bottles can be awkward to fill—you must hold them sideways or use a special funnel to pour in liquid. Price range: $3 to $4.

**Disposables.** With these, a sterilized, disposable plastic pouch, or liner, goes inside a rigid outer holder, called a nurser. The top edge of the liner is stretched over the nurser's rim. You pour in formula or breast milk and hold the liner in place by fastening the lid (a nipple and bottle ring). Price range: $10 to $15 for a starter set with 4- and 8-ounce holders and 10 liners.

**Natural-Flow bottles.** These bottles, made by Dr. Brown's, feature a patented internal strawlike vent system that is inserted into the center of the bottle and that's designed to eliminate air bubbles. Compared with other bubble-reducing bottles, such as angle-neck models, these have an extra piece or two to throw into the dishwasher. Again, the internal straw can be tricky to clean without a specialty wire brush.

## SOME LIKE IT WARM

Formula or breast milk is fine right out of the refrigerator, but many babies prefer it warmed up. The best way to accomplish that is to hold the bottle under a stream of warm water from the faucet or to place it in a bowl of warm water for several minutes. Shaking the bottle gently can help distribute the heat.

For about $30, you can buy an electric bottle warmer, which requires you to fill a chamber with water to produce steam heat. If you want one, look for a model with an on/off button and an automatic shutoff to prevent overheating.

Don't use a microwave to heat formula or breast milk. It can cause uneven hot spots you may not be able to detect. It can also destroy the immunological properties for which breast milk is heralded. And never put disposable bottles in the microwave—the plastic liner could explode when you take it out, possibly scalding both you and your baby.

Still, some parents swear by the system. "My second child never spit up and never had any gas problems whatsoever. I'm convinced it's because of Dr. Brown's," says Nikki Levin of Hickory, N.C., mother of two boys. Prices range from $12 to $16 for Dr. Brown's three-packs and starter kits.

**Standard bottles.** The classic shape with straight sides, these bottles are easy to fill and hold, can be used repeatedly, and allow you to accurately gauge formula amounts. They also offer many more nipple options compared with disposable bottles. Most breast pumps and all baby-bottle warmers are designed solely for use with standard bottles, although with breast pumps, you can easily transfer milk from a standard bottle to a disposable, if you like. There are two sizes of standard bottles: 4 or 5 ounces for infants and 8 or 9 ounces for older babies. Some bottles have compartments that allow you to postpone mixing powdered formula and water until serving time—at which point you simply rotate a portion of the bottle's top to release the powder into the water. Price range: $1 to $5.

**Nipples.** The bottle you choose is important. But sometimes it's the nipple, rather than the bottle, that makes all the difference to your baby. Nipples are sold separately from bottles or included as part of a starter kit. Many are compatible with different brands of bottles. For example, you can use Evenflo nipples on Gerber bottles, which gives you lots of mixing and matching opportunities. The major nipple brands are Avent, Dr. Brown's, Evenflo, Gerber, Munchkin, and Playtex.

Made of latex or silicone, nipples come in several shapes: the traditional "natural" bell, or dome shape, a slightly bulbous "orthodontic" design, or a flattened shape just for disposable bottles. Nipples also typically come in three different flow variations with different-size holes appropriate for your baby's age: slow flow (for babies 0 to 3 months), medium flow (for newborn to 12 months), and fast flow (for babies over 3 months). Dr. Brown's also makes a Preemie Flow nipple for feeding babies born prematurely.

Dr. Brown's and other brands, such as Playtex, also offer a Y-cut nipple for cereal or thick juices, but the American Academy of Pediatrics generally doesn't recommend feeding a baby this way because it can lead to excessive weight gain.

Nipples are usually sold in packs of two or three, ranging in price from $2 to $3.

# Recommendations

There are pluses and minuses with every type of bottle. Disposables spare you the chore of cleaning bottles, but end up costing more than standard or angle-neck bottles because of the need to buy liners (at roughly $7 a shot for a 100-count pack). Novelty shapes are relatively hard to clean and can harbor bacteria in their crevices; our advice is not to buy them. Standard glass bottles, although tough to come by these days, can break, of course, so they're not appropriate once your baby can hold a bottle on his or her own. Natural-flow bottles may indeed prevent gas and such but require a bit more time assembling and cleaning. They can also cost more than other types of bottles.

Your best bet is to choose the kind of bottle that's most comfortable for you and your baby. So experiment with different types and brands. If you're having a baby shower, you might register for a variety of starter kits, which include several bottles of various sizes and nipples in one set. They're often given as gifts. Start with, say, Dr. Brown's and Avent or Playtex, then take it from there. You'll know in due time which bottle your baby prefers. If your baby keeps spitting out a bottle or is especially fussy after eating, keep trying. (Some babies, incidentally, are equal opportunity feeders and will accept any bottle that comes their way.)

If you're predominately and exclusively bottle-feeding, a cache of six bottles in the 4- to 5-ounce size will get you off to a good start. If you're supplementing breast-feeding with only an occasional bottle, you may need only one or two bottles all told.

What nipple to offer your baby is often a matter of trial and error. So buy several different types, if the bottle you choose allows it, and go from there. Ultimately, you'll probably opt for whatever style and

## New-Age Nipples

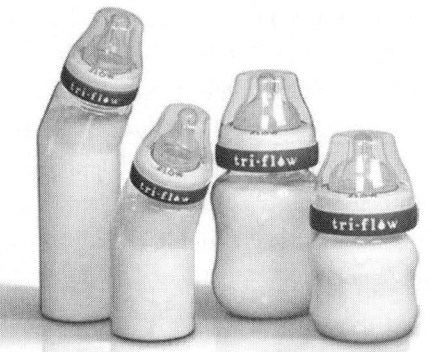

Even nipples have gotten into the high-technology act. Evenflo's Classic, Ultra, and Elite Nurser nipples, for example, come with "Micro Air Vents" that purportedly allow air to escape, reducing the amount baby might swallow. Munchkin's Tri-Flow nipple, at right, allows you to choose from three different flow speeds at the turn of a ring.

# BASIC BOTTLE DO'S AND DON'TS

## DO:

* Wash your hands before preparing your baby's bottle.
* If you're breast-feeding but want to begin to use a bottle, have someone else initially introduce your baby to the bottle at about four weeks into your nursing regimen. (Baby associates mom with breast-feeding and may resist if you try to introduce the bottle yourself.)
* Sterilize your bottles first by washing them in the dishwasher. Or wash bottles and other utensils in hot tap water with dishwashing detergent and then rinse them in hot tap water. Both of those options assume your water is chlorinated. If you have well water or nonchlorinated water or if you simply don't run your dishwasher that often, you'll need to use a sterilizer or boil bottles and utensils in water for 5 to 10 minutes. Avent makes a microwave steam sterilizer ($30 or so) that does the job in about 5 minutes. Boil nipples according to the manufacturer's instructions.
* Wean your baby from a bottle at 12 to 14 months of age. By that time, your baby, believe it or not, will be ready to drink from a training cup. Prolonged bottle use (after 14 months) can cause your baby to consume too much milk and not enough food and may delay the development of feeding skills (not to be confused with table manners, which will come into play in toddlerhood). It can also lead to tooth decay, which is painful and difficult to treat.

## DON'T:

* Give your baby a bottle of milk or formula to suck on during the night or at naptime. The habit can cause baby-bottle tooth decay. The best idea is to give your baby a bottle only at feeding times and not to mix bottles and bed.
* Prop up your baby with a bottle. This feed-yourself practice can lead to choking, ear infections, and tooth decay (yes, again), as well as less cuddling and human contact, which all babies crave.
* Give your baby a bottle to carry around and "nurse." This can lead to tooth decay, drinking too much, and sharing bottles with little friends, increasing the risk of colds and other infections. The contents of the bottle can also spoil, which can cause food-borne illness—aka, bad tummy bugs, which are no fun for your baby or for you.

material of nipple your baby will accept. A nipple should offer some resistance, but not so much that your baby has to struggle to get milk. Generally, younger babies prefer a slower flow, older babies, a faster one; although that's not always the case. In any event, never try to enlarge a nipple hole with a pin. That could cause the nipple to tear and become a choking hazard. Once you settle on a nipple, buy half a dozen so you have plenty on hand.

To avoid the remote possibility of a latex allergy, go with silicone over latex. Note, though, that newborns sometimes prefer latex nipples because of their greater flexibility. Latex nipples tend to swell and crack after two or three months of regular use, so if you choose to use them, discard old ones at that point. (They also tend to whiten when wet, which is harmless.) Saliva, heat, and sunlight can cause them to become sticky and clogged. To clean latex nipples, use hot soapy water and a special bottle brush (available where baby bottles are sold). Don't put latex nipples in the dishwasher.

Silicone nipples, on the other hand, are dishwasher safe. Clear, odorless, taste-free, and heat-resistant, silicone is also less porous than latex, so a silicone nipple may be better at resisting bacteria. Because silicone has a tendency to split and tear, you shouldn't use a bottle brush or nipple brush when cleaning it.

Whichever type of nipple you choose, inspect it regularly. For safety's sake, replace the nipple at the first sign of tearing or cracking. Your baby could accidentally inhale small pieces, which could cause injury. Before the first use, boil nipples according to the manufacturer's directions.

# Baby Food

O nce your baby is 4 to 6 months old, a whole new world of tastes and textures opens up. That's when most babies are ready to start mouthing and chewing "solid" food. It's mushy and messy but also an important and exciting milestone.

How will you know when your baby is ready? If you eat with your baby at meals, you'll begin to notice entrée envy. He or she may reach out and grab for the food you're eating. You'll also be able to spoon-feed your baby without resistance. At about 4 months, most babies  lose the tongue-thrust reflex, the tendency for an infant to push his tongue against the roof of his mouth when a spoon is inserted. Other signs include sitting with support, good head control, and doubled birth weight. Still, your baby has a way to go before he or she is nibbling from your plate.

The first solid food your baby will consume is likely to be a thin gruel consisting of a tablespoon or two of dry infant rice cereal mixed with breast milk or formula. (Breast milk or formula will continue to be on the menu until your baby is age 1 or so and makes the switch to soy or cow's milk.) If your baby doesn't demonstrate an allergic response after three to five days, you can gradually up the ante and make the cereal thicker. At that point you can also begin to introduce other foods, such as oatmeal, barley, and wheat, one at a time to check for allergies.

Typically, when your baby is 6 months or so, you can begin to add mashed fruits, yogurt, vegetables, and meats that you buy in jars or make yourself. Later, you can also try bite-sized foods, such as Cheerios, pieces of bread, avocado, cheese, and meats cut up for easy chewing.

Your pediatrician will be your best source of advice about what to feed your baby and when. At each well-child visit starting at about 4 months, you'll probably get a new list of foods your baby can eat and a list of what to avoid, such as peanut butter. (It's generally a no-no until age 2.) You may also be instructed to introduce foods one at a time to make sure your baby isn't allergic to them.

## Shopping Secrets

**Consider homemade.** Although commercial baby food is convenient, aside from rice cereal, you might want to make it yourself. Baby food is usually simple to prepare. You'll need only a fork to mash such foods as bananas or canned pears. A baby-food grinder (found in baby stores), food processor, or blender lets you process more fibrous foods such as sweet potatoes. Boil, bake, or steam first, then purée them well. (A time-saving tip: Pick one day a week to make a big batch, then freeze individual portions in ice-cube trays.) Add water, breast milk, or formula to smooth the texture, but omit butter, oil, sugar, or salt. Don't use honey as a sweetener for babies under 1 year old. It can harbor bacteria related to botulism.

One other caveat: According to the American Academy of Pediatrics (AAP), fresh beets, turnips, carrots, collard greens, and spinach may contain nitrates, chemicals that are rich in the soil in certain parts of the country and can cause an unusual type of anemia (low red-blood-cell count) in young infants. Unfortunately, you can't screen these vegetables for nitrates yourself by buying organic. For this reason, the AAP recommends buying commercially prepared forms of these foods, especially when your child is an infant. Baby food companies typically screen the produce they buy for nitrates and avoid buying these vegetables in parts of the country where the chemicals have been detected.

**Shop outside the baby-food aisle.** If you compare the prices

## KEEPING BABY'S FOOD SAFE

To keep baby's food free of bacteria and other food-borne pathogens that can cause illness:

* Wash your hands with soap and water before handling baby food or preparing formula. Not only will you be keeping your baby safe, you'll be less likely to get sick yourself.
* Don't feed your baby from the jar (or yogurt container) and then put the uneaten portion back in the refrigerator for another time. Harmful bacteria from your baby's mouth can grow and multiply in the jar. If your baby is likely to eat less than a full jar, spoon a portion into a bowl and put the jar in the refrigerator for later. You generally can keep opened jars in the fridge for up to three days in the case of fruits and vegetables, one day for meats, and two days for meat and vegetable combos. A permanent marker can be handy for dating those opened jars so you'll know what went into the refrigerator when.
* Don't leave perishable items out of the refrigerator (without a cold pack) for more than two hours. Throw them away if they've been sitting out longer than that.
* When you're traveling, transport food and filled bottles in an insulated cooler with frozen packs.
* Don't give your baby honey if he or she is less than 1 year old. It could contain bacteria associated with botulism, a potentially fatal form of food poisoning.
* Don't serve your baby or older child raw or unpasteurized milk, which may contain harmful bacteria. And no cow's milk before age 1.
* If you're making homemade baby food, use a brush to clean areas around the blender or food processor blades and parts. Trapped food particles can harbor bacteria.
* To freeze homemade baby food, put the mixture in an ice-cube tray. Cover with heavy-duty plastic wrap and freeze. Later, you can pop the frozen food cubes into a freezer bag or airtight container and date it. Store up to three months.
* Use dishwashing detergent, hot water, and a clean dishrag to wash and rinse all utensils, including the can opener, which comes in contact with baby's foods. Just wiping them with a paper towel isn't enough. It's soap, water, and friction that do the trick.

of commercial baby foods such as applesauce to the stuff you'd eat yourself, you're apt to find a significant price difference, ounce per ounce. The fresh and canned fruit and vegetable aisles of your supermarket offer easy, economical alternatives to commercial baby food. Canned pumpkin, for example, is well puréed, as are many types of applesauce (buy one without added sugar). You can purée anything further at home. Baby-food cookbooks have suggestions and recipes. You might also ask your pediatrician for advice.

**Come armed with coupons.** Aside from the coupons in newspapers and magazines, most major baby food manufacturers have special offers posted on their Web sites. Recently, for example, Gerber *(www.gerber.com)* was offering up to $45 in coupon savings on its products for parents who joined the Growing Up Gerber Club. Beech-Nut *(www.beech-nut.com)* had a special offer that entitled shoppers to special savings on baby food if they sent in labels from Beech-Nut baby food products.

## What's Available

The major brands of baby food are Beech-Nut and Gerber. The major organic lines are Earth's Best and Gerber's Tender Harvest.

Most pediatricians recommend starting your baby with commercial infant rice cereal. It's easy to digest and mixes easily with breast milk or formula. Some cereal has fruit added, which is appropriate after your baby has mastered the plain stuff.

Commercial makers of jarred baby food usually divide their product line into three stages: beginner (stage 1), intermediate (stage 2), and toddler (stage 3). Stage 1 foods are made for babies just starting on solids. They're usually a single food, puréed for easy swallowing. Beginner vegetables commonly found in jars include peas, carrots, green beans, potatoes, squash, and sweet potatoes. Fruits include apples, bananas, peaches, and pears. Stage 1 foods offer the most unadorned ingredients. Sweet potatoes are sweet potatoes and peas are peas, without the addition of sauces or flavoring.

Intermediate (stage 2) foods are intended for more experienced eaters (at about 7 to 8 months). At this point, the offerings get more interesting because foods are often combined to improve taste or minimize the need to open two jars, such as rice and carrots or beef and barley. Stage 2 foods have a smooth texture, but not as fine as beginner foods. Products made with meat juices may be labeled "with broth."

### The Dish on DHA

These days, some brands of baby food are fortified with DHA (docosahexaenoic acid), an essential fatty acid naturally found in breast milk and believed to promote mental and visual development. These fortified baby foods tend to cost more (as much as 30 percent extra per ounce), but the scientific evidence on them is mixed. So ask your pediatrician for a recommendation. DHA is also being added to some brands of infant formula, as we mention in chapter 22.

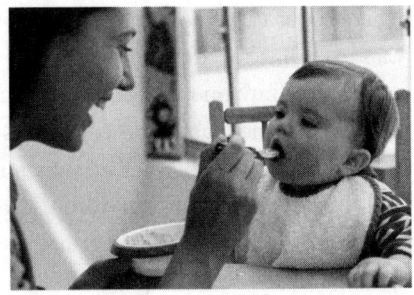

## SHOULD YOU GO ORGANIC?

Organic foods are a booming business in this country, and you'll find a cornucopia of organic options in the baby food section from two major brands: Earth's Best and Gerber's Tender Harvest. Natural foods markets often carry their own organic lines.

Baby food labeled "organic" must meet standards set by the United States Department of Agriculture and be at least 95 percent organic, meaning that all but 5 percent of the content was produced without pesticides and fertilizers. It also can't be irradiated (a one-time exposure to radiation intended to kill pathogens such as salmonella, listeria, or E. coli), genetically modified (a technique that alters a plant's DNA), or produced with hormones or antibiotics. Animals used for meat products are supposed to be raised on organically grown feed without additives. An independent organization, the National Organic Program of the U.S. Department of Agriculture, provides certification.

Do organically grown foods truly contain fewer pesticide residues than conventionally grown foods do? According to the evidence, the answer is yes. A study published in the peer-reviewed journal Food Additives and Contaminants and co-authored by a senior scientist at Consumers Union showed that organic foods had residues far less often than conventionally grown foods and also had fewer and lower levels of residues when they did.

A downside: The organic version will cost you. In our informal research we paid about 8 percent more for jarred, organic baby food than the nonorganic versions (which amounted to about 4 cents on each 2.5-ounce jar).

Whether it's worth it to feed your baby organic food is a personal choice. In general, foods produced organically or conventionally contain the same kinds and amounts of vitamins and minerals.

To get the full nutrient value of produce, organic or otherwise, try to give it to your baby when it's ripe—but not overripe. When produce sits too long, its cell walls start breaking down and nutrients leach out. To buy produce that isn't past its prime, choose fresh-looking fruits and veggies that aren't bruised or shriveled. Buy only what you need and use it within a few days. (For fruit that's fresh-cut, be sure to store it in the fridge along with all vegetables.) Whole fruit can be left on the counter if it needs more ripening time. Ripe fruit, with the exception of bananas and melons, for example, should be basically firm to the touch but have a little give. To reduce the risk of food-borne illness, wash all fresh fruits and vegetables with cool tap water before eating and cut away all bruised or damaged areas. To retain nutrients during cooking, steam fruits and veggies in a small amount of water.

Meat products with added starches will carry the words "with gravy."

Stage 3 foods are for children 9 months and older. This stage offers chunkier, larger-sized portions to keep up with growing appetites, such as Tender Harvest's Vegetable Medley with Pasta and the same company's Banana Apple Strawberry. At this stage, jarred baby food becomes more like the foods you whip up yourself. Indeed, some parents never bother with stage 3 but simply start giving baby more

# 15 FOODS YOU SHOULD EAT EVERY WEEK

When you're taking care of a new baby and juggling other challenges in your life, it's easy to let your own diet slide. Big mistake. "If you don't take care of your nutrition needs, you won't be able to do as good a job of taking care of your baby," says Felicia Busch, R.D., author of *New Nutrition: From Antioxidants to Zucchini* (John Wiley, 2000).

Busch, herself the mother of three, likens eating right to the oxygen mask demo on airplanes. Although it feels counterintuitive, parents of small children are instructed to strap on their own oxygen masks before attending to their child's.

Here are 15 foods that can boost your energy level and help keep you healthy.

**Milk.** Just one 8-ounce glass of skim or low-fat milk supplies one-third of your daily requirement for calcium, which is vital to strong bones and teeth. A diet rich in calcium can cut your risk of hypertension, colon cancer, and breast cancer, and possibly ease PMS (in the case of moms). Milk is also a valuable source of vitamin D, vitamin A, riboflavin, niacin, and vitamin B12, says Doreen Chin Pratt, R.D., director of nutrition services at Women & Infants Hospital in Providence, R.I.

**Bananas.** At about 100 calories each, bananas are a good source of fiber and the vitamins B6 and C. They're also loaded with potassium— a mineral that helps regulate blood pressure and is essential to muscle function. Eat one after a workout (when potassium levels are at their lowest), mix into smoothies, or add to your cereal for an all-day energy boost.

**Orange juice.** A stellar source of vitamin C (just one 8-ounce glass supplies 120 percent of your daily requirement), orange juice is also full of folate— which helps prevent birth defects and colon cancer— as well as potassium. Opting for the calcium-fortified kind can benefit your bones.

**Salad.** Tossing together a variety of greens (romaine and spinach are rich in vitamin A and folate, while iceberg has fiber), along with tomatoes, carrots, and cucumbers, is a smart way to sneak vegetables into your diet, says Joan Salge Blake, R.D., a clinical assistant professor of nutrition at Boston University. Studies have shown that getting at least three servings of vegetables a day can reduce your risk of cancer, heart disease, and diabetes. Just be sure to steer clear of high-calorie dressing!

**Peanut butter.** It's chock-full of protein, fiber, zinc, and vitamin E. It also contains mostly unsaturated fat, which lowers both total and LDL ("bad") cholesterol. "Peanut butter and jelly on whole-wheat bread with a glass of milk is a perfect meal," says Therese Franzese, R.D., director of nutrition at Chelsea Piers Sports & Entertainment Complex in New York City. But don't go for the reduced-fat version. "The fat is replaced with sugar, so it has the same calories as the regular stuff," she explains.

**Sweet potatoes.** These spuds—which are available year-round—should be a staple in your diet, not simply a holiday treat. They're an excellent source of potassium, fiber, and cancer-fighting antioxidants, such as beta carotene and vitamin C.

**Salmon.** This fish is a rich source of omega-3 fatty acids, which can lower your risk of heart disease. Eating salmon once or twice a week may also boost your immune system. "If you're pregnant or nursing, the fatty acids in salmon help aid fetal and infant brain and nervous-system development," says Andrea Crivelli-Kovach, Ph.D., an assistant professor of nutrition at Arcadia University in Glenside, Pa. However, the Environmental Protection Agency recommends limiting the amount of freshwater fish you eat that was caught by family and friends to one meal per week because of the mercury it may contain. Also, government agencies recommend that pregnant or nursing women not eat shark, swordfish, king mackerel, or tilefish.

**Broccoli.** It's low-cal and loaded with vitamins A and C, beta carotene, folate, and fiber—all of which can help reduce your risk of heart disease and certain kinds of cancer. Enjoy it raw or lightly steamed.

**Whole-grain cereal.** One bowl of fortified cereal typically supplies 10 or more vitamins and minerals, as well as complex carbohydrates (for energy), disease-fighting fiber, and phytochemicals—non-nutrient plant ingredients that help prevent disease. Choose cereals with at least 5 grams of fiber.

**Lean red meat.** Women, especially those who have given birth within the last two years, are at risk for low iron levels, which can lead to anemia. Red meat is an excellent source of iron that's easily absorbed by the body. Stick with lean cuts—anything with loin or round in the name—for their lower saturated-fat content, and eat no more than one 2- to 3-ounce serving (about the size of your palm) each day.

**Vegetable soup.** You get a slew of vitamins and minerals when you eat soup loaded with veggies such as carrots, potatoes, and onions. Even better, because it's mostly water (and also contains fiber), soup will fill you up on relatively few calories.

**Yogurt.** A good source of bone-strengthening calcium (an 8-ounce carton contains about 35 percent of your daily requirement), low-fat or nonfat yogurt also supplies protein and potassium. Choose plain yogurt, since the flavored kinds are often high in sugar, and make sure the label says the brand contains "live and active cultures," since these bacteria have been shown to benefit your gastrointestinal tract and may help prevent yeast infections.

**Eggs.** They're packed with the protein moms (and dads) need to help build and repair weary muscles. Eggs are also a good source of vitamin D, which helps the body absorb calcium. Still, because egg yolks are high in cholesterol, moderation is key. "It's fine to have one a day," says author Busch.

**Tomato sauce.** Tomatoes are loaded with lycopene, a powerful antioxidant that has been shown to help keep arteries clear and reduce your risk of heart disease. Most jarred sauces also contain fiber and vitamins A and C.

**Beans.** Canned or dried varieties, such as kidney, black, garbanzo, and navy beans, are a low-fat source of protein, iron, and soluble fiber, which can help lower your cholesterol level. "You'll make any meal healthier—from soups and stews to salads and pasta dishes—by adding a can of beans to it," says Blake. However, since canned beans can be high in sodium, rinse them well under cold water or buy the no-salt kind.

normal fare, still mashed and cut up for easy chewing and swallowing.

Infant juices are available, although they may be no different from the adult kind. Avoid citrus juice until your pediatrician gives you the go-ahead; it can upset little stomachs. In addition to fruit-juice basics such as apple and white grape, there are many combinations, some of which contain yogurt and fruit-vegetable blends. Some also have added calcium or vitamin C.

Go easy on the juice, though. Too much can cause diarrhea. And when babies drink juice, they may take in less breast milk or formula, which contain the nutrients they really need. Also, don't put baby to bed with a bottle of juice or milk; that can lead to tooth decay.

## Recommendations

Let your pediatrician be your guide about what to feed your baby and when to move to the next stage. Compare the ingredients and nutritional values on commercial baby food, and check expiration dates listed on the label or lid. All baby-food jars have a depressed area, or "button," in the center of the lid. Reject any jars with the button popped out—an indication that the product has been opened or the seal broken.

# 4

# Backpack Carriers

A-B-C

A backpack carrier can take you places you never thought you could go with a baby, such as on rugged, back-country hikes or cross-country skiing. But many parents report that they also use them for trips to far less exotic destinations, such as the mall, the zoo, or even Disney World.

Backpack carriers are intended for children old enough to sit up independently—usually at least 6 months old. They can be used for children up to a whopping 75 pounds, depending on the model, although 48½ pounds is more typical for weight maximums. You'll probably stop using a backpack carrier by the time your child is 3 years old, so you may never reach those upper weight limits.

Backpack carriers sport an aluminum or steel frame, which together with the waist or hip belt distributes a baby's weight along your back and waist, rather than putting it all on your shoulders and neck as do some front carriers that don't have a waist belt. Most backpack carriers come with built-in stands that help make loading and mounting easier, but they typically aren't stable enough to be used as baby seats on the ground. Seats and shoulder harnesses are

made of moisture-resistant fabric. Many models have multiple positions for the wearer and the child. Carriers typically have densely padded shoulder straps and hip belts, as well as storage compartments, vinyl weather shields, and toy loops. Some also have wheels and can convert to strollers.

On the negative side, backpack carriers can be more cumbersome and expensive than soft carriers. They shouldn't be used in your child's early months, but only when he or she can sit up unassisted and once the leg openings no longer present a slip-through hazard.

## Shopping Secrets

**Bring baby.** When your baby is about 6 months old, take him or her with you when you're shopping for a backpack carrier and do test runs in the store. If you don't have your baby with you when you're shopping, ask the salesperson to weigh down any carrier you try on with whatever is available so you can approximate the sensation of toting a baby in it.

**Practice, practice.** With the help of a knowledgeable salesperson, practice putting the carrier on and taking it off. Have your spouse do likewise to make sure it fits you both comfortably. Walk with it to make certain the frame doesn't hit the back of your head, that it's not too long for your height, that the straps are close enough together so they won't slip off your shoulders, and that the frame doesn't start to dig into your lower back after a few minutes.

## What's Available

Major brands of backpack carriers, in alphabetical order, include Baby Trend, Deuter, Evenflo (Snugli), Instep, Kelty Kids, and Madden. You'll find the best selection of these major brands through camping/outdoor outlets, specialty Web sites, and catalogs rather than in baby stores. Prices range from $75 to $275.

In general, a higher price will command a more padded, comfortable fit for you and your baby. That can be important if you plan to use the carrier more than just occasionally.

## Features to Consider

Your baby's comfort and safety (not to mention yours) are the most important issues when evaluating backpack carrier features. Many models within a brand differ only by a feature or two, which can add to the cost (or reduce it). Your best bet is to make a list of must-have features, such as those we cite below, then start trying on and comparing the various models.

**The cockpit.** Higher-end backpack carriers tend to offer a roomier ride for baby. Padding is also a key consideration. Although your baby may not complain, some parents believe that their children seem happier in a plusher ride.

**Fabrics.** Backpack carrier fabrics are likely to be durable nylon material similar to that used in modern suitcases. They vary from lightweight to heavy-duty. The fabric should be sturdy, moisture-resistant, and easy to clean by wiping with a mild detergent. (Allow the carrier a few days to air out when it gets wet.) If you plan to use your carrier daily, get one with heavier nylon for extra durability. Light-reflecting piping or stripes can help drivers see you in low-light conditions.

**Fasteners.** Carriers use a variety of buckles and fasteners for shoulder and waist straps and babies' seats. Buckles that hold shoulder and waist straps should be easy to adjust and not allow the straps to work loose when the carrier is in use. The most effective buckles are those that require two independent actions or considerable force by adult hands to squeeze and release them. Snaps should be sturdy and take a lot of force to unfasten.

**Foldability.** A backpack carrier that can be folded for storage in the trunk of your car is a plus.

**The frame.** Backpack carrier frames tend to be made of steel or aluminum. Aluminum is an advantage because it keeps the carrier's weight down. Some carriers offer rigid frame construction; others, especially those on the higher end, flex and give.

**Kickstand.** If a carrier has a kickstand (a definite plus for getting the carrier on and off by yourself), it should lock firmly in the open position and have hinges with spacers to prevent finger entrapment. When the carrier is on your back, the kickstand should close up so it does not snag on things as you walk. When the carrier is on the stand, it should be hard to tip over. However, don't use a carrier with a stand as a baby seat.

**Leg holes.** These should be wide enough not to bind baby's legs but not so wide that your baby could slip through them.

**Lumbar support.** Well-made carriers may have a special padded waist strap for adults that helps distribute the baby's weight from your shoulders to your hips and pelvic area. Carrying the weight lower is a definite comfort advantage. In the store, fasten the belt to test that it's long enough and neither too high nor too low when the carrier is in place. Padding should be dense rather than mushy.

**Padding.** Look for a backpack carrier with padding that covers the metal frame near your baby's face to protect him or her from bumping into it.

**Seat and seat belts.** Look for a seat that adjusts to different baby sizes, which is important so your baby can see over your shoulder from the beginning (but not so high that the carrier becomes unsafely balanced). You'll need to be sure the carrier has strong snaps or closures that will hold tight. A seat belt or other type of harness is essential to keep baby from scrambling out. Check all buckles and other securing hardware to be sure seams won't tear and straps won't slip.

**Shoulder and waist straps.** Shoulder-strap padding for you should be firm and wide. Putting your baby in and strapping the carrier on should be fairly simple. Straps should be positioned so they won't slip off your shoulders or chafe your neck. They should also be adjustable even while you're carrying your baby.

**Storage pouches.** If you can't leave your house without lots of toys, an extra bottle, snacks, and extra diapers, you'll need a carrier with ample storage, which is an area where models differ. Some are laden with pockets, pouches, and toy loops; others are streamlined for simplicity. Zippered pouches or those with a Velcro closure are better because things can't fall out. Plastic-lined pockets can be used for damp items. Some heavy-duty carriers for serious hiking offer a variety of removable pouch accessories so you can choose what to add or remove. The downside of too many pouches: You'll have to lug whatever you pack in the carrier, as well as your baby.

**Sun/weather shield.** Since a baby's eyes and skin are sensitive, you'll need to protect him or her from the sun and bad weather. Some carriers come with this important feature; others are sun/weather-shield compatible. If the carrier you select doesn't come with a shield, buy one separately on the spot. Not all sun/weather shields are created

## CERTIFICATION

**N**o certification program exists for these products. However, an American Society of Testing Materials committee, with Consumers Union's participation, is working on a standard, which could take effect by roughly 2005.

## CARRIER CAUTIONS

**W**hen toting a backpack carrier, the Consumer Product Safety Commission recommends that you:

- Use a carrier's restraining straps at all times so that your child isn't tempted to climb out when you're on the go.
- Keep your baby's fingers away from the frame joints, especially when you're folding the backpack.
- Check the backpack periodically for ripped seams, missing or loose fasteners, and frayed seats or straps. Repair them as needed (or throw the carrier away if it's on its last legs).
- Be sure to bend your knees rather than bending at the waist to keep your baby from falling out, when you're leaning over or stooping.

equal. The better shields are "hoods" that provide full coverage. And be sure to cover with sunscreen any part of your baby's skin that's showing.

## Recommendations

Before buying a baby carrier, think about how much you'll use it. That will help you in determining what to spend. A lower-priced version may be fine for quick jaunts. If you plan longer treks with your baby, consider a high-end model. In general, in the backpack carrier arena, you get what you pay for, but depending on your lifestyle, you may not need to go all-out.

In general, you want to buy a carrier that has enough depth to support your baby's back, with leg openings small enough to prevent your baby from slipping out but big enough to keep baby's legs from chafing.

# PRODUCT GUIDE • BACKPACK CARRIERS

**N**ote: These products were not tested by Consumers Union. This alphabetical listing does not include all models available but rather is a selection of some widely distributed ones. Descriptions are derived from the manufacturers' claims. Prices are approximate retail. For manufacturer contact information, see the Brand Locator, starting on page 283.

| Line/model | Price | Details |
|---|---|---|
| **BABY TREND** | | |
| **Compact Backpack Model 2510** | $50 | Has 6-pound steel frame, padded shoulder and hip straps, padded leg openings and head support, removable and washable heavy-duty nylon seat pad. Includes removable, tilt-top, adjustable canopy. |
| **Deluxe Backpack Model 2592** | $80 | Features 5-pound aluminum frame with stand, adjustable seat with five-point safety harness, padded leg openings, head support, and padded hip belt. Also has storage pouch, parent's zippered pouch, and two side cup-holders. Sun shield and rain cover included. |
| **DEUTER SPORT** | | |
| **KangaKid** | $120 | Functional day pack that converts to a child carrier. Has large main compartment, two front pockets, and child safety belt. Aluminum stays support the child seat and back system. |
| **Kid Comfort I Set** | $160 | Lightweight backpack. Features ventilated system padded hip belt, head rest, fold-out stand, zippered pocket, and height-adjustable seat with safety belt. Sun and rain-protecting roof included. |
| **Kid Comfort III** | $250 | Heavy-duty backpack. Has integrated sun roof, hip and mid-back ventilated padding, zippered pocket under seat, rear pocket, mesh pocket, fold-out stand, height-adjustable seat. Padded child seat features removable and washable chin pad. |
| **EVENFLO** | | |
| **Snugli Cross Roads** | $40 | Features five-point overhead child harness, retractable kickstand, mesh panels for ventilation. |
| **Snugli Cross Country** | $70 | Features adjustable hip belt, five-point padded child harness, sun/wind canopy, mesh panels for ventilation, retractable kickstand, storage compartment for baby gear. |
| **Snugli Cross Terrain** | $100 | Features adjustable hip belt, five-point padded child harness, sun/wind canopy, mesh panels for ventilation, retractable kickstand. |

# PRODUCT GUIDE • BACKPACK CARRIERS

| Line/model | Price | Details |
|---|---|---|
| **INSTEP** | | |
| **Stroller Backpack** | $75 | Converts from stroller to backpack. Stroller features large, zippered basket for storage, swivel front wheels, and parking brakes. Backpack features lightweight aluminum tubing, padded leg openings, "belly bar," and sun/wind canopy. |
| **Deluxe Stroller Backpack** | $100 | Converts from stroller to backpack. Stroller features swivel front wheels and parking brakes. Backpack features lightweight aluminum tubing, padded leg openings and "belly bar," and sun/wind canopy . |
| **KELTY** | | |
| **Meadow** | $100 | Introductory carrier features open child seat, adjustable padded waist belt, padded shoulder straps, mesh back panel, five-point child harness, automatic kickstand, and no-pinch hinge. Sun/rain hood not included. |
| **Base Camp** | $135 | Features an adjustable padded waist belt, padded shoulder straps, mesh back panel, five-point child harness, no-pinch hinge, and automatic kickstand. Sun/rain hood not included. |
| **Ridgeline** | $155 | Features expandable child seat, adjustable padded waist belt, molded shoulder straps, contoured padded back panel, five-point child harness, automatic kickstand, and no-pinch hinge. Sun/rain hood not included. |
| **Convertible** | $160 | Converts from stroller to backpack. Stroller has padded handle and storage bin under seat. Backpack features open child seat, adjustable padded waist belt, padded shoulder straps, mesh back panel, five-point child harness, no-pinch hinge. |
| **Back Country** | $185 | Features expandable child seat, adjustable padded waist belt, molded padded shoulder straps, molded padded back panel, five-point child harness, no-pinch hinge, automatic kickstand; storage compartments, and sun/wind hood. |
| **Summit** | $235 | Features expandable child seat, adjustable padded waist belt, molded padded shoulder straps, contoured padded back panel, five-point child harness, automatic kickstand, no-pinch hinge. Includes sun/rain hood and removable kid pack with shoulder straps. |
| **Pinnacle** | $275 | Features expandable child cockpit, adjustable padded waist belt, molded shoulder straps, contoured back panel, five-point harness, fold-out kickstand, no-pinch hinge, and storage. Sun/rain hood included. |

| Line/model | Price | Details |
| --- | --- | --- |
| **MADDEN MOUNTAINEERING** | | |
| **Voyager** | $150 | This entry-level backpack for around town but not for lengthy excursions features load lifter and stabilizing straps, laminated waist belt, and harnesses. Sunshade not included. |
| **Caravan (nonadjustable)** | $160 | Features fully padded bucket seat and sides, suspension frame system, removable day pack/diaper bag. Sunshade not included. |
| **Caravan** | $230 | Similar to Caravan model above but has adjustable frame system and also includes sunshade. |

# Bathtubs

**F**orget about the towel-lined sink you were probably bathed in as a baby. Although that's certainly still an option, there are plenty of portable bathtubs on the market these days that make the job of bathing your baby a whole lot easier—and more fun for both of you.

A baby bathtub provides an appropriately compact place for bathing. It can be placed in a sink, in a regular bathtub, on a counter or kitchen table, or right on the floor. However, if you put the tub anywhere higher than the floor, be sure to keep a hand on your baby at all times. With water around, bathtubs have a way of slipping and sliding.

Many of today's tubs have a removable mesh inner cradle so baby can't slide around too much. Others have a slip-resistant padded lining that allows a baby who can't sit up yet to relax in a semi-upright position.

You'll use a baby bathtub for less time than you may think. At about 6 months old, when your baby can sit up, he or she should no longer be bathed in an infant tub that sits in the sink. Instead, transfer baby to a slightly longer tub.

## Bath Basics

Before we get into the specifics of what's on the market, here are a few bath-time tips. For starters, don't worry about giving your baby a bath right away. Bathing doesn't officially start until the stump of your baby's umbilical cord falls off (about two weeks post-delivery). After that milestone, you can give your baby a bath every day if you like, although two to three times a week is a better idea because daily bathing can dry out your baby's tender skin. In addition to the tub, you'll need a soft towel (preferably hooded to cradle your baby's head), a baby washcloth, and baby body wash that doubles as shampoo to complete the mission.

There are a variety of baby bathtubs on the market. Keep in mind that just about any tub you buy will be awkward to use at first, mainly because bathing a squirmy baby—who may dislike temperature changes and being put in water—is awkward in itself. Expect your baby to protest the first time or two. After that, your baby will probably grow to enjoy bath time—and so will you. Also remember that your constant presence and attention is necessary any time your baby is in the bath.

## What's Available

Major brands of baby bathtubs include, in alphabetical order: Evenflo, The First Years, Graco, Leachco, J Mason, Primo, and Safety 1st. You'll see

### BE THERE ALWAYS

**A** baby can drown in as little as 1 inch of water, and each year the Consumer Product Safety Commission gets numerous reports of drownings that could easily have been prevented—if, for example, the caregiver hadn't left the bathroom to get the phone or answer the doorbell. Never leave your infant unattended in a tub—even for a minute. If the phone rings, let the answering machine pick up. If there's a knock on the door, ignore it. Always have your child within arm's reach.

You'll also need to be careful about scalding water. Before you place baby in the tub, the water should feel warm, not hot. When using a baby bathtub in the sink or in a regular tub, always turn the hot water off first and watch out for hot metal spigots. Swoosh the water around with your hand so that any hot spots even out. Although there are bath water thermometers you can buy or tubs that take the guesswork out of temperature control (the drain plug changes color if the water's too hot for baby), your wrist or your elbow should suffice.

Also make sure you have everything you need on hand before you start the bath. You don't want to have to scurry for, say, a washcloth or towel while baby is in the tub.

## DON'T BUY A BATH SEAT

There's one baby-bathing product you should absolutely avoid. That's a bath seat or bath ring. Basically a plastic baby seat with suction cups on the bottom for attaching to an adult bathtub, bath seats are supposed to make it easier to handle a baby during bathing. But more than 100 drownings have been associated with this product since 1983, and, as of this writing, the fatalities continue at a rate of six a year.

Bath seats can tip over when suction cups fail, and children can become trapped underwater. In many of these tragic cases, parents had just left the room momentarily, and in at least one case an adult was present.

In October 2003, the Consumer Product Safety Commission voted unanimously to propose a mandatory standard for baby bath seats to help prevent drownings. We estimate that a standard will be in effect by 2005. But in the interim, you're better off simply staying away from this product or returning it if one is given to you.

simple tubs that are flat on the bottom; tubs with contoured interiors that help position baby's head above water; tubs with supportive, internal nylon mesh slings that cradle newborns; contoured padded bath pillows filled with polystyrene beads that fit inside a regular tub; and tubs with an insert that can be taken out once baby is able to sit up unassisted and which can then be used until a child is age 2. You'll also find tubs with many of these features that fold in half like a suitcase for more compact storage. Bathtubs range from $13 to $30.

## Features to Consider

**Contoured design with slip-resistant padded lining.** In lieu of a sling, a contoured design is a must for keeping baby from sliding around too much; baby can still slip and slide, though, so you may want to pop in an additional foam cushion, which is sold separately.

**A drain with an attached plug.** This can make the tub easier to empty. One that's on the large side allows for quicker post-bath cleanup.

**Foldability.** Some tubs, like the Safety 1st Fold-Up Tub or The First Years 2-in-1 Fold-Away Tub & Step Stool (it folds into a step stool), collapse in two like a suitcase for easier storage. To make sure the tub won't leak, practice at first with a small amount of water.

**An internal mesh sling/cradle.** It's cozy and supportive, especially for a newborn. Some models, like the Graco Cuddle Tub, come with an adjustable pillow that attaches to the sling, an added comfort.

**A rounded crotch projection.** Found on the Evenflo Comfort

## Two tubs in one

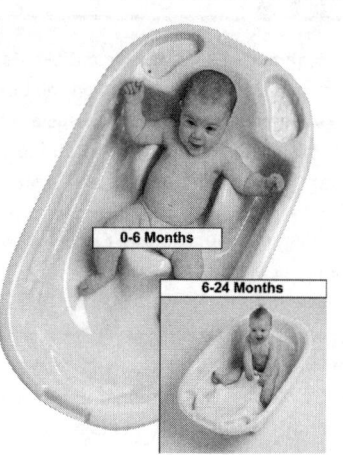

0-6 Months

6-24 Months

The Eurobath by Primo can be used to bathe a new-born. When baby is older, he can be seated facing the other direction at bath time.

Tub, an ergonomically contoured model, this feature can keep baby in a safer and more comfortable position.

**Shower curtain or towel hook.** Some models have a hook on the back to hang the tub up for draining or storage.

**A smooth, overhanging rim.** This feature makes it much easier to carry a heavy, water-filled tub from the sink to another location for bathing.

**Suction cups.** Some models have suction cups that attach the unit to the bottom of a regular bathtub.

**Temperature monitor.** If you're worried about getting your baby's bath water just right, some models, such as The First Years Sure Comfort Newborn-to-Toddler Tub, have drain plugs that change color to alert you if the water is too hot for a baby.

## Recommendations

Buy a bathtub made for a baby 6 months or younger that features a contoured design or an internal sling that cradles your baby in the water. Mildew-resistant pads are also a plus, although to prevent mildew and soap-scum buildup, you'll still have to clean the tub after each use. Tubs that convert and grow with your baby until age 2 or so are also a good idea.

Some parents report that collapsible tubs have problems with water leakage from the seams. A neater option is to buy a unit that doesn't fold and store it upright in your shower if you're short on space.

# Bicycle Trailers

H auling the laundry basket up and down stairs and chasing around a toddler-wannabe certainly qualify as exercise. Still, if you get the feeling it's not enough, a bicycle trailer can help you cover some ground in the name of fitness and fresh air without having to hire a baby sitter.

Trailers have two bicycle-type wheels and a long hitching arm that fastens onto your bicycle. Some can carry two kids, and others are designed for children with disabilities. They're promoted for towing a child big enough to sit up, usually starting at 6 months or so. But we think that's too young. For one thing, children of that age may not be physically equipped to withstand the forces they'll be exposed to in a trailer. For another, there are no helmets available at that age level—and a helmet is a necessity, in our view. If you want to use a trailer, our advice is to wait until your child is old enough to walk and can be properly fitted with a helmet.

Trailers give the impression of being safer than bicycle-mounted baby seats, since the passenger or passengers are seated, strapped in, and enclosed in a zippered compartment. Bicycle-mounted child seats can also make a bike unstable and hard to mount and dismount. As with trailers, they should not be used with very young children.

But trailers pose safety problems in their own right because their low profile makes them difficult for motorists to see, especially in limited light, even if they're

## CERTIFICATION

brightly colored. And trailers can tip over if you turn abruptly or happen to turn when one wheel is going over a bump. As your bike speeds up, braking becomes harder, even more so on wet surfaces. Trailers may also become snagged on bushes or other objects.

## Shopping Secrets

**Take a trailer for a test ride.** Put some weight in it, to find out if trailering is for you.

**Avoid buying a used bicycle trailer.** For safety's sake, also avoid one you're not able to examine carefully.

## What's Available

The major brands of bicycle trailers are, in alphabetical order: Bell Sports, Burley, Instep, and Schwinn. Yakima, once a major brand, is getting out of the bicycle trailer business.

All trailers have a rigid frame designed to protect young passengers if the unit rolls over. Prices range from $150 to $430 for both one- and two-passenger models.

## Features to Consider

**Assembly.** If you plan to put the bike trailer together yourself, you'll want clear instructions because assembly can be a challenge. If you need help, call the company or consult your local bike shop.

**Convertibility.** Some manufacturers offer conversion kits that allow you to turn a trailer into a jogging stroller. That's an attractive, expense-saving, two-for-one option. But we don't recommend the opposite—using a conversion kit to rig your stroller to your bike.

**Element defenses.** Many trailers come with plastic wind and rain shields, which protect against sun, wind, and rain. A zippered front shield can keep spray from the bicycle tires or mud from splattering onto your baby. But if the shield encloses the entire cabin, make certain there's some form of ventilation, such as breathable mesh windows. Your kids may appreciate tinted windows, which aren't available on all models. They can also help keep the "cockpit" cool.

**Folding mechanism.** Some trailers feature quick-release wheels and fold easily for storage (even in a hall closet), which can be an advantage if your riding is seasonal.

**Frame.** Frames are generally made of steel, but more expensive models may be aluminum or alloy, which are lighter. The frame should be firmly welded or bolted. Better models offer a roll cage to protect passengers in the event of a rollover.

**Harness.** Look for a padded, adjustable five-point harness (two straps over the shoulders, two for the thighs, and a crotch strap), much like a car seat's.

**Hitching arm.** The hitching arm should have a backup to prevent the trailer from accidentally breaking loose. Check the wheel mounting to be sure that it will hold securely. Look for a universal hitch, which will accommodate almost any bicycle. Some hitching arms are designed to help keep the trailer upright even if your bike goes down.

**Reflectors and safety flag.** Most trailers have side reflective strips, which are good if you're riding at twilight—although we don't recommend it. A safety flag, consisting of a pennant on a whip tall enough to make it visible to drivers, is a must.

**Seating.** The interior of the trailer should offer comfortable seating for young passengers, with adequate legroom and good back support. Storage pockets for toys or snacks are a plus. At the higher end of the price range, you'll find seats that recline, cushier padding, and on two-person trailers, a seat divider. The seat's protective cavity should be free of protrusions.

**Wheels.** They're typically made with rims of steel, which has the potential to rust, or aluminum, which doesn't. Look for high-quality rubber tires.

**Wheel guards.** Wraparound wheel guards are another safety feature to look for. They can help protect your kids while you ride and reduce mud spatter as well.

## Recommendations

For safety's sake, consider trailers to be "off-road vehicles" and use them only in parks and on safe, smooth trails where there's no risk of encounters with cars. Have your child wear a lightweight, well-fitting bike helmet, and follow the manufacturer's recommendations regarding weight and size limitations. That's typically 60 pounds for a one-passenger trailer and 100 pounds for a duo.

The better bicycle trailers have sturdy construction, tinted windows, a comfortable interior, and a wide wheel base. But before you decide to buy, ask yourself if you will use the trailer enough to justify the price. If you think you'll be using it only occasionally, buy the most durable trailer you can that's priced at the low end. Also, consider how much weight you'll tow. When the weight of the bicycle trailer plus the passenger or passengers exceeds 50 pounds, you may start to think of yourself as a beast of burden. At that point, maybe it's time for riders to get their own bikes.

CHAPTER

# 7

# Bouncer Seats

B abies like to be where the action is. A bouncer seat—also commonly called a "bouncy" seat—gives babies who can't sit up a place to hang out near you and the rest of the family during their first five or six months. For babies who need a little motion to fall asleep, a bouncer seat that vibrates can also be a big help.

Generally, a bouncer seat consists of a lightweight frame made from metal wire, tubular metal, or heavy-gauge plastic. Most are curved underneath to allow the seat to rock. Covered with a soft, removable, washable pad that conforms to a baby's shape, bouncer seats are somewhat springy, which may help keep your baby relaxed and amused. The fabric seat is rounded to support a baby's still-fragile spine, while a semi-upright tilt affords a view of the sur-roundings. Many parents report that their babies love to nap in a bouncer seat. The sitting angle also appears to be more comfortable for some babies after they've had a big meal than the flat posture demanded by a crib.

Most models of bouncer seats have a detachable, bent-wire play bar (sometimes covered with padding) that suspends plastic toys and teethers in front for your baby to kick, bat, and chew. Some models feature a set of colorful lights and sound effects that respond to a baby's movements and/or vibrate at two or three different speeds to lull baby to sleep. Some simulate the sound of a heartbeat as heard from the womb or play computer-chip-generated classical music. Others are simpler versions that transform your child's smallest movements into a soothing rocking motion, sans batteries.

## Shopping Secrets

**Consider either a bouncer seat or a swing–not both.** Many parents report that it's overkill to buy both pieces of equipment; one may end up going largely unused because the two essentially do the same thing for a baby—provide a secure place to relax and be gently lulled by motion.

**Keep this product's short life span in mind.** Your baby will only use a bouncer for five or six months—tops (and then, it's on to more interesting things, like sitting up and rolling). With that in mind, an inexpensive, lightweight model, provided it's stable, such as the Deluxe Bouncer by Delta Enterprise ($20, without vibrator, canopy, or netting), may serve you as well as a top-end design. In general, more money will get you a seat with toys, reclining and vibrating features, realistic (as opposed to tinny) music, plush fabric, and possibly the ability to rock as well as bounce. Still, more isn't always better. Parents report product satisfaction at both ends of the price spectrum.

## What's Available

The major brands of bouncer seats, in alphabetical order, are: Baby Bjorn, Baby Trend, Chicco, Combi International, Delta Enterprise, Dorel Juvenile Group (which includes Eddie Bauer and Safety 1st bouncers), Fisher-Price, Kolcraft, and Summer Infant. Prices range from $20 to $65. Many require batteries.

## BOUNCING ALFRESCO

**B**ouncer seats are typically meant for indoor use, although some models, such as the Eddie Bauer 2 in 1 Bouncenette and the Learning Patterns Play Dome by Fisher-Price, come with a sunshade and mesh netting, making them appropriate for outdoor activities, such as jaunts to the park or puttering in the garden. Still, when you're out with baby in a bouncer on a sunny day, keep it in the shade so your child doesn't become overheated and is fully protected from the direct sun.

## Features to Consider

**Convertibility.** Some bouncer-seat hybrids, like Chicco's Deluxe Musical Rocker Sofa, $65, accommodate babies up to 45 pounds and will grow with your child into the toddler years. Your toddler will probably appreciate having at least one seat in the house sized just for him or her.

**Cushiness.** Seat padding can vary from basic to extra-thick. Because wet diapers are bound to come in contact with the fabric covering, at the very least, upholstery should be removable and washable (check the label). There also shouldn't be any loose threads or gaps in the seams.

**Frame.** When you're in the store, give the various display models a "bounce." A bouncer seat should be stable and sturdy, but not stiff. Otherwise, some parents report, it won't bounce when baby is in it.

**Foldability.** Some models fold nearly flat, which is handy if you think you'll be traveling with your bouncer seat.

**Music and vibration.** If you choose a bouncer that vibrates or has music, opt for an automatic shut-off for the music/vibration feature.

**Outdoor accessories.** Some models have add-on features, such as a folding canopy that acts as a sunshade. Another option is mosquito netting, which may be important if you have a spring or summer baby. Both are useful protectors when the seat is used outdoors. Still, as we mentioned, use the seat only in the shade so your baby won't become overheated.

**Rockability.** Some bouncers are designed to rock as well as bounce, which parents may prefer because it gives a baby even more options. If you buy a rocking bouncer seat, make sure it has a stationary position, because your baby may not always be in the mood to rock.

**Seat belts.** Most models have a soft fabric three-point crotch strap as a restraint, although others feature a five-point harness, which is ideal for newborns because they tend to list to the side. If you don't buy a bouncer seat with a five-point harness, consider adding a head support—the kind you use with an infant car seat to stop your child's head from rolling to the side—but only if it's one supplied by the maker of the bouncer. For models with three-point harnesses, check the butterfly clips. They should be stiff enough to be safe without being so stiff that they pinch or are difficult for you to operate.

**Seat fabric.** Fabric patterns range from kid-friendly to sophisticated. But foremost, a seat cover should be removable and washable.

**Seat positioning.** Some bouncer seats recline more than others. The recline feature is necessary for infants, since they don't have the head control that sitting, even on a slight incline, requires. Some models let you select levels of reclining. Seats also vary in legroom and depth. Be sure your baby has enough wiggle room and leg support.

**Toy bar.** Besides watching you and your family from the sidelines, your baby may get pleasure from the toys that many bouncer seats come with. Toys are typically suspended from a removable play bar, although some models, such as the Kolcraft Tender Vibes Bouncer, feature a swing-away arm, which suspends toys in front of a baby in mobile fashion. Colorful spinning and squeaking toys and teethers are usually what's offered. Some toy bars have several positions and offer interactive noisemakers and lights. Most bouncers allow you to take the play bar off and use just the seat. Not all models have toy bars. We consider them an unnecessary feature, since your baby may not want to play with the toys all the time and during his or her early months won't know what to do with them.

## BOUNCER-SEAT SAFETY

Manufacturers will suggest a seat weight limit, usually ranging from newborn up to 20 or 30 pounds. Stick to it. Putting a child who is over the weight limit into the seat can make it tip. Here are some other safety recommendations:

- Never use a bouncer seat as a car seat.
- Stop using a bouncer seat as soon as your baby can sit up unassisted if it's not designed to be used by toddlers (some are); check the manufacturer's recommendations.
- Put the seat on the floor, which is the best place for it. Never use it on an elevated surface, such as a table.
- Don't carry your baby while he or she is in the bouncer.
- Always keep a close eye on your baby, even if you think he or she is completely safe and snug in the bouncer seat.

## CERTIFICATION

The Juvenile Products Manufacturers Association (JPMA) certifies for safety compliance one brand of bouncy seat, Kolcraft. The federal safety standard for small parts and other general hazards applies to bouncers as well. The industry's voluntary standard covers structural integrity as well as stability, restraint system, slip resistance, and safety instructions. Some models of infant activity seats have been recalled in recent years. Problems have included seats with an unstable base, handles with faulty locking mechanisms, kickstands that may not hold the seat stationary, and toys or play parts that may break off from the toy bar.

## Recommendations

Make safety your primary concern. You'll want a bouncer seat with a base or rear support that's wider than the seat itself for steadiness. Test the stability of a model in the store. When you press down on it from different positions, it shouldn't tip sideways. When you rock it front to back, it should stay in place. The bottom of the base should have rubber pads or other nonskid surfaces.

If you're buying a seat with toys attached to a toy bar, give them a squeeze and a tug. They should seem durable and unlikely to break off. The bar should stay in place when you bat at it (just like your baby will). If the frame is assembled with interconnecting parts, test by putting pressure on them to make sure they won't accidentally loosen.

**N**ote: These products were not tested by Consumers Union. This alphabetical listing does not include all models available but rather is a selection of some widely distributed ones. Descriptions are derived from the manufacturers' claims. Prices are approximate retail. For manufacturer contact information, see the Brand Locator, starting on page 283.

| Line/model | Price | Details |
|---|---|---|
| **BABY BJORN** | | |
| Baby Sitter 1-2-3 | $85 | Bouncer needs no batteries; bounces when baby moves. Includes crotch-strap restraint system and toy bar. Folds for travel and storage. |
| **BABY TREND** | | |
| Rock N Rest Bouncer | $40 | Includes three-point crotch-strap restraint system, rocking and nonrocking motions, two-speed vibration, three-position seat recline, removable headrest, and toy bar. Seat is removable and machine washable. Folds for travel and storage. |
| Euro Rock N Rest | $60 | Includes crotch-strap restraint harness, rocking and nonrocking motions, two-speed vibration, three-position seat recline, removable headrest, and toy bar with music and flashing lights. |
| **CHICCO** | | |
| Deluxe Musical Rocker Sofa | $65 | Plush bouncer seat with reclining backrest, crotch-strap safety harness, and rocking and nonrocking motions. Music box. |
| **COMBI** | | |
| Melody Bouncer | $40 | Features crotch restraint system, removable machine-washable seat cushion, adjustable toy bar, and acoustic canopy. Folds flat for travel and storage. |
| Deluxe Activity Rocker | $85 | Features three-position reclining seat with five-point safety harness, removable machine-washable seat cushion, and adjustable toy bar. Seat rocks, and vibrates. Requires one C battery. Folds to 6-inch thickness for travel or storage. |
| **DELTA ENTERPRISE** | | |
| Deluxe Bouncer | $20 to $30 | Padded bouncer on metal frame, with three-point crotch restraint system, one-speed vibration, and soft fabric toy bar that lights up and/or plays music. Seat is removable and washable. |

| Line/model | Price | Details |
| --- | --- | --- |
| **FISHER-PRICE** | | |
| **Soothe 'n Play Bouncer** | $20 | Features padded seat with three-point crotch restraint system, machine-washable seat, and removable toy bar. Vibration feature can be switched on or off. Requires one D battery. |
| **Cover 'n Play Bouncer** | $25 | Features padded seat with three-point crotch restraint system, removable toy bar, and attached blanket that stores underneath. Gentle bouncing motion is activated by baby's own movements. |
| **Classical Chorus Bouncer** | $25 | Features padded seat with three-point crotch restraint system, removable toy bar, and attached blanket that stores underneath seat. Vibration feature requires three C batteries. |
| **Learning Patterns Infant to Toddler Rocker** | $30 | Features padded seat with three-point crotch restraint system, two-position seat recline, and removable toy bar. Vibration feature requires one D battery. |
| **Kick & Play Bouncer** | $35 | Features padded seat with three-point crotch restraint system, removable toy bar, and vibration feature. Plays 10 songs, six sound effects, and dancing lights. Requires one D and three AA batteries. |
| **Learning Patterns Play Dome** | $40 | Baby lies down to play with overhead, adjustable toy bar. Toy bar requires one button cell battery (LR44 or equivalent), which is included. |
| **Ocean Wonders Aquarium Bouncer** | $40 | Features padded seat with three-point crotch restraint system, machine-washable seat pad, vibration feature, and removable toy bar. Plays lullabies and sound effects. Requires four D and three AA batteries. |
| **KOLCRAFT** | | |
| **Deluxe Tender Vibes Bouncer with Music** | $45 | Soft, fabric bouncer with three-point crotch restraint, reclining seat, and infant neck-roll support. Plays nursery rhymes. Toy bar is a swing-away mobile. Requires one D and two AAA batteries. |
| **SAFETY 1ST** | | |
| **Deluxe Musical Mobile Bouncer** | $25 | Soft fabric bouncer with three-point crotch restraint, infant headrest, vibration feature, machine-washable fabric seat, and musical mobile that converts to a toy bar. Requires one D battery. |
| **On-the-Go Cradle & Comfort Bouncer** | $30 | Soft fabric bouncer with three-point crotch restraint, headrest for support, vibration feature, machine-washable fabric, and toy bar. Requires one C battery. |

| Line/model | Price | Details |
|---|---|---|
| **2-in-1 Bouncenette** | $35 | A combination bouncer/portable bassinet. Includes built-in headrest support, two-speed vibration feature, and removable toy bar. Folds for travel or storage. Requires one D battery. |
| **Gentle Vibrations Reclining Bouncer** | $40 | Fully reclining fabric bouncer with three-point crotch restraint, vibration and adjustable canopy features, machine-washable fabric, and toy bar. Requires one D battery. |
| **Foot Start Super Bouncer** | $50 | Fabric bouncer that features two-speed gentle vibration, and machine-washable fabric. Lights, music, and bouncing motion are all activated by baby. Requires one D and two AA batteries. |

**SUMMER INFANT**

| Line/model | Price | Details |
|---|---|---|
| **Mother's Touch Bouncer Seat** | $30 | Fabric bouncer with three-point restraint features automatic rocking motion and gentle vibration, three-position reclining seat, adjustable head-support cushion, and toy bar. |
| **Reversible Starry Night Bouncer Seat** | $35 | Bouncer with reversible fabric has vibration feature, removable canopy, and toy bar. |
| **Flavia Bouncer Seat** | $40 | Fabric bouncer with three-point restraint features automatic rocking motion and gentle vibration, three-position reclining seat, head support cushion, and toy bar. |

CHAPTER

8

# Breast Pumps

A breast pump is indispensable in a number of scenarios: You want to continue breast-feeding but return to work; you need to formula-feed your baby temporarily for medical reasons but want to resume breast-feeding when you get the go-ahead from your doctor; you need to occasionally miss a feeding because you're traveling or otherwise away from your baby.

It also can come in handy during those first few days after you've delivered, when engorgement may be an issue. With engorgement, the breasts can become so full that a baby can have trouble latching on. "Things can be sailing along in the hospital, but when you get home, supply can outdo demand," explains Ann Darrah, director of maternal health at LaPorte Hospital in LaPorte, Ind. The solution is to express some milk with a breast pump—and to have one on hand before your baby is born, so the bottle is ready to go as soon as you return home after delivery.

A breast pump allows you to store milk (in bottles or storage bags) for later, then bottle-feed it to your baby or mix a little in cereal when he or she reaches the "solid" food stage. You can refrigerate breast milk safely for five to seven days, or freeze it for up to a year. A housekeeping note: Thaw it in warm water. Don't boil or microwave it; both of those heating methods can destroy valuable immunological components that make breast milk the liquid gold it is.

There are several types of breast pumps available—from large, hospital-grade and midweight "professional" pumps to handheld models that work one breast at a time. You'll want a pump that's appropriate to your particular situation.

A baby's natural sucking rhythm is 40 to 60 cycles per minute (one pull per second or a little less). Hospital-grade and midweight pumps typically operate at 30 to 60 cycles per minute. Other pumps are usually less efficient.

Speed is especially important if you plan to save a large quantity of milk. Mothers returning to work, for example, need to have much more breast milk on hand than those who stay home with their babies or are supplementing breast milk with formula.

Pumps also vary by the type of suction they apply. Intermittent action better imitates a baby than a constant vacuum—and is easier on mom.

Using a breast pump will take a little practice. You'll need to learn how to position it correctly and adjust the suctioning to get the best results. Don't worry—with the right pump, you'll soon get the hang of it. Pumps require some assembling and disassembling for cleaning. Wash any parts of the pump that touch your breasts or the milk containers in the dishwasher, or with hot, soapy water. Drain them dry before each use.

## Shopping Secrets

**Never buy a used breast pump.** Other than hospital-grade rental pumps, which are designed for multiple users (they have special barriers that prevent cross-contamination), all other breast pumps are made for one person only. To buy or borrow someone else's pump can put your baby's health in jeopardy because research suggests that bacteria and certain viruses can be transmittable through breast milk. And even if you buy your own tubing, bacteria and viruses can cling to a pump's internal diaphragm—the part that connects to the tubing—which can't be removed, replaced, or fully sterilized.

**Consider cyber-shopping.** A little research reveals that there are deals to be had in the online breast pump marketplace once you know what kind of pump you want. (Not sure where to start? Simply type in "breast pump" on a search engine like Google.)

**Browse at the hospital.** Many hospitals and birthing centers are now in the breast-pump business, offering competitive prices on a variety of pumps—plus advice that can help ensure breast-feeding success. It also wouldn't hurt to get a recommendation from your hospital's lactation consultant as to the right type of pump for someone in your particular situation.

## Parent-to-Parent

❝I'm renting the Lactina by Medela. It has worked great for the last five months. My only regret is that I didn't purchase a breast pump right from the start.❞

–**Jennifer Betts,** Lansing, Mich.

## What's Available

Now that breast-feeding is back in vogue (some hospitals are even organizing human breast-milk banks for babies who, for some reason, can't physically breast-feed), the options in breast pumps are dizzying. The major brands are, in alphabetical order: Avent, The First Years, Hollister, Medela, Whisper Wear, and Whittlestone.

Breast pumps come in these basic types: Large, hospital-grade dual-action models, which aren't typically available for sale (you rent them from the hospital where you deliver or from a lactation center); "professional" midweight, fully automatic models that can travel with you; small electric or battery-operated units that double- or single-pump; single or double pedal-pump models; one-handed manual pumps; and even "hands-free" pumps that you wear in your bra that pump while you work, do errands, or drive. (We told you the options were dizzying!)

Here's the lowdown on each:

### Hospital-grade breast pumps

These powerhouses are about the size of a car battery and can weigh 5 to 11 pounds. Manufactured for users in hospitals and for those who choose to rent, they have sensitive controls that allow you to regulate suction rhythm, intensity, and pressure. Some have a pumping action that's almost identical to a baby's natural sucking. Accessories permit dual pumping so you can empty both breasts at once. These are quite expensive to buy, but you can rent them from hospitals, medical-supply stores, lactation consultants, and some drug stores.

**Pros:** They're fast and efficient.

**Cons:** Some women may find these pumps noisy—they produce a rhythmic swishing sound. And even though some come with a rechargeable battery and an adapter for use in a vehicle, you wouldn't exactly want to lug one to and from work every day because they can be awkward and heavy.

To rent monthly, expect to pay $30 to $50.

## "Professional," midweight breast pumps

Usually no bigger than a briefcase, these breast pumps are slightly less efficient than the hospital-grade models, although you may notice little difference. "This one works as well as hospital pumps," says new mom Aimee Denman of Houston, Texas, referring to her Medela Pump In Style. "I know because I work in a hospital."

Most "professional" pumps offer intermittent suction, which mimics baby's natural sucking, although some use a constant vacuum. Many models include dual pumps for emptying both breasts at once. Many come in a black microfiber case to resemble a tote bag, which is ideal for working moms and those on the go. Some are also available in a backpack style, which leaves your hands free for your baby, when commuting, traveling, or shopping. They're often equipped with an adapter for your car's cigarette lighter or a battery pack, for times when you're not near an electrical outlet.

**Pros:** A quick and easy way to double-pump and fill up a bottle in minutes when you're on the go.

**Cons:** May be more breast pump than you need if you plan to pump only occasionally.

**Price range:** $160 to $300.

## Small electric or battery-operated units

These can be useful if you're away from your baby now and then—for a night out or a couple of hours during the day. Using widely available AA or C batteries or household current, these lightweight, compact devices can fit discreetly in a purse or briefcase. They're relatively quiet and can be used just about anywhere. But the suction can be slow and tedious, achieving only five cycles per minute. Some also have a constant vacuum that can cause nipple discomfort.

**Pros:** Portable and inexpensive.

**Cons:** If you use it more than occasionally, you may find that pumping takes too long. Consider one of these for occasional use only. **Price range:** $40 to $80.

## Manual breast pumps

With these small pumps, you produce the suction yourself by squeezing a bulb or lever or by manipulating a syringe-style cylinder. There are many different designs of manual pumps on the market. Cylinder, or piston-style, pumps usually allow you to control pressure and minimize discomfort. Some manual models let you operate them with one hand. They're easier to use than those requiring one hand to hold, one to pump.

**Pros:** These pumps are less expensive than electric models and don't need an electrical source or batteries.

**Cons:** Any small pump could tire your hand and arm and cause repetitive strain injuries if you use it frequently. Manual pumps are often markedly slower than other pumps. We recommend these only for occasional use.

**Price range:** $30 to $45.

Note: Some electric breast pumps, such as Medela's Pump In Style pumps (the Companion, the Traveler, and the Original) come with a manual breast pump, so you get two for the price of one.

## Pedal pump

These innovative breast pumps are powered by pushing a pedal with your foot and allow you to single- or double-pump.

**Pros:** Because your legs do the work, you won't have to worry about the wrist and hand discomfort that can occur with other manual, do-it-yourself pumps.

**Cons:** Some women find this type of pump too bulky and not easy to carry around. The pumping action also can be weak. After you've been nursing a while and expressing milk becomes more of a challenge (which tends to happen), this model may not be up to the job.

**Price range:** $35 to $55.

## Hands-free pump

Placed inside your bra, this battery-operated pump mimics the feel and sucking pattern of a baby. Milk travels through a flexible stem and collects in a self-sealing, spill-proof bag. Whisper Wear is the only brand of hands-free pump we know of on the market.

**Pros:** You don't have to drop everything you're doing to pump; it's the ultimate in multitasking.

**Cons:** Some women report that for this pump to work, you need a super-tight bra and must position the pump exactly (otherwise, milk won't collect properly). Also, since you're placing the pump inside your bra, your chest size will expand considerably, so you may need to wear a large sweater or blazer to camouflage the fact that you're pumping,if you do so in public. And we also hear that it's not exactly "whisper" quiet.

**Price range:** $119 (for a single pump) to $219 (double pump).

## Features to Consider

**Adapter/batteries.** If you're pumping on the road, you'll need a pump that has the option of running on batteries or that includes an adapter that can attach to your car's cigarette lighter. However, for models that aren't "hands-free," we don't recommend pumping while driving.

**Carrying case.** If you'll be commuting or traveling, a professional-looking pump "briefcase" or sporty backpack is the way to go. Most models other than the hospital-grade ones come in a chic, black case with a shoulder strap so you can travel incognito.

**Double-pumping.** If you'll be pumping at work or pumping often, get a double hospital-grade or midweight "professional" pump. By expressing both breasts at once, you can complete a pumping session in 10 to 15 minutes. Besides being fast, double pumps are superior because they're better for milk production. Double-pumping increases

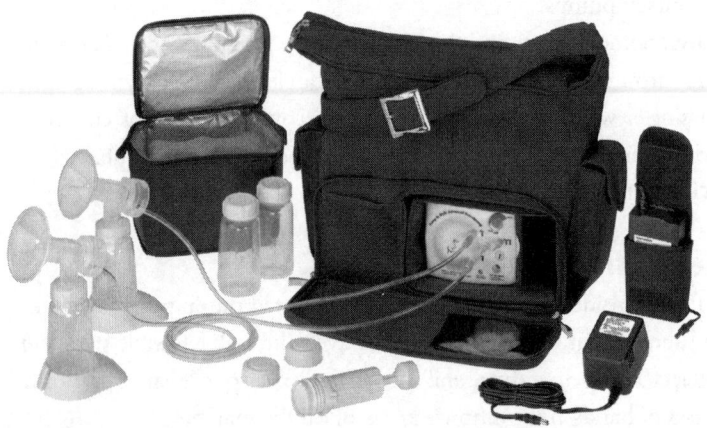

levels of prolactin, the hormone responsible for milk production. Smaller pumps or a single pump may not be able to maintain your milk supply long term.

**Insulated storage compartments.** Look for compartments in the pump's carrying case if you'll be pumping on the go and need to store your milk for later. But be sure to keep your breast milk in the storage compartment with an ice pack or two.

**Suction settings.** The best pumps mimic baby's natural nursing rhythm by pumping in two distinct modes: rapid, to simulate baby's rapid sucking to begin fast milk flow, and slower, to simulate baby's deeper sucking to maximize milk flow. Together, the two phases offer a more authentic breast-feeding experience with greater comfort, increased milk flow, and quicker nursing time.

Brands/models on the market that purport to pump "more like baby" include Medela's Harmony Manual Breast Pump, its Pump In Style Advanced, and its hospital-grade Symphony. A less well-known competitor on the market, but one worth a look, especially if you're uncomfortable (cracked, blistered, or bleeding nipples can come with the territory), is Whittlestone Breast Expresser. One online reader writes: "I was in terrible pain before I even left the hospital. At my follow-up appointment, they recommended the Whittlestone Breast Expresser. I was skeptical but willing to try it. It didn't hurt, and I got as much milk as with the Pump In Style."

## Recommendations

Consider renting a hospital-grade breast pump if you're not sure how long you'll need to use a pump or if you know you'll only need to pump for a short time. Still, since hospital-grade pumps aren't very portable, renting one is a realistic option only if you plan to be home with your baby. When you rent, you're given the pump, the bottles, and the suction cups. All you'll need to buy is the tubing that the milk flows through, which costs only a few dollars.

For information on pump rentals in your area and referrals to lactation consultants, contact the International Lactation Consultant

Association *(www.ilca.org)* or La Leche League *(www.lalecheleague .org)*. The hospital where you delivered your baby may have a lactation consultant on staff.

If you expect to use a breast pump regularly, especially if you plan to return to work, buy a midweight "professional" model. A professional pump will be your ally in getting a significant volume of milk in a given time and will also be your best bet for maintaining your milk supply.

Otherwise, if you plan to use a breast pump only occasionally, a manual pump or a small electric or battery-operated one will probably be all you need. They're appropriate for occasional use.

Since using a breast pump can be tricky, most manufacturers now supply informational brochures with their units. You can also call manufacturers' customer-service lines if you encounter problems with a specific pump. Many offer a 90-day warranty and will repair or replace a product without charge. But keep your receipt or the printout from your baby registry as proof of purchase.

There's also a host of information on the Internet about breast-feeding in general and specific guidance for issues such as continuing breast-feeding after returning to work. The La Leche League, at the Web address mentioned earlier, is a good place to start.

## PRODUCT GUIDE • BREAST PUMPS

Note: These products were not tested by Consumers Union. This alphabetical listing does not include all models available but rather is a selection of some widely distributed ones. Descriptions are derived from the manufacturers' claims. Prices are approximate retail. For manufacturer contact information, see the Brand Locator, starting on page 283.

| Line/model | Price | Details |
|---|---|---|
| **AMEDA** | | |
| **Cylinder Hand Breast Pump** | $30 | Two-handed single pump that operates by drawing down a central cylinder to create suction. Adjustable suction control. One-Hand Breast Pump |
| **One-Hand Breast Pump** | $40 | Single manual pump. Hand-squeeze design, no batteries needed. Similar model: Breastfeeding Starter Kit, includes pump, two cotton breast pads, and zipper bag. |

| Line/model | Price | Details |
| --- | --- | --- |
| **Nurture III Electric Breast Pump** | $130 | Electric double pump with adjustable suction strength. |
| **Purely Yours** | $250 to $300 | Dual or single breast pump that operates using an AC adapter, six AA batteries, or a car adapter. Adjustable suction and cycle speeds. |
| **AVENT** | | |
| Isis | $45 to $50 | Handheld manual pump. Milk flows into Avent bottles and storage containers. |
| **MEDELA** | | |
| **ManualElectric Pump** | $30 | Single manual pump or adapted for electric single pumping with two Medela electric rental models, the Classic and Lactina pumps. Adjustable vacuum control. |
| **SpringExpress** | $35 | Single manual pump operated by a spring piston action to create suction. Adjustable vacuum control. Attaches to any standard baby bottle. |
| **ManualEase** | $45 | Single manual pump with six vacuum settings. Features Autocycle pumping action, designed to simulate baby's nursing pattern. Pump can be mounted on a table or handheld. |
| **Harmony** | $50 | Single manual pump with action that mimics a baby's natural nursing rhythm. Compatible with most standard baby bottles. |
| **PedalPump** | $55 | Single or double breast pump operated by foot power. Works with Medela single- or double-pumping manual models. |
| **Single Deluxe Breast Pump** | $80 | Lightweight, portable handheld electric breast pump. Adjustable vacuum control. Simulates baby's nursing action. Similar model: Double Deluxe, $130. |
| **MiniElectric** | $85 to $95 | Electric single pump that can be powered from wall outlet or two AA batteries. Also comes with adapter to use manually. Similar model: Double Pumping MiniElectric, $150. |
| **DoubleEase** | $185 | Fully automatic double pump. Adjustable vacuum settings. Operates by wall electricity or two C batteries. Features Autocycle pumping action, designed to simulate baby's nursing pattern. |
| **Pump in Style** | $280 | Has nonremovable motor, AC adapter. Includes four bottles with lids and two bottle stands. Bag has storage and insulated compartments. Pump In Style Advanced with battery pack has two pumping phases. Also includes day carrying kit, $295. |

| Line/model | Price | Details |
| --- | --- | --- |
| **Pump In Style Companion** | $280 | Double electric pump. Adjustable suction pressure. Variable speed control to mimic nursing. Includes battery pack. Removable motor. Black carrying case. Includes separate cooler carrier. |
| **Pump In Style Traveler** | $300 | Double electric pump backpack-style case. Adjustable, padded shoulder straps. Removable motor and cooler carrier. |
| **THE FIRST YEARS** | | |
| **Easy Comfort Manual Pump** | $20 | Single manual pump with ergonomic handle. Includes two 5-ounce bottles. |
| **Natural Comfort Breast Pump** | $40 | Fully automatic single pump powered by electricity or batteries. Automatic pump-and-release action designed to mimic baby's natural sucking pattern. |
| **Easy Comfort Double Electric/ Battery Pump** | $150 | Dual pump that runs on batteries or wall electricity. T-handle allows one-handed double pumping. Suction/pressure control. Includes four 5-ounce bottles, insulated storage compartment, reusable ice packs. Black handbag style. |
| **WHISPER WEAR** | | |
| **Whisper Wear Single Breast Pump Kit** | $120 | Pump worn inside a standard bra. Operates on two AA batteries. Dual-phase motor mimics baby's sucking pattern. Adjustable suction control. Kit includes one pump and breast cup, one stem and two valves, plus 25 collection bags. Also includes carry bag and cooler pack. |
| **WHITTLESTONE** | | |
| **Whittlestone Breast Expresser** | $270 to $300 | Double electric breast pump that expresses milk through a low-vacuum foam cup design/massage action. Includes breast expresser, four milk storage bottles, two cooler packs, and instructional video. Black carrying case. |

CHAPTER

# 9

# Camcorders

F rom the moment your "star" is born, you may want to capture events on video. (Hospital or birthing center permitting, some parents even tape their baby's birth.) From those first sweet coos to your baby's homecoming and first birthday, you can relive the milestone events again and again and share them with your child when he or she gets older.

## Analog or Digital?

The least-expensive camcorders on the market are analog, which generally have good picture and sound quality and are less expensive than digital.

Digital camcorders, however, now dominate the market. They also get the highest marks in CONSUMER REPORTS' picture-quality tests. Reflecting the growth of DVD technology, some digitals now record directly onto a disk instead of tape.

In general, camcorder prices continue to fall. You can pay less than $250 for a basic analog model, less than $600 for a high-quality digital. The move to digital recording also means that

## The Digital Difference

In addition to very good sound and picture quality, a digital camcorder connects easily to a desktop computer for video editing. Some digital models weigh as little as a pound and are compact enough to fit in a pocket. Most have an LCD viewer of 2.5 inches on the diagonal; some viewers are as large as 4 inches.

camcorders may spend a little less time in the closet. Camcorders are historically one of the least-used pieces of hardware, averaging 12 hours a year, according to our reader surveys. But we've found that digitals see greater use—15 hours a year, on average.

One of the best things about digital technology is that with the right hardware and software, it's relatively easy to connect a digital camcorder to a computer for video editing. Your computer will need lots of hard-drive space and speed—a second of video from a digital camcorder occupies 3 to 4 megabytes—but even computers costing less than $1,000 are capacious and fast these days. You'll also need a 4-pin to 6-pin FireWire cable and matching input at the computer end, known as a FireWire, an IEEE-1394, or an iLink port. If your computer lacks such a port, you can buy an adapter card and FireWire cable.

Editing video shot on an analog camcorder may be slightly more cumbersome. Instead of using a FireWire port, you'll need to have a video-capture card installed in the computer. The card will have an analog video input. Or you can buy an outboard video capture device, which typically uses a USB connection to the PC.

## Recording Format

Once you've decided whether to go analog or digital and how much you want to spend, you need to pick a recording format. That determines not only how much you'll be paying for tape or disks but also how much recording time you'll get. No format is inherently superior in picture quality.

With analog, you can get 120 to 300 minutes of recording on a

Hi8 cassette; with the SVHS-C or VHS-C formats, you can get 30 to 120 minutes.

With digital formats that use MiniDV, Digital 8, or MicroMV tapes, you can get at least 60 minutes of recording on a standard cassette. MiniDV and D8 cassettes are the least expensive and easiest to find.

Digital DVD camcorders can accommodate either DVD-RAM disks, which can be reused but aren't compatible with all DVD players, or DVD-R, one-use disks that work in most DVD players. The standard setting yields 60 minutes of recording; the "fine" setting, 30 minutes. The lowest-rated digital model is equal to the best analog model that we've tested.

Our Ratings of camcorders, digital and analog, tape or disk, which start on page 80, show what you get for the money.

## Shopping Secrets

**Know what you want before you go to the store.** Don't depend on a store's sales staff for buying guidance. If our recent foray to the mall is any indication, you may not get much help. At a big-box electronics store, the only assistance to be had came from counter cards beneath each display-model listing, but not explaining, the many features. It was nearly impossible to figure out why one camcorder cost $300, another $600. At a smaller electronics store, we found a clerk who was up on all the buzzwords but not very helpful at interpreting them. We still couldn't figure out why one model cost $300, another $600. Bottom line: To simplify shopping, be clear on your budget and the features you want before you step into the store. You're on the right track by reading this chapter.

**Think about format.** If you're replacing an older camcorder, consider what you'll do with the tapes you've accumulated. If you don't stay with the same format you've been using, you will probably want to transfer the old tapes to an easily viewed medium such as a DVD. If you're buying your first camcorder, concentrate on finding the best one for your budget, regardless of format.

**Check the size, weight, and controls.** In the store try different camcorders to make sure they fit your hand and are comfortable to use. Some models can feel disconcertingly tiny. (You'll need to use a tripod if you want rock-steady video, no matter which camcorder you choose.) Most camcorders are designed so that the most frequently used controls—the switch to zoom in and out, the record button, and the tape controls for playback—are readily at hand. Make sure the controls are convenient and that you can easily change the tape or DVD and remove the battery.

**Consider supersizing the display.** Check the flip-out LCD viewer. Most measure 2.5 inches on the diagonal, but some are larger, adding about $100 to the price. If the viewer seems small and difficult for you to use or suffers from too much glare, consider moving up to a similar model or a different brand to get a better screen.

**Think about the lighting.** When taking videos of your baby, you won't always use your camcorder outdoors or in a brightly lit room. You can shoot video in dim light, but don't expect miracles. In our tests, using the camcorders' default mode, most produced only fair or poor images in very low light. Many camcorders have settings that can improve performance but are a challenge to use.

## What's Available

Sony dominates the camcorder market, with multiple models in a number of formats. Other top brands include Canon, Hitachi, JVC, Panasonic, Samsung, and Sharp. Most digitals come in the MiniDV format. Although some models can be slipped into a large pocket and weigh as little as 1 pound, their quality doesn't suffer. New formats, such as the disc-based DVD-RAM and DVD-R and tape-based MicroMV, have also appeared. Here are your basic format choices available today:

### Digital formats

**MiniDV.** These camcorders can record high-quality images. They use a unique tape cassette, and the typical recording time is 60 minutes at standard play (SP) speed. Expect to pay about $6 for a 60-minute tape. You'll need to use the camcorder for playback—it converts its recording to an analog signal so it can be played directly into a TV or VCR. If the TV or VCR has an S-video input jack, you can use it to get the best possible picture. Price: $600 to $2,000.

**Digital 8.** Also known as D8, this format gives you digital quality on Hi8 or 8mm cassettes, which cost $6.50 or $3.50, respectively. The Digital 8 format records with a faster tape speed, so a "120-minute" cassette actually lasts only 60 minutes at SP. Most models will also play your old analog Hi8 or 8mm tapes. Price: $400 to $800.

**Disc-based.** Capitalizing on the capabilities of DVD movie discs, these formats offer benefits that tape can't provide: long-term durability, a compact medium, and random access to scenes as with a DVD. The 3-inch discs record standard MPEG-2 video, the same format used in commercial DVD videos. The amount of recording time varies according to the quality level you select: from 20 minutes per side at the highest-quality setting for DVD-RAM up to about 60 minutes per side at the lowest setting. DVD-RAM discs are not compatible with DVD players, but the discs can be reused, which is good, considering that they cost about $25 apiece. DVD-R is supposed to be compatible with most DVD players and computer DVD drives, but the discs (about $3.50) are good for one use only. Price: $800 and up.

## Analog formats

Most analog camcorders come in one of three formats: VHS-C, Super VHS-C, or Hi8. They usually weigh around 2 pounds. Picture quality is generally good, though a notch below that of digital.

**VHS-C.** This format uses an adapter to play in any VHS VCR. Cassettes most commonly hold 30 minutes on SP and cost $3.50. Price: $250 to $500.

**Super VHS-C.** This high-band variation of VHS-C uses special S-VHS-C tapes. (A slightly different format, S-VHS/ET-C, can use standard VHS-C tapes.) One S-VHS-C tape yields 40 minutes at SP and costs $6.50. JVC is the only brand that offers models in this format. Price: $250 to $500.

**Hi8.** This premium variant of 8mm (an analog format that's virtually extinct) promises a sharper picture. For the full benefit you need to use Hi8 tape and watch a TV that has an S-video input. A 120-minute cassette tape costs about $6.50. Price: $200 to $400.

# Features to Consider

**Audio/video inputs.** These allow you to record material from another camcorder or a VCR. A digital camcorder must have such an input jack if you want to record analog material digitally.

**Autofocus.** This feature adjusts for maximum sharpness; manual override may be needed for problem situations, such as low light. (With some newer camcorders, you may have to tap buttons repeatedly to get the focus just right.) On many camcorders, you can also control exposure, shutter speed, and white balance.

**Backlight compensation.** This feature increases the exposure slightly when your subject is lit from behind and silhouetted.

**Digital still.** Camcorders with this capability allow you to take snapshots, which can then be downloaded to your computer. The photo quality, though, is generally inferior to that of a still camera.

**Flip-out liquid-crystal display (LCD) viewer.** This type of viewer is becoming commonplace on all but the lowest-priced camcorders. You'll find it useful for reviewing footage you've shot and easier to use than the eyepiece viewfinder for certain shooting poses. However, some LCD viewers are hard to use in sunlight, a drawback on models that have only a viewer and no eyepiece.

**Full auto switch.** This feature essentially lets you point and shoot. The camcorder automatically adjusts everything from the color balance to shutter speed, focus, and aperture (also called the "iris" or F-stop).

**Image stabilizer.** It automatically reduces most of the shakes that occur from holding the camcorder as you record a scene. Most stabilizers are electronic; a few are optical. Either type can be effective, though mounting the camcorder on a tripod is the surest way to get steady images. If you're not using a tripod, you can minimize shakiness by holding the camcorder with both hands and propping your elbows against the sides of your chest.

**Infrared-sensitive recording mode.** Also known as night vision, zero lux, or MagicVu, this feature allows shooting in very dim or dark situations, using infrared emitters. You can use it for nighttime shots, although colors won't register accurately.

**Light.** A built-in light provides additional illumination for close-ups when the image would otherwise be too dark.

**Microphone.** Unlike a built-in microphone, an external one that's plugged into a microphone jack won't pick up noises from the camcorder itself, and it typically improves audio performance.

**Preset auto-exposure settings.** These can be helpful for special lighting situations. A "snow & sand" setting, for example, adjusts shutter speed or aperture to accommodate high reflectivity.

**Quick review.** This feature lets you view the last few seconds of a scene without having to press a lot of buttons.

**Remote control.** Among other uses, a remote helps when you want to put your camcorder on a tripod and be in the picture yourself.

**Tape speed.** Regardless of format, analog or digital, every camcorder displays tape speeds the same way a VCR does. Every model, for example, includes an SP (standard play) speed. Digitals have a slower LP (long play) speed, which adds 50 percent to the recording time. A few 8mm and Hi8 models have an LP speed that doubles the recording time. All VHS-C and S-VHS-C camcorders have an even slower, EP (extended play) speed that triples the recording time. With analog camcorders, slower speeds worsen picture quality. Slow speed doesn't reduce picture quality on digital camcorders, though it may mean sacrificing some seldom-used editing options and it may restrict playback on other camcorders.

**Zoom.** This feature is usually activated by a finger control—press one way to zoom in, the other way to widen the view. Typical optical zoom ratios range from 10:1 to 26:1. The higher the ratio, the tighter you can zero in on your subject. A camcorder's optical zoom relies on lenses, just like a film camera. Many camcorders offer a digital zoom to extend the range to 400:1 or more, but at a lower picture quality.

Other features may be useful in editing your videos. They include a built-in title generator, a time-and-date stamp, and a time code, which is a frame reference of exactly where you are on a tape—the hour, minute, speed, and frame.

## Recommendations

If you don't want to spend a lot, an analog camcorder is a good value. Many are now priced at $250 or less. Analog models may also appeal to you if you have little interest in video editing. Otherwise, choose a digital model. Digital camcorders generally offer very good to excellent picture quality, along with very good sound capability, compactness, and ease of handling. Prices are continuing to fall.

# Ratings • Camcorders

ost people in the market for a camcorder choose a digital model. Digitals offer the widest range of tape formats, the best selection of models, and the best overall performance. Indeed, as the Ratings show, you can take fine picture quality pretty much for granted and base a choice on other factors: recording format, weight, size, or ease of use, for example.

A digital camcorder that uses MiniDV or D8 format is the best all-around choice, especially for people who don't want to spend a lot. Digitals that record directly onto a DVD are best-suited for those who can afford to spend upward of $900 and who want their home videos on a durable, easily stored medium. Analog camcorders' main advantage is a low price. Picture quality is about what you'd expect from a rental video.

| | | Excellent | Very good | Good | Fair | Poor |
|---|---|---|---|---|---|---|
| | | ◒ | ◒ | ○ | ◓ | ● |

**Within types, in performance order. Blue key numbers indicate Quick Picks.**

| Key number | Brand & model | Price | Format | Overall score (0–100) | Picture quality | Ease of use | Image stabilizer | Audio quality | Weight (lb.) | Battery life (min.) |
|---|---|---|---|---|---|---|---|---|---|---|
| **DIGITAL MODELS** | | | | | | | | | | |
| 1 | **Canon** Elura50 | $800 | MiniDV | | ◒ | ○ | ◒ | ○ | 1.0 | 60 |
| 2 | **Panasonic** VDR-M30PP | 800 | DVD-RAM, -R | | ◒ | ○ | ◒ | ◒ | 1.2 | NS |
| 3 | **Panasonic** PV-DV73 | 700 | MiniDV | | ◒ | ◒ | ◒ | ◓ | 1.4 | NS |
| 4 | **Panasonic** PV-GS50 | 700 | MiniDV | | ◒ | ◒ | ○ | ○ | 1.0 | NS |
| 5 | **Sony** DCR-TRV350 | 500 | D8 | | ◒ | ○ | ◒ | ◒ | 2.2 | 80 |
| 6 | **Hitachi** DZ-MV350A | 850 | DVD-RAM, -R | | ◒ | ○ | ◒ | ○ | 1.2 | 45-50 |
| 7 | **Sony** DCR-PC105 | 1,000 | MiniDV | | ◒ | ○ | ◒ | ◓ | 1.2 | 80-90 |
| 8 | **Sony** DCR-TRV80 | 1,500 | MiniDV | | ◒ | ○ | ◒ | ◒ | 1.8 | 95 |
| 9 | **Canon** ZR60 | 500 | MiniDV | | ◒ | ◒ | ◒ | ○ | 1.4 | 75 |
| 10 | **Canon** ZR70MC | 700 | MiniDV | | ◒ | ◒ | ◒ | ○ | 1.4 | 140 |
| 11 | **Hitachi** DZ-MV380A | 1,000 | DVD-RAM, -R | | ◒ | ○ | ◒ | ○ | 1.4 | 45-50 |
| 12 | **Sony** DCR-TRV22 | 700 | MiniDV | | ◒ | ○ | ◒ | ◒ | 1.4 | 90 |
| 13 | **JVC** GR-DX75 | 600 | MiniDV | | ◒ | ◓ | ○ | ◓ | 1.2 | 65 |
| 14 | **Sony** DCR-TRV33 | 800 | MiniDV | | ◒ | ○ | ◒ | ◓ | 1.4 | 90 |
| 15 | **Panasonic** PV-GS70 | 900 | MiniDV | | ○ | ○ | ◒ | ◓ | 1.2 | NS |
| 16 | **Sony** DCR-TRV38 | 900 | MiniDV | | ○ | ○ | ◒ | ◓ | 1.6 | 70 |
| 17 | **JVC** GR-DV500 | 600 | MiniDV | | ○ | ◒ | ○ | ◓ | 1.6 | 70 |
| 18 | **Canon** Optura 20 | 900 | MiniDV | | ○ | ○ | ◒ | ◒ | 1.6 | 60 |
| 19 | **JVC** GR-D70 | 480 | MiniDV | | ○ | ○ | ◒ | ● | 1.4 | 70 |
| 20 | **Sharp** VL-Z7U | 600 | MiniDV | | ○ | ◓ | ◒ | ◓ | 1.2 | 100 |
| 21 | **Samsung** SCD27 | 500 | MiniDV | | ◓ | ○ | ◒ | ◓ | 1.4 | 90 |

| | Excellent | Very good | Good | Fair | Poor |
|---|---|---|---|---|---|
| | ⊖ | ⊖ | ○ | ◔ | ● |

**Within types, in performance order. Blue key numbers indicate Quick Picks.**

| | Brand & model | Price | Format | Overall score | Test results | | | | Features | |
|---|---|---|---|---|---|---|---|---|---|---|
| **ANALOG MODELS** | | | | | | | | | | |
| 22 | **Sony** CCD-TRV318 | $300 | Hi8 | ▬▬▬ | ◔ | ⊖ | ⊖ | ⊖ | 2.0 | 120 |
| 23 | **JVC** GR-SXM250 | 250 | SVHS/ET-C | ▬▬▬ | ◔ | ⊖ | ◔ | ● | 2.4 | 75 |
| 24 | **Canon** ES8600 | 280 | Hi8 | ▬▬▬ | ◔ | ○ | ◔ | ◔ | 2.0 | 90 |
| 25 | **Samsung** SCL810 | 230 | Hi8 | ▬▬▬ | ◔ | ⊖ | – | ◔ | 2.0 | 90 |

## Guide to the Ratings

**Overall score** is based mainly on picture quality; ease of use, image stabilizing, and audio quality carried less weight. **Picture quality** is based on the judgments of trained panelists who viewed static images shot in good light at standard speed (SP) for tape and "fine" mode for DVDs. Picture quality in low light was nearly always fair or poor. **Ease of use** takes into account ergonomics, weight, how accurately the viewfinder frames scenes, and contrast in the LCD viewer. **Image stabilizer** indicates how well that circuitry worked. **Audio quality** represents accuracy using the built-in microphone, plus freedom from noise and flutter. **Weight** includes battery and tape or disk. Optical zoom range is as stated by the manufacturer. **Battery life** is as stated by the manufacturer, using the LCD viewer. Turning off the viewer typically extends battery life by 10 to 40 minutes. "NS" indicates that the manufacturer did not provide the specification for battery life. **Price** is approximate retail.

# Quick Picks • Camcorders

**Best values among digital camcorders:**
3 **Panasonic** $700
4 **Panasonic** $700
5 **Sony** $500, CR Best Buy
9 **Canon** $500

The Panasonics (3, 4) offer high overall performance and good reliability. The Sony (5), the only D8 model we tested, can play 8mm and Hi8 tapes, has an excellent image-stabilizing system, and the best low-light performance among the digital camcorders. Sony D8 models have also been reliable. The Canon (9) is lighter and somewhat easier to use, but Canon has been among the more repair-prone brands of digital camcorders.

**A bargain-priced DVD camcorder:**
2 **Panasonic** $800

The least-expensive DVD recorder we tested, it has an excellent image stabilizer. DVD camcorders are too new for us to know how reliable they are likely to be.

**Best value in an analog camcorder:**
22 **Sony** $300

This model is one of the easiest to use and has the best low-light performance of the analogs we tested. Sony Hi8 camcorders have been among the more reliable of that format.

CHAPTER

# 10

# Cameras
## Film and Digital Models

**L**ights! Camera! Action! From your baby's birth to all of those firsts—first smile, first tooth, first step—each day with a new baby is a photo opportunity that can bring on the urge to run for your camera. Now's the time to get ready to capture the memories you'll enjoy for years to come.

## FILM CAMERAS

Today's film cameras are convenient, easy to use, and produce pleasing photographs. Unlike digital cameras (more on those later in this chapter), a point-and-shoot film camera doesn't require learning, buying, or doing anything new. Just drop off the film and pick up your prints. Nearly all can produce snapshots of your baby that are sharp and well-lit, with little distortion or other drawbacks.

You can also get some of the benefits of digital cameras, such as storing the images in your computer where you can use software to crop, brighten, or otherwise improve them. When you drop off a roll for processing, simply ask for the photos to be stored digitally on a floppy disk or a photo CD. Other options include scanning negatives or prints using a scanner and computer.

## Shopping Secrets

**Try before you buy.** A camera that's easy to grip is a plus. Be sure that you can see the viewfinder's image clearly. If you wear glasses, you might want a camera with a diopter adjustment to help you see through the viewfinder without them.

**Think small.** You never know when you're going to want to snap a picture of your baby. A camera that's lightweight, portable, and fits into your purse or diaper bag is your best bet for taking treasured, impromptu shots—at the zoo, at grandma's house, at the supermarket. Some of our readers even keep disposable cameras in various rooms of their homes just so they never miss a baby-photo opportunity.

## What's Available

Major brands of point-and-shoot cameras include, in alphabetical order: Canon, Fujifilm, Kodak, Minolta, Nikon, Olympus, and Pentax. Many make point-and-shoot cameras in both 35mm and APS (Advanced Photo System) formats. Many also make SLR (single-lens reflex) 35mm cameras, which are somewhat larger, use interchangeable lenses, and let you see exactly what the lens sees. All three camera types automatically handle focusing, exposure, and shutter-speed settings. Flashes are built into practically all point-and-shoot models and some SLRs. The lowest-priced film cameras are fixed-focus, like an old-fashioned box camera. Many of these are "disposable" models; you send the camera to a lab to get the film developed.

### Compact 35mm cameras

Small, light, and inexpensive, these point-and-shoot cameras are capable of producing exceptional photos.

**Pros:** Since you don't have to worry about focus or lighting, you can just grab the camera and snap away—handy when your baby suddenly performs a feat you simply must get on film. And if you request digital storage when you have the film processed, you can then crop and edit the shots with computer software.

**Cons:** Because you don't see exactly what the camera sees when you look through the viewfinder, you may have trouble framing the shot so it contains exactly what you want, with no cut-off heads or noses.

**Price:** $6 to $12 for a disposable camera; $20 and up for fixed-focus models; $60 and up for automatic, nonzoom cameras; $80 and up for a model with a zoom lens.

## APS cameras

Advanced Photo System cameras closely resemble 35mm point-and-shoot models but with one important difference: They use a unique cartridge that holds the film at all times, from loading to shooting to processing. The film frames are smaller than 35 mm, but the cameras make the most of each frame.

**Pros:** Variety. You can get an APS camera to make a normal snapshot ("S" in APS parlance), a slightly wider view ("H"), or a panorama ("P"). You can change from one view to another with each new frame. And whenever you order reprints, you can order different views—a panoramic version of a standard shot, for example. Most APS cameras have autofocus and a zoom lens. There are very few single-use APS models.

**Cons:** The negative is approximately half the size of 35mm, so each photo has less detail than a 35mm negative. As a result, pictures can look grainy, especially when they're enlarged. Otherwise, the quality of the prints rivals those from 35mm cameras. Because the format is relatively new, the film can also be harder to find than 35mm.

**Price:** A few dollars more than comparable 35mm models.

## 35mm SLR cameras

Bulkier than point-and-shoot models, SLR cameras not only offer the option of interchangeable lenses, but also let you see what the camera sees. (Even the best point-and-shoot cameras show only about 90 percent of the area that will actually appear in your photo.) So with an SLR, you can compose a shot precisely.

**Pros:** The generally high-quality optics deliver the best image quality. If your SLR has both autofocus and a built-in flash, it can be as quick to use as a point-and-shoot camera. For advanced photographers, SLRs allow hands-on control over things like shutter speed and aperture setting when set in manual mode.

**Cons:** If you're new to the world of photography, an SLR and its manual features may be too much camera for you.

**Price:** $200 and up for the camera body plus another $100 and up for a moderate-range zoom lens.

## Features to Consider

**Aperture.** Indicated by an f-number (such as f 2.8), an aperture governs how wide the camera will open the lens when you take a photo. (The smaller the f-number, the larger the opening.) A wider aperture allows more light to reach the film, so it can increase your odds of taking good pictures indoors without a flash. A wider maximum aperture also raises the price of the camera.

**Autofocus.** This feature lets you obtain crisp images without having to manually focus, a plus for capturing a squirmy baby. Low-end cameras typically cover preset ranges, permitting quick shots but dispensing with the more precise focusing of higher-priced models. Multiarea autofocus reduces the risk of focusing on the background of a scene by accident. Focus lock lets you freeze the focus onto whatever appears at the center of the viewfinder. This means you can keep the focus on your baby while you move around to change the angle of the shot. Compact film cameras typically use an infrared beam to focus. In-the-viewfinder signals in many models will let you know when your subject is too close to be in focus or when you've gone out of flash range.

**Built-in flash.** These cover various distances, from 4 or 5 feet to 10 feet or more. The smartest ones track with the zoom lens to broaden or narrow the beam. A fill-flash setting lets you "fill in" harsh shadows in sunlit portraits.

**Date stamping.** This feature imprints photos with the date they were taken, thereby saving you from having to hand-date batches after they're developed. This task can easily fall by the wayside when you've got a hungry baby to feed and diapers to change.

**Motorized film handling.** This feature automatically advances the film, then rewinds it when you reach the end of the roll. With a 35mm camera, you drop in the film, pull out the leader, and close the camera; with APS, you merely drop in the cartridge. Mid-roll change, a feature found in some APS cameras, lets you reload partially exposed rolls of film—useful if you often switch between different film speeds.

**Programmed auto exposure.** Common on all but the cheapest models, programmed auto exposure allows the camera to regulate both the shutter speed and the aperture to achieve a properly exposed photo, in either bright or low light. An exposure-compensation feature lets you make up for any brightness differences between the background and the subject to prevent underexposing your subject when the background is bright—that sunny day in the park, for example—or overexposing when the background is unusually dark. SLRs and more advanced compact models may also offer several preset exposure modes that suit various situations.

## TAKING BETTER BABY PHOTOS

**B**abies and toddlers make challenging subjects for photos. After all, they don't necessarily smile when you want them to or look at the camera, and they've been known to wiggle right out of a shot. Here are some things you can do to get better baby shots.

**"Get into your child's environment,"** urges Bob Watts, owner of Enterprise Photo, a professional photography business in Kimberly, Idaho. If your baby is playing on the floor in the living room, you (the photographer) should get down there too. "You don't want to be standing up, shooting from above," says Watts. Your baby will think, "What's Mommy or Daddy doing now?" That may yield a confused or fearful expression.

**Respect your baby's personality.** Don't expect a shy baby to turn into a ham just because you have a camera in hand. Overall, "you want to capture your baby's personality so that later, you'll say, 'I recognize that look or that attitude,'" Watts says. For a shy child, for example, you might want to click the shutter when his or her chin is down a bit. If your baby is a spark plug, you want to capture those bright eyes and big smile.

**Recruit an assistant.** Have your spouse, a sibling, friend, aunt, or uncle play with your baby while you wield the camera. "You'll get a more natural shot if your baby is doing something rather than simply looking at you," Watts says.

**Use the power of distraction.** When you want your baby to look at the camera (while playing with a toy, for example), "say, 'show that toy to me,' or 'show it to Mommy,' " Watts suggests. But don't hold the toy yourself because babies tend to reach for whatever you're presenting. "You'll get hands in the picture," Watts says.

**Schedule picture time when your baby is happiest.** That could, for example, be right after meals rather than immediately post-naptime.

**Keep a camera handy for spontaneous moments.** You might have several disposables, as we mentioned, strategically located around the house—on the mantel, on top of your refrigerator, in your bedroom.

**Practice, practice, practice.** If you aren't a veteran photographer, take lots of pictures until using the camera becomes second nature. "That way, when you get that magic moment, you're not fumbling around, trying to figure out how to turn the camera on," Watts says.

**Engage toddlers and older children in make-believe.** If you're trying to get a shot of them in their Halloween costumes, for example, initiate a game of trick-or-treat in which you ring the doorbell and they hold out their candy sacks. "And have them say their name instead of cheese," says Watts. "I don't know why it works, but right after they say their name, they usually smile."

**Red-eye reduction.** "Red eye" occurs when a flash reflects off your subject's retinas. Since you'll want to capture those baby blues or big browns, consider red-eye reduction, which typically uses a light before the main flash to constrict the subject's pupils. A flash located farther from the lens also reduces red eye. (If necessary, you can retouch a print to eliminate red eye, using a black fine-point marker or a special red-eye correction pen. If you opt for digital storage, you may be able to remove red eye as you edit the photos on your computer.)

**A self-timer.** This feature delays the shutter so you can be in a picture yourself and not go unrepresented in the family photos. Certain models offer a wireless remote shutter release.

**Shutter speed.** This determines how long the aperture stays open during a single shot. A fast shutter speed (1/1000 to 1/8000 of a second or so) lets you freeze a moving subject, such as a toddler on the go.

**Zoom lens.** Available on many models, it will typically magnify your subject two to four times. For example, a 3x lens zooms from about 35 mm (for a fairly wide angle) to about 105 mm (for a moderate telephoto). Generally, the higher the zoom ratio (4x as opposed to 2x, for example) and the larger the maximum aperture, the higher the cost of a zoom lens.

## Recommendations

Spending more gets you more features and often better optics. Nevertheless, you can expect a fairly high level of quality from 35mm point-and-shoot models—even from a very low-priced one. For maximum versatility and image quality, however, SLR models still remain the best (if bulkiest and most expensive) choice.

Don't expect too much from the built-in flash that's standard on point-and-shoot cameras. External-flash units (such as the detachable ones available for some compacts and SLRs) provide more light for your subject than do the built-in flashes.

See the Ratings on page 95 for our advice on specific models of 35mm and APS cameras.

# DIGITAL CAMERAS

Compared with film cameras, digital models provide a greater level of creative control over your images. And there's no suspense: You can preview your pictures right away on the camera's liquid-crystal display (LCD).

Digital cameras record images on reusable memory cards instead of film. If you want to shoot 50 pictures in a day— and as a new parent you probably will— you can do that and just keep two. You're not out film costs, and there's no penalty for getting familiar with your camera as well as lighting.

Once you've taken a digital photo, you can transfer it to your computer, crop or enlarge it, adjust the color, then make prints, greeting cards, and even T-shirts. You can also post it on a Web site or send images to family and friends via e-mail—all using the image-handling software included with the camera.

Every digital camera comes with a program, such as Adobe Photoshop Elements, that lets you crop an image, fix color, add "punch" to dingy tones, and organize your photo collection for storage and presentation. Such software gives even the most technically challenged beginners unprecedented creative command. Plus, you can store all your photos as computer files, which don't take up shelf space as do negatives and are easier to browse and share with others than prints. And you need only print your favorites. Photos saved as files can be uploaded to Web pages or printed months, even years, later without losing quality.

## Resolution and print quality

A digital camera captures an image in the form of millions of tiny picture elements called pixels. Most cameras have a resolution of at least 2 megapixels (2 million pixels); the most expensive have 4 or more. In general, the higher the pixel count, the sharper and more detailed the image can be.

The downside is that the higher the resolution you use to shoot a photo, the more space it will take up on your camera's storage card, and

# DIGITAL PROS AND CONS

**W**ith a digital camera, you don't have to buy film or pay for developing it. However, digital photography has its own ongoing costs, such as regular supplies of ink cartridges and photographic paper. Digital cameras are also much harder on batteries than film cameras, so much so that you should carry spares while on extended outings.

On the plus side, most digital cameras come with user-friendly features, such as automatic exposure control, autofocus, automatic flash, and a zoom lens. Most have both an optical viewfinder and a color LCD viewer. LCD viewers are essentially 100 percent accurate in showing what you get–better than most of the optical viewfinders–but they gobble up battery power. You can also view shots you've already taken on the LCD. Many digital cameras provide a video output, so you can see your pictures on a TV screen.

The file format most commonly used is the highly compressed JPEG. (It's also used on the Internet for photos.) Some cameras can save photos in TIFF format, but this uncompressed setting yields enormous files.

If you're considering a digital camera because you think its advantages outweigh the drawbacks, or you've decided it's time to step up from an aging digital model, you should be able to find cameras to your liking among the models we list (see page 97). They range in price from less than $220 to more than $1,000.

**If you're new to digital photography, the controls may take some getting used to.**

the fewer such photos the card will hold. To compensate, cameras let you shoot at resolutions lower than the maximum.

Typically, you should shoot at a camera's highest resolution if you expect to make large prints, but you can use lower resolutions for snapshots or images you plan to e-mail or put on the Web. Often the number of high-resolution shots that will fit on the memory card supplied with a camera is so small that you'll need to buy a larger card.

The resolution at which you shoot limits how large a print you can make if you want it to be razor sharp. That's especially true if you crop a photo tightly and use just a part of the total image. Shoot at too low a resolution for the size of print you want and the resulting image will look coarse, "dotty," or jagged. Cameras that are 2- to 3-megapixels provide sufficient detail to print 8x10s from uncropped images.

Higher resolution isn't necessarily synonymous with higher print quality. Image clarity can be affected as much by lens quality or other factors.

## Shopping Secrets

**Try before you buy.** In the store pay particular attention to how a camera feels to hold in shooting mode for more than a few seconds. Even the best performing camera won't serve you well if you're not comfortable using it. And keep in mind how you'll use the camera. If you'll be toting it along with your baby on outings, consider a compact model. Some digital cameras are scarcely bigger than a deck of cards. Others are the size of traditional film cameras. Weight can range from several ounces to more than a pound.

**Look for a model with an optical zoom of 3x or more.** That lets you zero in and frame shots flexibly. Manufacturers sometimes list a camera's digital zoom instead of, or along with, its optical zoom. But digital zoom is an electronic trick and not a true zoom. If the type of zoom being claimed isn't obvious from the camera or its packaging, check the manufacturer's Web site. Also look for an LCD that tilts or whose brightness you can adjust, which might make it easier to view in bright sunlight.

**Choose a camera that recycles quickly.** If a camera takes too long to recycle between shots, you can miss an important moment. Just how long is too long depends on the subjects you're shooting. The most responsive cameras in the Ratings recycled in just 2 seconds.

## What's Available

The leading manufacturers of digital cameras include, in alphabetical order: Canon, Fujifilm, Kodak, Minolta, Nikon, Olympus, Pentax, and Sony are . Prices for 3-megapixel models range from $220 to $450; for 4-megapixels and up, $260 to $1,000 or more. To spend less than $200, you'll need to opt for a 2-megapixel model. In general, for basic, nonprofessional use, CONSUMER REPORTS has found the best value to be 3-megapixel cameras, though 4-megapixel models are now becoming more affordable.

# Features to Consider

**Batteries.** Most digitals use proprietary rechargeable batteries. Some, however, conveniently use standard AAs.

**LCD viewer.** Look for an LCD that tilts or that can be adjusted for brightness, which can make it easier to use in harsh sunlight.

**Navigational menus and buttons.** With some cameras, you use menus to navigate. Some featured models have an extensive system of menus that take time to master using buttons to step through choices on an LCD. Others have an easy-to-use control wheel for selecting basic functions. One Toshiba model's LCD doubles as a touch screen: You tap desired options and settings as you would on a PDA or an ATM at your bank. However, we found this approach of no practical advantage. Navigational design factors are a matter of personal preference, so try out a camera in the store before you buy.

**Recycling time.** Since babies and toddlers are always on the go,

## ESSENTIAL EXTRAS

**M**ost digital cameras come with at least a few accessories, such as a basic memory card and batteries. But if you shoot more than the occasional family gathering or more than a few photos at a time, you'll probably need to buy at least one of these accessories:

**Card reader.** Tethered to your PC (usually via a USB port), this device accepts memory cards for transfers, so you don't have to hook up the camera to the PC. That can help conserve batteries. If you shoot large numbers of high-resolution photos, a card reader can also save transfer time, provided you have one designed to take advantage of the fastest computer connections, such as FireWire or USB 2.0. Some readers have slots for two or more types of cards. Prices: $20 to $40.

**Higher-capacity memory storage.** The memory storage card that cameras include seldom holds many high-resolution photos. With most cameras, a 128-megabyte (MB) card, which costs about $50, increases your capacity. Depending on the type of memory storage device your camera uses—CompactFlash, Memory Stick XD, SmartMedia, Secure Digital, or other—you may be able to buy sizes such as 512 MB or higher.

**Rapid charger.** In-camera charging is often slow and cumbersome, and it ties up the camera. A rapid charger, if available for your battery type, frees the camera and may revive batteries in just a couple of hours. Price: $25 to $35.

**Rechargeable batteries.** Use these when traveling or as backup to your regular batteries. If your camera accepts nickel-metal hydride (NiMH) AA cells, they're a good choice because they're widely available and can be recharged many times. Some brands now offer batteries with extra capacity, which should last a bit longer. Whichever ones you buy, make sure the charger you have works with that type. Price: $10 (four batteries).

The following accessories, though not essential, can enhance your photographs or save you time:

**External flash.** This extends the range at which you can shoot flash photos. It can eliminate red eye or allow you to tilt up the flash to reflect it off ceilings for a softer, more pleasing look. It requires a camera with a flash outlet known as a "hot shoe." Price: $40 to $100.

**Laptop PC Card adapter.** An adapter lets you plug a camera's memory card into a laptop's PC Card slot so you can download photos. Price: $10.

**Tripod.** Putting your camera on a sturdy tripod will allow you to use a slower shutter speed and avoid camera shake. It may also eliminate the need for a flash. You can operate the shutter via the camera's self-timer or a cable you purchase separately. Most cameras have a threaded socket on the bottom made to accommodate a tripod. Price: $20 to $50.

you'll probably want a camera that takes less time to recycle between shots. For comparisons see the Ratings on page 97.

**Red-eye reduction.** As with a film camera, this feature shines a light toward your subject just before the main flash. (A camera whose flash unit is farther from the lens also produces less red-eye. Computer editing may correct it, too.)

**Zoom lens.** A zoom lens provides flexibility in framing shots and closes the apparent distance between you and baby—ideal if you want to quickly switch to a close shot. A 3x zoom is comparable to a 35 to 105mm lens on a film camera; a 2x zoom to a 35 to 70mm lens. Optical zooms are superior to digital zooms. Digital models double or triple the zoom range, but only by magnifying the center of the frame without actually increasing picture detail, resulting in a somewhat coarser view. Look for a model with an optical zoom of 3x or more.

## Recommendations

Going digital makes it easy to take photos of your baby and share them with friends and relatives who are also computer users. Most models have a 3x zoom, manual controls to adjust the aperture and shutter speed, self-timer, tripod socket, software for Windows and Mac OS, and a one-year warranty on parts and labor. Most use AA batteries. We tested cameras that take AA batteries using alkaline batteries. (Lithium batteries generally last longer but cost more.)

As to photo software, the package that comes with your camera (or computer or scanner) could be all you need. If you find that you want

# PRINTS OF YOUR PRINCE (OR PRINCESS)

**E**ven if you have a terrific camera, you need a way to produce high-quality prints from your favorite baby photos. That means different things to different users.

Casual film photographers may be satisfied with prints from a one-hour lab or with an extra-cost picture-CD backup of the prints. Digital-photography enthusiasts, however, may want to do it all themselves, mastering image-handling software on the computer and relying on a high-quality inkjet printer for prints.

Inkjets dominate the printer market for home users because of their low prices and prowess with color photos and graphics. You'll also find inkjet technology used in multifunction machines—home-office hardware that puts printing, faxing, copying, and scanning in one reasonably compact box. Laser printers, a mainstay in offices, are costly and mainly for black-and-white printing.

the kinds of features that only a separately purchased retail package offers, we recommend the following products, based on our testing:

- ACD Systems ACDSee 5.0, $45
- Jasc Paint Shop Photo Album 4, $50
- Microsoft Picture It! Photo 8.0, $30

These products are good choices for people who want to improve their photos and manage image files. Microsoft's Picture It! Photo was among the easiest to use of the programs we evaluated, but it works only with Windows.

ACDSee and Paint Shop Photo Album are both easy-to-use programs that emphasize organizing, filing, and storage, but they're light on editing and drawing tools. Either one is worth considering if you plan to share lots of photos via e-mail or post them on a Web page as many proud new parents now do.

Still more advanced programs are:

- Adobe Photoshop Elements 2.0, $100
- Microsoft Picture It! Digital Image Pro 7.0, $90

They are for people who want to create masterpieces the way pros do. They're not expensive, and you can easily learn many of their features. Picture It! Digital Image Pro works only with Windows, while Photoshop Elements works with Windows or Mac OS. The ultimate tool for editing photographs is Adobe's Photoshop CS, $600. But fully mastering it requires so much training and expertise that it's strictly for professionals.

# Ratings • Film Cameras

**W**hether they use 35mm or APS film, these cameras have attained a fairly high level of quality. Nearly all can produce very pleasing snapshots–sharp, properly focused, with little distortion or other drawbacks. They're very easy to use, and they're moderately priced; most sell for less than $200, and many models worth considering are less than $150. The higher-priced cameras tend to have the widest zoom-lens range, but otherwise aren't superior to the others. Most of the cameras in the Ratings are 35mm; only two are APS models. That's a reflection of the dominance that 35mm has in the market, making it the safest choice in terms of availability over the long term. Film format aside, use factors such as price, weight, or the zoom-lens range to narrow your choice among models.

| | Excellent | Very good | Good | Fair | Poor |
|---|---|---|---|---|---|
| | ⊖ | ⊖ | ○ | ◐ | ● |

Within types, in performance order. Blue key numbers indicate Quick Picks.

| Key number | Brand and model | Price | Overall score | Picture quality | Convenience | Flash | Viewfinder | Shutter delay, sec. | Flash range, ft. | Zoom | Weight, oz. | Battery (L=lithium, A=alkaline) |
|---|---|---|---|---|---|---|---|---|---|---|---|---|
| **35 MM CAMERAS** |
| 1 | **Minolta** Freedom Zoom 160 | $170 | | ⊖ | ⊖ | ⊖ | ○ | 0.2 | 21 | 4.3x | 8 | L |
| 2 | **Fujifilm** Zoom Date 90SR | 100 | | ⊖ | ⊖ | ⊖ | ◐ | 0.4 | 13 | 2.4x | 9 | L |
| 3 | **Samsung** Fino 120 Super | 150 | | ⊖ | ⊖ | ⊖ | ○ | 0.5 | 21 | 3.2x | 8 | L |
| 4 | **Fujifilm** Zoom Date 1300 | 240 | | ⊖ | ⊖ | ⊖ | ○ | 0.5 | 13 | 4.6x | 8 | L |
| 5 | **Minolta** Freedom Zoom 130 | 150 | | ⊖ | ⊖ | ⊖ | ○ | 0.5 | 20 | 3.5x | 9 | L |
| 6 | **Olympus** Infinity Zoom 80 QD | 120 | | ⊖ | ⊖ | ⊖ | ○ | 0.4 | 14 | 2.1x | 9 | L |
| 7 | **Samsung** Evoca 90W NEO | 140 | | ⊖ | ⊖ | ⊖ | ○ | 0.4 | 24 | 3.2x | 10 | L |
| 8 | **Minolta** Zoom 110 Date | 100 | | ⊖ | ○ | ⊖ | ○ | 0.5 | 26 | 2.9x | 7 | L |
| 9 | **Fujifilm** Zoom Date 115SR | 110 | | ⊖ | ○ | ⊖ | ○ | 0.4 | 15 | 3x | 7 | L |
| 10 | **Leica** C2 | 300 | | ⊖ | ○ | ⊖ | ◐ | 0.2 | 20 | 2x | 9 | L |
| 11 | **Minolta** AF50 Big Finder | 55 | | ⊖ | ○ | ⊖ | ⊖ | 0.3 | 13 | - | 8 | A |
| 12 | **Pentax** IQZoom EZY-80 Date | 70 | | ⊖ | ⊖ | ⊖ | ◐ | 0.5 | 12 | 2.1x | 9 | L |
| 13 | **Pentax** IQZoom 115V | 100 | | ⊖ | ⊖ | ⊖ | ○ | 0.5 | 18 | 3x | 10 | L |
| 14 | **Olympus** Stylus 100 Wide | 200 | | ⊖ | ○ | ⊖ | ○ | 0.4 | 21 | 3.6x | 8 | L |
| 15 | **Minox** CD 150 | 200 | | ⊖ | ○ | ⊖ | ⊖ | 0.5 | 13 | 3.9x | 7 | L |
| 16 | **Olympus** Infinity Zoom 105 QD | 100 | | ⊖ | ○ | ⊖ | ○ | 0.4 | 26 | 2.8x | 9 | L |
| 17 | **Olympus** Stylus 120 | 180 | | ⊖ | ○ | ⊖ | ○ | 0.4 | 21 | 3.2x | 8 | L |
| 18 | **Canon** Sure Shot Z155 | 170 | | ⊖ | ⊖ | ⊖ | ◐ | 0.4 | 17 | 4.2x | 9 | L |
| 19 | **Canon** Sure Shot 130u | 120 | | ⊖ | ○ | ⊖ | ⊖ | 0.2 | 15 | 3.4x | 7 | L |
| 20 | **Minox** CD 155 | 200 | | ⊖ | ⊖ | ⊖ | ◐ | 0.4 | 18 | 4.1x | 11 | L |
| 21 | **Canon** Sure Shot 115u | 110 | | ⊖ | ○ | ⊖ | ○ | 0.6 | 19 | 3x | 7 | L |
| 22 | **Fujifilm** Zoom Date 160EZ | 180 | | ⊖ | ⊖ | ⊖ | ⊖ | 0.5 | 15 | 4.2x | 7 | L |
| 23 | **Minolta** Zoom 160c Date | 160 | | ⊖ | ⊖ | ⊖ | ○ | 0.5 | 23 | 4.3x | 7 | L |

**Within types, in performance order. Blue key numbers indicate Quick Picks.**

| Key number | Brand and model | Price | Overall score | Picture quality | Convenience | Flash | Viewfinder | Shutter delay, sec. | Flash range, ft. | Zoom | Weight, oz. | Battery (L=lithium, A=alkaline) |
|---|---|---|---|---|---|---|---|---|---|---|---|---|
| | | | 0 ———— 100 | | | | | | | | | |
| | | | P F G VG E | | | | | | | | | |

**35 MM CAMERAS** *continued*

| Key number | Brand and model | Price | Overall score | Picture quality | Convenience | Flash | Viewfinder | Shutter delay, sec. | Flash range, ft. | Zoom | Weight, oz. | Battery |
|---|---|---|---|---|---|---|---|---|---|---|---|---|
| 23 | **Minolta** Zoom 160c Date | 160 | ▬▬▬ | ⊖ | ⊖ | ⊖ | ○ | 0.5 | 23 | 4.3x | 7 | L |
| 24 | **Samsung** Fino 80 Super | 90 | ▬▬ | ⊖ | ⊖ | ⊖ | ⊖ | 0.7 | 18 | 2.1x | 8 | L |
| 25 | **Fujifilm** Zoom Date 125SR | 135 | ▬▬ | ○ | ⊖ | ⊖ | ○ | 0.4 | 17 | 3.3x | 8 | L |
| 26 | **Pentax** ESPIO 140V | 150 | ▬▬ | ⊖ | ⊖ | ⊖ | ○ | 0.5 | 14 | 3.7x | 8 | L |
| 27 | **Nikon** One Touch Zoom 90s/QD | 115 | ▬▬ | ○ | ⊖ | ⊖ | ◐ | 0.3 | 16 | 2.4x | 9 | L |
| 28 | **Canon** Sure Shot 90u | 90 | ▬▬ | ⊖ | ○ | ⊖ | ⊖ | 0.2 | 18 | 2.4x | 7 | L |
| 29 | **Yashica** EZS Zoom 105 | 100 | ▬▬ | ○ | ○ | ⊖ | ◐ | 0.4 | 18 | 2.8x | 11 | A |
| | **APS CAMERAS** | | | | | | | | | | | |
| 30 | **Kodak** Advantix F620 | 80 | ▬▬▬ | ⊖ | ⊖ | ⊖ | ◐ | 0.6 | 24 | 2x | 7 | L |
| 31 | **Canon** Elph Z3 | 150 | ▬▬ | ⊖ | ⊖ | ⊖ | ◐ | 0.5 | 15 | 2.3x | 6 | L |

## Guide to the Ratings

The Ratings reflect our judgments, based on tests conducted for our counterpart in Europe, the International Consumer Testing and Research Organization. **Overall score** is based on picture quality and convenience. **Picture quality** is based mainly on image sharpness and focusing accuracy. **Convenience** covers ease of operating the camera's controls. Differences here are not large. **Flash** performance is based on exposure accuracy and uniformity of illumination. **Viewfinder** accuracy indicates how closely the viewfinder's framing matches that of the print. The viewfinders invariably show less than you'll see in the print. A lower score here means prints will suffer from extraneous content on the edges. **Shutter delay** indicates the minimum time elapsed between pressing the shutter release and the picture's actually being taken. **Flash range** is the maximum distance claimed by the manufacturer when using ISO 200 film with the lens set at wide angle. The larger the **zoom** range, the greater the range of wide-angle and telephoto effect available. **Weight** includes camera, battery, and film. **Battery type:** Lithium batteries last much longer and charge the flash more quickly than alkalines. **Price** is the estimated average.

# Quick Picks • Film Cameras

**Best all-round choices:**
1 **Minolta** $170
3 **Samsung** $150
5 **Minolta** $150
7 **Samsung** $140
8 **Minolta** $100
9 **Fujifilm** $110

These six have excellent or very good picture quality and flash, a generous flash range and zoom-lens range, and they sell for less than $200. They weigh about half a pound, typical for cameras like these. The Minolta (1) has the longest zoom range and the fastest-acting shutter. The Samsungs (3, 7) have an adjustable viewfinder. Of the six, only the Fujifilm (9) is designed so that the flash zooms with the lens to minimize falloff in flash performance when the lens is at its telephoto setting.

**If you want an APS camera:**
   **30 Kodak** $80

Your choices are much more limited than for 35mm cameras. The Kodak (30) is the less expensive of the two APS cameras tested.

# Ratings • Digital Cameras

| | Excellent | Very good | Good | Fair | Poor |
|---|---|---|---|---|---|
| | ⊖ | ⊖ | ○ | ◒ | ● |

**Within types, in performance order. Blue key numbers indicate Quick Picks.**

| Key number | Brand & model | Price | Overall score | Print quality | Weight (oz.) | Flash range (ft.) | Next-shot delay(sec.) | Optical zoom |
|---|---|---|---|---|---|---|---|---|
| 1 | **Kodak** DX 6490 | $500 | | ⊖ | 14.0 | 16 | 2 | 10X |
| 2 | **Fujifilm** FinePix S7000 | 700 | | ⊖ | 21.0 | 28 | 2 | 6X |
| 3 | **Kodak** DX 4530 | 300 | | ⊖ | 9.0 | 11 | 3 | 3X |
| 4 | **Kodak** EasyShare DX6440 | 380 | | ⊖ | 9.0 | 17 | 3 | 4X |
| 5 | **HP** PhotoSmart 945 | 500 | | ⊖ | 17.0 | 8 | 2 | 8X |
| 6 | **Pentax** Optio 555 | 500 | | ⊖ | 9.0 | 17 | 3 | 5X |
| 7 | **Canon** PowerShot A80 | 400 | | ⊖ | 12.0 | 14 | 3 | 3X |
| 8 | **Minolta** Dimage A1 | 900 | | ⊖ | 23.0 | 12 | 2 | 7X |
| 9 | **Olympus** Camedia C-5000 | 400 | | ⊖ | 10.0 | 12 | 3 | 3X |
| 10 | **Fujifilm** FinePix A310 | 250 | | ⊖ | 7.0 | 16 | 4 | 3X |
| 11 | **Pentax** Optio 33WR | 300 | | ⊖ | 8.0 | 10 | 3 | 2.8X |
| 12 | **Canon** A300 | 180 | | ⊖ | 8.0 | 7 | 3 | None |
| 13 | **Gateway** DC-T50 | 350 | | ⊖ | 8.0 | 10 | 9 | 2X |

## Guide to the Ratings

**Overall score** is based mainly on print quality, along with weight and the presence of useful features. **Print quality** is based on expert judgments, using 8x10 prints made with each camera's default resolution and image-compression settings and printed on a high-rated inkjet printer. **Weight** includes battery and memory card or disc. **Flash range** is the maximum claimed range for a well-lighted subject. **Next-shot delay** is the time the camera needs to ready itself for the next photo. **Optical zoom** refers to the range of focal lengths. A 3X zoom is comparable to the 35-to-105-mm zoom lens on a film camera; 5X to 10X provides greater magnification. **Price** is approximate retail. All cameras have 3 to 5 megapixels except the Fujifilm FinePix S7000, which is a 6-megapixel camera.

# Quick Picks • Digital Cameras

### Good all-around choices

1 **Kodak** $500

9 **Olympus** $400

Fully featured cameras with manual controls and a short delay between shots. The Kodak has a powerful 10X optical zoom lens.

### Compact and low-priced

3 **Kodak** $300

11 **Pentax** $300

The Kodak is a 5-megapixel camera that delivers excellent image quality and has a short delay between shots. The Pentax is water resistant in up to two feet of water for up to 30 minutes—especially useful for taking snapshots at the beach. Both lack manual controls.

**CHAPTER**

# 11

# Car Seats

A child car seat should be high on your to-buy list. You'll need one to bring your baby home from the hospital and for every car trip thereafter. In fact, hospitals and birthing centers generally won't let you leave by car with your newborn if you don't have one.

To protect children in the event of a crash, every state requires that kids up to 4 years of age ride in a car seat (and about a third of the states require booster seats, some for children as old as 8). There are two main types for transporting infants: rear-facing-only infant car seats and convertible car seats. The latter can be used rear-facing until the maximum limits (weight and height) that the seat is rated for are reached; after that, you use them forward-facing.

If you start with an infant car seat, as many parents do and as we recommend, your baby may outgrow it quickly. At about 6 to 9 months your baby will probably become too heavy to carry in an infant seat, and you'll want to switch to a convertible seat, which also gives baby additional room. But be sure to keep your child's convertible seat facing the rear of the vehicle until he or she reaches the weight and height limits specified by the manufacturer.

Under no circumstances should you switch the convertible car seat to a front-facing orientation for a child younger than 1 year and weighing 20 pounds or less. That can result in death or serious injury in a crash. Some children ride rear-facing beyond their second birthday.

The safest place for a child is in your vehicle's rear-center seat. The car seat should never be installed on a front seat that has an air bag. Two exceptions: If your car doesn't have a back seat, or if your child has a medical condition that requires constant monitoring, you can have an on/off switch installed for the front-passenger air bag or have it disconnected so the child's car seat can go next to the driver. But to have that done you'll need a letter of authorization from the National Highway Traffic Safety Administration (NHTSA). To obtain one, contact the agency via its Web site, *www.nhtsa.dot.gov.*

## A Look at the LATCH System

Since Sept. 1, 2002, all child car seats with an internal harness and nearly all passenger vehicles sold in the U.S. have been required to include equipment designed for simpler buckling. This system, called LATCH (Lower Anchors and Tethers for Children), shown below as typically installed, consists of child car-seat connections that attach to anchor points in the vehicle, eliminating the need to use a vehicle's safety belts to install the seat. You can still use safety belts to install a LATCH-equipped child car seat—for example, in an older car that lacks LATCH anchors. You can also retrofit some non-LATCH car seats with LATCH features. (Go to *www.ConsumerReports.org* and click on the "Babies and Kids" section for a report on LATCH retrofit kits.)

According to NHTSA, four out of five car seats are installed incorrectly. It's no wonder. Although LATCH-equipped child car seats are

### A Tight Fit

When installing a LATCH car seat, attach the lower anchor **(A)** and the tether **(B)**. A secure car seat shouldn't be able to move more than 1 inch forward or sideways.

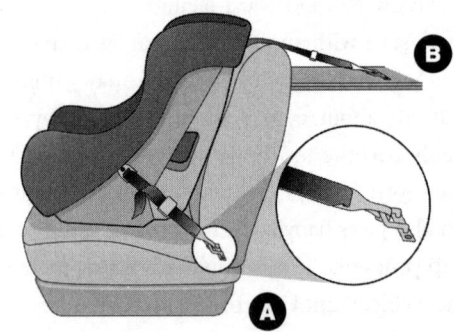

supposed to be easier to install and more compatible with a wide range of vehicles, some of the car-seat models we tested (see results on page 109), while excellent or very good overall, were harder to use or install than is ideal to ensure a secure fit. Most of the difficulty resulted from poor lower-anchor design in the cars. But our tests of child car seats showed that a surprising number had design flaws or were difficult to make fit securely. Children who ride in those seats may not be protected to the fullest extent possible.

## Shopping Secrets

**Make sure the seat is compatible with your car.** One of the first things you should do in choosing a seat for your child is to check the fit of any models you're considering in your own car. Even before that, though, we suggest placing similar-looking models side by side in the store to compare features. (If you've already had your baby, place your child in it, to get a sense of the ease of buckling and unbuckling.) Then, if possible, bring the floor model to your car for a mock installation. Be aware that some vehicle seats are too short, indented, or excessively sloped to allow a good fit of a child car seat.

If you're considering a convertible car seat, try the floor model in both the rear- and front-facing positions. Check out the harness release button in the rear-facing position; in some models, it may be too low to reach comfortably.

If you're considering an infant car seat/stroller combination, also known as a travel system, check to be sure it fits in your trunk or vehicle cargo area. If the store won't let you take the seat out to your car to try it, make sure you can return any car seat you buy—or go to another store.

**Insist on new.** Although there are many baby items you can borrow or buy secondhand, don't make a car seat one of them if you can avoid it. A used seat may have been in a crash or recalled. The manufacturer's instructions may be missing. If, for some reason, you must use a secondhand seat, avoid those with an unknown history or that are older than six years. In the world of car seats, a six-year-old model is a relic—and risky. You'll also want to avoid recalled models. For more, see Product Recalls starting on page 327.

**Send in the registration card.** You should be notified by the manufacturer if the car seat is recalled. To play it extra safe, you can also sign up for the Consumer Product Safety Commission's e-mail subscription list at *www.cpsc.gov/cpsclist.asp*. Updated recall information will be sent directly to your e-mail in-box. Or check monthly issues of CONSUMER REPORTS or visit *www.ConsumerReports.org*. Other sources of information on car-seat recalls include NHTSA's Web site (*www.nhtsa.gov*) and the Consumer Product Safety Commission site, *www.recalls.gov*.

**Check the store's return policy.** If you're not happy with a particular car seat for whatever reason, it's important to know that you can return it and try again with another model. Be aware that a badly soiled or damaged seat may not be exchanged.

**Replace a car seat that has been involved in a crash.** Although the seat may look perfectly fine, it could have suffered structural damage. As the National Safe Kids Campaign, a nonprofit organization, puts it: "If a restraint system has already protected a passenger in a crash, it has done its job." California residents should be aware that in the event of a crash, their insurance carriers are required to pay to replace any child car seat with a new one.

## What's Available

The major brands of car seats you're likely to encounter are, in alphabetical order: Baby Trend, Britax, Century/Graco, Cosco, Eddie Bauer, Evenflo, Peg Perego, and Safety 1st. Combi has also recently entered the car-seat market. There are also car beds for preemies and other very small newborns if there's a concern that a car seat may not provide a secure fit or that it may exacerbate breathing problems. In addition, there are specially designed car seats for children with physical disabilities. (For more information, check out *www.snugseat.com, www.columbiamedical.com, www.britaxusa.com,* and *www.ezonpro.com.*) Every model of car seat sold in the U.S. must meet federal safety standards. These are your basic choices:

### Infant seats

These rear-facing, cradle-type seats are for babies up to 20 or 22 pounds, depending on the model. They allow infants to recline at an angle that doesn't interfere with breathing and protects them best in a crash. Many strollers are now designed to accommodate infant car seats. All infant car-seat models come with a handle, and nearly all have a base that secures to your vehicle with LATCH connections or a safety belt, a convenience that lets you remove the seat and use it as a carrier. You can strap most infant seats into a car without a base, using the vehicle safety belts. Our crash tests, the results of which begin on page 109, included the base because most people use them that way.

## DISCOVER A DEFECT?

To report a possible defect with a car seat you bought or with a vehicle's attachment system, call the National Highway Traffic Safety Administration (NHTSA) hotline at 888-327-4236 or go to *www.nhtsa.gov.*

Today, infant seats have either a three-point harness—two adjustable shoulder straps and a lock between the child's legs or—even better—an adjustable five-point system—two straps over the shoulders, two for the thighs, and a crotch strap. An infant seat's handle usually swings from a position behind the seat's shell when in the car to an upright position for carrying. Slots underneath most seats help them attach to the frame of a shopping cart.

**Pros:** They fit small infants best. With an infant car seat, you also can move your baby from car to house without waking him or her up—a plus for both of you.

**Cons:** Your baby may outgrow an infant car seat quickly and become too heavy for you to use it as a carrier. As a result, you may find yourself having to buy a convertible car seat after your baby is 6 to 9 months old. However, our advice is still to start with an infant seat before moving up to a convertible seat.

**Price range:** $30 to $180.

## Travel systems

Most manufacturers of car seats offer combination strollers/infant car seats, called travel systems. With a travel system, you create a carriage by snapping an infant car seat into a stroller. The car seats of travel systems also come with a base, which stays in the car. The snap-on car seat is generally positioned atop the stroller so the infant rides facing the person pushing. Your baby can also ride in the stroller seat alone when he or she is big enough.

A new generation of travel systems have strollers that are infant-ready; that is, you can transport a newborn safely in one. See page 229 for more on travel systems' configurations as strollers. There are also lightweight strollers and stroller frames with no seat that can accommodate various brands of infant seats.

**Pros:** Travel systems offer one-stop shopping: You get an infant car seat and a stroller all in one.

**Cons:** Most travel-system strollers can be used only with a car seat from the same company. They can also be bulky, so if you're a city dweller who negotiates more subway stairs than highways or if the trunk of your car isn't too roomy, you may be better off with a separate car seat and a compact stroller that is appropriate for a newborn.

**Price range:** $40 (stroller frame only) to $400.

### Convertible seats

With a convertible seat, the child faces rearward as an infant, then toward the front as a toddler. The seat can function as a rear-facing seat for infants up to 22 or 35 pounds, depending on the model, and as a front-facing seat for toddlers generally up to 40 pounds (a few have a 65-pound limit). Models typically have an adjustable five-point harness system—two straps over the shoulders, two for the thighs, and a crotch strap between the legs. Some models have a tray shield that lowers over the baby's head and fastens with a buckle between the legs. However, our tests show that children, especially small ones, are better restrained with a five-point harness.

**Pros:** A convertible car seat can be a money saver, taking your child from infancy to kindergarten. We advise starting with an infant seat first, though, as mentioned earlier.

**Cons:** Convertible seats are not compatible with strollers, so you will have to transfer your baby from the car seat to a carriage or stroller when you're ready to set out on foot. Such jostling can wake a sleeping baby, a problem if you need to take baby on frequent shopping expeditions or other errands.

**Price range:** $50 to $250.

### Down the Road

Here are more seating options for children riding front-facing. These seats are not for rear-facing use and are not rated in this book.

**Toddler/booster seats.** Looking like large versions of convertible seats, these front-facing seats are used with an internal harness for toddlers 20 to 40 pounds. They're either LATCH-attached or can be secured using the vehicle belts and tethers. When kids reach 40 pounds, the seat becomes a belt-positioned booster seat, which children can use until they're 80 or 100 pounds. With a belt-positioned booster seat, the child is restrained using the vehicle's lap and shoulder belts.

**Booster seats.** These are generally for children weighing 40 to 80 pounds. They use the vehicle's own safety belts to restrain the child.

**Built-in seats.** Some U.S. and foreign automakers offer on select cars and minivans an integrated, forward-facing child seat that has a harness and accommodates toddlers weighing more than 20 pounds. There are also some booster-seat versions. Built-in seats must meet the same performance standards as add-on child seats. However, they offer little or no side protection and they're usually located next to a door, instead of in the center—the safer position. You may also need a regular car seat for when your child travels in other vehicles.

## Features to Consider

**The fabric.** Today's car seats cater to every possible taste—plain colors, plaids, animal and paw-print motifs, "cowmooflage," and patriotic red, white, and blue. Remember that, style aside, babies tend to be messy, so washable fabric is a plus, especially if your car seat will be with you beyond the first year, when training cups and eating on the go can kick into high gear. Some leading brands, however, require hand washing and line drying. Make sure you're up for that; most coverings are rigged through the belting system and are held in place with elastic so they can be removed for laundering. But in some cases extracting the fabric from the seat can require extensive dismantling. Check the seat's manual for how-to's.

Extras such as add-on seat covers ("boots"), thicker padding, addi-

### EASY RIDERS

Recognizing that some car seats are more user-friendly than others (with or without the LATCH system), the National Highway Traffic Safety Administration recently created the Ease of Use ratings program. It evaluates seats based on criteria such as whether the seat is preassembled or requires assembly after purchase, the clarity of installation instructions, and how easy it is to secure a child in the seat. Under this new rating system, child restraints are given an overall ease-of-use rating of A, B, or C, with A being the easiest to use, and C the least easy. Because the Ease of Use rating system doesn't correlate directly with safety, consider using it as a cross-referencing tool with our car seat Ratings on page 109. For more information, log onto *www.nhtsa.gov/CPS/CSSRatings/Index.cfm*

# HOW TO TOTE AN INFANT SEAT/CARRIER

If you opt to use your infant seat as a carrier, realize that it can be a killer on your wrists, elbow, lower back, and neck if you tote it by the handle or string it on your forearm like a handbag.

"I've got bursitis in my shoulders, which came on nearly seven months ago when my last child was born," says Sandy Cummings, mother of three from Dedham, Mass. The culprit: Cummings' infant car seat (10 pounds) plus her baby (21 pounds at his 6-month checkup).

But even a much lighter baby-plus-car-seat duo can be damaging because the weight is at the end of your arm, putting maximum force on your wrists, elbow, neck, and shoulders. "The greater the horizontal distance from the weight you're carrying to your torso, the more stress on your joints, discs, ligaments, and muscles," says Mary Ellen Modica, a physical therapist at Schwab STEPS Rehabilitation Clinics in Arlington Heights, Ill. "It's equivalent to walking around with three or four full paint cans in one hand—something most people wouldn't do, but yet, they'll carry a car seat that way."

A better idea: "Carry the car seat in front of you so that you have both hands on the handle," advises Diane Dalton, orthopedic clinical specialist at Boston University's Sargent College of Health and Rehabilitation. With the weight of the seat and your baby centered and close to your trunk, the force on your body will be reduced, Dalton says. Another option: Leave the infant seat in your car and transfer your baby to a soft infant carrier (more about those on page 213) or a stroller (see page 225).

Or simply carry your baby in your arms, and you and your baby will both benefit. Infants transported that way use their head, neck, and shoulder muscles to stabilize themselves. "Those muscles may develop sooner in babies who aren't carried around in a car seat," says Patrice M. Winter, owner of Trinity Physical Therapy in Fairfax, Va., and a spokeswoman for the American Physical Therapy Association.

tional reclining options, or adjustable head-support cushions may offer greater comfort. But buy them only if they are sold by the same maker as the seat and for that specific seat, since they were tested that way; mixing brands is very risky. Some models have elastic side pockets for toys, bottles, or snacks. As your baby grows, they can come in handy, but they're not absolutely necessary.

**Level indicator.** Some infant seats and convertible seats have a level indicator on the side to help you install them facing the rear at a safe angle.

**Seat shell.** Typically, manufacturers use the same shell of molded plastic for all seats of a particular model.

**Top tether.** This webbed strap can be used with all front-facing seats for children up to 40 pounds and with some up to 65 pounds. It's located on the back of a convertible or toddler seat and hooks into an eye bolt in a vehicle's rear deck, floor, roof, or seatback. New passenger vehicles have the anchors in place in their rear seats, but older models may need to have the hardware added. Obviously, you can't use a tether with cars that lack a top-tether anchor or that have no provision for a retrofit.

## Recommendations

Start with an infant seat for a newborn and pay close attention to the height and weight limits as your child grows. When your baby reaches the infant seat's limits for height and weight, use a convertible seat in the rear-facing orientation up to the seat's limits in that mode. Then use the convertible seat front-facing until your toddler reaches the next weight limit. After that, use a booster seat until your child is tall enough to use the car's safety belts. Buying three seats instead of two may cost more, but it can pay off in protection and peace of mind. The Ratings that begin on page 109 have information on specific models.

## Installation: Getting It Right

When installing a seat for the first time, give yourself a good half-hour. If you can recruit a helper, even better. Here are a few pointers for making installation easier.

**Read all about it.** Consult the instructions that come with the seat as well as your vehicle owner's manual for information on how to use your car's safety belts with that car seat. Some car manufacturers also have a free how-to brochure or video that can help.

**Position the seat.** As we've mentioned, the center rear seat is the safest spot. You may have to place the seat next to a door if you have more than one small child; if there isn't a shoulder belt in the center (for use with a booster seat); if your LATCH-compatible vehicle lacks lower anchors in the center rear position and you don't want to use the center-seat vehicle belt; or if using the center rear seat would make the child seat unstable, among other reasons.

**Secure the seat.** Use your weight to push the child seat into your vehicle's seat (you may want to use a knee) while pulling the slack out of the car's safety belt or LATCH strap. With a rear-facing seat, adjust the angle as directed by the manufacturer, using the level indicator or other means to get the backrest of the car seat close to a 45-degree incline. With a front-facing seat for a toddler up to 40 pounds, use the top tether. If the top tether is not in use, such as with a toddler/booster seat used as a booster, remove the top-tether strap or secure it so it doesn't fly around and injure your child in a crash. When you're securing an infant or toddler seat with a car's safety belt, you may need a locking clip so the lap belt remains tight. See the manufacturer's instructions for details.

**Adjust the harness.** Harness straps in a rear-facing car seat should be at or slightly below the infant's shoulders. For front-facing toddlers, harness straps should be at or slightly above the toddler's shoulders. If a harness is properly snug, you should not be able to insert more than one of your fingers behind it.

**Check the seat every time you use it.** Whenever you buckle your child in, try shifting the car seat from side to side and back to front. It shouldn't move more than an inch in either direction. Make sure the harness straps fit snugly.

**Double-check with the experts.** After you've installed the seat, make sure it's correct. Visit the NHTSA *(www.nhtsa.gov)* Web site and click on "child-seat inspections" to find an inspection site near you. At the National Safe Kids Campaign site *(www.safekids.org)*, you'll find a list of your state's Safe Kids Buckle Up Check Up events. You can also find child passenger safety information, including where to get your child's seat inspected, at 866-SEAT-CHECK (866-732-8243) or *www.seatcheck.org*.

# Ratings • Car Seats

**A**t a time when child car seats have been redesigned and passenger vehicles modified to make them simpler to install—and thus more likely to be used correctly—our tests show that a surprising number had design flaws or were difficult to make fit securely. Children who ride in those seats may not be protected to the fullest extent possible. The good news is that our Ratings include recommended models in both car-seat categories.

Rating key: Excellent ⊖ | Very good ⊖ | Good ○ | Fair ◐ | Poor ●

**Within types, in performance order. Blue key numbers indicate Quick Picks.**

| Key number | Brand & model | Price | Overall score (0–100, P F G VG E) | Crash protection — Latch | Crash protection — Belt | Ease of use — Latch | Ease of use — Belt | Fit to vehicle — Latch | Fit to vehicle — Belt |
|---|---|---|---|---|---|---|---|---|---|
| | Similar models in small type. | | | | | | | | |
| **INFANT SEATS** | | | | | | | | | |
| 1 | **Graco** SnugRide | $85 | | ⊖ | ⊖ | ⊖ | ⊖ | ⊖ | ⊖ |
| 2 | **Peg Perego** Primo Viaggio | 150 | | ⊖ | ⊖ | ⊖ | ⊖ | ⊖ | ⊖ |
| 3 | **Combi** Tyro | 130 | | ⊖ | ⊖ | ⊖ | ○ | ○ | ◐ |
| 4 | **Safety 1st** (Cosco) Designer 22 | 80 | | ⊖ | ⊖ | ◐ | ◐ | ⊖ | ⊖ |
| 5 | **Evenflo** PortAbout 5 | 80 | | ○ | ○ | ⊖ | ○ | ⊖ | ⊖ |
| 6 | **Baby Trend** LATCH-LOC | 80 | | ○ | ⊖ | ⊖ | ⊖ | ◐ | ⊖ |

| Key number | Brand & model | Price | Overall score (0–100, P F G VG E) | Crash protection — Latch infant | Crash protection — Latch toddler | Crash protection — Belt infant | Ease of use — Latch infant | Ease of use — Latch toddler | Ease of use — Belt infant | Ease of use — Belt toddler | Fit to vehicle — Latch infant | Fit to vehicle — Belt infant |
|---|---|---|---|---|---|---|---|---|---|---|---|---|
| | Similar models in small type. | | | | | | | | | | | |
| **CONVERTIBLE SEATS** | | | | | | | | | | | | |
| 7 | **Britax** Roundabout | $230 | | ⊖ | ⊖ | ⊖ | ⊖ | ⊖ | ⊖ | ⊖ | ⊖ | ⊖ |
| 8 | **Britax** Marathon | 249 | | ○ | ⊖ | ⊖ | ⊖ | ⊖ | ⊖ | ⊖ | ⊖ | ⊖ |
| 9 | **Evenflo** Titan 5 Vanguard 5CT | 70 | | ⊖ | ⊖ | ⊖ | ⊖ | ⊖ | ⊖ | ⊖ | ⊖ | ⊖ |
| 10 | **Evenflo** Triumph 5 | 130 | | ⊖ | ⊖ | ⊖ | ⊖ | ⊖ | ⊖ | ⊖ | ⊖ | ⊖ |
| 11 | **Graco** Comfort-Sport 8433 _8431, 8432, 8437, 8439_ | 75 | | ○ | ⊖ | ⊖ | ⊖ | ⊖ | ⊖ | ⊖ | ⊖ | ⊖ |
| 12 | **Safety 1st** (Cosco) Comfort Ride 22-400 | 70 | | ○ | ⊖ | ⊖ | ○ | ⊖ | ○ | ⊖ | ○ | ⊖ |
| 13 | **Cosco** Touriva 22-100 | 50 | | ○ | ⊖ | ⊖ | ⊖ | ⊖ | ⊖ | ○ | ⊖ | ⊖ |
| 14 | **Cosco** Alpha Omega 22-150 | 135 | | ○ | ⊖ | ⊖ | ⊖ | ○ | ⊖ | ○ | ⊖ | ⊖ |

## Guide to the Ratings

**Overall score** is based on crash protection, ease of use, and fit to vehicle in LATCH mode. To judge **crash protection** we had an outside laboratory perform crash tests in which dummies of varying sizes and weights were strapped into seats and run through a simulated 30 mph head-on crash. **LATCH** means using the Lower Anchors and Tethers for Children system to attach to the vehicle; **belt** means using a vehicle

*Continued on page 110*

*Continued from page 109*

safety belt to attach the car seat. Car seat **ease of use** includes installation, adjusting harness positions, placing the child in the car seat, securing the harness, and removing the child. Seats were installed in cars with various seat configurations and safety-belt designs to assess **fit to vehicle.** All infant car seats rated fit children up to 20 or 22 pounds; convertible seats fit children up to 30 or 35 pounds rear-facing, up to 40 pounds front-facing, except as noted. All convertible seats, when placed in the toddler position, scored an excellent for latch and belt fit to vehicle. **Price** is approximate retail.

# Quick Picks • Car Seats

## Infant seats

1 **Graco** $85
2 **Peg Perego** $150

The Graco (1) is a good seat that fits properly in most vehicles. The Peg Perego earned high marks overall. If you're considering the Viaggio, make sure it fits in your car; fit was sometimes a problem in our tests.

## Convertible seats

7 **Britax** $230
8 **Britax** $249

The top-rated Britax (7) is costly but earned high marks overall. Its brandmate (8) is designed to accommodate children up to 65 pounds using the internal harness: rear-facing up to 33 pounds, front-facing with LATCH up to 48 pounds, and front-facing with belt attached up to 65 pounds.

CHAPTER

# 12

# Changing Tables & Dressers

Y ou can diaper a baby just about anywhere you have room and where the baby is safe from falling, even on the floor. But since you'll change 2,000-plus diapers by the time your baby is potty trained, your back will benefit from something made for the task—either a standard changing table or a dresser that doubles as one.

Besides being able to diaper your baby at a comfortable level (most changing tables stand 40 inches high), you'll have diapers, wipes, diaper rash ointment, and a toy or two (to keep baby busy) within easy reach. Unlike the crib or the floor, changing tables also have shelves, and dressers have drawers you can use to store diapering essentials.

A third option you may see in stores is a removable changing table that simply sits on top of a regular dresser. That's a precarious position when you've got a squirmy baby on board, which is the reason we

**S**eptember is traditionally a month when baby-store proprietors create money-saving promotions on baby furniture. It's a good time to buy, as is January, when retailers are motivated to aggressively clear inventory to pay Christmas bills. At these pivotal times of the year in the baby furniture business, watch for sales.

don't recommend them at this time. However, safer designs may evolve as a result of a safety standard now being developed with Consumers Union's participation.

## Shopping Secrets

**Go for girth.** If you're planning to use a combination changing table and dresser, think short and fat, not tall and thin. A dresser that's wider and lower to the ground will be less likely to fall forward when you place extra weight on top (your baby). If you do end up with a taller dresser, mount it to the wall so it won't tip over. Several manufacturers make mounting hardware for this purpose that's as simple as a plastic strap and two screws. (You'll need to find a stud in the wall to drive the screws into.)

**Check any drawers.** Most changing tables have open shelves that make it easy to reach diapers and clothing, but some have drawers instead. Make sure drawers are not used by an older sibling to climb the table and cause it to tip.

**Opt for barriers on four sides.** A changing table is usually surrounded by a restraining barrier made of rails or wood slabs on three or four sides. Protection on all four sides is better.

## What's Available

The major makers of changing tables and dressers include, in alphabetical order: Alta Baby, Badger Basket, Bellini, Child Craft Industries, Delta Enterprise, Jenny Lind, and Sorelle.

Changing tables are sold solo or as part of a nursery suite, along with a crib, chest, and armoire. Sometimes, a changing station is built on top of a chest or inside an armoire.

Most models have wooden frames, but you may find some constructed of wicker. A safety belt—a single strap with a wide buckle— is usually included. If it isn't, buy one and install it separately. Models that coordinate with other pieces of baby furniture may be appealing but are more expensive.

Changing tables range from $100 to $250 for models that coordinate with other furniture.

## Features to Consider

**Safety strap.** The changing table pad you're considering should have a safety strap. Buying one separately and installing it is possible, but a factory-supplied and installed strap is a better choice.

**Sturdiness.** Like other pieces of furniture, a changing table or dresser shouldn't wobble when you give it a light shake. Go ahead and test the floor model in the store, if possible.

**Wheels.** Some tables come on wheels, designed to be moved from room to room, as a mobile changing station.

**Wood.** You may want to seek out a good pedigree. Pricier changing tables tend to be made of solid hardwood like birch, beech, and maple rather than particle board with a wood finish.

### Changing Table Safety

Each year thousands of babies are injured in changing table accidents. It only takes a second—the time it takes to turn for diapers and wipes—for an active baby to roll over and tumble to the ground. To prevent falls, use the safety straps on your changing table and never leave your baby unattended to answer the phone or the doorbell (even if he or she is strapped on). In fact, make it a practice to keep one hand on your baby, no matter what.

## Recommendations

Consider all the furniture you plan to include in the nursery—you may decide that you don't need a changing table at all or simply don't have room for one. If you think you need or would like a changing table, try before you buy. Test the table in the store, as if you were changing a baby. If you see a backache in your future because that changing table is too low, try another brand or model.

CHAPTER

# 13

# Clothing

A-B-C

**W**arning: It will take every ounce of willpower not to load up your shopping cart with teeny-tiny Levi's, Zen wrap dresses, peasant tops, and a romper in every color. Baby clothes, trendier than ever and oh-so-scrumptious, are as irresistible for parents (and thankfully, for well-meaning friends and relatives) as a hot fudge sundae when you're trying to lose weight. Not that your baby cares. All he or she wants is to be comfortable. And that's an important distinction to keep in mind. The basic necessities—even if they're "preowned"—will keep your little cutie content. Still, you may not want to dress your baby in just any old thing.

## Shopping Secrets

**Be clothing conservative.** During your first forays into the baby department, buy only a few items in newborn size, such as one or two sleepers. You'll want to focus more on 6-month size clothing—your baby will grow into it quickly. But even then, try to hold back and fill in after you've reaped the post-birth-announcement bounty. That strategy—to anticipate clothes from generous friends and relatives—may get you through the first year, since you'll probably receive a lot of them. Rest assured that knowing gift-givers, such as friends who are already parents, grandmothers, and aunts, will buy in bigger sizes, understanding how fast babies grow.

**Watch for sales and specials on brands you like.** You may do especially well at the end of each season. Sales are everywhere: in stores, in catalogs, and online. Buy in your baby's current size and also stock

## THE WELL-DRESSED BABY

**H**ere's a review of the Baby Basics list from the Introduction. Use your own judgment on how much you want to buy yourself, and what you can expect as gifts.

### Basics

_____ Four sleeping outfits, sleeper sacks, or one-piece sleepers, preferably with attached feet. Sleepers and sacks are preferable to covering a baby with blankets, which can be a suffocation hazard. Snug-fitting cotton and flame-resistant sleepwear are the safest choices for children.

_____ Six side-snap T-shirts.

_____ Four to six undershirts that snap around the crotch.

_____ A small baby cap (although the hospital will probably give you one).

_____ Six pairs of socks/booties.

_____ Two to three soft, comfortable daytime outfits.

_____ Cotton sweater or light jacket.

### Summer babies

_____ Brimmed hat with elasticized chin strap to keep baby from batting it off.

### Winter babies

_____ Either a snowsuit, heavy zip-up bunting with legs, a sack with sleeves, legs, and a hood, or a hooded jacket. Make sure the garment you buy isn't so bulky that your baby no longer fits into his or her child car seat or stroller. Also, remove strings from hooded jackets or sweatshirts; strings are a strangulation hazard.

_____ Warm knit hat with an elasticized chin strap.

## FOOTWEAR FOOTNOTES

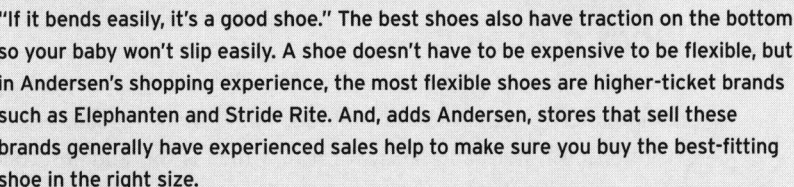

**W**ait until your child is a confident walker—at about 13 or 14 months—before buying his or her first shoes. That's when a child really needs them.

Jane Andersen, D.P.M., a spokeswoman for the American Podiatric Medical Association, recommends picking a first shoe with flexibility, which helps the foot develop its arch. "Try to bend the shoe in half," she says. "If it bends easily, it's a good shoe." The best shoes also have traction on the bottom so your baby won't slip easily. A shoe doesn't have to be expensive to be flexible, but in Andersen's shopping experience, the most flexible shoes are higher-ticket brands such as Elephanten and Stride Rite. And, adds Andersen, stores that sell these brands generally have experienced sales help to make sure you buy the best-fitting shoe in the right size.

In the meantime, resist the shearling moccasins and other designer booties you'll see everywhere. Otherwise, you'll be forever retrieving them. Many babies kick off anything and everything other than elasticized baby socks that cling to the feet.

Another option is machine-washable, soft fabric shoes called Padders (*www.padders.com*) or wrap-and-snap fleece booties by Zutano (*www.zutano.com*). For best results, buy in your baby's exact size rather than slightly bigger.

up on larger ones. Major chain stores have promotions regularly, sometimes even weekly.

**Consider used.** If you've never bought anything secondhand, you might want to start now. You can easily get away with it (and nobody will know), especially when your child is an infant. "My biggest money saver is the local mom's group sale," says Laura Winblade of Bellevue, Wash., mother of a preschooler and a toddler. "In my area, there's one for mothers of multiples, and they have a sale twice a year. Babies go through clothes so quickly, the small stuff is always in good condition. But I've found that as my children get older, it's harder to find quality used clothes."

Winblade has a point. As babies become toddlers, and messy activities such as finger painting come into play, clothing gets more wear and tear and isn't as easy to pass along or pass off as new. But infant clothing is another story; it's not unheard of to pay 50 cents for a pair of infant pants that would cost you $12 or more new.

Besides checking the local tag or garage sales and browsing *www.ebay.com*, put the word out among parents you know. You may get quite serviceable clothes delivered by the box load to your front door. Check out any local baby consignment stores for good deals on clothes for special occasions, such as fancy dresses, since they're likely to have been worn only once or twice. But inspect hand-me-downs carefully for unraveling thread, small buttons, loose snaps, or scratchy appliqués and elastic bands. To avoid putting your child at risk, don't dress him or her in anything that's not as good as new or that appears unsafe to you.

## What's Available

In baby clothes, you'll find " boy" and "girl" clothing in every imaginable pattern, color (besides pink and blue, think mocha, powder, buttermilk), style, and fabric. Cotton, which is soft and absorbent, continues to be the most common fiber, although many garments are made of cotton/polyester blends, which dry quickly and resist wrinkles, or cotton/spandex for maximum give. You'll also find thick, soft knits and fleece made of microfiber.

Major brands of infant wear include, in alphabetical order: Baby Gap, Baby Gund, Baby Lulu, Carter's, Chicken Noodle, First Impressions, Flapdoodles, Gerber, Good Lad, Gymboree, Halo Innovations (sleep sacks), Kushies, Little Me, New Potatoes, and Zutano. As with adult clothing, prices run the gamut.

Sizes are usually based on age, although they typically fit babies younger than indicated: preemie, 0 to 3 months, 3 to 6 months, 6 to 9 months, 9 to 12 months, 12 months, 18 months, and 24 months. However, one manufacturer's 6 to 9 months, for example, may be different from another's.

Except for sleepwear, which should always fit snugly, a good general rule for buying the right clothing size is to double your baby's age. A 3-month-old, for example, will likely fit quite nicely (with a little room to grow) in clothing that says it's for a 6-month-old. If you're buying

## RECALL REMINDER

Occasionally, baby garments are recalled because of safety hazards such as snaps coming off or sleepwear that's marketed as flame-retardant when it's really not. For updated recall information on infant products, including baby clothes, consult monthly issues of CONSUMER REPORTS or visit the Consumer Product Safety Commission's Web site at *www.recalls.gov* and click on Recalls. You can also get on the CPSC's e-mail subscription list for recall information at *www.cpsc.gov/cpsclist.asp*.

**T**he Consumer Product Safety Commission allows manufacturers to make sleepwear without added flame retardants for sizes under 9 months. The only condition is that the sleepwear be tight-fitting to avoid trapping the amount of air needed for fabric to burn, as well as to reduce the chances of contact with a flame. Similarly, our recommendation is for you to use sleepwear that fits snugly.

for a 6-month-old, buy clothing sized for a 12-month-old, and so forth. Or read the weight and length charts found on the back of many garment packages. You can also consult a size chart, which many baby-clothing stores, especially those that sell garments in European sizes, keep on hand.

## Features to Consider

Your primary concerns should be dressing ease, softness and safety, then style. Since most babies dislike having anything pulled over their heads, look for garments that are easy to take off and put on, such as those with front-opening or side-snap tops. Snaps are easier (and faster) than buttons. Quick access to the diaper area is also essential, so opt for snap-open legs or loosely elasticized waists. Velcro closures are particularly quick and convenient. Before washing, close them so that they don't fill up with lint and threads and lose their holding power.

**Comfort.** Check the seams on the inside of the garment. On all clothing, seams should be smooth, not rough, and lie flat rather than sticking out. Don't buy clothes with tight elasticized bands on arms, legs, neck, or waist. They can irritate your baby's skin and also restrict circulation. Bypass anything that could be scratchy—unpainted metal zippers, appliqués, or snaps with rough or uneven backings. If an appliqué is made of heat-welded plastic, check for rough edges on the back. Give buttons or snaps a quick tug to make sure they can't easily come off, posing a choking hazard. But don't pull so hard that you weaken the attachment in the process.

**Fabric.** As with adult clothing, labels on baby apparel must state fiber content and care instructions.

All-cotton knits may look large when new, but they can shrink as much as 10 percent with repeated washing. Polyester/cotton blends are less expensive than pure cotton and more resistant to wrinkles and shrinkage. Avoid thin, semitransparent items or garments that show signs of poor finishing such as unclipped thread. Although babies grow fast, you'll need clothing that's durable enough to last several months or more.

## Recommendations

When stocking up on a few basics before baby arrives, purchase very little in newborn size. Your baby will outgrow these tiny garments quickly—sometimes in less than a month. It's more practical to buy in the 3- to 6-month or 6- to 9-month size. But if saving money is your mission, do most of your shopping after friends and relatives have had the chance to respond to your birth announcement. Then just fill in any gaps in your baby's wardrobe.

Also, consider safety. Be wary of tiny buttons, hooks, snaps, pompoms, bows, and appliqués. They can be choking hazards. Routinely check clothes and fasteners for these loose items. Avoid knitted clothes—sweaters, booties, or hats—that look like they might trap a baby's tiny fingers or toes. Cut all dangling threads before your baby wears a garment and avoid clothing that has seams with very few stitches per inch. Before you put socks or booties on baby, turn them inside out to look for small threads that could capture toes.

If you're value-minded, remember that low-priced and midpriced garments often have soft but sturdy fabrics, competent workmanship, and plenty of baby style. They're also usually machine washable. Upscale baby clothes cost more (sometimes amazingly more) than standard garments, without a proportionate increase in quality and durability. If you buy such clothes, know you're doing it for style. In addition, high-fashion clothes may require hand laundering, even dry cleaning. Remember that your baby will quickly outgrow anything you buy—and, no matter how carefully you monitor, will manage to spill on everything as he or she becomes more mobile.

# 14

# Cribs

O f all the items on your baby-shopping list, you'll probably find a crib among the most challenging to select. That's because there's a vast array of cribs on the market, ranging from economy and midpriced models to high-end custom cribs that up the style ante. Manufacturers also offer cribs that convert to a toddler bed and even to a full-size one (after you purchase a few additional items like bed rails). One, the-new-to-the-U.S. Stokke Sleepi System oval crib, even morphs into two children's chairs.

Whether you have your baby sleep in a crib from the get-go or start with a bassinet, cradle, or the like (an alternative for your baby's first four months or so), you'll want a crib that's durable and safe and matches your own taste and budget. You'll also need to buy a mattress, which is usually sold separately. For more on that topic, see Crib Mattresses, starting on page 141.

Despite the dizzying array of cribs you'll find at mass merchandisers, in baby boutiques, and online, all cribs are basically a rectangular box with a mattress support on legs with wheels. The sides and sometimes the end boards are made of bars or slats so you can see inside—and baby can see out. Cribs usually have one or two drop sides—sides you lower with a lift-and-press action, a foot release, or a two-hand-operated latch mechanism, which makes it easier to reach in and tend to your baby.

Over the past few years, however, a new crib design has emerged—a crib without a drop side—that is, all sides are stationary so there are no moving parts that could loosen and entrap baby or hinges to potentially pinch little fingers. On a no-drop-side crib, which industry insiders see as the wave of the crib future, one side is set at waist level so you can reach in without straining. As with drop-side models, you lower the mattress as your baby grows to prevent him or her from climbing out, although tending to your baby can become decidedly challenging if you happen to be short in stature.

Since the turn of the new century, most cribs have been produced to meet the latest voluntary safety standard (and efforts are under way to further strengthen the current one). So you can be reasonably assured that a crib bought new today is as safe as it can be. In fact, in our latest crib tests, Consumer Reports started with a safety plateau of "good," since we consider the current crop of cribs on the market to be at least at that level. Those Ratings start on page 130.

Most cribs are constructed of wood, which can range from porous and easily dented pine in lower-priced cribs to strong and durable hardwoods such as ash, beech, oak, and hard maple in top-of-the-line models. As a rule, a crib made from harder wood is heavier and more costly. Cribs may also be constructed of other materials such as steel, brass, or molded plastic. Some manufacturers are experimenting with "engineered wood" such as medium-density fiberboard, which can be

## SAVE YOUR BACK

**O**ver time, lifting your baby out of a crib the wrong way can take a toll on your back. To prevent problems, don't lock your knees or hold your baby at arms' length as you pick him or her up. "This puts extreme pressure on your spinal discs," says Nicholas Warren, Sc.D., ergonomics coordinator at the University of Connecticut Health Center in Farmington.

Do plant your feet shoulder-width apart, lower the crib railing (if the crib has one), and bend your knees. Then bring your baby as close to your body as possible before lifting, to minimize the stress on your back.

difficult to distinguish from natural wood.

Some cribs offer a drawer that fits underneath, which is handy for storage. However, it can also present a hazard if, for example, an inquisitive toddler decides to use it as a step for climbing.

## Shopping Secrets

**Don't buy a "pre-owned" crib at a yard sale, thrift shop, or online.** Older cribs may not meet current safety standards. Buying new helps you know you're creating the safest and most secure sleep environment for your baby. The date of manufacture is always stated somewhere on the crib.

**Decide first whether you want a crib with one, two, or no drop sides.** That will narrow the selection considerably and make your crib shopping easier.

**If you're considering a crib with no drop sides, be sure to test display models in the store.** Use the mattress's lowest setting to see how easy it is for you to bend in to retrieve your baby. In our tests we found no-drop-side cribs nearly as easy to use as drop-side models for accessing a child when the mattress was in the highest or infant position. After that, with either type, you'll need to reach deeper and deeper into the crib, which may not be comfortable, especially if you're on the short side.

**If you're shopping for a crib with drop sides, operate them in the store to make sure they raise and lower smoothly and quietly.** Models that open with a lift-and-leg-press action or those with a lift-and-foot-release mechanism can usually be opened with one hand—an advantage when you've got a baby in the other. Still, most parents raise and lower the side of the crib only during the first few months. Once babies get bigger and stand up in the crib, many parents pick them up without lowering the side. So, a crib that doesn't have the best drop-side mechanism but is satisfactory in other ways can still be a good option.

**Consider buying a crib that converts to a toddler bed only if you don't plan on having more children any time soon.** Otherwise, you'll need the crib for your next baby (and so on) and never get the chance to convert it. Also, consider buying a convertible crib if you don't mind that the toddler bed you'll end up with may look very criblike. Many convertible cribs make the switch simply by having one drop side removed, and the basic look of the crib remains. Some

# SAFER SLEEPING

To reduce the risk of Sudden Infant Death Syndrome (SIDS), always place your baby to sleep on his or her back (unless your pediatrician advises otherwise). Stomach sleeping doubles the likelihood of SIDS. In fact, since the beginning of the "Back to Sleep" campaign in 1992, which recommended that babies sleep on their backs with no soft bedding items in their sleep area, SIDS rates have dropped by more than 50 percent.

Also known as crib death, SIDS typically happens to babies under 6 months of age, peaking at 2½ months. Boys are slightly more prone to SIDS, and deaths are two-thirds more likely during winter months. The cause of SIDS isn't completely understood, although recent research suggests that some SIDS babies may have had unusual heart rhythms or brain-signaling abnormalities. Breast-feeding appears to offer a baby some protection from SIDS.

Overheating may also be a contributor to SIDS. Keep the temperature in baby's room between 67° and 71° F. Also ban smoking around your baby. Exposure to cigarette smoke increases the risk of SIDS.

Other ways to keep your baby safer during a snooze:

• Don't put your baby to sleep on a waterbed, sofa, soft mattress, pillow, or bean bag chair. The fluffy bedding materials and soft surfaces can allow a dangerous buildup of carbon dioxide around a sleeping baby from the baby's own breath. Rebreathing exhaled carbon dioxide has been identified as a leading cause of death in SIDS incidents.

• Don't share a bed with your baby. In addition to the risk that you might roll onto your baby, adult beds pose other hazards. For example, your baby could get trapped between the bed and a wall, headboard, bed frame, or other object. Accidental suffocation in soft bedding is another danger, as is the possibility of falling off the bed. If you breast-feed your baby in your bed, be sure to return him or her to the crib afterward. (For safer alternatives to bed sharing, see page 133.)

• Position the crib away from window blinds, wall hangings, or draperies. Children can strangle on the cords.

• Don't use an electric blanket, heating pad, or even a warm water bottle to heat your baby's crib. An infant's skin is highly heat-sensitive and can be burned by temperatures comfortable to an adult.

parents, on the other hand, report that since the conversion to a toddler bed is so minimal, it's less taxing for toddlers to make the transition to a "big girl" or "big boy" bed.

**Check construction and workmanship.** The simplest in-store test is to give the crib a slight shaking and see if the frame seems loose rather than solid. But be aware that display models aren't always as tightly assembled as they could be. Without applying excessive pressure, try rotating each bar to see if it's well secured to the railings. You shouldn't find loose slats on a new crib.

## What's Available

Major brands of cribs include, in alphabetical order: Alta Baby, Angel Line, Babi Italia, Baby's Dream, Bellini, Child Craft, Childesigns, Delta, Dorel Juvenile Group (Cosco), Evenflo, Fisher-Price (Storkcraft), Jardine, Kindercraft, Simmons, and Storkcraft. Crib prices range from $100 for economy models to $3,000 for custom cribs with a canopy. Paying more is largely an aesthetic issue. "You're buying quality of the finish, quality of the lumber, the detail that went into the lumber, and the crib's operating mechanism," says Seth Berger, owner of Baby & Toy Superstore in Stamford, Conn. Here's more on what you'll get at the various price points.

**Economy cribs** (in the $100 to $150 range). Models at the low end of the price scale can be perfectly adequate. Prices are low because manufacturers use cheaper materials and simpler finishes and designs. These models tend to be lighter in weight compared with top-of-the-line ones. White or pastel paint or shiny lacquer-like finish may be used to cover wood defects, such as knots and variations in shading. You may notice minor finishing flaws, such as poorly sanded rough spots, uneven patches of paint, and the heads of metal brads or glue residue at the base of the slats. On a low-priced model, typically only one side can be released, which is also the more stable approach.

Loosely fitting hooks may hold the metal mattress support at each corner. The springs making up the mattress support are lighter in construction than those in pricier models. When you shake the crib, it may seem rattly rather than sturdy. One $110 crib, the Delta Luv Jenny Lind crib (model 4750), with a solid masonite mattress support, is a

## HOW LONG SHOULD YOUR BABY SLEEP IN A CRIB?

Some sleep experts, like Jodi Mindell, Ph.D., author of *Sleeping Through the Night: How Infants, Toddlers and Their Parents Can Get a Good Night's Sleep* (Harper Resource, 1997), suggest keeping children in a crib until they're 2½ or so. "The confined nature of a crib provides a cocoon of security and can help your child get a good night's sleep," she says. And until age 2½ or so, children don't understand boundaries. Move them into a bed too soon and you can find them roaming about the house or into your bedroom. ("Hi Mommy. Hi Daddy.")

For safety's sake, our suggestion would be to monitor your child's development closely and discontinue crib use as soon as he or she shows an ability to climb out. Don't put your child back into the crib after the first "escape," regardless of his or her age. Falls that result from a child attempting to climb out of a crib can cause serious injury.

**SAFETY TIP**

**C**heck all crib hardware from time to time and replace anything that's loose (a strangulation hazard). Tighten all nuts, bolts, and screws. Check mattress support attachments regularly to make sure none are broken or bent. After you move a crib, double-check that all mattress support hangers are secure.

CONSUMER REPORTS Best Buy (see page 130).

**Midpriced cribs** ($150 to $450). At this price level, it becomes increasingly difficult to discern quality differences from brand to brand. These models are sturdier and more decorative than economy models. They come in an array of wood finishes, from Scandinavian-style natural to golden maple and oak shades, reddish-brown cherries, and deep mahoganies. End boards may be solid and smoothly finished, and many models have slats on all sides. The gentle curves of the end boards are well finished with rounded edges. Slats are thicker than those of economy models and may be round or flat with rounded edges.

The mattress supports on these models tend to be sturdy, the springs heavier. These cribs have single, double, or no drop sides. Locking wheels or casters (sometimes optional) provide stability. There may be a stabilizer bar or two running underneath for greater rigidity. The best-made cribs in this category have recessed guides for the drop side, no exposed brads or glue residue where the slats are fastened to the rails, and a uniform finish. There may be extra-high posts, canopies, or a storage drawer underneath the unit.

**High-end cribs** ($450 on up). These models, many of them imported from Europe, have hand-rubbed, glazed, or burnished finishes. You'll see sleigh styles with curved end boards and hand-painted details, as well as some models hand-crafted from wrought iron. These cribs may have single, double, or no drop sides. On some with drop sides, the hardware is recessed and may be so well hidden that it's difficult to tell whether the side lowers or not. Mattress supports use heavy-gauge springs and heavyweight metal frames and may adjust to four heights. These cribs may also include a drawer and convert to a daybed/toddler bed or other nursery furniture. At the highest end, a fairy-tale-like canopy may be part of the ensemble.

## Features to Consider

**Convertibility.** If you're interested in buying a crib that converts to a toddler or full-size bed, keep in mind that some require parts that aren't typically included in your original purchase, such as bed rails, stabilizing rails, or support rails (for converting to a full-size bed).

Convertibility can stretch the life of a crib into the toddler years and beyond. Some parents, however, prefer to start over when their baby is beyond the nursery stage with a completely new set of "big girl" or "big boy" furniture.

**Drawers.** Some models include a drawer or two under the mattress. Under-crib drawers are not usually attached to the crib frame. Some are freestanding and roll out from under the crib on casters. Before buying, pull any drawer all the way out to inspect its construction. You may find that it has a thin, cardboardlike floor that could bow and give way when loaded with linen or clothing. A drawer floor made of a harder material, such as fiberboard, is more likely to hold up over time. Other cribs have a set of drawers attached to the short end of the unit.

**Drop sides.** Many cribs have a single side that lowers, which is the more stable approach. Some claim "one-hand operation," which can be helpful, but check the store model to be sure it delivers on this benefit. Some cribs, including expensive heavyweight models, have double drop sides, which is something to consider if you'll be approaching your baby's crib from either side. (Many parents have no need for a second drop side.) The newer designs have relatively quiet releases that require you to lift the rail while you push the release with your leg. The older design requires you to lift the side while pressing a metal lever or tab under the railing with your foot. The foot maneuver is awkward since you have to stand on one leg to do it. Metal components often rattle and squeak. A third, though rare, type of release mechanism uses latches at each end of the top rail that must be pulled out at the same time. Federal regulations require that lowering mechanisms be built to prevent accidental release by a baby or sibling.

**Finish.** The look of dark wood stains is currently gaining popularity, although you'll also see lighter stains such as maples and cherries. White, however, remains the most common crib color. Other painted colors include off-whites, washed whites (revealing the wood's grain), and green, blue, or yellow pastels. A little roughness in the finish isn't a problem as long as there are no serious defects such as splintering or peeling paint.

**Mattress height.** All full-size cribs offer at least two mattress

**T**he following companies are currently in the Juvenile Products Manufacturers Association (JPMA) certification program: Alta Baby, Baby's Dream Furniture, Bassett Furniture Industries, Bellini, Child Craft, Delta Enterprise, Dorel Juvenile Group, Evenflo, Forever Mine, Generation 2 Worldwide, Million Dollar Baby, P.J. Kids LLC, Simmons Juvenile Products Co., Simplicity, Status Furniture, Storkcraft, Young America, and Yu Wei Co. Ltd. That means that any model they manufacture must be certified to the American Society for Testing and Materials (ASTM) voluntary safety standards. You may or may not find a certification sticker displayed on a crib or its packaging. Note, however, that models made by companies that are not in the certification program may not necessarily be less safe.

height positions; more expensive models have three to four. To prevent your baby from falling out of the crib, adjust the mattress support to its lowest height position when he or she is able to sit or pull up, usually between 6 and 8 months. Many models don't require tools for adjusting mattress height positions, though some do. Accessing the screws or bolts can be difficult in some models.

**Mattress supports.** Most mattress supports consist of a metal frame with springs. With some cribs the mattress support is a one-piece board; with others it's a grid with wood slats. The mattress supports are adjustable so the mattress can be raised or lowered depending on the size of the child. Mattress supports need to be held securely in place so they aren't dislodged when you're changing a crib sheet or when another child or large pet pushes up from underneath.

**Sides and railings.** Crib sides are constructed by fitting bars (or spindles or slats) into mortised holes in the top and bottom rails, then securing each bar with glue and one or two metal brads. The small holes made by the brads or pins are usually filled and covered with a finish so they're invisible. As per the mandatory safety standard, crib slats should be no more than 2⅜ inches apart, so slat width shouldn't be an issue.

**Structural integrity.** Sturdiness is a sign of construction quality. One or more stabilizer bars—metal rods fastened to both end boards beneath the crib—can help make the frame more rigid.

**Teething rails.** These are smooth, plastic coverings for the top of the side rails to protect the crib and a gnawing baby's gums. The voluntary industry standard says teething rails should be built to stay in place and not crack or break.

**Wheels/casters**. Made of plastic or metal, a crib's wheels can be standard rollers or round, multidirectional, ball-shaped casters, which swivel and make it easier to haul a crib from one room to another. Not all cribs come with them, which isn't an issue if your crib won't be venturing out of the nursery. If your baby's crib will be on bare wood or tile floors and you choose a crib with wheels, make sure they lock to prevent the crib from "walking" across the room or tempting other children to take baby on a joy ride when your back is turned.

## Recommendations

Buy a crib that's unused, made after 1999, and Juvenile Products Manufacturers Association (JPMA) certified or certified to meet the American Society for Testing and Materials (ASTM) voluntary standards (ASTM F-1169 and ASTM F-996). Certification can assure you that your crib conforms to the latest federal and voluntary safety standards. Buying new will help protect your baby from hidden dangers such as drop sides, slats, or hardware that may have been weakened as a result of previous rough use, or excessive dampness or heat during storage. By law, the production date of the crib has to be displayed both on the crib itself and on its shipping carton.

Cribs are shipped unassembled, so if you're not certain about your ability to put a crib together correctly (typically a two-person job that requires a full hour—from unpacking to complete assembly), ask to have the retailer send a qualified assembly crew to your home. This can mean an extra $70 or more unless the cost is built into the retail price, but it can give you valuable peace of mind for your baby's safety. Besides saving tempers and fingers, having the store assemble the crib allows you to inspect it on the spot—and reject it if you discover flaws. If you do choose to assemble the crib, do it in the baby's room. Once put together, the crib may not fit through a small door.

# Ratings • Cribs

All of the cribs we tested meet current safety standards. Those with the highest safety scores did well in our assessments of additional factors, including certain strangulation risks, hardware, mattress supports, and the clarity of instructions. The most convenient cribs tended to have one or two drop sides that could be raised or lowered with one hand. They were also easy to assemble and to adjust the mattress height. Cribs judged least convenient had drop sides that required two hands to operate, or sides that didn't lower at all. They may also have been difficult to assemble.

Excellent Very good Good Fair Poor
⊜ ⊜ ○ ◔ ●

**Within types, in performance order. Blue key numbers indicate Quick Picks.**

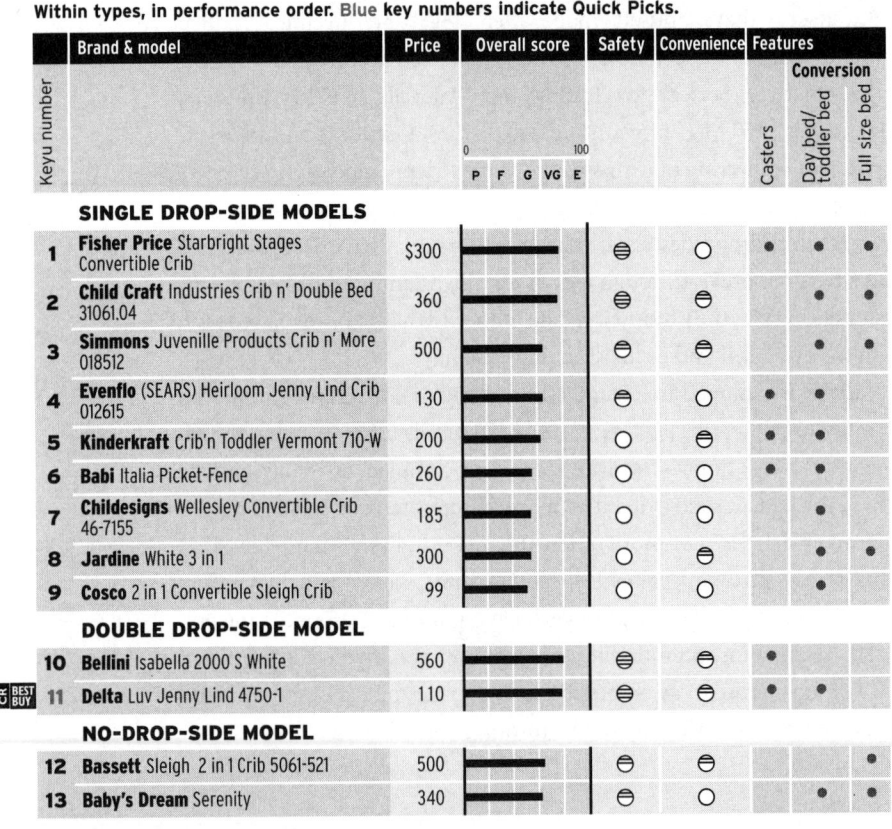

| Keyu number | Brand & model | Price | Overall score | Safety | Convenience | Casters | Day bed/ toddler bed | Full size bed |
|---|---|---|---|---|---|---|---|---|
| | **SINGLE DROP-SIDE MODELS** | | | | | | | |
| 1 | **Fisher Price** Starbright Stages Convertible Crib | $300 | | ⊜ | ○ | • | • | • |
| 2 | **Child Craft** Industries Crib n' Double Bed 31061.04 | 360 | | ⊜ | ⊜ | | • | • |
| 3 | **Simmons** Juvenille Products Crib n' More 018512 | 500 | | ⊜ | ⊜ | | • | • |
| 4 | **Evenflo** (SEARS) Heirloom Jenny Lind Crib 012615 | 130 | | ⊜ | ○ | • | • | |
| 5 | **Kinderkraft** Crib'n Toddler Vermont 710-W | 200 | | ○ | ⊜ | • | • | |
| 6 | **Babi** Italia Picket-Fence | 260 | | ○ | ○ | • | • | |
| 7 | **Childesigns** Wellesley Convertible Crib 46-7155 | 185 | | ○ | ○ | | • | |
| 8 | **Jardine** White 3 in 1 | 300 | | ○ | ⊜ | | • | • |
| 9 | **Cosco** 2 in 1 Convertible Sleigh Crib | 99 | | ○ | ○ | | • | |
| | **DOUBLE DROP-SIDE MODEL** | | | | | | | |
| 10 | **Bellini** Isabella 2000 S White | 560 | | ⊜ | ⊜ | • | | |
| 11 | **Delta** Luv Jenny Lind 4750-1 | 110 | | ⊜ | ⊜ | • | • | |
| | **NO-DROP-SIDE MODEL** | | | | | | | |
| 12 | **Bassett** Sleigh 2 in 1 Crib 5061-521 | 500 | | ⊜ | ⊜ | | | • |
| 13 | **Baby's Dream** Serenity | 340 | | ⊜ | ○ | | • | • |

## Guide to the Ratings

**Overall score** is based on safety and convenience of the tested models. **Safety** scores include results of tests for the potential for hardware failure, strangulation from nonvertical protrusions, errors in assembling and reassembling the crib, mattress-support safety, and errors in converting to a day bed/toddler bed or full-size bed. **Convenience** is based on the use of tools and whether or not they were supplied; access to the infant; and ease of assembling the crib and converting it to its other uses, following the instructions correctly, using the drop side(s), moving the crib, adjusting the mattress height, and maintenance. **Price** is the price we paid at retail stores in the fall of 2003. **Features** provide information on drop side operation, casters, and whether the model converts to a toddler/day bed or full-size bed.

## Quick Picks • Cribs

**Best value**

**11 Delta Luv** $110

This double drop-side model received an excellent safety score, although it was less convenient than some, requiring two hands to raise or lower the side. It can convert to a toddler bed and also to a full-sized bed.

**CHAPTER**

# 15

# Crib Alternatives

For the first four to five months of your baby's life, you have some options other than putting him or her to sleep in a crib. These alternatives—bassinets, bedside sleepers, cradles, miniature cribs, non-full-size cribs, and portable cribs (play yards)—offer a cozy nest near a parent's bed for a newborn or young infant. A small baby may seem more at home in a compact space than in a large, airy crib. And there's something to be said for keeping your baby close by for nighttime feedings and diaper changes, although that's also possible with a full-size crib.

However, once your baby begins to move around more and seems uncomfortable (or nears the upper weight limit recommended by the manufacturer), it's time to move to a crib. So think of these crib alternatives as options just for the short term.

There is an American Society for Testing and Materials (ASTM) safety standard for bassinets and cradles, but currently no company that produces them is in a certification program. Crib alternatives that fall into the non-full-size crib category are subject to a federal standard similar to the one for full-size cribs. Companies that produce non-full-size cribs are in the Juvenile Products Manufacturers Association (JPMA) certification program. For more information on crib safety, see Cribs, starting on page 121.

## What's Available

**Bassinets.** These compact baby beds, some with wheels, are made of fabric, wicker, or woven wooden splints. Most have a rigid hood that can be attached on one end. They take up little space and can be moved easily from room to room. Some may convert into another piece of furniture, such as a changing table, when baby has outgrown the bassinet.

Bassinets present some safety issues. Some models have relatively rough, sharp inside edges. Models with soft sides may pose entrapment dangers. (The soft, thin mattress found in many models is limited in thickness to reduce the hazard of suffocation, and additional bedding should be avoided for that reason.) And bassinets are not as inherently stable as portable cribs.

The hinged legs on folding bassinets have been known to give way accidentally. Your baby will outgrow a bassinet after about three months. Price: about $100.

**Bedside sleepers.** These are so compact they could be called "cribettes." They can be made to fit flush against the side of a bed, at about the same height as the adult mattress. The side next to the bed usually has an opening with a "lip" that's a few inches high to prevent the infant from rolling out. Bars or a high, padded rim enclose the other three sides. The connector between your mattress and the sleeper is usually a length of fabric or strapping secured between the mattress and the bedsprings. Leg extensions are available with some models to raise them to a height matching the adult bed. The floor pad, however, has to be lower than the adult mattress surface.

A bedside sleeper requires much more care to keep in a safe setup position than a full-size crib or other crib alternative. If it is not completely joined with your bed or isn't at the appropriate height, a gap or ridge could form that can trap a baby's head, neck, or torso. Your baby will outgrow a bedside sleeper after a few months; you should stop using it when baby is able to roll over or pull up to a kneeling/sitting position. Price range: $100 to $200.

**Cradles.** Although a cradle has a charming, old-fashioned look about it, we suggest that you resist buying one. Babies do love rhythmic movement, but experts advise that the most effective rocking direction is a head-to-toe motion, similar to what a baby experiences when held on your shoulder in a rocking chair. The side-to-side motion of a cradle can also press a tiny baby against the side of the unit. Cradle frames suspended on hooks have a gentler motion but can still cause a baby to roll from side to side.

Babies should never be left unattended in freely rocking cradles. Locking pins should be bolted in place so the cradle can't tilt at an angle greater than 5 degrees. Your baby will outgrow a cradle after four to six months.

**Miniature or non-full-size cribs.** Sometimes called "grandma cribs" (not to be confused with play yards, see page 201), these are small, rectangular wooden or metal baby beds that mimic full-size cribs but are more compact and fit through doorways more easily. Some have legs that lower, so the bed portion can sit close to the floor. Miniature cribs are safer than bassinets, cradles, and bedside sleepers and fold compactly for traveling. Your baby will outgrow a miniature crib as soon as he or she is able to push up on all fours—usually between 4 and 6 months. Price: about $80.

## Recommendations

The ability to keep your baby in a cozy space near where you're sleeping is the primary attraction of all these crib alternatives, whose essential differences are outlined above. However, their period of usefulness is relatively brief, and they don't provide the same level of safety as a full-size crib, which can also be located in an adult bedroom, though it will probably take up more space.

View any crib alternative with some caution. Evaluate construction, looking for a model with a sturdy bottom and a wide, stable base. Make sure the mattress and padding are smooth and extra firm and fit snugly. If fitted sheets (or any additional parts) are needed, obtain them from the same company that made the crib alternative, if possible. Other tips to keep baby safe:

**Follow manufacturer guidelines.** Always adhere to the manufacturer's weight and size specifications. They are usually printed on the product's carton, or you may need to consult the instruction book. Warnings are usually on the product, and they may be numerous.

**Check any folding mechanisms.** If the legs or frame fold for storage, make sure they lock into place effectively when the unit is set up. Otherwise, the unit could accidentally fold while it's in use.

CHAPTER

# 16

# Crib Bedding

ight up there on the excitement scale with gathering your list of baby names is pondering the endless possibilities for making your baby's room special. Some expectant couples elect to learn the gender of their baby ahead of time just so they can get a head start on decorating—not that we're suggesting that, of course.

All told, making a big deal out of the baby's room is part of the fun of parenthood, although you can certainly be low-key if you wish. "It's much easier and less expensive to choose cheery paint with a few prints or a lamp shade to let everyone know 'this is a baby's room,' " says Jennifer Renton of Albany, Calif., mother of a toddler, who decided to stick with a minimalist motif.

Angela Harrigan-Flores, the owner of Jackandjill.com, an online furniture store, agrees. "You can do so much with accessories, such as lamp shades, mirrors, frames, and wall hangings, to make a baby's room special, especially if at least one of the accessories you choose is personalized with your baby's name," she says.

However you decide to approach the task, keep in mind that everything, including the room's color scheme, typically revolves around the bedding you select. In fact, it's often much easier to pick a paint color or wallpaper after you've chosen your baby's bedding, rather than the other way around. You can otherwise find yourself having to repaint or repaper.

Colors and styles of sheets run the gamut—from licensed character themes like Winnie the Pooh that adorn not only sheets but also curtains, wallpaper, rugs, laundry bags, and wall hangings as part of nursery "ensembles," to simple and subdued prints, checks, and pastels in muted tones. Beyond traditional bedding fabrics like 100 percent cotton, you'll also find piqué, velour, fleece, fake suede, corduroy, chenille, and country quilting. Take one step into the bedding department, especially at specialty baby stores, and we think you'll agree. Babies' rooms never looked so good—and parents' choices have never been so overwhelming.

## What's Available

Major brands of crib bedding include, in alphabetical order: Amy Coe, Baby Martex, Babystyle, Bebe Chic, Blue Moon Baby, Brandee, California Kids, Celebrations, Cotton Tale, Danielle, House Inc., Kidsline, Kimberly Grant & Co., Lambs & Ivy, Laura Ashley, Mount Vernon Mills, OshKosh, Patch Kraft, Regal Lager, Sumersault, Sweet Potatoes, Wamsutta, and Wendy Bellissimo.

Prices for bedding sets range from $50 to $700 (the upper end is for custom-made, an option often available through specialty retailers such as Poshtots.com). This doesn't include a fitted sheet or a diaper stacker; the latter, in our opinion, is completely optional.

Although you may still see large, puffy quilts, comforters casually draped over cribs, and luxuriously stuffed bumpers in stores, catalogs, and online, the Consumer Product Safety Commission has deemed them unsafe for use in cribs because they're a suffocation hazard. Consumer Reports recommends that you keep pillows, quilts, comforters, sheepskins, stuffed toys, and other soft products out of your baby's crib. In general, kids under 1 year old should sleep in a crib that's nearly bare—with just a mattress and fitted sheet and perhaps one thin blanket, tightly tucked at the corners.

We don't recommend bumper guards for infants. If you do buy one, be sure to remove it as soon as your baby can pull up to a standing position so he or she can't use it as a step to climb out. Also, if you use a bumper, it should fit around the entire crib and tie or snap securely in at least six locations. Bumper ties should be 9 inches or less in length.

If you choose to use a thin blanket, tuck it around and under the crib mattress and slide your baby into the pocket that it forms only as far as his or her armpits. Your baby's head should remain uncovered during sleep. Or consider using a sleeper such as the Halo SleepSack as an alternative to blankets of any kind.

## Bedding Basics

To outfit your baby's crib, you'll need:

**Fitted sheet.** Most crib sheets are elasticized and have fitted corners. Fabrics range from woven cottons and cotton blends to lightweight flannel. Two to three should get you off to a good start.

**Mattress pad.** These quilted pads should be thin, if you use one at all. They're usually made of cotton or a synthetic material and should cover the mattress securely. Most, like fitted sheets, are elasticized all the way around. Many are moistureproof, but that's not absolutely necessary because all mattresses have some form of waterproofing. Buy one or two pads. Never use a plastic bag as a mattress cover. Plastic is a suffocation hazard.

**Receiving blankets.** These very thin blankets are typically made of woven cotton. You'll use them to swaddle your newborn during nap and nighttime for the first few months (the ultimate security blanket). They also make great mops for spit-ups and camouflage for discreet nursing. Get a half-dozen large waffle-weave blankets made of 100 percent cotton for good absorbency (or put them on your shower gift list).

**Thin crib blanket.** Use this for tucking into the corners of your baby's crib and then tucking your baby into, with or without a sleeper sack, depending on the season.

**Wearable sleep blanket.** The Halo SleepSack, which typically retails for about $13, is endorsed by the SIDS Alliance, an organization that provides information on Sudden Infant Death Syndrome and seeks ways to reduce the risk of infant death. Still, there are other brands, including the Large Beddie Bye Zip Around Safety Blanket by Kiddopotamus (also roughly $13). A wearable sleep blanket slips over a regular sleeper or diaper and provides plenty of room for little legs to stretch and kick. Look for flame-retardant fabric. Use in conjunction with or in place of a thin crib blanket.

## What's Optional

**Coverlet (blanket) or comforter.** Even though you shouldn't use either of these as a crib component, a blanket/comforter can come in handy as a play mat or exercise pad for tummy time under your watchful supervision. Tummy time (that's parent lingo for the time your baby spends on the floor during the day doing "push-ups") helps develop upper body coordination.

**Crib skirt.** It's not necessary, but it does add a touch of style to the crib and your baby's room.

## Recommendations

Whether you decide to do it up lavishly or decorate your baby's room simply, make safety your main concern. Purchase tightly fitting sheets, then recheck the fit after each laundering, since washing can cause shrinking or weaken the elastic. Also, check for loose threads or ties that could catch a baby's head or neck. Plan to launder sheets twice before the first use to remove any chemical residue left over from the fabric-treatment process and to ensure correct fit. Use a fragrance-free, dye-free liquid or powder laundry detergent, such as Dreft.

To avoid potentially irritating your baby's delicate skin, don't use liquid fabric softener or dryer sheets. Whatever you wash with, be sure to rinse baby clothes and bedding thoroughly; if you use a washing machine, opt for a second rinse cycle.

Don't use a bumper pad or any fluffy crib bedding. Remember that bare is best.

Follow the suggestions in the Cribs chapter for safer sleeping, such as putting your baby to bed on his or her back and keeping puffy quilts and comforters out of the crib.

CHAPTER

# 17

# Crib Mattresses

Whesn you're shopping for a crib, you'll also need to choose a mattress, which is typically sold separately from the crib. Aside from safety, which is paramount, the firmness of the mattress and the quality of its covering (or ticking) are your main concerns.

There are two general types of crib mattresses: foam and innerspring. Both tend to keep their shape well. There are differences, of course. For one, foam is lighter. The densest foam mattress is usually no more than 10 pounds, compared with 20 to 25 pounds for some innerspring mattresses. So changing your baby's sheets may be easier with a foam unit. Foam is also less springy and therefore less apt to encourage your baby to use the mattress as a trampoline. Still, innerspring crib mattresses remain the most popular.

If you're considering a foam mattress, keep in mind that low-priced models tend to be mushy and flimsy, with a thin vinyl covering and vinyl edging. They may also be unsafe. Putting a baby to sleep on a soft mattress increases the risk of Sudden Infant Death Syndrome (SIDS). Higher-priced models tend to be firmer (and therefore safer), with thicker, reinforced vinyl or cotton coverings.

To assess foam density (which has a direct relation to firmness), compare the weight of different foam models. That's not always easy to do in a store, but if you're able to lift several different mattresses, do it. In general, the heavier the foam mattress, the denser the foam. You can also give the mattress a squeeze test in the center by pressing your palms into both sides of it at once. A dense mattress won't allow you to press very far. A denser foam mattress is also likely to have firmer edges, which is another important performance factor.

To judge the quality of an innerspring mattress, don't go by the sales gimmick of "coil count." While the cheapest innerspring baby mattresses have about 80 coils and the most expensive can have 600 coils, a high coil count doesn't always mean a firmer mattress. In fact, a model with 150 coils can be firmer than one with 600. You can judge by picking up mattresses to compare their weight and by squeezing them to test for firmness. Innerspring models generally have firmer edges than foam mattresses, but squeeze the edges to do a comparison. You may also feel border rods at the top and bottom perimeter, which provide extra edge support for safety and durability.

The number of layers of padding, what that padding is made of, and the quality of the covering add to the price and increase comfort. The cheapest innersprings, like low-end foam mattresses, have thin vinyl coverings and edgings, which can tear, crack, and dry out over time. As prices go up, coverings become thick, puncture-resistant reinforced double or triple laminates, and edgings have fabric binding, which is a sign of quality. Beyond that, reversibility, the presence of ventilators, and thickness are factors that differentiate one model from another.

### KEEP IT CLEAN

**F**ollow the manufacturer's instructions, which usually suggest wiping it clean with a warm, moist cloth and mild soap. It's also a good idea to air the mattress out periodically and keep it in a dry place during periods of storage.

The mattress you select should also be in compliance with a new flammability law that went into effect on Jan. 1, 2004. Though this is a state law applying only to California, crib mattresses sold in other states are expected to comply with it.

## Shopping Secrets

**Compare mattresses in the store.** Do this by squeezing them.

**Confirm store return policies.** And keep your receipt. A store's return policy is more important than a mattress maker's warranty. The store should be willing to exchange a mattress that doesn't fit properly, which is a major safety concern.

## What's Available

The major brands of foam and innerspring mattresses are, in alphabetical order: Child Craft, Colgate, Evenflo, Kolcraft, Sealy, and Simmons. Prices range from $30 to about $230.

## Recommendations

You don't have to spend the most to get a good quality mattress, but don't skimp, either. A budget somewhere between $90 and $150 will generally serve your baby well. A good, firm mattress may also promote proper posture and is more likely to be durable, which is important if your baby will be using the same mattress as a toddler bed or you'll be passing it down to future siblings.

In the case of innerspring models, look for a firm mattress with good support from border rods. Border rods provide extra firmness, durability, and edge support. A mattress with reinforced or embossed vinyl is leakproof; it is also less likely to tear on the metal edge of a mattress foundation and should hold up better over time. Also look for air vents along the sides of the mattress, which not only help keep the mattress ventilated but may prevent seams from splitting when your tot inevitably starts jumping.

When selecting a foam mattress, go for one with high-density foam. Do the squeeze test for firmness in the center and at the edge. Pinch the mattress covering or ticking; it should feel thick, not flimsy.

## CERTIFICATION

There is no certification program for crib mattresses by any independent organization, but there are flammability standards. A federal flammability standard for adult mattresses applies to crib mattresses as well. A newer California law went into effect on Jan. 1, 2004; it applies to mattresses sold in that state, but manufacturers are likely to meet it regardless of where they sell their products.

Make sure any mattress you buy passes the two-finger test for fit in the crib. Check that fitted sheets fit snugly and securely, overlapping the corners so that you can't easily pull them up at the corners. Ill-fitting crib mattress sheets are a strangulation and suffocation hazard. And never use an adult sheet as a crib sheet, not even in a pinch.

## PRODUCT GUIDE • CRIB MATTRESSES

**N**ote: These products were not tested by Consumers Union. This alphabetical listing does not include all models available but rather is a selection of some widely distributed ones. Descriptions are derived from the manufacturers' claims. Prices are approximate retail. For manufacturer contact information, see the Brand Locator, starting on page 283.

| Line/model | Price | Details |
|---|---|---|
| **CHILD CRAFT** | | |
| **Child Craft Baby Comfort Extra-Firm Foam** | $65 | Extra-firm foam-core mattress with ventilators. Weighs 7 pounds. |
| **Legacy Peaceful Dreamer Extra-Firm Foam** | $65 | Extra-firm foam-core mattress with ventilators. Weighs 7 pounds. |
| **Child Craft Baby Comfort Innerspring** | $75 | Innerspring mattress with ventilators. No border rods. Weighs 16 pounds. |
| **Legacy Peaceful Dreamer Innerspring** | $75 | Innerspring mattress with ventilators. No border rods. Weighs 16 pounds. |
| **Legacy Lifetime Mattress** | $150 | Innerspring mattress with two sides, one designed for infants (with extra-firm padding) and one for toddlers (with convoluted foam). Has ventilators and border rods. Weighs 22 pounds. |
| **Child Craft Posture Craft Super-Firm Innerspring** | $155 | Innerspring mattress with ventilators, and border rods. Weighs 25 pounds. |
| **Legacy Precious Posture Super-Firm Innerspring** | $155 | Innerspring mattress with ventilators and border rods. Weighs 25 pounds. |
| **Child Craft Baby Natura Latex** | $200 | Foam mattress with breathable, open-cell latex as its core. No ventilators. Weighs 17 pounds. |

| Line/model | Price | Details |
| --- | --- | --- |
| **COLGATE** | | |
| **Foam Supreme II 5-inch** | $70 | 5-inch foam mattress with border rods, no ventilators. Weighs 6 pounds. |
| **Crown Imperial I 5-inch** | $80 | Firm foam mattress with quilted cover, ventilators, and border rods. Weights 6 pounds. |
| **Little Aristocrat IV** | $90 | Innerspring mattress with ventilators and border rods. Weighs 10 pounds. |
| **Super Luxury 5 -inch** | $90 | Foam mattress with ventilators and border rods. Weighs 7 pounds. |
| **Slumbertyme 5-inch** | $90 | Firm foam mattress with ventilators and border rods. Weighs 6 pounds. |
| **Little Aristocrat I** | $90 | Innerspring mattress with ventilators and border rods. Weighs 10 pounds. |
| **Premier 6-inch** | $90 | 6-inch foam mattress with ventilators and border rods. Weighs 7 pounds. |
| **Crown Imperial III** | $100 | Innerspring mattress with ventilators and border rods. Weighs 11 pounds. |
| **Classica III 5-inch** | $100 | Two different types of foam, with ventilators and border rods. Weighs 7 pounds. |
| **Classica I 5-inch** | $120 | Firm foam mattress with ventilators and border rods. Weighs 8 pounds. |
| **Grand Premier 5-inch** | $130 | Firm foam mattress with ventilators and border rods. Weighs 8 pounds. |
| **Classica Supreme 5-inch** | $130 | Two different types of foam, with ventilators and border rods. Weighs 9 pounds. |
| **Baby Regal I by Colgate (exclusive to BuyBuy Baby)** | $150 | Innerspring mattress with ventilators and border rods. Weighs 22 pounds. Similar models: BuyBuy Baby Regal II, 25 pounds, $120; BuyBuy Baby Sophisticate, 25 pounds, no ventilators, $220. |
| **2-N-1** | $150 | Innerspring mattress with ventilators and border rods. Weighs 16 pounds. |
| **CradleTyme Ultra II** | $150 | Innerspring mattress with ventilators and border rods. Weighs 15 pounds. |
| **Diploma** | $170 | Innerspring mattress with ventilators and border rods. Weighs 17 pounds. |
| **3-N-1** | $180 | Innerspring mattress with ventilators and border rods. Weighs 21 pounds. |

| Line/model | Price | Details |
|---|---|---|
| Elegance | $190-$200 | Innerspring mattress with border rods. No ventilators. Weighs 20 pounds. |
| Visco-Classica | $200 | Foam mattress, with 5 inches of firm foam topped with 1 inch of viscoelastic (a foam cushion). Has ventilators and border rods. Weighs 9 pounds. |
| Ultimate | $230 | Innerspring mattress with border rods, no ventilators. Weighs 26 pounds. |
| **KOLCRAFT** | | |
| Baby Prestige | $30 | Innerspring mattress. No border rods or ventilators. Weighs 11 pounds. |
| Ortho Rest | $40 | Innerspring mattress with border rods, no ventilators. Weighs 15 pounds. |
| Pediatric 1000 | $40 | Innerspring mattress. No border rods or ventilators. Weighs 14 pounds. |
| Baby Sealy | $50 | Innerspring mattress with border rods, no ventilators. Weighs 15 pounds. |
| Pediatric 1500 | $50 | Innerspring mattress. No border rods or ventilators. Weighs 12 pounds. |
| Baby Soft Ultra | $60 | Innerspring mattress with border rods, no ventilators. Weighs 16 pounds. |
| Supreme Sleep | $60 | Innerspring mattress with border rods, no ventilators. Weighs 16 pounds. |
| **SIMMONS** | | |
| Baby Slumber Deluxe | $50 | Innerspring mattress with ventilators, no border rods. Weighs 15 pounds. |
| Baby Beauty Supreme | $70 | Innerspring mattress with ventilators, no border rods. Weighs 17 pounds. |
| Super Maxipedic | $90 | Innerspring mattress with ventilators, no border rods. Weighs 22 pounds. |
| Baby Beautyrest Elegance | $100 | Innerspring mattress with ventilators and border rods. Weighs 21 pounds. |
| Baby Beautyrest Backcare VII | $110-$120 | Innerspring mattress with ventilators and border rods. Weighs 21 pounds. |
| Sleep 'n More (exclusive to Babies "R" Us) | $120 | Innerspring mattress with ventilators and border rods. Weighs 23 pounds. |

# 18

# Diapers

Y ou'll change thousands of diapers by the time your child is 2 to 3 years old and he or she is ready for the potty. Fortunately, diaper quality is better than ever, which makes the task easier.

Your first major decision in the diaper department will be cloth vs. disposable. Both kinds of diapers have their benefits and drawbacks. On the one hand, disposable diapers are undeniably convenient, and the vast majority of babies today wear them. But they're also costly: You can expect to spend $1,500 or more on disposables by the time your baby is out of them.

Cloth diapers are less expensive to use than disposables, especially if you do the laundering yourself. Cloth "diapering systems," with water-resistant outer coverings that close with snaps or Velcro, are almost as easy to use as disposable diapers. But you still have to wash the cloth diaper insert, of course.

Despite a resurgence in the popularity of cloth diapers, disposable diapers

remain the most popular choice among today's parents, as well as day-care centers and hospitals. A disposable diaper has gel and other super-absorbent materials between the lining and the outer shell that absorb many times their weight in liquid. Disposables draw liquid into the gel layer and away from baby's skin, so you can leave your baby in one longer than you could a cloth diaper, without causing discomfort.

All disposables are not the same, however. You'll see differences in fit and the ability to control leaks from brand to brand. For this book we tested 10 brands of disposables on 79 children in three day-care centers. More than 6,500 diapers were used in the course of testing. Although all disposables are absorbent, name-brand diapers performed better than store-brand (or private label) ones in our tests. Pampers, Huggies, and Luvs rated Excellent overall. Store brands ranged from Good to Very Good.

As a whole, disposable diaper quality has improved since we last tested diapers for CONSUMER REPORTS in 1998. They're generally less leaky than they've ever been, feel less moist when they're wet, and provide a better fit. They're also one absorbent bunch (as they've traditionally been). Any of the diapers or training pants we tested will absorb far more liquid than a child is likely to produce during the time a single diaper is worn.

Diapers are often sized according to baby's weight, beginning with

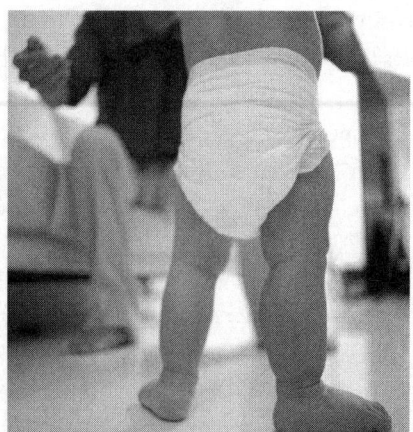

preemie and newborn and progressing to sizes 1 through 6. Some store brands are simply marked small, medium, large, and extra large, with weight ranges listed on the package. The biggest diapers fit children 35 pounds and over.

As the sizes increase, you get fewer diapers for the same price. A large package might give you 68 diapers in size 1, but only 32 in size 6. As with many things, buying the largest packages can reduce your per-diaper costs.

# DISPOSABLE DIAPERS

## What's Available

Major brand names of disposable diapers include Huggies, Luvs, and Pampers. Major store brands include America's Choice (A&P), Baby Basics (Albertson's), Little Ones (Kmart), Loving Touch (Target), Simply Dry (Stop & Shop), Ultra Comforts (Kroger), and White Cloud (Wal-Mart). Prices for disposables range from 19 to 32 cents per diaper; you'll generally save by buying a store brand over a name brand. Saving pennies per diaper may not seem like much, but with five diaper changes a day, you'd save about $15.50 per month and $186 per year.

## Features to Consider

**Fasteners.** The type of fastener varies from brand to brand. Most now use Velcro fasteners, which, unlike tape, don't lose their sticking power when they come in contact with baby creams or powders.

**Leak guards.** These elastic barriers and flaps of material improve fit around the waist, legs, and thighs to help prevent leaks.

**Lotion.** Many diapers have a lotion on the liner that is supposed to protect baby's skin. But you'll still want to keep zinc oxide diaper cream on hand for the inevitable outbreaks of diaper rash.

**Stretch sides.** These help the diaper do a better job of fitting a baby's unique contours, which can help stop leaks. Your baby may find diapers with stretch sides more comfortable, too.

**Shells.** The shells of many diapers have a clothlike feel that minimizes moisture.

## Recommendations

Plan on using plenty of diapers for your newborn, but don't load up on the newborn size. Babies with higher birth weights may not fit the smallest size at all. Start with a package of newborn and a package of size 1—about 48 diapers in all. Then buy in volume after you see which size fits your baby.

For starters, select the smallest diaper your child can comfortably wear—a larger diaper not only costs more, but it also may not fit your baby as well, allowing leaks. You may have to experiment a bit to find a diaper that fits your baby's quickly changing body. Diaper sizes vary from brand to brand. One brand's size 3 may fit children 12 to 24 pounds, while another's fits those 16 to 28 pounds. A brand's weight ranges usually overlap: Size 2 in one brand covers 12 to 18 pounds; size 3, 16 to 28 pounds, and so forth.

Stores often put disposable diapers on sale as "loss leaders" to induce parents to shop there. So watch for specials and stock up when the time comes. Take advantage of freebies and coupons, and consider joining a warehouse club, such as Costco or Sam's Club. You might also want to call the toll-free customer-service lines or register at the Web sites of disposable diaper companies for their new-parent programs, which often include coupons and free samples. (But keep in mind that your name may get on mailing lists.) Also, experiment with store brands, especially if your budget is tight. While they don't rate as highly as name brands, they can do an adequate job, and your savings will add up over the years you'll be in the diapering trenches.

## CLOTH DIAPERS

### What's Available

Cloth diapers are made from different types of absorbent cotton fabrics: terry (like towels, but softer), bird's-eye (similar to old-fashioned tea towels), gauze (thin and lightweight), and flannel (similar to the material used in flannel sheets and pajamas, but denser and thicker). Flannel is the softest against the skin as well as the most absorbent. A combination of terry and flannel is also quite absorbent.

Diapering systems (basically a diaper with a protective outer shell) are superior to plain diapers in terms of absorbency, fit, and leak control and spare you the hassle of safety pins. But they are also more expensive. Major brands of cloth diapers and cloth diapering systems include Basic Comfort, Bellies and Buns, Bumkins, Earthwise Basics,

## DIAPER-WASHING BASICS

**W**ash cloth diapers two dozen at a time. Presoak first, using your washer's highest water level and the hottest water. Launder with a hot wash and cold rinse. You don't have to use a special laundry detergent—any detergent labeled free of perfume or dyes will work fine. As long as you presoak, you don't need to use chlorine bleach, which shortens diaper life. To remove stains, use chlorine-free bleach or washing soda. If your baby is prone to diaper rash, rinse diapers twice, adding three-fourths of a cup of white vinegar to the second rinse.

Don't use liquid fabric softener or dryer sheets. Your baby may have an allergic reaction to the fragrance. Fabric softener can also leave a waxy buildup on diapers, making them water-repellent instead of absorbent.

Fuzzi Bunz, Gerber, Hana's Generation, Kushies, and Sweet Pickles. Cloth diapers and diapering systems are available at baby, toy, and mail-order stores, as well as on Web sites such as *www.kushies.com.*

## Features to Consider

No question, cloth diapers are much less convenient than disposables. If you don't use a diaper service, you have to soak the soiled diapers between laundry loads. And the demands of a new baby can make keeping up with the diaper onslaught a daunting proposition. But there are ways to lighten the burden if you decide to go this route.

A diaper service can make cloth diapers easier to deal with, although the expense can boost your diapering costs to the same level as disposables. For that reason you may want to drop hints with friends and relatives that you'd welcome diaper service as a shower gift.

**Diaper types.** There are three main types of cloth diaper: unfolded, prefolded, and preshaped. Unfolded diapers are rectangles of flat fabric that you fold to fit your baby's shape, holding them in place with diaper pins.

Prefolded diapers are also rectangular but have extra or absorbent layers in the center. Contrary to their name, they may require some folding when you put them on your baby. They also require pinning. With both folded and prefolded diapers, you'll also need to use water-proof pants.

Preshaped diapers have a narrow crotch and wide wings that wrap around baby's waist. Some require diaper pins, but others have snaps. With preshaped diapers, you have to buy different sizes as your baby grows. Some have a moisture-resistant vinyl outer covering sewn onto

**D**iaper services are available mainly in metropolitan areas. For a monthly fee the service will deliver two to three dozen fresh diapers once or twice a week and take away the soiled ones. Diaper services wash at high temperatures, so the diapers are virtually sterilized. Most services designate a set of diapers to be used solely by your baby and guarantee no commingling. They'll also give you a diaper pail fitted with a plastic bag (no presoaking required). Price: $50 to $70 per month.

the diaper, eliminating the need for waterproof pants. But the outer covering may not launder thoroughly (allowing detergent to remain or bacteria to grow), and the diaper may take longer to dry.

Prices for diapers range from $1 to $2 each, waterproof pants, $2 and up.

**Diapering systems.** Diapering systems are the most expensive cloth option. They include a moisture-resistant covering of nylon or polyester into which you insert a folded diaper or washable liner.

The outer covering comes in a range of sizes to accommodate a baby's growth. Velcro fasteners or several rows of snaps (for different fits) keep the covering closed. The most absorbent inserts use multiple layers of thick flannel resembling dense cotton velvet.

## Recommendations

The type of cloth diaper you choose (as well as whether you go with cloth at all) is a matter of personal preference. If you choose cloth diapers, you will need two to three dozen to begin with, plus four to six waterproof outer pants. Most companies that sell diapering systems offer sample packs of their various brands, so you can determine which works best for you.

# Ratings • Disposable Diapers

**A**ll diapers in our tests were far more absorbent than they need to be if you change your child's diaper every 2 to 2½ hours, as is typical. The best diapers in our tests fit well and also prevented leaks the best. They kept children feeling dry and had fasteners that stayed put. Lower-rated diapers seldom leaked, but the worst left children feeling wet a bit more often, didn't fit well on a variety of body types, or had fasteners that were somewhat less secure. Our advice is to try a highly rated store brand first, checking the diaper often until you know whether the brand works for your child. If you're not satisfied, try a lower-priced, national-brand diaper. If you still have qualms, consider top-rated premium diapers, which fit the best.

| | Excellent | Very good | Good | Fair | Poor |
|---|---|---|---|---|---|
| | ⊖ | ⊖ | ○ | ◖ | ● |

**In performance order. Blue key numbers indicate Quick Picks.**

| Key number | Model | Price | | Overall score | | Test results | | | |
|---|---|---|---|---|---|---|---|---|---|
| | | Per diaper | Per month | 0 ... 100 / P F G VG E | | Resists leaks | Keeps baby dry | Fits a variety of kids | Fastener quality |
| 1 | **Pampers** Custom Fit Cruisers | $0.30 | $46.50 | | | ⊖ | ⊖ | ⊖ | ⊖ |
| 2 | **Huggies** Supreme | 0.32 | 49.60 | | | ⊖ | ⊖ | ⊖ | ○ |
| 3 | **Pampers** Baby-Dry | 0.28 | 43.40 | | | ⊖ | ⊖ | ○ | ⊖ |
| 4 | **Huggies** Ultratrim | 0.29 | 44.95 | | | ⊖ | ⊖ | ⊖ | ○ |
| 5 | **Luvs** Ultra Leakguards | 0.23 | 35.65 | | | ⊖ | ⊖ | ○ | ⊖ |
| 6 | **Baby Basics** Ultra Leakage Protection (Albertson's) | 0.21 | 32.55 | | | ⊖ | ⊖ | ⊖ | ⊖ |
| 7 | **America's Choice** Ultra Thin Stretch (A&P) | 0.22 | 34.10 | | | ⊖ | ⊖ | ○ | ⊖ |
| 8 | **Ultra Comforts** (Kroger) | 0.21 | 32.55 | | | ⊖ | ⊖ | ⊖ | ○ |
| 9 | **White Cloud** (Wal-Mart) | 0.21 | 32.55 | | | ⊖ | ⊖ | ○ | ⊖ |
| 10 | **Simply Dry** (Stop & Shop) | 0.19 | 29.45 | | | ⊖ | ⊖ | ⊖ | ⊖ |
| 11 | **Loving Touch** (Target) | 0.21 | 32.55 | | | ⊖ | ⊖ | ⊖ | ⊖ |
| 12 | **Little Ones** (Kmart) | 0.22 | 34.10 | | | ⊖ | ⊖ | ○ | ⊖ |

## Guide to the Ratings

The **overall score** reflects performance with our day-care panel, which comprised three day-care centers. Judgments of leakage and dryness figured much more prominently into the overall score than did the other categories. All regular diapers were tested by 79 children of both sexes, ranging in age from 2 months to nearly 3 years. Day-care testers changed the diapers on a schedule, with additional changes as needed. **Resists leaks** is as reported by the day-care testers. **Keeps baby dry** reflects how often children felt wet to those testers. **Fits a variety of kids,** also as reported by the day-care testers, reflects how well diapers fit various body types. **Fastener quality** incorporates how well the fasteners performed. **Price per diaper** is the manufacturer's suggested retail price or the published price of size 4 (large) diapers in the jumbo package; **cost per month** assumes 155 diapers used.

# Quick Picks • Diapers

**Best value:**

5 **Luvs** $0.23

6 **Baby Basics (Albertson's)** $0.21

7 **America's Choice (A&P)** $0.22

While Baby Basics (6) and America's Choice (7) were excellent, America's Choice prevented leaks slightly better. If neither brand is available in your area, consider the excellent Luvs (5), the least-expensive national brand in our tests.

**If your child is prone to leaks:**

1 **Pampers** $0.30

2 **Huggies** $0.32

Both offered excellent fit on a variety of bottoms, though they are costly.

CHAPTER

# 19

# Diaper Bags

W hen you're on the go, a diaper bag will likely be your constant sidekick—your changing table away from home, as well as a portable kitchen and baby-entertainment center. So consider size, comfort, and durability, just as you would with any purse or tote you carry frequently. Any bag, of course, will work, such as a basic tote. But chances are, you'll be happier with one that's specifically designed for baby gear.

Manufacturers offer diaper bags in a wide variety of colors, fabrics, and designs, some more practical and durable than others. Diaper bags have come a long way from the traditional, rectangular pastel bags adorned with Pooh and other animated characters (although babyish diaper bags are still very much an option).

The trend today, however, is toward more discreet diaper bags, ones that can be handed from mom to dad without embarrassment, and that could easily double as an adult backpack, stylish purse, or gym bag. Features such as a pocket for your cell phone,

insulated bottle pockets, and padded shoulder straps have also become de rigueur. Ditto for a large, wipe-clean, detachable changing pad.

## Shopping Secrets

**"Test drive" models in the store.** Visualize where you'd put diapers, a change of clothes for your baby, wipes, the changing pad, an insulated lunch bag, your keys and wallet, and whatever else you typically carry with you. Everything should be within easy reach, a necessity when you're grabbing for things on the go. Comfort is also key. If you can, try on the bag you're considering to see how well it fits your body. Wide or well-padded straps can make carrying the bag more comfortable. There should also be a loop for carrying by hand. The handles of a tote-style bag should be short enough so that the bag doesn't drag on the ground when you carry it like a suitcase, but long enough so it can be slung over your shoulder. A backpack's shoulder straps should be adjustable for proper fit.

**Don't think bigger is necessarily better.** You want a good size diaper bag, yes. But you don't want one that's so roomy that you're constantly losing things in its caverns. An overnight or duffel diaper bag, for example, may be too big for your everyday needs, unless you have more than one child's things to carry with you. And even if you don't have a lot of stuff, there's a tendency to fill the void. Before you know it, a large diaper bag can easily outweigh your baby.

**Look for side zipper compartments.** Babies are a demanding lot. External zippered pockets offer fast access to tissues, pacifiers, toys, and your keys. You want to be able to grab and keep going, without having to break stride or put your baby down to find what you need.

## What's Available

Major brands, in alphabetical order, include: Babies' Alley, Burberry, Combi, Dolly, Eddie Bauer, Kate Spade, Lands' End, L.L. Bean, Little Company, Maclaren, Mommy's Helper, Regal Lager, Safeline, Samsonite, and Trend Lab.

Fabrics and patterns run the gamut from frolicking teddy bears and pastel backgrounds to sophisticated solids, checks, plaids, and stripes in roadworthy nylon and microfiber. Designs include backpacks, tote-style bags that could pass for briefcases, handbags with shoulder straps, fanny packs, urban slings, messenger bags, and duffels (also known as "dude diaper bags"). Some diaper bags unfold like a garment bag and

**Y**ou'll want to be fully prepared when you and baby venture away from home. But don't go overboard—you've still got to carry that bag. Restock the bag as soon as you return home, so you don't forget anything the next time you go out. You want a bag that's good to go. Here are some ideas on what to pack.

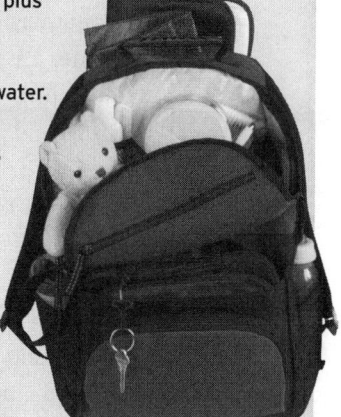

- Diapers, of course. At least five or six if you'll be out most of the day.
- A travel pack of baby wipes.
- Changing pad.
- Zinc oxide diaper-rash ointment.
- Plastic bags for disposing of soiled disposable diapers.
- Leak-proof bag for soiled cloth diapers or wet clothes. (Some diaper bags come with one of these.)
- A complete change of baby clothes (including socks), plus a hat, sweater, and/or jacket if it's chilly out.
- Sunscreen—if it's summer.
- If you're bottle-feeding, extra formula and sterilized water.
- Snacks, such as cereal and crackers, in lidded plastic containers and/or an insulated lunch bag for cold items such as yogurt or juice.
- A bib or two.
- Two clean pacifiers if your baby uses one.
- A favorite small toy or two.
- A book that baby can hold and/or chew on.
- Teething toys, if your baby is teething.
- Tissues.
- Cloth diaper or small towel to mop spit-ups and spills.
- Baby pain and fever reliever or even a small first-aid kit.
- Extra baby blanket.
- Reading material for you. If you have a few minutes, you can catch up on that magazine or newspaper you never got to read at home.

hang over door frames and crib railings or in bathroom stalls and closets, displaying their contents in neatly zippered pockets.

Diaper bags range from $20 for a low-end fabric or vinyl model to $300 or more for well-appointed designer bags.

## Features to Consider

**Changing pad.** All bags come with a rectangular changing pad that folds up and fits in the bag and can be wiped clean. But some are cushier than others. (Cushy is better.) Many fold to fit into a designated pocket. Some have a semirigid interior that helps maintain the pad's shape. With some fanny-pack styles, the changing pad unfurls when you unzip a special compartment.

**Construction.** Look for strong, adjustable straps (nylon webbing is a smart choice) and well-reinforced seams.

**Fabric.** Bags made of quilted fabric are often favored by gift givers, but heavy-duty, moisture-resistant nylon or microfiber is more practical, especially if you're planning to have more than one child and you want the bag to go the distance. You'll also want a diaper bag that's as washable inside as it is out since things have a tendency to spill from both directions. Some manufacturers continue to offer "baby colors"—pastels and light-colored prints. But dark shades are less likely to show stains and wear. And if you go for a more adult look, you can consider retasking the bag for other purposes after your diapering days are over—assuming it has held up well enough.

**Storage.** Easy-to-access, zippered exterior compartments, which can function as a wallet and as storage for things you constantly need (like tissues and pacifiers), are a convenient plus. Make sure the zippers are heavy duty so they'll hold up. Clear vinyl or mesh pockets inside can stow diapers, wipes, and other baby gear, although they're not absolutely necessary. Some bags, such as the Maclaren, have an internal zip PVC bag for wet items. But too many pockets can be confusing—*Which one did I put her toy in?*—and a diaper bag should make your life easier, not more complicated. In general, sportier style bags (think backpacks) tend to have lots of inside and outside compartments. Designer bags tend to be relatively simple with just one or two inside pockets, perhaps none on the outside.

## Recommendations

If in doubt, opt for a backpack-style diaper bag so you won't get stuck having to balance your baby in one hand and a shoulder bag in the other. It's healthier for your neck and shoulders too when the weight you're carrying in your diaper bag is centered at your core.

If value is what you're after, midpriced models (in the $35 to $100 range) offer the best mix of sound construction and generous storage. Low-end models (in the $20 range) skimp on quality and durability, leaving you with a bag that may tear, fray, or get stained or sticky and soon have to be replaced.

Designer diaper bags are a class unto themselves. If you want a certain look or designer label, you'll pay for it. But you're apt to get a good-quality bag, too.

**CHAPTER**

# 20

# Diaper Pails

Changing diapers, of course, is one of the least glamorous aspects of having a baby. But it's got to be done many times a day, and the right diaper pail can make the job easier, especially if you use cloth diapers. That's particularly true if you have more than one baby in diapers at a time, whether that means twins or triplets or children close in age.

The type of diaper pail you'll need depends on whether you're using cloth diapers or disposables, although some diaper pails, like the Diaper Champ by Baby Trend, can go either way. The standard cloth diaper pail is a sturdy plastic vessel for soaking cloth diapers before laundering. The typical disposable-diaper pail is also plastic, but it may be rigged with special liners or regular garbage bags that lock in diapers and odors at the twist or flip of a handle.

## What's Available

**Cloth.** The best pails for cloth diapers are strong enough to hold a considerable amount of water but also easy to carry, with a comfortable handle and a spout for pouring out soaking solution. If you use cake deodorizers in your cloth diaper pail, store unused amounts out of the reach of children. They can be poisonous.

**Disposables.** For disposable diapers, the major brands of pails are, in alphabetical order: Diaper Champ, Diaper Dekor, Diaper Genie, and Safety 1st.

The Diaper Genie, the veteran of the bunch, uses a plastic funnel insert that allows you to twist each diaper into an individual pouch, which forms an odor-blocking seal. You shove the diaper into the funnel, twist the top of the pail to seal the diaper in place, then close the lid. To empty the pail, you open the bottom, pull out a chain of encased diapers, and throw them away.

Strong competitors to the Diaper Genie are the Diaper Champ, which accepts both cloth and disposables, and the Diaper Dekor. They're simpler models that require no twists or turns and work with ordinary kitchen trash bags. You can open and close the Champ with one hand, which is a plus for when you have a baby to guard with the other. The Dekor offers a hands-free design. You simply step on a pedal to open the lid. It's available in a plus-size model, which holds up to 46 diapers instead of the usual 25 to 30; that can be useful if you have more than one child in diapers at a time.

## Features to Consider

Here are some features and qualities to consider that can help you choose one brand or style over another.

**Capacity.** Diaper pails typically hold between 24 and 46 diapers, although their capacity decreases as your baby grows into bigger diapers.

**Child-resistant lid.** Look for a pail with a lid that has a child-resistant locking button or a mechanism that makes it difficult for little people to break in, such as a step pedal opener. If you use cloth diapers, the issue becomes very important because of the liquid involved. Not just any plastic kitchen garbage can will do. You'll need a cloth-diaper pail with a securely locking lid to prevent your baby and other curious little ones from possibly falling in.

**Comfort.** If you're going the cloth route, pick a pail with a pouring lip and comfortable handles.

**Ease of use.** Some diaper pails require two hands; you have to shove the diaper into the plastic-bag insert, then twist. Others can be operated with one hand or have a hands-free pedal.

**Liners or bags.** Some pails require special plastic liners, while others use regular garbage bags.

# Doorway Jumpers

I n case you've never seen one, a doorway jumper is a bouncy seat that can hang from the top of a door frame to accommodate infants from 5 to 15 months in age. Think of it as bungee jumping for babies.

Bungee-style cords or springs suspend the seat from a nonslip clamp so pre-walking babies can jiggle themselves up and down when they push off the floor. It's a cheap thrill that can delight them—and burn off steam, getting babies primed for their morning or afternoon nap.

Like stationary entertainers and walkers, jumpers require babies to stay upright. That does nothing to strengthen their thigh and back muscles, which are critical to crawling and walking. And while many infants enjoy jumpers, others actually get "seasick" from the motion. More worrisome, a jumper's straps or clamps can break, allowing the apparatus to fall. A poor design also may allow babies to bump into the sides of the door frame, either because vigorous jumping causes them to bob around or because a sibling tries to swing them.

Jumpers have straps that adjust to a child's "jumping height." Most have a removable, washable seat. Some feature support bars in the front and back of the seat, while others have solid, molded frames that encircle the baby. There might be a small tray to hold snacks or toys, but that's not necessary since most children don't eat while they're jumping or play with other toys.

## What's Available

Major brands of doorway jumpers include, in alphabetical order: Evenflo (OshKosh), Graco, and Jolly Jumper. Jumpers usually lack seat belts, but there is little likelihood of a child falling or climbing out. Prices range from $30 to $40.

## Recommendations

Think carefully before you invest in a doorway jumper. While the idea of giving a very active baby an outlet for his or her energy may be appealing, the suspension nature of a jumper can invite trouble. No amount of supervision can keep an infant from crashing to the floor, and that may happen no matter how many times your baby has used the jumper successfully in the past. You'll also find quality differences in the construction of the springs, suspension cords, supports, and seat.

Parents report mixed results with all brands and types. Some say they love their jumper and haven't looked back. Others report design flaws that surfaced when their infant was in action—frontal crossbars that nearly "choked" a small child or suspension straps that broke, much to everyone's surprise. We think there are plenty of other—and safer—alternatives to help your baby get a little exercise.

That said, if you decide to use a jumper, here are a few things to keep in mind:

Buy one with specifications that match your door frame. Not all door frames are constructed in a way that can adequately support a doorway jumper.

Inspect the jumper every time you put baby inside to be sure the straps are securely fastened and the clamp will hold.

Limit jumping time to 15 minutes at a stretch, so your baby doesn't become nauseated.

Never push a jumper as if it were a swing (or let others do it). Even though swinging in the house sounds like fun, it can cause your baby to strike the side of the doorway. Jumpers are not a good choice in a multi-kid environment.

Finally, keep a close eye out for trouble and don't leave the room while your child is jumping.

## CHAPTER

# 22

# Formula

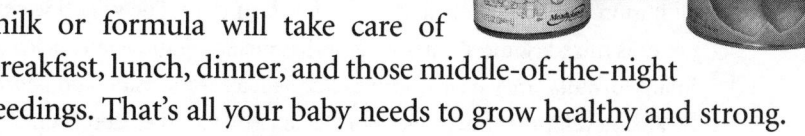

**A**s the parent of a newborn, you'll have a million things to do. But planning gourmet meals for your baby won't be one of them. Until your child is about 6 months old, breast milk or formula will take care of breakfast, lunch, dinner, and those middle-of-the-night feedings. That's all your baby needs to grow healthy and strong.

Still, the decision about whether to go with breast milk or formula (or both), can be complicated. The short answer: Try to breast-feed your baby if you can. Even the infant-formula companies will tell you, as Nestlé does on its Web site, "breast milk is best for babies." That's because breast milk contains immunity-enhancing antibodies and white blood cells. Nursing helps guard against infections, allergies, diarrhea, pneumonia, meningitis, urinary-tract infections, and Sudden Infant Death Syndrome (SIDS). Studies show that it may also enhance your baby's brain power and help protect against insulin-dependent diabetes, Crohn's disease, colitis, and certain forms of cancer later in life. Colostrum, the thin yellow "premilk" that flows from the breasts during the first few days after birth, is especially rich in disease-fighting antibodies, says Charles Shubin, M.D., director of the Children's Health Center at Mercy Family Care in Baltimore, Md.

The American Academy of Pediatrics recommends that moms breast-feed for a year. If this commitment isn't realistic, aim to breast-feed for as long as possible to supplement the immunity your baby receives in utero. (If you decide to wean your baby before age 1, you'll need to use formula.)

If you want to breast-feed but for some reason it isn't working, don't give up or feel you have to go it alone. There are lots of sources of help—from other mothers and hospital lactation consultants to the International Lactation Consultant Association *(www.ilca.org)* and La Leche League *(www. lalecheleague.org).*

Still, breast-feeding sometimes isn't an option, or you simply may not want to breast-feed full time or for a full year. That's when formula comes into play. Usually derived from cow's milk, formula provides most but not all of the crucial components of breast milk. If your baby is exclusively formula-fed as a newborn, he or she will probably need six to eight feedings in 24 hours, with about 2 to 4 ounces of formula per bottle.

Many brands of formula are now fortified with DHA (docosahexaenoic acid) and ARA (arachidonic acid), essential fatty acids that are naturally found in breast milk. The fortified formulas tend to cost a bit more, and whether they're worth it is unclear. The scientific evidence is mixed; some studies suggest that including these fatty acids in infant formulas may have positive effects on a baby's vision and neural (brain) development over the short term. Other studies don't confirm these benefits. So ask your doctor for a recommendation. And keep in mind that even formulas with DHA and ARA aren't a perfect match for breast milk because the exact chemical makeup of breast milk—like many other foods—still isn't known.

In any event, the formula that you buy should be fortified with iron unless otherwise directed by your pediatrician. Although there are low-iron formulas available, the American Academy of Pediatrics discourages their use because they can increase the risk of infant iron deficiency.

If you're planning to use formula, hold off on buying it until after your baby is born. Your baby may prefer one type of formula over another or may be able to tolerate only a particular brand. Because formula is big business, many companies are generous with free samples. In fact, you can almost certainly count on the hospital loading you up with samples when you go home. If you register at a baby store for gifts or word somehow gets out that you're expecting, you may also receive unsolicited samples from formula companies in the mail right around your due date.

No matter what brand you settle on, if your baby shows signs of intolerance to the protein found in milk-based formulas—a rash, persistent vomiting, and diarrhea, or any other unusual symptom—call your pediatrician. You may need to experiment with different brands or have to switch to a soy-based formula.

Also, talk to your pediatrician before using any type of bottled water for formula. Bottled water intended for infants must meet standards for tap water established by the Environmental Protection Agency. It may have fluoride added, but too much fluoride can be toxic. The bottles warn against using if your baby is already getting fluoride some other way. Just as with tap water, it's recommended that you heat bottled water until it reaches a rolling boil before mixing it with formula.

## Shopping Secrets

**Use coupons.** Breast milk is a bargain—but formula and baby food can add up. In fact, the annual cost of using formula exclusively is

## STORING MILK AND FORMULA SAFELY

To make sure the formula and breast milk you feed your baby are safe, follow these Food and Drug Administration guidelines for how long either liquid lasts in the refrigerator and freezer. To protect your baby from potentially harmful bacteria, never put an unfinished bottle back in the refrigerator for another time. To play it safe, throw it away and start fresh.

| Liquid | Refrigerator | Freezer | Special Instructions |
|---|---|---|---|
| Expressed breast milk | 1 day | 3 to 4 months if freezer is at 0°F | Label it with a date to be sure |
| Formula | 1 day | Not recommended | For unopened cans of formula, observe "Use by" dates printed on the container. |

likely to run $1,500 to $4,000, depending on your baby's nutritional requirements. To keep costs down, use coupons and shop at discount retailers, such as Wal-Mart, Costco, Sam's Club, Toys "R" Us, or the large chain pharmacy or supermarket in your area.

**Prefer powder, if possible.** When stored as directed, powdered formulas are the least expensive option among the formula lineup and, when unopened, last the longest. Next in terms of cost comes concentrated liquids. Ready-to-feed liquid formulas are the most convenient and fastest; you don't have to boil water and you don't have to worry about the formula clumping up. But they're also the biggest drain on your billfold.

**Consider a store brand.** You'll find store brands at mass merchandisers such as Kmart and Wal-Mart. The savings they offer can be substantial. In our informal research, the store brand of formula at a local Wal-Mart (Parent's Choice) cost 40 percent less per ounce than a leading national brand (Nestlé's Good Start).

According to the Food and Drug Administration (FDA), all formula marketed in the United States must meet the same nutrient specifications, which are set at levels to fulfill the needs of infants. Although infant-formula manufacturers may have their own proprietary formulations, brand-name and store-brand formula must all contain at least the minimum levels of all nutrients specified in FDA regulations, without exceeding maximum levels, where those are specified.

## WHY BABIES DON'T NEED WATER

**A**side from breast milk and/or formula, you may wonder if it's OK to give your baby water, or if your baby needs it, especially in the summer. The answer is no. During the first year of life, you don't need to supplement formula with bottles of water—even on hot days. "Babies don't need any additional fluids beyond formula or breast milk," says Michael Farrell, M.D., chief of staff at Children's Hospital Medical Center of Cincinnati.

In fact, giving infants water can be dangerous because they can easily suffer from water intoxication, a condition in which their developing kidneys can't excrete water fast enough. As a result, water builds up in the body and dilutes the electrolyte balance of the blood, possibly causing seizures, coma, or even death. To avoid water intoxication, simply give your baby a little extra breast milk or formula instead of water if you sense he or she is thirsty on especially hot days. And never dilute formula; that's another potential cause of water intoxication. Check the label for proper mixing instructions. Be sure to instruct caregivers to do the same.

# FORMULA COMPLAINTS AND CONCERNS

If you have a general complaint or concern about a food product, including infant formula, contact the Food and Drug Administration via its Web site, *www.fda.gov /opacom/backgrounders/problem.html*. If you think your infant has suffered a harmful effect from an infant formula, call your pediatrician and ask that he or she report your concern by calling the FDA's MedWatch hotline at 800-332-1088 or online at *www.fda.gov/medwatch*. The MedWatch program allows health-care providers to report problems possibly caused by FDA-regulated products such as infant formula.

**Check the "use by" date.** When buying formula, look for the "use by" date on the label required by the FDA. Until that date, you can be assured that the formula will contain no less than the amount of each nutrient declared on the product label and will otherwise be of acceptable quality.

**Be brand loyal.** Although the major brands of formula are roughly equal, it's generally recommended that you stick with one brand, whichever your baby is used to. Still, it's fine to use liquid and powder interchangeably.

**Order from the manufacturer.** Many formula companies, such as Enfamil *(www.enfamil.com)*, offer this convenient option.

**Join the club.** Some formula companies, such as Similac *(www.similac.com)*, have a new-parent club you can join by filling out an online form. After you enroll, you're eligible for various offers, which may include discounts and formula samples.

## What's Available

The major brands of formula are, in alphabetical order: Carnation, Enfamil, Nestlé Good Start, and Similac/Isomil. Formula comes in three versions: powder, concentrated liquid, or ready-to-feed liquid. Most formulas contain added iron, while others, such as soy formulas, are for babies allergic to cow's milk. Lactose-free formulas are available for babies who have problems digesting milk sugar. There are also hypoallergenic formulas for problems such as allergies to protein in cow's milk or soy formulas. Your pediatrician is the best source of advice on what to feed your baby. But your baby's preferences will drive the choice, too. Sometimes it simply amounts to trial and error.

### Powdered formula

**Pros:** It's the least costly of the lot.

**Cons:** Both powders and concentrated liquids (see below) require care in measuring the added water to be sure that your baby gets the right concentration of nutrients. But you can prepare several bottles at a time to use within 24 hours.

### Concentrated liquid formula

**Pros:** Slightly faster than powdered to prepare because you don't have to mix a solid with a liquid.
**Cons:** More expensive than powder, and you still have to boil water.

### Liquid formula

**Pros:** It's convenient. With water already mixed in, you're good to go.
**Cons:** It's the most expensive option. According to our informal cost analysis, you'll pay about 40 percent more for liquid than powder.

When preparing formula, follow label directions exactly and instruct caregivers to do the same. And if you should happen to use different brands of powdered formula, don't mix up the scoopers. They often have different measurements/proportions.

Never try to stretch formula with extra water. Improperly diluted formula can cause malnutrition and water intoxication, which is potentially life threatening. Too little water can produce a mix that, over time, may damage the baby's kidneys.

# Gates

With an active baby on the loose, your home can resemble a gated community. Still, a gate or two can help keep a child contained in an area or away from potential hazards, such as stairs. You can also use a gate to keep a pet away from a child (and vice versa). Child safety gates are intended for children between 6 months and 24 months of age. All of the gates CONSUMER REPORTS tested (see page 173 for test results) can be opened and closed by an adult but use various designs to prevent children from opening them.

Child safety gates come in two basic types, based on the method of installation. A hardware-mounted or permanent gate requires screws for installation in an opening such as a doorway. If properly secured to the doorjamb or between two walls with the supplied plates and screws, hardware-mounted gates are the more secure choice, although no gate can be guaranteed to keep a child in or out. To install, you must drill holes into the door frame or the wood frame behind the dry wall of another opening. (You can fill in the holes later with putty or sealer when you no longer use the gate.) You can also remove many of these gates from the mounting hardware for times when you want the doorway or opening free. Hardware-mounted gates that are intended for stair locations install so that they will swing open only one way—such as away from the stairs—for maximum safety.

A pressure-mounted gate is held in an opening by pressure against the door frame or walls. Pressure-mounted gates usually have two sliding panels that adjust to make the gate fit the opening. A pressure bar or some other locking mechanism then wedges the gate into place. Pressure gates were designed for doorways measuring between 28 and 32 inches. Many houses and apartments have wider door openings, so about 10 years ago manufacturers began offering elongated models— some as wide as 48 or even 60 inches. Some models have optional extensions you purchase separately. Pressure-mounted gates are useful in areas where falling isn't a major concern, such as in a doorway separating two areas with same-level floor, or at the bottom of a stairway to discourage a child from venturing upstairs.

Simple to install, pressure-mounted gates can also be surprisingly easy to dislodge. Even the most stable pressure-mounted gate will work loose over time, so inspect it frequently. Manufacturers now recommend that you not use a pressure-mounted gate at the top of stairs. Take that recommendation seriously.

Both types of gates can also offer a swing open/close feature. They're usually designated as "swing gates."

## Shopping Secrets

**Make sure the gate will fit.** Bring width measurements of doors or openings along with you when you shop. Take heed if your door or opening is at a gate's upper width limits. Although many gates claim they can accommodate wide doorways, they may be wobbly when they're stretched to the max. Keep in mind that some gates are designed to be mounted with either pressure or hardware, which is good if you can't decide which type to buy.

**If possible, test gates in the store.** Make sure they're easy for you to open and close. Try them from both directions. Many open with one hand or feature a hands-free operation (you press on a pedal)— good for when you have a wiggly baby in your arms and for thwarting a curious toddler, who won't be able to put enough weight on the pedal to release the gate.

## What's Available

The major brands of child safety gates are, in alphabetical order: Cardinal Gates, Evenflo, The First Years, GMI, KidCo, North States Industries, and Safety 1st. Some gates are made with vertical wood slats and top and bottom rails. Others are constructed of enamel-coated steel or aluminum tubing, or molded plastic with plastic mesh. Gates of plastic or wire mesh may be framed with end tubes and top rails of either wood or coated metal. A few gates are made with transparent plastic center panels. Gate prices range from $20 to $100.

## Features to Consider

Gate safety depends on solid construction, reliable hardware, and the absence of entrapment hazards.

**Construction.** Look for sturdy construction and an even finish. Wood surfaces should be smooth, splinter-free, and fashioned with rounded rather than sharply squared edges. Vertical slats or bars should be no more than $2\frac{3}{8}$ inches apart. Gates shouldn't have openings or protrusions at the top edge that might snag clothing or necklaces or present head- or neck-entrapment hazards. Metal is more durable than wood. Note that some metal gates have a support bar that crosses the floor beneath the gate, which could cause tripping when the gate is open.

**Height.** To prevent an adventurous child from climbing over, a gate must stand a minimum of three-quarters of the child's height. Most gates measure 22 inches or more from top to bottom. When a child is taller than 36 inches or weighs more than 30 pounds (typically at about 2 years of age), consider a gate no longer adequate or safe.

## CERTIFICATION

Located on the frame or packaging, a certification sticker shows that the gate meets the minimum requirements of the American Society for Testing and Materials' voluntary standard and that its manufacturer participates in the pass/fail certification program administered by the Juvenile Products Manufacturers Association (JPMA). The standard addresses issues including the size of typical doorway openings, gate height, and the strength of top rails and framing components.

Some gates have been recalled in recent years. Problems have included plastic parts that break, posing choking hazards. The following brands of gates bear the JPMA seal: Cardinal Gates, Dorel Juvenile Group (Safety 1st), Evenflo, The First Years, GMI, Kidco, North States Industries, Regal Lager, and Summer Infant Products.

**Installation flexibility.** Many gates can be installed over uneven surfaces or over baseboards and moldings and adjust to fit openings as wide as 60 inches. Some hardware-mounted gates can be slid out of their wall mountings, which is a bonus when, say, you're entertaining and don't want the gate in the way. Some pressure gates include a pressure indicator, which allows you to check for proper installation, a definite plus.

**Latches.** A certified gate must have a latching mechanism that requires two actions to release. Often a dual-action latch can be opened with one adult hand. There are different types of latches. A gate with a squeezing mechanism opens by compressing parts of the gate, but such a latch can be uncomfortable to use, so test it in the store. Other options include a pressure-release handle and one that lifts up. Some models use a foot pedal—but it requires strong pressure to release.

**Sound.** Many gates click when they're shut, signaling that they're doing their job.

**Travel.** Some pressure-mounted models are marketed for travel and come with a carrying case. They can be useful to quickly make a motel room or a relative's home more child-friendly.

## Recommendations

For shielding stairs and steps, choose a hardware-mounted gate. Never use a pressure gate at the top of stairs—no matter how much you want to avoid drilling holes into your woodwork. Pressure-mounted gates are suitable for less hazardous locations, such as between rooms. Also, choose a gate with a straight top edge and rigid vertical filler bars or a mesh screen. Avoid gates with horizontal slats or similarly tempting footholds; they're an invitation for a child to climb. If you choose a model with mesh panels, look for a fine weave—wide-holed mesh may provide a foothold for climbing or could entrap fingers.

Follow mounting instructions carefully. (Allow yourself a good hour for installing hardware-mounted gates.) If you suspect your gate-installation skills aren't up to snuff or you don't have an electric drill, which is typically required, consider recruiting a handy friend or relative. After you've installed a gate, frequently check hardware where it attaches to the gate and wall. Loose hardware not only makes a gate less effective but may also be a choking risk. Keep large toys, such as stuffed animals or riding toys, away from the gate so they can't be used as a step stool for climbing over the gate.

Avoid old-fashioned, accordion-style wooden gates with large "V"s at the top and diamond shape spaces between the slats; they are an entrapment hazard for heads and necks. Although these types of gates haven't been manufactured for nearly 20 years, you can still find them in thrift shops and yard sales. If you have this type of gate, replace it with a new model. And finally, remember that a gate is only a deterrent, not a replacement for adult supervision. You'll still have to keep a close eye on your child.

# Ratings • Gates

Select a gate primarily by where you will place it. Hardware-mounted gates require tools to install and, when installed correctly, are the more secure type. Always use a hardware-mounted gate at the top of a stairway. If you want to avoid permanent installation, consider a pressure-mounted gate. This type should only be used to divide level areas or to block the bottom of a stairway. Although easy to install, this type is also fairly easy to dislodge.

| | Excellent | Very good | Good | Fair | Poor |
|---|---|---|---|---|---|
| | ⊖ | ⊖ | ○ | ◔ | ● |

**Within types, in performance order. Blue key numbers indicate Quick Picks.**

| Key number | Brand & model | Price | Overall Score | Maximum opening | Minimum opening | Safety | Convenience | Width range (in.) | Height (in.) | Weight (lbs) | Hands-free open & close | One-hand open & close | Can be used on uneven surfaces |
|---|---|---|---|---|---|---|---|---|---|---|---|---|---|
| | | | **Test results** — Security | | | | | **Specifications** | | | **Features** | | |
| | **HARDWARE-MOUNTED** | | | | | | | | | | | | |
| 1 | **The First Years** Simple & Secure Gate 3620 | $60 | | ⊖ | ⊖ | ⊖ | ○ | 29.5-44 | 29 | 10 | | • | • |
| 2 | **KidCo** Safeway Gate G20 | 60 | | ⊖ | ⊖ | ⊖ | ○ | 25-43.5 | 31 | 7 | | • | • |
| 3 | **Evenflo** Secure Solutions Swing Gate 1050 | 35 | | ⊖ | ⊖ | ⊖ | ○ | 28-42 | 31 | 5 | | • | |
| 4 | **Cardinal** Gates The Stairway Special SS-30A | 80 | | ⊖ | ⊖ | ◔ | ○ | 27-42.5 | 30 | 6 | | • | • |
| 5 | **North States** The Great Gate 8686 * | 40 | | ◓ | ⊖ | ⊖ | ○ | 29-42 | 27 | 9 | | • | |
| 6 | **Safety** 1st Swing'N Lock Gate 41780 * | 30 | | ◓ | ○ | ⊖ | ○ | 26-41.5 | 29 | 6 | | • | |

*Continued on page 174*

*Continued from page 173*

# Ratings • Gates

| | Excellent | Very good | Good | Fair | Poor |
|---|---|---|---|---|---|
| | ⊖ | ⊖ | ○ | ◒ | ● |

**Within types, in performance order. Blue key numbers indicate Quick Picks.**

| Key number | Brand & model | Price | Overall Score | Test results — Security — Maximum opening | Minimum opening | Safety | Convenience | Width range (in.) | Height (in.) | Weight (lbs) | Hands-free open & close | One-hand open & close | Can be used on uneven surfaces |
|---|---|---|---|---|---|---|---|---|---|---|---|---|---|
| | **PRESSURE-MOUNTED** | | | | | | | | | | | | |
| 7 | **KidCo** Gateway G11 | $55 | | ○ | ○ | ⊖ | ⊖ | 30-36 | 30 | 10 | | ● | ● |
| 8 | **KidCo** Gateway To Go G14 | 55 | | ◒ | ◒ | ⊖ | ⊖ | 28-36 | 29 | 5 | | ● | ● |
| 9 | **Evenflo** Easy Swing Gate 545 | 33 | | ◒ | ○ | ⊖ | ⊖ | 28-39 | 28 | 8 | | ● | ● |
| 10 | **The First Years** Hands-Free Gate 3600 | 50 | | ◒ | ◒ | ○ | ⊖ | 29-34 | 31 | 11 | ● | | ● |
| 11 | **Safety** 1st Swing'N Lock Gate 41780 * | 30 | | ◒ | ◒ | ⊖ | ○ | 26-42 | 27 | 6 | | ● | |
| 12 | **Safety** 1st Easy-Fit Security Gate 41817B | 21 | | ● | ◒ | ⊖ | ○ | 28-42 | 27 | 6 | | | |
| 13 | **North States** The Great Gate 8686 * | 40 | | ● | ◒ | ○ | ○ | 29-40 | 27 | 9 | | ● | |
| 14 | **Cardinal** Gates Pressure Gate PG-5 | 102 | | ● | ● | ○ | ◒ | 28-36 | 30 | 8 | | ● | ● |

*\* Gate is mountable with hardware or pressure, was tested in both modes, and is listed as tested in both categories.*

## Guide to the Ratings

**Overall score** is based primarily on security. **Security** indicates how well the gate resisted being dislodged at its maximum and minimum openings. **Safety** reflects the gate's adherence to the ASTM standard and how easily the gate could be climbed. **Convenience** reflects features and versatility. **Price** is the average price paid.

# Quick Picks • Gates

For the top of the stairs or a permanent installation choose a hardware-mounted gate.
   1 **The First Years** $60.
   2 **KidCo** $60.

For less permanent installation in less hazardous locations—between rooms or at the bottom of a stairway—choose a pressure-mounted gate.
   7 **KidCo** $55.

For traveling or visiting choose a gate that packs compactly.
   8 **KidCo** $55.

# CHAPTER
# 24

# High Chairs

**F**eeding a hungry baby in a high chair isn't always a picnic. But the right high chair can help contain mealtime madness and make the whole experience a lot more enjoyable, both for you and for your baby.

You'll want a stable, sturdy model that can stand up to spilling, kicking, and regular cleaning for at least a year (some babies can't bear to sit in a high chair after that). A chair with a tray that can be released with one hand is also a plus. Picture your baby occupying your other arm while you're opening and closing the tray; it's just one of the many physical feats you'll be asked to master as a parent.

A high chair usually consists of a frame of molded plastic or metal tubing and an attached seat with a safety belt and a footrest. There are still a few old-fashioned wooden high chairs out there with a removable tray or arms that lift the tray over a baby's head, although they aren't always as comfortable for babies as the modern, form-fitting models on the market now, and most of them aren't certified as meeting the latest safety standards. You'll also find a few hybrid units, which can double as a swing or convert into other types of gear, such as a chair for an older child or a play table.

## Shopping Secrets

Look for a chair that has a waist strap and a strap that runs between the legs. If a tray is used, there should be a passive restraint, such as a crotch post, used in conjunction with the harness straps. A high chair, like a car seat or a stroller, is one of those shake-rattle-and-roll buying experiences. We suggest visiting the baby store near you with the broadest selection. Then do the following:

**Open and close the fastener** on the seat's safety harness (try it one-handed) to make sure it's easy to use. If it's not, you might be tempted not to use it every time your child is in the seat, although that's imperative.

**Adjust the seat height** to see how well that mechanism works. Some seats come with as many as seven possible heights. You may only use one or two, but you can't know for sure at this point.

**Assess the seat cover.** Look for a chair with upholstery made to last. It should feel substantial, not flimsy. Make sure upholstery seams won't scratch your baby's legs.

### Bon Appetit, Baby

Restaurant high chairs are notorious for having broken safety restraints and other defects. One option: Bring your own portable hook-on chair (or at least have one in your trunk just in case, if you're traveling by car). The Graco Travel Lite Table Chair *(www.graco baby.com)*, which retails for about $33, is the only portable table chair on the market certified by the Juvenile Products Manufacturers Association (JPMA). Its locking mechanism provides a secure fit on certain table tops so you and your baby can enjoy your meals.

Another option is to bring your infant car seat into the restaurant. Many parents have found that if you take the restaurant high chair, turn it upside down, and securely park the car seat within the legs of the high chair, baby can join the adults at the table at nearly tabletop height.

**Make sure wheels can be locked** (if you're buying a model with wheels) or that they become immobilized when there is weight (like a baby) in the seat.

**Watch out for rough edges.** Examine the underside of the feeding tray to make sure it's free of anything sharp that could scratch your baby. Also look for small holes or hinges that could capture little fingers.

**Check for the absence of small parts.** Make sure the caps or plugs that cover the ends of metal tubing are well secured. Parts small enough for a child to swallow or inhale are a choking hazard.

**Know when to fold 'em.** If you plan to fold up your high chair as often as every day, practice in the store. Some chairs that claim to be foldable can have stiff folding mechanisms. Technically they may be foldable, but they're not user-friendly.

## What's Available

Major brands of high chairs include, in alphabetical order: Baby Trend, Chicco USA, Dorel Juvenile Group (Cosco), Evenflo, Fisher-Price, Graco, J. Mason, Kolcraft, Peg Perego, and Scandinavian Child. There are three general price ranges:

### Basic High Chairs

High chairs at this end of the price range (under $70) are simple, compact, and generally work quite well. Essentially plastic seats on plastic or steel-tubing legs, such models may or may not have tray and height adjustments and tend to lack bells and whistles, such as wheels, foldability for storage, one-handed tray removal, or the capacity to recline, which you may not use anyway unless you're bottle-feeding. The seat is usually upholstered with a vinyl covering or bare plastic, and the pad may be removable and washable. The tray is typically kept in place with pins that fit into holes in the tubing.

**Pros:** For the money, a basic high chair can serve you and your baby well. But it pays to comparison shop, as some brands may be more suitable to your needs than others.

**Cons:** Watch for chairs in this price range with grooves in the seat's molded plastic (a gunk trap); cotton seat pads rather than vinyl, which tend not to hold up as well over time; and trays with side release buttons that are accessible to your baby. Some parents report that their babies can remove such trays—food and all—as early as 9 months of age.

### Midpriced High Chairs

In this price range ($70 to $150), you'll find many of the features of higher-end chairs, which include multiple tray and chair-height positions; casters for mobility, with a locking feature for safe parking; a reclining seat for infant feeding; one-hand removable tray; foldability for storage; and a three- or five-point harness plus a passive restraint when used with the tray. Most have cushioned, vinyl seat pads that can be removed for washing, although you'll also still see models with cloth covers in this price range; those are a challenge to keep clean. Frames and seats are typically made of molded, rigid plastic or steel.

**Pros:** This price range generally offers sturdier chairs with more usable features, although, depending on the model, price isn't always aligned with quality.

**Cons:** Some models are bulky and can eat up space in a small kitchen, although a large footprint provides greater stability. Just watch out that you don't trip on the protruding legs.

### High-End High Chairs

In this price range ($150 to $250), you'll find European imports and traditional solid-wood high chairs. Chairs at this end of the market tend to have thick, tubular frames topped by densely padded seats upholstered in vinyl. As a result, they may have a more solid feel and cushier digs for baby. Some models come with add-on fabric covers that are removable for laundering. These chairs can be adjusted to many different heights and reclining positions with a simple squeeze-release mechanism. Some have folding "A"-shaped frames to make them easy to store.

**Pros:** You'll get extra features, such as seven height positions instead of five, and often better quality, which is important to consider if you want the chair to last through another baby or more. Another bonus: Many parents report that companies that sell higher-end chairs tend to have responsive customer service, which helps if you have a problem.

**Cons:** Chairs in this range can be bulky because they tend to have a wider base for stability. That's good because it reduces the risk of tipping. However, you'll need more space to accommodate the footprint, which tends to be more like that of a baby swing.

## Features to Consider

**Crotch post.** To help prevent a baby from slipping out under the tray and getting his or her head caught, high chairs now typically have a center crotch post attached to the tray or to the seat. It's not meant to replace the safety belt, though. A center post that attaches to the chair rather than to the tray is better because it enables you to push your child up to the table without the tray but still have that center-post support.

**Foldability.** Some high chairs fold for storage. If that's important to you, make sure there's a secure locking system to prevent accidental folding while your child is in the chair or being put into it. Such a system should automatically engage when you open the chair.

**Safety belt.** As we mentioned, this is an important feature. When buying a high chair, examine the restraining straps to make sure the waist belt has a buckle that can't be fastened unless the crotch strap is also used. Safety belts should hold your baby securely in place, with no leeway for standing up or climbing out. Some high chairs offer an adjustable three-point harness—two adjustable shoulder straps and a lock between the child's legs—or an adjustable five-point harness— two straps over the shoulders, two for the thighs, and a crotch strap, which is ideal.

**Seat adjustment.** Seats can move up or down to as many as seven

## CERTIFICATION

Often located on a high chair's tray or frame, a certification sticker shows that the model meets the minimum requirements of the American Society for Testing and Materials (ASTM) voluntary standard and that its manufacturer participates in the pass/fail certification program administered by the Juvenile Products Manufacturers Association (JPMA). Certified high chairs are required to have a passive restraint, such as a crotch post; a locking device that prevents accidental folding; secure caps and plugs; sturdy, break-resistant trays; wide legs to increase stability; and no springs or dangerous scissoring actions that could harm little fingers. Safety belts have to pass force tests. High chairs are also covered by the federal safety standard for small parts.

The certification sticker may not be on all high chairs or their packaging, so it's important to know which brands are JPMA-certified. They are: Baby Trend, Chicco USA, Combined Resources International, Dorel Juvenile Group, Evenflo, Fisher-Price, Graco, J. Mason, Kolcraft, Peg Perego, Scandinavian Child, and Stokke (which makes the Kinderzeat, a toddler chair). Note: ASTM is, at the time of this writing, revising its high-chair standards. The last revision was in 1999, and it's best not to buy a high chair made before that year. For updates on certified high chairs, visit *www.jpma.org*.

## A Chair That Grows the Distance

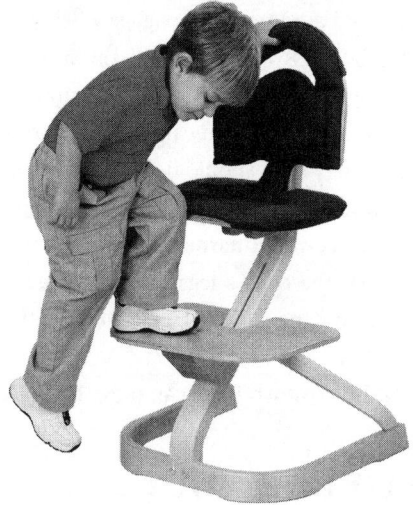

One of the newest trends in high-chair design is a chair that follows your baby into other stages of life. The Svan Chair by Scandinavian Child, for example, is made to convert from a high chair to a toddler chair to a computer chair for a teen. Made of molded wood, it features a minimalist Swedish design and comes with a three-point harness and wood safety guard. The chair retails for about $250.

height positions on some chairs. They may also recline (in case your baby falls asleep right after eating). However, except for bottle feeding, don't use a seat in the reclining position while feeding your baby—that's a choking hazard. With a height-adjusting chair, the seat slides along the chair frame, locking into various positions. Height options range from nearly floor level to standard high-chair level, with the middle height low enough to allow the seat (with the tray removed) to be pushed up to a dining-room table.

**Toys.** Some high chairs have toys that attach to the tray, an option your baby will likely enjoy, although you can certainly buy toys separately that fasten to high-chair trays. But avoid strings when attaching them.

**Tray.** In general, you'll want a lightweight tray you can take off with one hand or that swings to the side when not in use. Certain designs help contain spills: a tray that surrounds baby on all sides, a tray angle that channels liquids away from baby, or a tall rim all around the tray. Some chairs have two trays: a big tray with a deep rim for feeding and a smaller one for snacking or playing. Don't be lured by a claim that the tray is "dishwasher safe"—most trays are too large to fit in a dishwasher. One exception: Many parents report that the dishwasher-safe feeding tray that snaps off the base of the Fisher-Price Healthy Care High Chair (about $70) really does fit in their dishwashers.

**Upholstery.** Many models have seat coverings—or entire seat panels—that come off for easier cleaning. Be sure fasteners won't cause upholstery to tear as you pull off the seat or coverings. Opt for a seat cover with a pattern rather than a solid color; patterns are better at concealing spills. Some covers look like cloth but are really vinyl, which is easier to spot clean than cloth.

**Wheels.** Wheels may make it easier to move the high chair around, which is important if you'll frequently be hauling your high chair from, say, the kitchen to the dining room. On the other hand, wheels can also be a nuisance because they may allow the chair to move as you're trying to pull a tray off, or as you put your baby in. Older children may be tempted to take the baby for a joyride when you turn your back.

## TIPS FOR SAFER SEATING

Always use a high chair's safety restraints rather than just depending on the tray alone to do the job. That won't be adequate. According to the Consumer Product Safety Commission, thousands of children are treated in hospital emergency rooms each year for injuries associated with high chairs. Deaths can also occur. Most of the injuries have resulted from falls when the restraining straps weren't used and parents turned their backs. Children can stand in the chair and topple. They can also slip under the tray and strangle when their heads become trapped between the tray and the chair seat. Here are some other safety tips:

• Never leave your baby unsupervised in a high chair, even for a moment.

• With chairs that fold, be sure the locking device is locked each time you set the chair up.

• Don't let older children hang onto a high chair or its tray, play around it, or climb into it unassisted, especially when your baby is in it. The chair could tip over.

• Keep the high chair away from a table, counter, wall, or other surface from which your child could push off with feet or hands. That can also lead to tipping.

• Inspect the high chair often. After your baby has been using the chair for a while, check to make sure it's still in good shape. You'll want to be sure the seat-belt buckles are secure, the chair still locks into place, and that any small parts remain firmly attached.

Wheels on some models appear to make the chair less stable. If you decide on a wheeled model, look for locks on the wheels, preferably on all four. Some models come with locking casters. Still others have just two wheels and stay in place unless you tilt them on their wheels for rolling around.

## Recommendations

There are pluses and minuses with every price range of chair. All can be tough to clean because, let's face it, baby food has a way of getting into every possible nook and cranny (and most seats have them somewhere). High-end models, such as Chicco, Peg Perego, and Scandinavian Child, offer flexible positioning, extra-thick seat padding, and attractive upholstery.

Midpriced models, such as the Baby Trend Breckenridge, generally represent the best value, however. And, like high-end models, they usually have an easy-to-remove tray, a sturdy safety belt, a tip-resistant frame, and a crotch post. But even some basic chairs, such as the Graco Neat Seat High Chair, can compete with higher-end models in terms of safety and other features. No matter what your budget, buy a chair of recent production that's certified (see page 179) so you can be sure it meets the current voluntary safety standard. Also do the in-store road-testing we suggest earlier in this chapter.

Note: These products were not tested by Consumers Union. This alphabetical listing does not include all models available but rather is a selection of some widely distributed ones. Descriptions are derived from the manufacturers' claims. Prices are approximate retail. For manufacturer contact information, see the Brand Locator, starting on page 283.

| Line/model | Price | Details |
|---|---|---|
| **BABY TREND** | | |
| **Taylor Square Vista High Chair** | $50 | Features six-position height adjustment, four-position seat recline, adjustable one-hand removable tray, padded seat with five-point harness and footrest, and caster wheels with brakes. Folds for storage. |
| **Trend High Chair Breckenridge** | $90 | Features six-position height adjustment, four-position seat recline, adjustable one-hand removable tray, padded seat with five-point harness and footrest, and caster wheels with brakes. Folds for storage. |
| **Trend High Chair Tahoe** | $90 | Features six-position height adjustment, four-position seat recline, adjustable one-hand removable tray, padded seat with five-point harness and footrest, and caster wheels with brakes. Folds for storage. |
| **CHICCO** | | |
| **Chicco Mamma Double Tray** | $130 to $150 | Six-position height adjustment, three-position seat recline, five-point harness, one-hand tray release, and vinyl seat cover. Seat comes with a detachable infant insert. |
| **COSCO** | | |
| **High Chair 03-330** | $70 | Features three-point safety restraint, reversible vinyl padding, wide leg base, and molded footrest. Has snap-on, compartmentalized tray that holds baby food jars, drinks, and utensils. T-bar restraint can fold under tray. |
| **EVENFLO** | | |
| **Envision High Chair** | $60 to $80 | Features seven height positions, three seat recline positions, safety T-bar restraint, one-hand tray, and removable cloth pad for cleaning. Folds for storage. |
| **Envision Plus High Chair** | $60 to $80 | Features seven height positions, three seat recline positions, four locking casters, one-hand tray, safety T-bar restraint, and removable cloth pad for cleaning. Folds for storage. Some models include snack tray. |

| Line/model | Price | Details |
| --- | --- | --- |
| Simplicity Plus High Chair | $80 | Features eight height positions, four reclining seat positions, four locking casters, safety T-bar restraint, removable cloth pad for cleaning, and one-hand tray with attached T bar that swings out. Folds for storage. |
| Steps to Grow High Chair | $100 | Molded plastic high chair that converts to a booster seat and later to a table and chair for a toddler. Features two height adjustments, large tray with one-hand release, and cushioned padding. |
| **FISHER-PRICE** | | |
| Cozy Fit Infant-to-Toddler High Chair | $50 | Features multiple height adjustments, four-position recline, three-point restraint, one-hand tray release, and wipeable and machine-washable pad. Seat has cushioned, adjustable "wings" for a secure fit. Converts to a booster. |
| Healthy Care High Chair | $70 | Features seven height adjustments, three-position seat recline, five-point restraint, vinyl-coated pad, and compartmentalized feeding tray. Folds for storage. |
| Deluxe Healthy Care High Chair | $90 | Features seven height adjustments, three-position seat recline, five-point restraint, four locking casters, vinyl-coated pad. Includes three food trays that snap on and off. Folds for storage. |
| **GRACO** | | |
| Easy Chair 3190 | $30 | Features three-position seat recline, tray with snack compartments and cup holders, removable vinyl seat padding, and T-bar seat restraint. |
| Easy Chair 3195 | $40 | Features three-position seat recline, pull-out tray insert and compartmentalized server tray, removable vinyl seat pad, and seat T-bar restraint. |
| Harmony 3920 | $70 | Height-adjustable chair with four-position seat recline. Features tray insert, wipeable seat pad, and three- and five-point harness. Folds for storage. |
| DoubleTray 3856 | $80 | Features six height positions, three-position recline. Comes with two seat pads: one cloth, one vinyl. Folds for storage. |
| Harmony 3940 | $90 | Height-adjustable model with four-position seat recline, tray insert, wipeable seat pad, three- and five-point harness, and storage basket. Folds for storage. |
| DoubleTray 3868 | $90 | Features six height positions, three-position recline, meal and snacking trays, and reversible cloth seat pad with a secondary vinyl pad. Folds for storage. |

| Line/model | Price | Details |
| --- | --- | --- |
| **Baby Classics Harmony 3940** | $110 | Height-adjustable model features four-position seat recline, tray insert, wipeable seat pad, three- and five-point harness, and storage basket. Folds for storage. |
| **Baby Classics Harmony 3960BC** | $140 | Height-adjustable model features four-position seat recline, tray insert, wipeable seat pad, three- and five-point harness, inner baby booster for sitting support, tray cover and place mat, and storage basket. Folds for storage. |
| **KOLCRAFT** | | |
| **Perfect Recliner High Chair** | $60 to $100 | Features six height positions, three-position seat recline, one-hand tray release, three-point safety straps and T-bar, removable tray toys, and washable cloth slipcover. Can convert from high chair to table chair. |
| **Perfect Height High Chair** | $60 to $100 | Features six height positions, one-hand tray release, three-point safety harness and T-bar, and contoured seat back. Converts from high chair to table chair. |
| **PEG PEREGO** | | |
| **Prima Pappa DT** | $130 | Features seven height and four recline positions, adjustable tray, four caster wheels with brakes on the rear wheels, and wipeable vinyl upholstery. Folds for storage. |
| **Prima Pappa Roller** | $190 | Features seven height and four recline positions, padded leatherette upholstery, adjustable tray, and four casters with brakes on the rear wheels. |
| **Prima Pappa Double Upholstery** | $250 | Features seven height and four recline positions, removable slipcover over wipeable vinyl upholstery, five-point harness, adjustable tray, and four caster wheels with brakes on the rear wheels. Folds for storage. |
| **ROCHELLE** | | |
| **Lexington** | $190 | Made of ash with oak finish. Features spoked seat back, three-point harness, and footrest. Seat padding sold separately. |
| **Charlotte** | $190 | Made of maple. Features spoked seat back, three-point harness, and footrest. Seat padding sold separately. |
| **Windsor** | $190 | Made of maple. Includes spoked seat back, three-point harness, and footrest. Seat padding sold separately. |
| **Nostalgia** | $190 | Made of ash with oak finish, spoked seat back, three-point harness, and footrest. Seat padding sold separately. |

| Line/model | Price | Details |
|---|---|---|
| **Memphis** | $190 | Made of maple with a choice of three light finishes. Includes three-point harness and footrest. Seat padding sold separately. |
| **SCANDINAVIAN CHILD** | | |
| **The Svan Chair** | $250 | Natural, bentwood construction that converts from a high chair to a toddler chair. Cushions are machine-washable. |

# Monitors

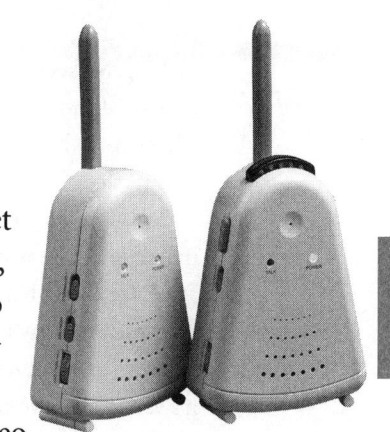

**B**aby monitors are an extra set of ears—and in some cases, eyes—that allow you to keep tabs on your sleeping baby when you're not in the same room. There are two basic types: audio and video.

Audio monitors operate within a selected radio frequency band to send sound from the baby's room to a receiver. Video monitors use a small wall- or table-mounted camera that transmits images to a TV-set-like monitor.

Still another way to keep tabs on baby is with movement sensors, under-the-mattress pads that alert you when his or her movement completely stops for more than 20 seconds. While some parents may find movement sensors reassuring, bear in mind that they're not medical devices and shouldn't be used in place of prescribed heart or breathing monitors to detect conditions such as sleep apnea. Nor should you rely on them to prevent Sudden Infant Death Syndrome (SIDS), the cause of which is still unknown.

A baby monitor's challenge is to transmit recognizable sound over a distance with minimal interference from other wireless devices. Using a variety of environments, CONSUMER REPORTS tested seven audio monitors ranging from $20 to $50; an

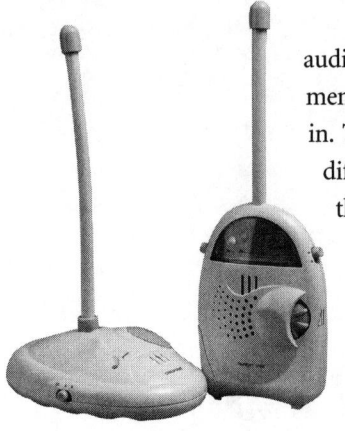

audio/video monitor, $100; and an audio monitor/movement sensor, $90. All are fine for the basic job of listening in. They differ a lot in other attributes, however. Those differences are noted in the Ratings on page 191, and in the Features to Consider.

## Shopping Secrets

**Decide how much you want to monitor.** The latest generation of baby monitors claims to allow the constant surveillance of baby's every whimper, breath, and movement. One model, the Everywhere Rechargeable 900 MHz Monitor (The First Years, $50), even lets you eavesdrop on your baby when you're in the shower because it's battery-operated and water-resistant. For some parents, that may be comforting. For others, such nonstop monitoring is apt to be nerve-racking. So keep in mind that a monitor isn't a must-have. If you live in a small house or apartment or feel as though you'd like a break when your baby is sleeping—which is legitimate—it's OK to go monitorless.

**Consider your home and lifestyle.** In many situations you may appreciate a monitor with both sounds and lights so you can also "see" your baby's cries. If you'll be taking business calls during naptime, you may want to be able to turn the sound down very low and rely on the lights. A video monitor can also serve the same purpose, but it's very expensive and not very portable. Similarly, if you live in a large house, you may want a monitor with two receivers rather than just one—although that can be a convenience in a small home as well. And, in general, look for monitors with features that make them easy to move about, such as a compact parent unit that clips onto your belt. (Try it on before buying, if possible; we found the antennas tend to poke the wearer.)

**Choose between audio or audio/video.** A good audio monitor will let you know whether your baby is awake or asleep, moving or stationary. Our tests showed only so-so picture quality from the one video monitor we rated. You can tell that your baby's eyes are open, for example, but you can't distinguish much detail.

**Mind the frequency.** None of the baby monitors CONSUMER REPORTS tested was immune from static. The closer your monitor's frequency is to that of another device, such as a cordless phone, the more likely you'll hear static or cross talk. You may reduce interference if your monitor lets you switch to a different channel within its frequency band, as did all the models CONSUMER REPORTS tested. The Evenflo 3000 and Summer Infant have more separation between channels than the others, for a greater chance of reducing interference.

**Consider your phone.** Choose a monitor that operates in a different frequency band than your cordless phone. Most newer cordless phones are either 2.4 gigahertz or 900 megahertz. If you have a 900 MHz cordless phone and a 900 MHz monitor, they can interfere with each other.

**Check the range.** All the models CONSUMER REPORTS tested that claimed a signal-distance range met or exceeded it in our open-air test; the maximum claimed distance was up to 500 feet for The First Years Crisp & Clear Plus. Pick a model with an appropriate signal range for your home. Some home-construction materials, such as concrete and metal, can reduce the range, however.

**Learn the return policy.** Since you often can't test monitors before you buy them (there usually aren't display models available, and conditions in the store may be very different from those in your home), learn the return policy of the store or Web site where you're buying or registering. You'll want to be able to take back a monitor if you're unhappy with it for any reason. (Common problems include static and interference from cordless phones or answering machines, even the ambient sounds of an air conditioner or a neighbor's barking dog.)

## What's Available

The major brands, in alphabetical order, are Evenflo, The First Years, Fisher-Price, Graco, Safety 1st, SBC/Phillips, Summer Infant, and Unisar/BebeSounds. Baby monitors we tested ranged in price from $20 to $50 for audio monitors, $100 for audio/video, and $90 for movement sensors.

## Features to Consider

**Battery for the child unit.** All of the child units tested can be plugged into the wall for power, but four also can use either 9-volt,

AAA, or AA alkaline batteries. All the parent units have this option. The battery option is useful in the event of a power failure and also allows you to take the unit where there are no outlets, such as outdoors.

**Compact parent unit.** The smallest parent units are about the size of a fat wallet. You can use the integral belt clip to free your hands, but the antenna may poke you.

**Extra parent unit.** This unit can stay in, say, your bedroom while the other is carried about the house.

**Low-battery indicator.** A light or tone warns of the need to recharge or replace batteries in the parent unit.

**Rechargeable batteries included.** This money-saving feature is provided with some parent units. You can buy rechargeable or alkaline batteries for other parent units.

## Nice But Not Necessary

**Intercom.** Pushing a button and speaking into the parent unit lets you reassure your baby that you're on your way.

**Video monitor.** Summer Infant has one. But its so-so picture quality limits its usefulness.

## Works Better in Theory

**Finder feature.** Press a button on the child unit to make the parent unit beep. Unfortunately, it doesn't work if the lost unit has been switched off.

# Ratings • Monitors

A n audio monitor should be sufficient for most people. All the baby monitors we tested did an acceptable job of transmitting sounds within a typical home and yard, and all were easy to use. But they differed in battery life, features, and range. The audio/video monitor we tested had only so-so picture quality. Consumer-grade movement sensors should not be used for medical monitoring. The sensor we tested included an audio monitor that performed very well, but it was overpriced for that function alone.

| | Excellent | Very good | Good | Fair | Poor |
|---|---|---|---|---|---|
| | ⊖ | ⊖ | ○ | ◑ | ● |

**Within types, in performance order. Blue key numbers indicate Quick Picks.**

| Key number | Brand & model / Similar models, in small type, comparable to tested model. | Price | Overall score | Performance | Range | Sound | Battery life | Compact parent unit | Extra parent unit | Battery for child unit | Rechargeable batteries incl. | Low-battery indicator |
|---|---|---|---|---|---|---|---|---|---|---|---|---|

**AUDIO MONITORS** *All use the 49-megahertz frequency band except (1), which uses 900 megahertz.*

| 1 | **The First Years** Crisp & Clear Plus 3813B | $40 | | ⊖ | ⊖ | ○ | • | | • | • | • |
| 2 | **Evenflo** Constant Care 3000 | 50 | | ⊖ | ⊖ | ⊖ | | | • | • | • |
| 3 | **The First Years** Safe & Sound 3808 | 25 | | ⊖ | ⊖ | ⊖ | • | | | • | • |
| 4 | **Safety 1st** Super Clear 2 Receiver / 49243 🄳 Safe Glow 2 Receiver | 30 | | ○ | ⊖ | ⊖ | • | • | | | • |
| 5 | **Graco** UltraClear 2755GM | 50 | | ⊖ | ⊖ | ◑ | | • | | | |
| 6 | **Evenflo** Constant Care 1500 | 20 | | ⊖ | ○ | ⊖ | • | | • | | |
| 7 | **Fisher-Price** Sounds 'n Lights 71624 🄳 / B9637 | 30 | | ⊖ | ⊖ | ○ | • | | | | |

**AUDIO/VIDEO MONITOR** *Uses the 900-megahertz frequency band.*

| 8 | **Summer Infant** Baby's Quiet Sounds / 02010 | 100 | | ◑ | ⊖ | — | | | | | |

**AUDIO MONITOR/MOVEMENT SENSOR** *Uses the 49-megahertz frequency band.*

| 9 | **Unisar/Bebesounds** / Angelcare Sensor with Sound AC201 | 90 | | ⊖ | ⊖ | ⊖ | | | | • | • |

🄳 *Discontinued, but similar model is available. Price is for similar model.*

## Guide to the Ratings

**Overall score** is based on ease of use, range, sound, and battery life. **Range** was measured outdoors and in the line of sight. **Sound,** for parent and child units, includes measurements of sound level and sensitivity to sounds from different directions. **Battery life,** as measured, was excellent (more than 20 hours), very good (15 to 20 hours), good (10 to 15 hours), or fair (5 to 10 hours). **Price** is approximate retail. All audio-only monitors have: Two-channel select switch, sound-activated lights, volume control, power "on" light, and belt clip for parent unit.

# Quick Picks • Monitors

**QUICK PICKS**

### Best value, with excellent battery life:
**3 The First Years** $25

Batteries on the parent unit lasted 24 hours. This very compact unit also has a low-battery indicator and rechargeable batteries, a money saver.

### Good for multifamily residences:
**2 Evenflo** $50

This monitor had better separation than most between its two channels, so you may have an easier time finding a signal without interference from neighbors' wireless devices.

### Good choice for a big house:
**1 The First Years** $40

The lone audio-only monitor we tested that uses 900 MHz. In optimal conditions it transmitted farther than the up to 500 foot range claimed on the box. The unit includes a compact receiver and rechargeable batteries.

CHAPTER

# 26

# Nursing Bras

I f you decide to breast-feed, you won't necessarily need bottles, a bottle sterilizer, or formula. But you will need a nursing bra. It will be your key piece of equipment to get the job done quickly and easily at feeding time.

Nursing bras look like regular bras except that the cups of the bra open or lower from the front when you unsnap or unhook the closure. The latches that open the cup for nursing should be simple to operate with one hand. Most manufacturers have several nursing-bra lines, including models that are comfortable for sleeping or lounging; traditional, seamless "soft cup" and underwire styles; and super-supportive sports nursing bras that can take a pounding on the tennis court.

Whatever style you choose, proper fit is the key to breast-feeding success, says Lynne Andrako, a certified bra fitter for Medela, the breast pump and nursing bra manufacturer. A poorly fitting bra will not only be uncomfortable but also may increase the risk of mastitis, a milk-duct infection. (The ill-fitting bra can put pressure on milk ducts, which may cause them to become clogged—and a magnet for infection-causing bacteria.)

Based on her experience, Andrako estimates that 80 percent of women buy the wrong size nursing bra. Where do many pregnant women go wrong? To accommodate their changing breasts (even early on, your breasts will enlarge and become heavier as fatty deposits increase and new milk ducts grow), women often increase

M-N-O

their bras' band size but go up only one cup size.

In actuality, says Andrako, the rib cage enlarges a bit during pregnancy but generally not enough to warrant increasing the band size you normally wear. (You can easily accommodate for any increase by adjusting the hooks in the back.) So if you're a 34 before pregnancy, chances are you'll be a 34 during and after, she says. But if you wore a C cup pre-pregnancy, you may go up to an F—or higher. Cup sizes typically go from A through D, then DD, DDD, F, G, H, and I.

In addition to a nursing bra, you'll need disposable or washable cotton pads that you can tuck inside the bra to absorb any leakage. The disposable types are typically made of super-absorbent material that wicks moisture away from the skin. They're higher-tech than cotton nursing pads but also more expensive. Both kinds prevent clothing stains and skin irritation and don't show to the outside world. You can find nursing pads at drug stores, maternity and baby stores, and Web sites.

Other accessories that you may or may not need include adjustable bra strap pads that easily attach to any bra to relieve strap pressure and special bra shells that can protect sore nipples from irritation or help draw out inverted nipples. Those are also available at maternity stores and Web sites.

## Shopping Secrets

**Get fitted by a certified bra fitter.** Yes, there's even a certification program for that. When you're bra shopping at a maternity store, ask the saleswoman if there's one on staff. This service, if offered, is typically free of charge. If a certified bra fitter isn't available, a lactation consultant, perhaps one affiliated with the hospital where you'll deliver,

## ARE NURSING CLOTHES NECESSARY?

In addition to a nursing bra, you can buy special nursing shirts and nightwear that have strategically placed slits and flaps in the front to facilitate breast-feeding. Although nursing clothes make breast-feeding easy, they're certainly not essential. A button-down blouse, stretchy T-shirt or sweater, and two-piece pajamas—in other words, your regular clothes—can be just as easy. Regular clothes can be even more discreet, if that's important to you. Because of their front flaps, which consist of two extra pieces of fabric, nursing shirts tend to advertise the fact that you're nursing, although no one, except other mothers, may notice. Still, they're an added expense, and their life span tends to be short.

can usually help. Many lactation consultants are also certified bra fitters.

When you're being fitted, you'll be measured around your midsection, just under your arms. The tape will also be wrapped around your torso at the fullest point of the bust. The difference between the two measurements is your cup size. Once you get your bra size (and don't be surprised if the saleswoman keeps that to herself), you can start trying on bras until you find a style you like and feel comfortable in.

**Plan on buying three to five bras.** That should be enough to meet your needs, allowing you to have a couple on deck with one or two in the wash. Plan on at least one of those bras being a sleep/loungewear bra for the early days of nursing when you'll want to wear your nursing bra to bed for leakage control.

**Shop as early as six weeks predelivery.** By that time, your breasts will be nursing size, so you can be assured that you'll get the correct size bra.

**If you're especially large-breasted,** you may need to shop around. If the bras available in your local maternity store aren't large enough, try a specialty lingerie or "foundation" store instead. They can usually accommodate your needs and even custom-make bras in your size, if necessary.

## What's Available

Major brands, in alphabetical order, are Bravado, Fancee Free, Leading Lady, Medela, Olga, and Promise. Nursing bras range from about $12 (sleeping/lounging bras) to about $40 (sports nursing bras).

## Recommendations

The best nursing bras are stretchy, absorbent, and don't bind the breasts in any way that could interfere with milk flow. Look for bras that are cotton, machine washable, and have no special laundering or care requirements. You'll be busy enough in the days to come.

Since the right size bra is so important to getting breast-feeding off to a good start and reducing the risk of complications, such as clogged milk ducts, shop at a specialized maternity store or seek out a lactation consultant/certified bra fitter for at least your first bra. To find a lactation consultant in your area, contact the hospital or birth center where you'll deliver, or log onto the International Lactation Consultant Association at *www.ilca.org*. A professional fitting will ensure a comfortable fit and the correct size. After you've bought one properly fitting bra, you can order more at a department store or online, if you'd like. Many Web sites offer especially competitive deals.

CHAPTER

# 27

# Pacifiers

A pacifier can be a sanity saver, especially when your baby is fussy. "The sucking action will calm babies and can even help some of their jaw muscles develop properly," says Julie Barna, a dentist and spokeswoman for the Academy of General Dentistry in Lewisburg, Pa. Of course, sucking from a bottle or breast-feeding will do the job, too.

A pacifier consists of a latex or silicone nipple mounted on a plastic shield that's wide enough to not be sucked into your baby's mouth. (In the highly unlikely event that should happen, pacifiers are required to have at least two ventilation holes in the shield, which can admit air.)

Some pacifiers have knobs on the back; others have rings. Available separately are carrying cases, as well as short, clip-on ribbons that attach the pacifier to clothing and prevent it from ending up on the floor or the street.

For some parents, a pacifier is the thing that finally quiets their baby and makes everything all right with the world. For others, it's just a waste of money because some babies, especially those who are breast-feeding, simply don't like pacifiers and will repeatedly spit them out, no matter which brand or type you try.

Will your baby crave a pacifier or be satisfied with the breast or bottle? You'll

P-Q-R-S

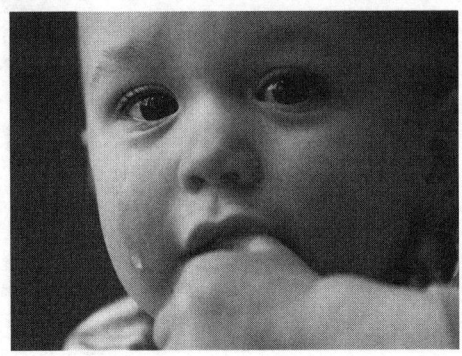

know which kind of baby you have soon enough, perhaps even before you leave the hospital.

## So Many Pacifiers, So Little Time

If you find yourself in the pacifier aisle, you'll see a large variety—from angled pacifiers with a wide tip, frequently called "orthodontic," to a basic, round-tipped pacifier, which is advertised as "most like mother." Incidentally, all pacifiers sold in the U.S., whether or not they're labeled "orthodontic," are orthodontically correct, Barna says. (To be sure, look for the American Dental Association Seal of Approval on the pacifier package.)

"Orthodontic means that your baby's top and bottom jaw are in a correct position when he's sucking on it," Barna says. That position doesn't interfere with normal jaw growth and development and, in fact, may promote it.

Pacifiers come in several sizes. They're classified by age on the package, so it's easy to see which size to buy.

## Banning the Binky

Between your child's first and second birthday, it's a good idea to wean him or her off the pacifier. (Cold turkey is one possible method. Out of sight, out of mind.) You'll save on dental and doctor bills later because prolonged use of a pacifier can change the shape of your baby's growing jaw and palate. The sucking action can narrow it in the wrong places and incorrectly widen it in others. If pacifier use continues into the preschool years, "we can pretty much guarantee that your child will need orthodontic treatment," Barna says.

There's another reason to ditch the pacifier, even closer to the one-year mark. Recent studies have shown that using a pacifier after age 1 can double the risk of middle-ear infections. "When a child is sucking on a pacifier, the auditory tube in the middle ear actually opens, allowing bacteria that naturally reside in the mouth to pass through, which causes infection," Barna explains.

If you find your toddler wants something to suck on, Barna recommends graduating to a water-filled training cup with a collapsible rubber straw. The suction action will promote normal muscle development and hand-eye coordination and not lead to ear infections. But don't fill that spill-proof cup with juice, soda, or even milk between meals. The sugar and phosphoric acid in these beverages can foster tooth decay.

## What's Available

Major brands of pacifiers include, in alphabetical order: Avent Naturally, Evenflo, Gerber, Mam (Sassy), Playtex, and Tommee Tippee. Pacifiers range from $4 to $6 for a package of two.

## Recommendations

If you decide to go the pacifier route, buy several in infant size. Try different brands and nipple shapes. We recommend silicone over latex because babies can develop an allergy or sensitivity to latex, although it's rare. Silicone eliminates that potential problem and also tends not to deteriorate as quickly.

## PACIFIER SAFETY

To prevent choking, the Consumer Product Safety Commission (CPSC) requires that pacifiers be able to pass a "pull test." The test ensures that a pacifier is strong enough (after boiling and cooling) not to separate into small pieces that could choke or suffocate a baby.

Pacifiers sold with a ribbon, cord, string, or yarn attached must also be labeled with this warning: "Do Not Tie Pacifier Around Child's Neck as It Presents a Strangulation Danger." Pacifiers have a tendency to gravitate to the floor or disappear when you need them most. Still, no matter how frustrated you get, take that concern seriously. Each year, the CPSC receives reports of infants strangling on pacifier cords or ribbons tied around their necks. A baby can catch a pacifier cord on crib posts, doorknobs, and many other objects when you're not looking. It takes only a second for a serious pacifier accident to occur.

Over time, pacifiers can crack and tear. Check them carefully, and if you discover any problems, throw them away.

Use a pacifier between meals when you sense your baby just needs something but isn't hungry. Giving a pacifier to a baby who wants food isn't a good idea, however. That can make baby so distraught that he or she will have trouble calming down enough to eat.

Once you settle on a brand/type, buy several so you don't waste time scouring the house for that precious pacifier. Keep two in your diaper bag—you'll need an extra in case you drop one or your baby spits it out onto the floor (that's inevitable). And if you're traveling together, make sure your spouse is armed with one, too. Have several dispersed in key locations around your home, such as the living room, baby's room, and the kitchen.

Before you use a new pacifier, boil it for five minutes to remove any chemical residue. After that, wash your baby's pacifiers often with warm soapy water by hand or in the dishwasher. Frequent washing is particularly important for babies younger than 6 months; their immune systems are especially immature.

# Play Yards

**T**hese updated versions of yesterday's playpen can be handy for your home or when you travel. Play yards provide babies with an enclosed place for playing or napping. Many multitask by, for instance, including a changing table insert, a bassinet (perhaps one that vibrates to lull baby to sleep), and storage pouches on the side.

How necessary are they? You can certainly live without one. But a play yard can also fill a need you may not know you have until you start using it. One online reader, the father of a toddler and an infant, writes, "Our version features a changing table insert, a bassinet, and the overall 'playpen.' It doubles as a portable crib and can be rolled from room to room throughout the house. We use ours most of the time as a 'remote nursery.' It saves us from having to run up a flight of stairs to the children's rooms for every diaper or quick clothing change."

Most play yards are designed for portability, whether that means simply fitting them through a door, moving them from one room to another, or folding them up

# A WARNING ON THE GRACO PACK 'N PLAY

In cooperation with the U.S. Consumer Product Safety Commission, Graco Children's Products, maker of the widely sold Graco Pack 'n Play portable play yard, provided new instructions for about 538,000 Pack 'n Plays with raised changing tables.

As part of the recall action, Graco says it intends to warn consumers about this hazard and to provide labels to affix to the changing station. The new instructions and the label tell users never to put a child in these portable play yards when the changing table is still in place.

Why? A child within the play yard (not the bassinet) could get under the changing table and lift the table up. If this occurs, a child's head and neck can potentially become wedged between the changing table and the yard rail, possibly resulting in strangulation. The commission and Graco are aware of a 13-month-old girl who died this way.

The Pack 'n Play play yards with raised changing tables have model numbers 2016, 35235, or numbers that begin with 9531 or 9533. The last three digits of the model number will vary. The model number can be found on a label on the white plastic center cone, under the play yard. The play yards were sold in discount, department, and juvenile product stores from October 2001 to September 2003. Models sold since then should carry the warning label about the hazard.

You can contact Graco at 800-233-1546 or visit the company's Web site at *www.gracobaby.com* for a free label that can be affixed to the changing table (to warn your child's other caregivers). And, of course, always remove the changing table when your child is using the play yard.

to fit in the trunk of your car. They're typically 28 inches wide and 40 inches long and resemble a short golf bag when folded. Most weigh between 20 and 25 pounds without the bassinet or changing station insert; 30 to 35 pounds with it.

Play yard frames are made of metal tubing. Mesh on at least two and sometimes all four sides provides ventilation but little protection from the sun and the wind. Roll-down curtains on some models function as sun and wind shades. You can also buy an optional canopy to help keep insects out, but the canopy may concentrate heat.

Some models include bassinet inserts that slide over the play yard's frame. Don't use these once your baby can push up, pull up, roll over, or has reached the manufacturer's stated weight limit (which is about 15 pounds or 3 months old). Changing-station inserts, which also slide over the frame usually include safety harnesses. Be sure to remove the insert when your baby is playing in the play yard.

For safety's sake avoid using a hand-me-down or garage-sale play yard. Instead, buy a new model that meets the current voluntary safety standard, which addresses the design problems of earlier models. A play yard's top rails are typically hinged at the center to allow for folding. Many play yards sold in the 1990s had rails that could collapse at the hinges, forming a steep V-shaped angle that put children at risk of entrapment and strangulation. Fourteen children were killed when play yards collapsed, according to the Consumer Product Safety Commission.

To address the hazard, the industry's voluntary standard, updated in 1999, now requires that hinges automatically lock when rails are pulled upright, and the rails won't lock unless you follow sequential setup steps. Once rails are locked and the floor is pushed down, the rails remain securely locked until you pull the floor up again. The rails must also undergo a strength test that mimics the force of an adult leaning on them. At least one company, J. Mason, avoids hinged rails altogether by employing a nonfolding top frame. The rail is a tubular rectangle with plastic fittings for screw-in legs. To set it up, you slide its legs through nylon sleeves on the play yard's corners and screw them into the top rail fittings.

The CPSC has recalled models that pose a rail-collapse hazard. However, many may still be in use in hotels, day-care centers, and people's homes.

Most play yards carry the warning, "Never leave your child unattended." That would appear to rule out using the play yard for overnight sleeping—yet that's what many play yards are used for, especially when families travel. The industry is now rethinking that warning statement and may not be using it in the future.

If you use a play yard for overnight sleeping, keep in mind that the mattress pad is thin for a reason: to prevent a child from becoming wedged between the pad and the sides. Never add extra mattresses or padding, and don't use blankets or other types of soft bedding, which pose a suffocation hazard. Instead, layer your baby for warmth with a T-shirt and a footed sleeper or wearable sleeper sack.

## Shopping Secrets

**First consider how you're likely to use your play yard.** If it's going to function mostly as a playpen, you can probably go with the basic model and skip the extras. If you travel often, you'll want a play yard that's especially light in weight, folds compactly, and is easy to tote. It may even be possible to roll the packed unit.

If you plan to have your newborn take naps in the play yard, you'll want to compare the bassinet options. Some play yards offer a full-size bassinet, which runs the entire length and width of the play yard. Others have an abbreviated three-quarters version, which is adequate for the length of time your baby is likely to use it. Some models have a canopy and one or more side curtains to help shield your baby from sun and wind, which can be helpful if you plan to take the play yard outside. A pair of lockable wheels or swivel casters on one end will make it easier to move from room to room.

**As always, try the product in the store** before you buy. Play yards are popular shower gifts; if you're planning to include one on your registry list, be sure to select the model yourself.

**Go with a model that has storage compartments** that attach to the outside so they're out of your baby's reach.

**Be sure to check the floor pad.** It should be one that the manufacturer supplied for the model. It should also be no more than 1 inch thick, snug-fitting, and firm enough to protect the baby from falling into the loose mesh pocket that can form between the edge of the floor panel and side (a suffocation hazard). For the same reason, never add a second mattress. Follow the manufacturer's height and weight guidelines for use.

**Check the production date** on the play yard and its packaging. Buy one with the latest date.

**Check to see that the model has a certification sticker** from the Juvenile Products Manufacturers Association (JPMA) indicating that it meets the American Society for Testing and Materials' current voluntary standard for play yards.

## What's Available

The major brands, in alphabetical order, include Baby Trend, Cosco, Dorel Juvenile Group, Eddie Bauer, Evenflo, Fisher-Price, Graco, Kolcraft, and J. Mason.

Most models have hinges and lock buttons in the center of the top rails. To set one up, you typically pull the top rails up so they're locked, then push the floor down. To fold this design, you pull the floor up, then press the lock buttons and raise the top rails slightly. On some you first turn the handle in the center of the floor and then pull up. An alternative design from J. Mason eliminates the top-rail hinges. Play yards range from $80 to $135.

# Features to Consider

**Attachable bassinet.** This provides a place for a newborn to nap. Look for a design that's easy to use. Stop using the bassinet when your baby either reaches the manufacturer's recommended weight limit or can sit up, pull up, or roll over (at about 3 months old and 15 pounds). Because an attachable bassinet may become dislodged, you should keep older siblings away from it when the baby is in there.

**Canopy.** Made of a combination of mesh and moisture-resistant (and sometimes heat-reflective) fabric, a canopy can help shield baby from the sun and flying insects. Because of the potential for heat buildup, however, don't use a canopy in direct sun.

**Carrying case.** Most consist of a fabric bag. The four sections of the folded-up floor provide sturdiness. A handle or strap is helpful for carrying. Some have the added convenience of rolling while folded. If you're flying, consider shipping the play yard ahead of you.

**Changing station.** These typically attach to the top of the top rail. When using one, always keep your hand on your baby; the safety harness is helpful with wiggly toddlers. Remove the changing station once the child is in the play yard itself, to avoid potentially fatal entrapment between the station and the yard's top rail.

**Floor pad.** The floor pad is about 1 inch thick and is usually made up of four fabric-covered masonite panels. The panels fold into a box for carrying the folded unit. The floor pad should stay in place so there's no danger of your baby slipping or getting trapped between it and the floorboard.

**Foldability.** If you'll often be traveling with your baby, the ease of folding and reassembling your play yard becomes an issue. Some models claim to set up in less than 1 minute. Try it for yourself in the store if possible.

**Side curtains.** Included with some play yards, they provide protection from the sun and wind. The curtains roll up when not needed to allow for greater air circulation.

**Storage.** Storage for toys and other baby items is provided on some models, with zippered side pockets, hook-on fabric storage pouches, and clip-on parent organizer bags. They should be big enough to actually hold something and also stay out of baby's reach.

**Toys.** A few play yards have tactile toys sewn into an inside wall. These are an added bonus. But avoid tying any items across the top or corner of the play yard or hanging toys from the sides with strings or cords. That can be a strangulation hazard.

**Wheels or casters.** A pair of lockable rubber wheels or swivel casters on one end makes moving the play yard easier. With some designs, the unit can also be rolled when folded.

## Recommendations

We urge you to consider only play yards made recently, say in late 2000 or later, that meet the current safety standard. Look for the date of manufacture and the certification sticker on the packaging. With older models, there's a possibility that a top-rail hinge may collapse during use and trap your child. Those models have been recalled, but many may still be out there. If your child uses a play yard at a day-care facility or in a hotel, be sure it's a recent model.

Each time before using it, examine padded sides and all areas where mesh and fabric are sewn together to be sure there are no loose threads that could entangle little fingers and toes. The floorboard should fit snugly against the springy mesh sides—gaps are an entrapment hazard. Heed maximum height and weight limits—usually 35 inches and 30 pounds. Stop using a play yard when your child attempts to climb out. And as your child becomes mobile, remove any large items from the inside of the play yard. They can be used as a stepping stool for climbing out.

**N**ote: These products were not tested by Consumers Union. This alphabetical listing does not include all models available but rather is a selection of some widely distributed ones. Descriptions are derived from the manufacturers' claims. Prices are approximate retail. For manufacturer contact information, see the Brand Locator, starting on page 283.

| Line/model | Price | Details |
|---|---|---|
| **BABY TREND** | | |
| **Nursery Center & Playard** | $70 | Includes bassinet with padded mattress and changing table. Folds for travel and includes travel bag. |
| **Santa Fe Nursery Center & Playard LE** | $80 | Features automatic locking top rails with one-hand, bottom rail safety lock. Includes removable combination bassinet and changing table with safety strap, padded mattress, clip-on parent organizer, and travel bag. |
| **Baby Trend Nursery Center** | $100 | Features braking wheels on one end, removable bassinet with padded mattress, clip-on parent organizer, removable musical mobile, and night-light. |
| **Tahoe Nursery Care Center & Playard** | $120 | Includes portable bassinet with padded mattress, removable hood and three-pocket organizer, two-pocket parent organizer, changing table with safety straps. Folds for travel and includes travel bag. |
| **EVENFLO** | | |
| **BabyGo Portable Playard** | $70 | Features large side pouch, padded floor and top rails, and caster wheels. No bassinet. Other models ($80 and up) add bassinet, changing table, organizers, and toy bars. |
| **FISHER-PRICE** | | |
| **Nursery Care Center** | $100 | Features padded, removable changing table and half-size bassinet. Has removable mobile, storage/organizer, and mesh sides. |
| **GRACO** | | |
| **Pack 'n Play 9340** | $50 | Basic rectangular model features removable, hammock-style changing table, side diaper stacker, push-button folding mechanism, and mesh on all four sides. Includes carrying bag for travel or storage. Other models ($60 and up) add bassinet, toy bar, and mobile. |
| **Pack 'n Play 9261** | $80 | Basic square design comes with four toys and folds for storage or travel. Another square model (9265, $100) adds overhead toy "gym" and other features. |

| Line/model | Price | Details |
| --- | --- | --- |
| **J. MASON** | | |
| **J5419 Sports Play Yard** | $100 | Basic model with mesh sides. Folds flat for storage. Other models ($115 and up) include removable bassinet and changing table, canopy, and other features. |

# Rocking Chairs & Gliders

f you've considered buying a rocking chair but weren't sure you'd use it, or were turned off by the grandmotherly image, think again. Babies and rocking chairs go together like macaroni and cheese.

"A rocking chair, which I resisted at first, actually turned out to be invaluable. There's lots of feeding with a baby, and having a chair that's easy to get in and out of and rocks to boot, is comforting," says Sarah Goralski of Pleasantville, N.Y., mother of a toddler. Indeed, the rocking motion of the chair will maximize the soothing effect your baby feels when being held.

Basic hardwood rocking chairs have been around for ages. A more modern variation (and many would say an improvement) is the glider, a chair that's designed to rock in a parallel motion like a porch swing rather than forward and backward in an arc. Most gliders also come with cushions (although be aware that they may be sold separately and not included in the glider price).

An ottoman you can prop your feet up on when not rocking or gliding is also

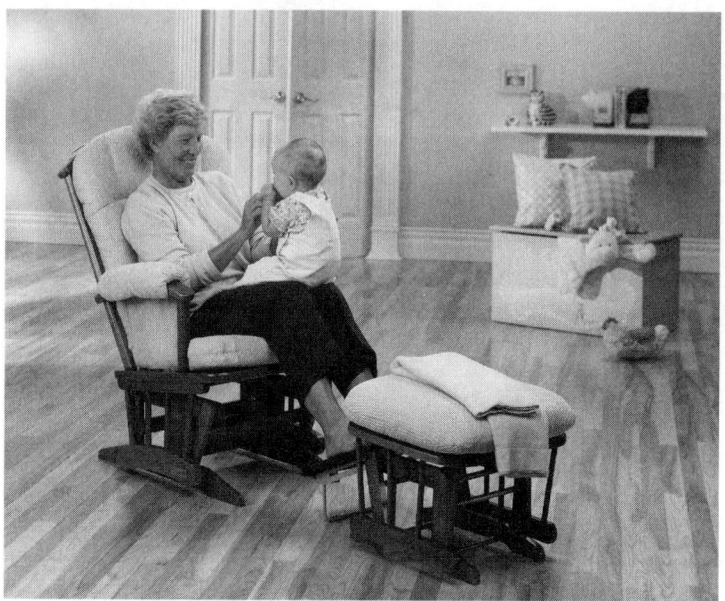

usually available as a stand-alone item and is purely optional. "Very few actually buy the ottoman," says Seth Berger, a third-generation owner of Baby & Toy Superstore in Stamford, Conn. So don't feel like you're missing out if you skip it. In fact, you may be better off. Because your feet are elevated and you'll tend to be sitting for long periods, "ottomans tend to make feet fall asleep," Berger says.

## Shopping Secrets

**Test it in the store.** This is an item you don't want to research solely on the Internet (although you can certainly buy online if you know what you're getting). Sit in the chair and rock away. That's the best way to tell if a chair's seat fits your bottom.

**Ask about warranties.** In the case of a glider, you'll want to know if the bearings, which run the gliding mechanism, have a warranty. They take the brunt of a person's weight over time. Ten years is a good warranty length, although a lifetime warranty is, of course, better.

**Get a rocker or glider with an extra wide seat** if you plan to use a nursing pillow. You'll need the room. In fact, practice in the store with a display-model nursing pillow to make sure everything fits. If a glider you're considering has well-padded arm rests, however, those may be all you need to support and comfortably feed your baby.

**Choose a glider that locks in place** if you have a toddler or plan on more than one child. When you're feeding your newborn with a toddler underfoot, little fingers can get caught in the gliding mechanism.

**Go for a darker color.** Stay away from natural beige or pastel fabrics. Furniture fabric can pick up a soiled appearance even from just normal wear and tear. And, of course, washable fabrics are a plus.

## What's Available

The major brands of rocking chairs, in alphabetical order, are: Angel Line, Jenny Lind, Kidcraft, and Nicholas and Stone. Major glider makers are: Dutailier, Jardine Enterprises, and Shermag.

Rocking chairs and gliders range in price from $150 to $600. In general, a higher price tag reflects solid wood construction. In the case of gliders, you'll probably get more durable cushions, a higher quality gliding system, a spring-supported seat, and a positional lock you can use to keep it from gliding. Some gliders even have a recline feature. "We used that a lot in our daughter's first weeks, when she adored sleeping on our chests and we were able to get a little sleep, too," says Jennifer Reston of Albany, Calif., mother of a toddler. Although you get what you pay for, you don't have to go whole hog. There's quality and solid construction in the midrange as well.

### Glider 101

FEATURES TO LOOK FOR:

- Solid wood construction
- Cushions that won't lump and that are covered in woven fabrics that won't fray
- High padded back for support
- A spring underneath the seat for support
- Smooth gliding mechanism
- Mechanism bearings with a warranty
- Locking mechanism
- Recline option

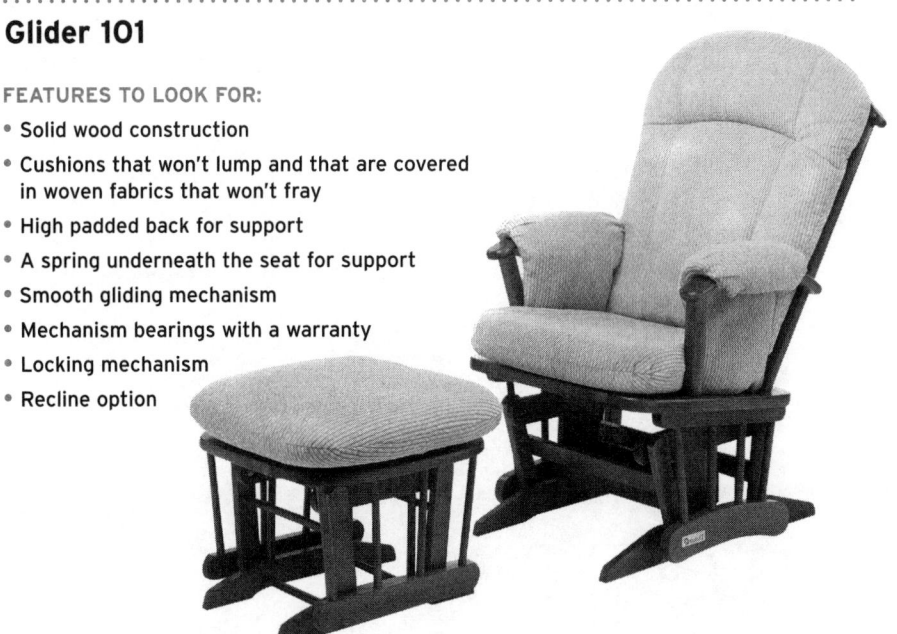

## GLIDER IN DISGUISE

**A**lthough you may be rocking your baby well into the toddler years, rocking chairs and gliders tend to have a limited use. Once your baby goes to sleep without rocking, you may find that you sit in the chair less and less—at least until the next baby comes along. To address this concern, manufacturers are now making gliders that are fully upholstered to look like a bedroom chair or one that might warm the corner of a living room if done in the right fabric.

## Recommendations

If in doubt, choose a glider over a rocker. For one thing, gliders are more comfortable, and you'll use one more than you think. You also may be able to integrate it more easily into your living room later on. Secondhand is an option, but if you opt to buy new, allow plenty of time for it to arrive before your baby is born. Although many baby stores have gliders in stock, others require ordering. Allow up to 10 weeks for delivery. Minimal assembly may be required.

If you're having a baby shower, put a glider on your wish list. While it's an expensive item, friends and family may get the idea to chip in as a group.

# Soft Infant Carriers

**B**abies love and need to be held, and carriers are a great way to keep your baby close and cozy even when you're on the go. In a sense you wear your baby, which may make him or her feel secure and ease any fussiness. If you like using a carrier (and your baby likes it too), you may even be able to postpone buying a stroller for a few months, until your baby can sit up.

The basic types of soft infant carrier are strap-on models and slings. Both are made of fabric. Strap-on carriers, as their name implies, strap onto you in front or on your back. They're the most widely used type. Slings essentially consist of a length of fabric you wrap over your shoulders. Those we've seen aren't secure enough during activities more rigorous than walking. With a primal feel to them, slings form a comfy, portable nest for infants and can be adjusted to tote toddlers. They're an option for babies who haven't reached the minimum 7 to 8 pound weight requirement of many strap-on carriers.

Some slings are made for especially small babies. "We couldn't have managed without our Weego Preemie," says Beth Klingner of Pleasantville, N.Y., mother of 1-year-old Ben, referring to a soft carrier for babies as little as 3 pounds. "Our baby was often soothed to sleep in it during the early days when nothing else seemed to work."

Many slings and strap-on carriers offer just the basics: an intimate, supported mode of transportation for baby. Others have extras such as insulated zippered pouches, toy loops, a bib, and even a diaper changing pad so you don't have to carry a separate one.

Strap-on soft carriers are an equally good option for toting a baby during the first few months. Some even allow for easy and discreet nursing, as do slings. Infants riding in a strap-on carrier face inward, while older babies can face either inward or outward. Some soft carriers can also be worn on your back.

Models with leg openings big enough for a child to slip through have been subject to recalls. Some models now come with a seat insert for newborns to guard against that, which is a feature you should look for.

## Ready to Ride

The length of a sling typically adjusts with two "O" or "D" rings worn over one shoulder. For maximum comfort, a baby should ride above your waist and below your bust line. Mastering the adjustment of rings and pleats so everything fits correctly takes time, even with clear, printed directions. If you experience back or neck discomfort from carrying most of a baby's weight on one side, give that shoulder a break by putting the sling on with the strap on the opposite shoulder.

A sling or a strap-on soft carrier can be especially useful during the early weeks and months after birth. Cranky babies can often be soothed by riding in one. "It never fails to calm my granddaughter down," says Barbara Perkins, of Lebanon, Tenn., who owns a Baby Bjorn soft carrier (not pictured).

Soft carriers offer less structural support for babies over 6 months—and less for you, too—than framed backpack carriers. Your baby will probably become too heavy and uncomfortable for a soft carrier before reaching the upper weight limits specified for most, which is typically 30 to 40 pounds. That's why, if you like carriers, we suggest switching to a framed, backpack-type carrier after your baby can sit up. (For more information, see page 39.)

Other models use straps or other means to narrow the openings. Most new strap-on models are now made to be in compliance with the leg-opening requirements of an upcoming American Society for Testing and Materials standard.

## Getting the Hang of It

You may feel a little awkward the first few times you use any type of infant carrier. To begin with, you have to figure out how to put it on. Then you have to adjust the straps or fabric so the carrier will fit your body comfortably. Last—and this is the fun part—you have to get your baby inside the carrier without provoking a fuss, then learn to trust your carrier and get used to the initially uneasy feeling of having your baby suspended.

Some manufacturers recommend that you practice with a teddy bear or doll until all steps become natural. That's not a bad idea.

Learning how to move with a sling or strap-on carrier can also take practice. You can't lean over, and your back, shoulders, and legs must adjust to the extra weight. You'll also have to be mindful of your extra dimensions when you go through doorways and around corners so your baby won't bump into anything. Although many carriers are designed to adjust and "grow" with your baby, some parents complain of lower back pain with front carriers once their baby reaches about 20 pounds. A simple rule is to stop using a carrier when you sense you're approaching your own physical limits. (You'll know.)

## Shopping Secrets

**Read the instructions in the store.** If you don't understand how to adjust and use your carrier, chances are you'll be frustrated once you get it home. Be sure to note and follow the manufacturer's weight and size limits.

**Try on a floor model.** And have your spouse do the same if you're both going to use it. (Incidentally, there are carriers designed for large-stature parents.) You'll want to be able to see if you like wearing it, and whether it will fit your baby comfortably. Keep in mind that some babies dislike any carrier that makes their head feel confined. Test for softness to make sure the carrier won't chafe your baby's skin.

**Keep your receipt.** If you or your baby don't like the sling or strap-on carrier you select, you'll want to be able to return it.

# What's Available

The major brand of sling is NoJo. Strap-on soft-carrier makers include, in alphabetical order: Baby Björn, Evenflo (Snugli), Infantino, Kelty K.I.D.S, Maclaren, Theodore Bean, and Weego.

## Slings

Made of fabric (sometimes pleated), a sling forms an over-the-shoulder "hammock" for holding a young baby across your front in a semireclined position. Some claim a maximum child weight of 30 pounds. And there is one made for twins.

**Pros:** A sling mimics the way you'd naturally carry your baby, but frees up your arms. Such a position may soothe a fussy baby. As with other kinds of carriers, you can get around easily in tight spaces where a stroller might not be able to go.

**Cons:** Having your baby's weight in the diagonally frontal position may be uncomfortable, especially if you're petite and your baby is large. Slings aren't secure enough for activity more rigorous than walking.

**Price range:** $35 to $40.

## Strap-on soft carriers

A soft carrier holds a young baby in an upright position (facing outward or inward), which he or she may like less than the curled position provided by a sling. Some soft carriers can also be worn on your back.

**Pros:** A soft carrier helps keep your hands free and allows you to hold baby snugly against your chest. With a soft carrier, as with a sling, you can take your baby where strollers can't easily go, such as on stairs and cramped elevators.

**Cons:** Our online readers report that wearing an infant carrier can put a strain on the lower back once baby weighs more than 20 pounds. Models that have a waist belt can better support the weight.

**Price range:** $20 to $100.

# Features to Consider

**Fabric**. Slings and strap-on carriers are made of fabrics such as cotton, corduroy, flannel-like materials, or moisture-resistant nylon, and come in a variety of colors and patterns. Slings and front carriers should be completely washable. If you like, wash your carrier a few times before use to soften it and remove chemical odors. Bear in mind that drying time may be long, and some carriers can be line-dried only.

**Fasteners.** Carriers have a variety of buckles and fasteners for shoulder and waist straps and babies' seats. Buckles that hold shoulder and waist straps should be easy to adjust and not allow any straps to work loose when the carrier is in use. The most effective buckles are those that require two separate actions by adult hands to unlatch. Snaps should be sturdy and require a lot of force to unfasten, which may make them inconvenient to use.

**Lumbar support.** Well-made carriers may have a special padded waist strap that helps distribute baby's weight from your shoulders to your hips and pelvic area. This is a definite comfort advantage. Fasten the belt to test that it's long enough and neither too high nor too low when the carrier is in place. Padding should be firm rather than mushy.

**Shoulder and waist straps.** Shoulder-strap padding should be firm and wide. Straps should be positioned so they won't slip off your shoulders or chafe your neck, and they should be adjustable even while you're carrying your baby.

# Recommendations

Think about how much you'll use a soft carrier. That will help you determine what to spend. A low-priced version may be fine for quick jaunts. If you foresee longer treks with baby or expect to be using your carrier a lot, consider a higher-end model. You might also wait until after your baby's born to see if the need for a carrier arises. There are carrier parents and then there are those who mostly leave their carriers hanging on a hook in the closet. Time will tell which one you are.

# Ratings • Soft Infant Carriers

**S**trap-on soft carriers are designed for babies weighing as little as 7 or 8 pounds and toddlers weighing up to 40 pounds, depending on the model. Soft carriers offer less structural support for babies over 6 months—and less for parent, too—then framed backpack carriers. Your baby will probably become too heavy and uncomfortable for a soft carrier before reaching the upper weight limits specified for most.

| | Excellent | Very good | Good | Fair | Poor |
|---|---|---|---|---|---|
| | ⊜ | ⊖ | ○ | ◒ | ● |

Within types, in performance order. Blue **key numbers indicate Quick Picks.**

| Key number | Brand & model | Price | Weight (lb) | Overall Score 0 ... 100 P F G VG E | Test results Ease of use | Comfort |
|---|---|---|---|---|---|---|
| 1 | **Kelty K.I.D.S.** The Kangaroo Soft Infant Carrier | $80 | 8 to 25 pounds | | ⊜ | ⊜ |
| 2 | **Baby Björn** Baby Carrier Active 26063 | 120 | 8 to 26 pounds | | ⊜ | ⊜ |
| 3 | **Baby Björn** BB 230 | 90 | 8 to 25 pounds | | ⊜ | ⊜ |
| 4 | **Theodore Bean** Infants & Toddlers Carrier 36201 | 50 | 8-12 pounds with newborn insert; 10 to 40 pounds | | ⊜ | ⊜ |

## Guide to the Ratings

**Overall score** is based on use as a front carrier and reflects ease of use and comfort (judged with the aid of parents). Child **weight range** is per the manufacturer. **Ease of use** considers how well the carriers fit the adult and the child, and ease of loading/unloading the child. **Comfort** considers the comfort of the straps and other parts and how balanced the carrier felt to the adult. **Price** is approximate retail.

# Quick Picks • Soft Infant Carriers

**1 Kelty** $80
**2 Baby Björn** $120

Both models come with a waist belt for the adult that helps distribute baby's weight from your shoulders to your hips and pelvic area.

CHAPTER

# 31

# Stationary Activity Centers

**T**hese all-in-one, molded-plastic play stations resemble walkers—but without the wheels. That makes them a safer alternative to traditional wheeled walkers. Most activity units have a circular frame with a rotating, high-backed seat recessed in the center and a surrounding flat tray with a variety of attached toys. Babies can use them as soon as they begin to sit up independently (some starting at about 4 months and most by 6 months). They'll outgrow them when they become fairly confident toddlers (between 12 and 15 months).

A stationary activity unit keeps your baby relatively safe in one spot while you do other things. "After our first child started crawling, a stationary unit was great because of all its toys. With it we could make dinner and maybe eat some of it, too," says Joe L. of Virginia, father of Megan, 7, and 6-month-old twin boys.

Most stationary activity centers adjust to different heights to grow with your child. The effect of those height adjustments may be reflected in the manufacturer's age recommendations, going as high as 3 years. But in most cases that's overly optimistic, in our view. You'll get the most use from a stationary activity center when your baby is between 6 and 10 months old.

## Shopping Secrets

**Do your in-store research.** The better stationary activity centers have a sturdy frame; no accessible sharp edges or hardware underneath or on top; comfortable, soft fabric edging on the sides and legs of the seat cushions; and well-designed, well-secured toys for little hands. The seat should swivel smoothly without any hitches, and there should be no gaps in the rim between the edge of the swivel mechanism and the tray that could conceivably capture small fingers. If the activity center's bottom is a saucer, its flip-down braces, which prevent it from rocking, should be sturdy.

**Go with an activity center with fewer bells and whistles** if you're worried that your baby will become overstimulated. Spending more money will get you a model with many toys and battery-operated sounds and lights. Some of them offer as many as 11 separate activities. Although many babies enjoy a wide range of options, some parents worry that the infants will become overstimulated themselves from the constant noise. Some motions may also be too much (such as swivel actions) for young children.

## What's Available

The major brands, in alphabetical order, are: Evenflo, Fisher-Price, Graco, and Safety 1st.

Models come with a solid flat base or a rocking one; some fold at the push of a button for storage. Some activity centers are bare-bones, with only a few toys, while others are more elaborate, with six or more play items vying for baby's attention. With a few adjustments, one model, the Bouncin' Baby Play Place by Safety 1st, becomes a play set for toddlers, with a small track for cars. Prices range from about $60 to $90.

## Features to Consider

**Foldability.** Some models fold—a plus for storage and travel.

**Motion.** Some activity centers are merely a stationary seat with a toy or two. Others feature a seat that swivels 360 degrees, with springs allowing the unit to bounce when baby moves as well as providing a rocking motion.

**Pushdown tabs.** These anchor the seat in a stationary position. They're a must to keep a rocking activity center from becoming too turbulent or if you want to feed your baby in his or her activity center.

**Seat.** Many models have seat heights that adjust to three or four levels, which allows an activity center to grow with your baby. More expensive models have thicker padding. Seat pads are often removable for cleaning, which is a plus.

**Toys.** All activity centers feature a play tray with attached interactive toys, such as a spinning ball, mirrors, clackers, and rings. You'll also find models that come with soft toys and electronic gizmos that produce sounds and lights. Some models have a detachable keyboard/sound-maker. In general, more expensive models are loaded with toys and produce more sound. The Step and Play Piano by Fisher-Price, for example, which retails for $90, lets babies move forward and back along a track system to play four different-colored keys at their feet— reminiscent of the movie *Big* with Tom Hanks. Meanwhile, baby can also play the same keys at hand level as well as various other musical toys, such as a squeaky trumpet.

## Recommendations

Stationary activity centers with a solid, flat base are the most stable. Examine any attached toys for size. To reduce the risk of choking, they should be too large to fit through the center of a toilet-paper roll (about 1¾ inches in diameter).

Although most babies enjoy being in one of these, some don't. If you can, have your baby test-drive a unit in the store or during play dates at other parents' homes to get a sense of how he or she fares. If you settle on one, resist the urge to routinely park your baby in it. Having your child in a stationary activity center for more than 30 minutes at a time can tax a baby's naturally weak back and leg muscles.

And even though a stationary activity center can give you a chance to grab a bite (sans a baby in your lap) or even take a quick shower, always keep an eye on your baby while he or she is in it. Also, keep the stationary entertainer away from hot surfaces, dangling appliance cords, window blinds, and sources of water such as a swimming pool.

Two brands of activity centers bear the Juvenile Products Manu-facturers Association (JPMA) certification seal: Graco (Little Tikes) and Dorel Juvenile Group (Safety 1st).

Note: These products were not tested by Consumers Union. This alphabetical listing does not include all models available but rather is a selection of some widely distributed ones. Descriptions are derived from the manufacturers' claims. Prices are approximate retail. For manufacturer contact information, see the Brand Locator, starting on page 283.

| Line/model | Price | Details |
|---|---|---|
| **EVENFLO** | | |
| MegaSaucer | $60 | Features three-position seat-height adjustment, three flip-down stabilizers, and removable, washable seat pad. Baby can swivel, bounce, rock, and play with nine surrounding toys. Plays 15 sounds and lights. |
| ExerSaucer Classic | $60 | Features three-position seat-height adjustment, three flip-down stabilizers, and removable, washable seat pad. Baby can rock, spin, and/or bounce, and play with seven surrounding toys. |
| Portable Fun UltraSaucer | $80 | Features three-position seat-height adjustment, three flip-down stabilizers, built-in carrying handle, and removable, washable seat pad. Baby can swivel, bounce, rock, and play with 11 surrounding toys. Plays sounds and songs. Folds for travel or storage. |
| **FISHER-PRICE** | | |
| Step and Play Piano | $90 | Features a seat that glides along a track. Baby can press colored piano keys with his or her feet. Same keys are represented at hand level as are several other musical instruments, such as a squeaky trumpet. |
| **GRACO** | | |
| Rocking Entertainer | $50 | Saucer-shaped unit rocks slightly, and its three-height-position seat swivels so baby can reach toys from all angles. Features seven interactive toys. |
| Little Tikes Ocean Friends | $60 | Saucer-shaped unit rocks slightly or can be stabilized by engaging its push-down feet. Three-height-position seat swivels so baby can reach toys from all angles. Features nine surrounding interactive toys. |
| Nursery Rhyme Entertainer | $70 | Saucer-shaped unit rocks slightly or can be stabilized by engaging its push-down feet. Three-height-position seat swivels so baby can reach toys from all angles. Features six surrounding interactive toys. |

| Line/model | Price | Details |
| --- | --- | --- |
| **Little Tikes Convertible Entertainer** | $80 | Saucer-shaped unit rocks slightly or can be stabilized by engaging its push-down feet. Three-height-position seat swivels so baby can reach toys from all angles. Features 14 surrounding and overhead interactive toys with lights, sound, and voice recognition. Cloth seat is machine-washable. |
| **SAFETY 1ST** | | |
| **Bouncin' Baby Play Place** | $50 | Saucer-shaped unit bounces with baby's movements. Three-height-position seat swivels 360 degrees. Features 10 interactive toys, three sounds, and six songs. Converts to a floor play set for toddlers. Padded seat is machine-washable. |

CHAPTER

# 32

# Strollers

Having a new baby can be a walk in the park—with the right stroller, of course. In fact, a stroller is one of the most important pieces of baby gear you'll buy. And as your baby grows, you may end up with more than one. Many parents buy a traditional stroller for everyday use plus a lighter-weight one for traveling. You may even want a more rugged stroller for jogging or simply negotiating uneven sidewalks and curbs. City streets are deceptively hard on strollers.

There are dozens of choices on the market, including umbrella strollers, carriages, travel systems, jogging strollers, and models designed to carry two or more children. You can also find a bare-bones frame that accepts almost any infant seat.

For a newborn, consider a fully reclining stroller with leg holes you can close. Another option is buying a stroller that is not for a newborn but that allows you to attach an infant car seat, usually made by the same manufacturer. When your child outgrows the infant seat—typically at about 6 months or 20 pounds—you then can use the stroller alone. Another alternative is a travel system, which consists of an infant car seat, a car-seat base, and a stroller. They are increasingly popular.

Pricier strollers now have air-filled tires for a more comfortable ride. Five-point harnesses, a safety feature that better secures baby, are almost standard on higher-priced models. Most strollers these days also have cup holders and trays for parents and for the child. Some are even rigged for sound, an added feature that will, of course, cost you.

Strollers that don't fully recline or that can't accommodate an infant car seat are fine for babies older than 6 months, when they are no longer vulnerable to slipping through the leg openings.

## Shopping Secrets

**Select it yourself.** Strollers are popular baby gifts and shower presents. Still, you should shop for a stroller yourself then register for it at a department or baby store if you want to receive it as a gift because you're the best judge of how you intend to use it. If you receive a stroller you didn't select yourself, make sure you want to keep it. Strollers, like cars, are highly personal buying decisions. You'll probably use your stroller often, and your baby will spend a lot of time in it. You should love the one you end up with.

**Don't go by price alone.** A higher price doesn't always mean higher quality. CONSUMER REPORTS' tests have shown that some economical strollers can perform as well as or even better than models priced hundreds of dollars more. Even the most sophisticated models can suffer typical stroller flaws: malfunctioning wheels, frames that bend out of shape, locking mechanisms that fail, safety belts that come loose, or buckles that break.

**Don't assume lighter is better.** Thanks to design changes during the past decade or so, strollers have become smaller, lighter, and easier to maneuver. Increasingly, manufacturers are forgoing steel for aluminum, which can reduce stroller weight by a few pounds, though it raises the price substantially. But lighter strollers may not hold up as well, especially if you're an urban dweller. You'll need a model that can take cobblestones, curbs, and disjointed sidewalks—again and again.

**Give it a test drive.** When you're shopping, take the models you're considering for a spin in the store. Practice the one-arm open-close move. Try opening, folding, and lifting the stroller with one hand, because your other arm will often be holding your baby. Make sure you can stand tall when you push the stroller and that your legs and feet don't hit the wheels as you walk. If both you and your spouse are going to be using the stroller, you should both try it out. Some models have adjustable handles, an important feature if one parent is significantly taller than the other.

If possible, take the floor model of the stroller you're considering out to your car to be sure that it will fit in your trunk when it's folded. Also, jiggle the stroller. The frame should feel solid, not loose. Compare maneuverability.

**Consider your baby's age.** Newborns can't sit up, so they need a stroller that allows them to lie on their backs for the first few months of life or one that accepts an infant car seat. Avoid traditional strollers that don't recline—including umbrella-style strollers—until your child can sit up, usually at about 6 months of age. Some strollers that do fully recline aren't appropriate for newborns because they have large leg openings that could trap and possibly strangle a baby.

**Think about where you'll do most of your strolling.** City dwellers who rely on subways, buses, and cabs are going to need a sturdy stroller that folds quickly and compactly. Suburban parents who drive a lot may find that a travel system better suits their needs. It's easier to get baby in and out of the car and stroller in the detachable infant car seat. If you're athletic, you might also want a jogging stroller to use during runs or serious walking workouts. If you live in the country, on the beach, or in a snowy climate, an all-terrain model may be what you need.

**Size up storage capabilities**. A stroller with a

**"**We purchased the Graco Leisure Sport Travel System, a three-wheel stroller with large inflatable tires. It's perfect for the dirt/sand roads where we live.**"**

–**Rebecca Havourd,** Pinckney, Mich., mother of 18-month-old Rocco

large shopping basket makes life easier for those who get around town mostly on foot. If you opt for a model that reclines, make sure you can reach the basket if the seat back is reclined, or, if it's a travel system, when the infant car seat is in place.

**Evaluate warranties and return policies.** Most stroller manufacturers and retailers have warranties that cover poor workmanship and inherent flaws. But they won't necessarily take the unit back if it malfunctions in some way. Manufacturers may either refer you to the store for a replacement or insist that you ship the stroller back for repair—at your expense—leaving you stranded without baby wheels. Your best bet is to purchase the stroller from a store, catalog, or Web site that offers a 100 percent satisfaction guarantee.

**Check certification.** Somewhere on a stroller's frame or carton there should be a certification sticker showing that the stroller meets the minimum requirements of the American Society for Testing and Materials voluntary standard and that its manufacturer participates in the pass/fail certification program administered by the Juvenile Products Manufacturers Association. The key tests are for safety belts, brakes, leg openings, and locking mechanisms that prevent accidental folding, as well as for stability and the absence of sharp edges. The program is voluntary, and models from uncertified companies may be as safe as those from certified ones. But all things being equal, choose a certified model. Companies that are certified as of this printing are: Baby Trend, Britax, Bugaboo, Delta, Dorel, Evenflo, G&A USA Group, Graco, J. Mason, Kidco, Kolcraft, Maclaren, and Peg Perego.

## What's Available

The biggest selling brands of single strollers are, in alphabetical order: Baby Trend, Combi, Evenflo, Graco, Kolcraft, Maclaren, and Peg Perego. Newer boutique brands that are gaining ground include Bugaboo and Mountain Buggy.

Because newborns can't sit up without support, they can't ride in a standard stroller. You'll find the following basic choices for babies younger than 6 months:

## Seat carrier frames

These lightweight, empty frames are designed to roll an infant car seat around, using it as the passenger compartment.

**Pros:** Inexpensive, compact, and convenient.

**Cons:** Both the car seat and the frame can no longer serve as your stroller once your child outgrows the seat (typically at 6 months to a year).

**Price range:** $50 to $60.

## Carriage/strollers

These models have backrests that fully recline, providing sleeping space for infants. Once your child can sit up—at about 6 months — this type can convert to a stroller configuration. Some units have large, spoked wheels and compartments that can be removed and used as a bassinet. We didn't test these for this book since they are no longer very popular and few manufacturers produce them.

**Pros:** Can be used for newborns and are convenient.

**Cons:** Difficult to carry on public transportation, and you still need a car seat.

**Price range:** $50 to $600.

## Travel systems

These combine a stroller and infant car seat and are for use with newborns to toddlers. With some models you can use either the stroller or car seat with a newborn; in others, you use the car seat until the child outgrows it, usually at about 22 pounds, then switch to using the stroller alone.

**Pros:** Allows you to move a sleeping baby in the infant car seat undisturbed from car to stroller.

**Cons:** If you select the car seat first, you have to live with the stroller it mates with (and vice versa). An alternative is to choose a stroller that accepts car seats from a number of different manufacturers.

**Price range:** $100 to $400.

## Multiseat strollers

Similar to other strollers, these give you a relatively efficient means of taking twins or triplets (or young siblings of different ages) for a ride.

Most companies that manufacture strollers for one also make a version with two or more seats. Multiseaters offer the same features as strollers for a single rider, just a larger-scale construction. Alternatives include strollers with a standing bench or small seat in the rear that lets a second child hitch a ride. The major brands of multiseat strollers are Cosco, Graco, and Kolcraft, as well as higher-end imports such as Combi, Maclaren, Mountain Buggy, and Peg Perego.

Multiseat strollers usually come in one of two configurations: tandem or side-by-side. Tandem models, the most common type of multiseat stroller, have one seat directly behind the other. They're the same width as single-passenger strollers and the best choice overall. However, while the backseat can recline, the front one usually can't without infringing on the space of the rear passenger. Some tandem strollers let you set the seats so that the children face each other; others have a "stadium seat" arrangement that allows the child in back to see over the one in front.

**Pros (tandem):** Tandems easily go through standard doorways. A folded tandem takes up just a little more space than a folded standard midweight stroller.

**Cons (tandem):** Steering can be difficult, and it can be tricky getting over a curb. Some models offer limited leg support and very little legroom for the rear passenger.

**Price range (tandem):** $100 to $500.

Side-by-side, the other configuration, consists of two seats attached to a single frame or a unit resembling two strollers bolted together. You can also create your own by joining two umbrella strollers with a set of screw-on brackets—available at baby discount chains and specialty stores. The features on side-by-side strollers are similar to what you'll find on single-passenger models. This type works best for children of about the same weight, such as twins. Each of the seats has an independent reclining mechanism.

**Pros (side-by-side):** A side-by-side model goes up curbs more easily than a tandem, although when children of different weights ride in the unit, it may veer to one side.

**Cons (side-by-side):** Most side-by-side models can't be used with infant car seats. A folded side-by-side stroller requires twice as much space as the equivalent single-occupant version. Although manufacturers may claim that a stroller is slender enough to go through a standard doorway, you'd be wise to measure both the stroller and any doors or other openings you plan to wheel it through.

**Price range (side-by-side):** $100 to $500.

## Down the Road

Stroller types appropriate for babies older than 6 months include:

### Traditional strollers

This category runs the gamut from lightweight umbrella strollers (named for their curved, umbrella-like handles), which typically weigh less than 12 pounds, to more heavy-duty conventional strollers that weigh 17 to 35 pounds. The latter are somewhat bulky but quite stable, deep, and roomy. Higher-end models may have shock absorbers on all wheels as well.

For folding, many strollers employ a one-handed release embedded in the handlebar. You flip a lock switch or move the casing of the latch mechanism to one side, then push the handlebar forward until the frame begins to fold.

**Pros:** Many are lightweight and convenient.

**Cons:** Heavier models are difficult to carry on public transportation and to lift into car trunks or minivan cargo areas. And you still need a car seat. The small wheels on low-end models don't perform well on uneven sidewalks or rough terrain. The compact size of umbrella strollers and other lighter-weight models may cramp toddlers, especially when they're dressed in heavy winter clothes.

**Price range:** $20 (umbrella strollers) to $300 (high-end conventional strollers).

### Jogging or all-terrain strollers

These three- and four-wheeled strollers or traditional-style strollers with heavy-duty suspensions and/or air-filled tires let you push your child semireclined in a canvas pouch while you walk (or in some cases, jog or even race). The larger the wheels, the easier it is for the pusher. Like a bicycle, a jogging or all-terrain stroller is made of metal tubing, has wheels with spokes, and rides on air-filled tires. It has large wheels that are 12 to 20 inches in diameter—two in the rear and one or two in front. The long, high handlebar is designed to help keep your running feet and legs away from the stroller's frame and legs, but you still may have to adjust your gait to avoid bumping into the unit.

The appropriate minimum age for children to ride in a jogging or all-terrain stroller is a matter of debate, although one brand, Mountain Buggy, makes an all-terrain stroller that can be used as a carriage. For more conventional jogging/all-terrain strollers, manufacturers typically suggest 8 weeks, but our medical consultants say a baby should be at least 6 months, able to sit up, and have some head support to withstand the potentially jarring ride.

**Pros:** Good for off-road use; provides a relatively smooth ride over obstacles such as rocks, potholes, and uneven sidewalks. A jogging/all-terrain stroller typically has a longer useful life than a plain stroller, with some models able to accommodate a child as heavy as 75 pounds. Several companies offer double- and triple-sports strollers with a total weight limit of up to 100 pounds or 150 pounds, respectively.

**Cons:** Can be unstable when the rear wheels are lifted over a curb. Not suitable for infants younger than 6 months (unless it converts from a carriage convertible). They also require more space than other strollers, and you may need to remove the stroller's wheels to fit it in the trunk of your car. Bicycle-type tires can go flat and require reinflating with a bicycle pump or a gas-station hose.

**Price range:** $120 to $600, depending on the number of seats.

## Features to Consider

**Brakes.** Brakes are especially important with jogging and all-terrain strollers since you may be using the stroller at a good clip and need to slow down quickly. Most have two types of brakes: a bicycle-style hand brake for slowing down and a foot-applied brake, used when the stroller is parked or to hold it on a sloping surface.

**Canopy.** Meant to protect baby from sun or rain, canopies range from a simple fabric square strung between two wires to deep, pull-down versions that shield almost the entire front of the stroller. Some canopies also have a clear plastic "peekaboo" window on top so you can keep an eye on your baby while you're strolling. The window (or viewing port) is a nice feature; you'll use it more than you think you might.

**Cup holders.** Many strollers have a cup holder for the pusher as well as one for the small passenger. They're a welcome feature for both.

**Five-point harness.** The best models offer an adjustable five-point harness (two straps over the shoulders, two for the thighs, and a crotch strap), much like those found in car seats, which help keep a baby or toddler from slipping out (or climbing out when you're not looking). The straps should be height-adjustable for proper fit, and they should be securely anchored.

**Footrests.** Footrests can help a child sit more comfortably without legs dangling. Even the flimsiest strollers offer some type of footrest, yet most are too low to help any but the tallest toddlers. For that reason, make certain that the seat rim is soft and won't press uncomfortably into the back of your child's legs.

**Handlebars.** Adjustable handlebars can be extended or angled to accommodate parents of different heights. Reversible handles allow you to swing them over the top of the stroller, then lock them into a front position so baby rides facing you. A single crossbar not only allows for one-handed steering but also generally makes the stroller more stable and controllable. Umbrella strollers and other models with two independent handles almost always require two hands to maneuver.

**Large shopping basket.** A roomy, easily accessible storage basket underneath the stroller makes errands with baby much easier. Sizes of baskets vary. Try to choose one that's at least big enough to accommodate a diaper bag. When shopping for a stroller, press on the storage basket's floor—it shouldn't drag on the ground when loaded. Some strollers also offer storage pouches, with elastic top edges, in back. With other strollers, you can buy a net bag that fastens onto the handle—

good for carrying snacks, but nothing much heavier than that.

**Leg holes.** Carriage/strollers, which fully recline, must have leg holes that close so an infant can't slip through one of them. Typically, manufacturers use mesh shields or hinged, molded footrests that raise and clamp over the leg holes. According to the industry's voluntary standard, a stroller with leg holes that can't be closed off shouldn't be able to fully recline, which is meant to prevent its use with a newborn.

**One-handed opening/folding mechanism.** Essential for when you need to open or fold the stroller with one hand while holding baby with the other. The best strollers fold compactly in a matter of seconds.

**Play tray.** Strollers may have a tray where babies can play, dribble milk, drop crumbs, or just rest their hands. If the tray comes with attached toys, check their size and make sure they are securely fastened. Some strollers have been recalled because small parts on their play trays' toys pose a choking hazard. Instead of a tray, other models have a front

## TIPS FOR SAFER STROLLING

* Never leave children unattended in a stroller, especially when they're asleep. They may slip into a leg opening and strangle.
* Use the safety belt or harness to restrain children and prevent tipping.
* To avoid the possibility of injuries, don't overload the stroller with a child heavier than the manufacturer's weight limit, and don't put more children in the stroller than its design allows.
* Don't hang heavy bags on stroller handles, which can cause the stroller to tip.
* Make sure the frame locking mechanism is properly engaged to avoid collapse, and use the parking brake when you're stopped, especially on an incline.
* Keep your child away from the stroller when you're folding and unfolding it to avoid pinched fingers.
* Never use a pillow, folded quilt, or blanket as a mattress in a stroller or baby carriage. They're a suffocation risk.
* Return the stroller warranty card so you can be notified of a recall, or sign up for the Consumer Product Safety Commission's e-mail subscription list at *www.cpsc.gov/cpsclist.asp*. Updated recall information will be sent directly to you via e-mail.

bar to help keep baby restrained with the attached crotch strap. To make it easier to get a squirming baby or toddler seated, the bar should be removable or swing open rather than be permanently attached.

**Shock absorbers.** Air-filled tires or tires molded from foam can help give baby a smoother ride. So can shock absorbers—covered springs or rubber pads above the wheel assemblies. In all strollers the frame reduces some jarring.

**Wheels.** The larger the wheels, the easier it is to negotiate curbs and rough surfaces. But big wheels eat up trunk space. Most strollers have double wheels on the front that swivel to make steering easier. Front wheels often have two positions: full swivel for smooth surfaces or locked in one position for rough terrain. Misaligned and loose wheels are a chronic stroller problem. One sign of good construction is that the wheels of a stroller contact the floor uniformly when there's a baby inside. Some manufacturers have created wheel assemblies that can be completely slipped off the frame for easy replacement, which is a plus.

## Recommendations

Your first decision is which of the types of strollers discussed earlier in this chapter you want to buy. As we mention, you may want to have more than one—such as a traditional stroller and a lighter-weight model for traveling. After you've made that decision, consult the Ratings on the next page for advice on specific makes and models.

# Ratings • Strollers

**N**ow that parents tote their children practically everywhere, there seem to be strollers for all occasions, lifestyles, and budgets: from $20 umbrella strollers to $800 European prams, with joggers, tandems, and even sport-utility-inspired models priced in-between. Increasingly, many parents are choosing car seat/stroller combinations in which the car seat fits in the stroller. Pricier strollers now have air-filled tires. Five-point harnesses, a safety feature that better secures baby, are almost standard on higher-priced models. Formerly deluxe extras such as cup holders and trays now appear on most models.

|  | Excellent | Very good | Good | Fair | Poor |
|---|---|---|---|---|---|
|  | ⊖ | ⊖ | ○ | ◑ | ● |

**Within types, in performance order.** Blue **key numbers indicate Quick Picks; see page 237.**

| Key number | Brand & model | Price | Overall score | Car-seat compatible | Ease of use | Safety | Durability |
|---|---|---|---|---|---|---|---|
|  | Similar models in small type. |  | 0 ————— 100  P F G VG E |  |  |  |  |
|  | **TRADITIONAL STROLLERS** |  |  |  |  |  |  |
| 1 | **Peg Perego** Aria | $170 |  | ✔ | ⊖ | ⊖ | ⊖ |
| 2 | **Graco** MetroLite 6111 | 135 |  | ✔ | ⊖ | ⊖ | ⊖ |
| 3 | **Graco** CitiLite 6474 **D** 6479 | 100 |  |  | ⊖ | ⊖ | ⊖ |
| 4 | **Maclaren** Volo | 110 |  |  | ⊖ | ⊖ | ⊖ |
| 5 | **Kolcraft** GS Cruiser 46843 | 50 |  |  | ⊖ | ⊖ | ⊖ |
| 6 | **Peg Perego** Pliko Trek SNG | 260 |  | ✔ | ◑ | ⊖ | ⊖ |
| 7 | **Combi** Perfect Match 6630 | 120 |  | ✔ | ⊖ | ⊖ | ⊖ |
| 8 | **Combi** Travel Savvy 2120 | 80 |  |  | ⊖ | ⊖ | ◑ |
| 9 | **Fisher-Price** Comfort Lite LX | 80 |  |  | ○ | ◑ | ⊖ |
| 10 | **Bertini** M5 Shuttle | 310 |  |  | ○ | ◑ | ○ |
|  | **ALL-TERRAIN AND JOGGING STROLLERS (THREE-WHEEL STYLE)** |  |  |  |  |  |  |
| 11 | **Safety 1st** (Cosco) Two Ways 01-648 | 115 |  |  | ○ | ⊖ | ⊖ |
| 12 | **Kolcraft** Jeep Liberty Limited 55157 | 120 |  |  | ○ | ⊖ | ⊖ |
| 13 | **Baby Trend** Expedition 9112 | 110 |  |  | ◑ | ⊖ | ● |
|  | *The following jogging stroller lacks an effective parking brake. We don't recommend it if you expect to park it.* |  |  |  |  |  |  |
| 14 | **Baby Jogger** SJ3-16 | 300 |  |  | ○ | ● | ⊖ |
|  | **DOUBLE STROLLERS (SIDE-BY-SIDE STYLE)** |  |  |  |  |  |  |
| 15 | **Maclaren** Twin Traveller | $350 |  |  | ○ | ⊖ | ⊖ |
| 16 | **Combi** Twin Savvy 7030 | 335 |  |  | ○ | ⊖ | ⊖ |
| 17 | **Baby Trend** Expedition Double 9192 | 170 |  |  | ○ | ⊖ | ⊖ |
|  | **DOUBLE STROLLERS (TANDEM STYLE)** |  |  |  |  |  |  |
| 18 | **Peg Perego** Ganciomatic Duette | 500 |  | ✔ | ○ | ⊖ | ⊖ |
| 19 | **Fisher Price** Comfort Lite Tandem LX | 95 |  |  | ○ | ⊖ | ○ |

| | Brand & model | Price | Overall score | Car-seat compatible | Ease of use | Safety | Durability |
|---|---|---|---|---|---|---|---|
| | **TRAVEL SYSTEMS (SCORES ARE FOR THE STROLLER ONLY)** | | | | | | |
| 20 | **Evenflo** Journey Premier 5441383 | 180 | ▬▬▬▬ | ✔ | ⊖ | ⊖ | ⊖ |
| 21 | **Graco** Sterling 7425 | 180 | ▬▬▬▬ | ✔ | ⊖ | ⊖ | ⊖ |
| 22 | **Eddie Bauer** (Cosco) Lightweight 01-754 | 200 | ▬▬▬ | ✔ | ⊖ | ⊖ | ○ |
| 23 | **Evenflo** PortAbout 5 | 150 | ▬▬ | ✔ | ⊖ | ⊖ | ● |

## Guide to the Ratings

**Overall score** is based on ease of use, safety, and durability. **Ease of use** was judged by trained staffers and includes feature evaluations and assessments of opening, folding, pushing straight, pushing through turns, going up/down curbs, loading baskets, and using the stroller with a car seat where applicable. **Safety** was assessed on the basis of safe design for this age group. To assess durability, we exposed the strollers to static loads of up to 100 pounds in the seat, opened and closed each stroller 400 times, and cycled each with a maximum load over the equivalent of about 50 miles of bumpy pavement. **Price** is approximate retail. Travel-system Ratings do not include tests of the car seats included with the system.

# Quick Picks • Strollers

**Traditional stroller**
> 1 **Peg Perego** $170
> 2 **Graco** $135

The top-rated Peg Perego is an excellent, lightweight choice that is very easy to use, although its harness is tricky. It can accommodate a car seat. The lower-priced Graco is also a very good car-seat-compatible model.

**All-terrain**
> 11 **Safety 1st** $115

This stroller was best in the category, although all three-wheel strollers, including this model, can become unstable when lifted to mount curbs.

**Double stroller**
> 17 **Baby Trend** $170
> 18 **Peg Perego** $500

Expect some compromises. The Baby Trend, a three-wheel, side-by-side model, performed well but was unstable when the rear wheels were lifted to mount curbs. The Peg Perego was the top-rated tandem model and works with infant car seats from the manufacturer, but it's pricey.

**Travel system**
> 20 **Evenflo** $180

This stroller, which comes with the PortAbout 5 car seat, is our top-rated model. It has a visual indicator that lets you know when the car seat is secured in the stroller. Note: Early production models (fall 2003) had front wheels that came off during folding/unfolding. Evenflo provided new wheels to consumers who experienced this problem. Evenflo informed us that it is now using different wheels and has resolved the issue.

# 33

# Swings

A baby swing can be handy for soothing a crying baby or occupying him or her while you get things done nearby. "Graco's six-speed swing was our 'drug of choice' when my daughter was 3 months old and counting," says Kelly Spallone of Reno, Nev., mother of a baby girl. "It allowed me to cook dinner and do other kitchen activities while I kept an eye on her."

Designed for indoor use, baby swings typically consist of a seat suspended by a pair of arms attached to a frame with wide-standing, tubular-metal legs. Swings come in windup and battery-operated models. To make a windup model swing, you crank a handle at the top or side of the frame, which provides 20 to 30 minutes of movement. Battery-operated swings are driven by a motor that generally uses four D batteries. Such models emit a low churning noise with each passage of the swing. Most of the swings on the market today are battery-operated.

With either a windup or battery-powered mechanism, swings are lightweight and can be easily moved from room to room, although some are more maneuverable than

## Swings on the Go

If you think you'll be moving your swing from room to room often, are short on living space, or want the option of throwing your swing into the car for road trips, consider a travel version, which has a low profile and a sturdy carrying handle.

The Fisher-Price Deluxe Take-Along Swing ($60) is just one example of a travel swing that has all the options of a full-size swing in a compact, portable design.

others. Standard-size swings eat up a fair amount of room, so they may not be for you if floor space is scarce.

Some parents of colicky babies swear by swings. Other parents say they get by just fine without one. You may find that a swing comes in handy if your baby needs to sleep in a semi-upright position due to a cold or stuffy nose (although a bouncer seat may do the trick as well).

## Shopping Secrets

**Decide whether you want a windup or battery-operated swing.** A windup model may be perfectly adequate as long as it's stable and has a well-padded, reclining seat that affords easy access. Battery-operated models usually have a sleeker design plus more features, such as speed controls, baby-sound activation, and toys attached to a front play tray. However, many parents find the motors noisy. If possible, try display models in the store (with batteries) or double-check the store's return policy. Then, test the swing as soon as you get home so you'll have the option of taking it back within the time allowed.

**Try your baby out in a friend's swing or bring baby to the store with you for test runs** when you're shopping. Keep in mind that your baby may not like the motion of a swing at first, although that could change after a few tries. Your baby's reactions may help you decide on one brand over another, or whether you're even a candidate for a swing in the first place.

## What's Available

The major brands of baby swings are, in alphabetical order: Fisher-

Price, Graco, J. Mason, and Kolcraft. Prices for windup swings range from $40 to $65. The price range for battery-operated swings is $70 to $100.

## Features to Consider

**Crotch post.** A built-in crotch post prevents a baby from sliding out of the seat—an extra safety measure. There should also be a safety belt, which most models have.

**Frames.** Swings without a top crossbar make it easier to put your baby in and take him or her out again. At the very least, look for a swing that has a wide, sturdy stance and folds or dismantles for storage.

**Seat cover.** Look for plush padding that's machine-washable.

**Seat settings.** Multiple reclining positions can help you find the most soothing posture for your baby, which is especially important if baby likes to nap while swinging (a common combo).

**Speeds.** Some battery-operated swings give you up to eight speeds, but more than four is overkill. The faster speeds may annoy rather than relax your baby.

**Swinging motion.** Some swings, such as the Fisher-Price Ocean Wonders Aquarium Cradle Swing, have two swinging motions: side to side and front to back. That's nice but not essential.

**Timer.** Some models feature a time-remaining indicator that can help you keep tabs on the action.

**Toys.** Many swings come equipped with toy bars or trays, which is an option your baby may enjoy. But make sure they're within reach so your baby can actually touch them. Also check that they're safely attached and have no small parts that might cause choking.

### SWING SAFETY

- Never leave your baby unattended in a swing.
- Always use the safety belt provided.
- Limit the amount of time your baby swings, especially at a high or fast setting. More swinging time can make some babies dizzy. If you're drowsy while your baby's swinging, turn the swing off before you fall asleep. You don't want to wake up and find that your baby has been swinging for hours.
- With battery-powered swings, start with the lowest setting—high settings may be too rough for your baby.
- Always follow the manufacturer's age and weight specifications.
- Stop using the swing when your child attempts to climb out.

The following companies make Juvenile Products Manufacturers Association-certified infant swings: Fisher-Price, Graco, J. Mason, and Kolcraft. Swings are also covered by the federal safety standard for small parts. Some models of baby swings have been recalled in recent years. Problems have included loose screws on the swing's support arm that caused the seat to separate and drop to one side, a seat that wasn't properly attached, swing frames that weren't stable, frames or seats with sharp edges, harnesses that could entangle a child, and hazardous toys.

Nice but not necessary extras include a front tray, with or without attached toys; sound (classical music and lullabies), which may or may not be soothing to little ones and grown-ups; a light display; storage baskets on the side to hold toys and accessories; and a remote control to activate the swinging action, music, or both. Some swings, such as the Deluxe Smart Response Swing by Fisher-Price, try to sense when baby needs comforting and respond automatically. A built-in sound sensor "hears" baby's sounds and responds by swinging and/or playing music.

## Recommendations

Look for a swing that has a sturdy, stable frame with strong posts and legs as well as a wide stance to prevent tipping. The bottom of the legs or frame should not protrude so far that you're likely to trip over them, however. Examine the seat. It should be well padded and have a crotch post (if it's not a travel version) to prevent your baby from sliding out. It should also offer a partially reclined position for snoozing. You'll also want a secure safety belt.

If you buy a model with a cradle or bassinet attachment, make sure it's well mounted underneath, with no potential for breaking loose. If you opt for a battery-operated swing, come equipped with four C or D cell batteries to test products in the store and hear the sound of the motor (a deal-killer for many parents). As a rule, swings don't come with batteries included.

**N**ote: These products were not tested by Consumers Union. This alphabetical listing does not include all models available but rather is a selection of some widely distributed ones. Descriptions are derived from the manufacturers' claims. Prices are approximate retail. For manufacturer contact information, see the Brand Locator, starting on page 283.

| Line/model | Price | Details |
|---|---|---|
| **FISHER-PRICE** | | |
| Open Top Take-Along | $40 | Portable, folds compactly. Five speeds. Baby sits low to ground. Open top for easy in and out. Requires four C batteries. |
| Deluxe Take-Along | $60 | Portable. Eight swing speeds. Baby sits low to ground. Twinkling lights. Plays five songs with volume control. Pull toys activate music and lights. Requires four C batteries. |
| Smart Response model B2108 | $70 | Sound sensor automatically responds by swinging and playing music. Five swinging speeds. Three-position seat recline. Three-position interactive toy bar. Requires four D batteries. Similar B1636 includes folding canopy with three plush toys, $70. |
| Deluxe Smart Response | $80 | Sound sensor automatically responds by swinging and playing music. Interactive, removable toy tray. Five swinging speeds. Three-position seat recline. Requires four D batteries. |
| Quick Response Swing with Remote Control | $90 | Five swing speeds. Three-position seat recline. Remote control activates swinging and/or music. Three-position toy bar with detachable toys. Requires four D batteries. Similar: Deluxe Quick Response with Remote Control, and toy tray, $90. |
| Ocean Wonders Aquarium Cradle | $100 | Swings side to side or front to back. Six speeds. Two-position reclining seat. Motorized mobile with four plush toys. Eight songs and three soothing sounds. Removable toy tray. Requires four D batteries. Similar: Cradle Swing without ocean theme, music, or sounds, $80. |
| **GRACO** | | |
| Quiet Wind-Up model 1143 | $40 | Quiet wind-up design. Three-position seat recline. Tray with two toys. Similar: Quiet Wind-Up 1130 with no toys on tray, $30. |
| 2-Speed OpenTop model 1481 | $50 | Battery-operated, two-speed control. Three-position seat recline. Two toys on tray. Requires four D batteries. Similar 2-Speed OpenTop 142 includes flip-open tray, mobile with three soft toys, and four-position seat recline, $70. |

| Line/model | Price | Details |
|---|---|---|
| **Travel Lite model 1850** | $60 | Stores compactly. Sits low to ground. Reclining seat. Rotating canopy and handle. Flashing lights and music. Swings with baby's momentum. No batteries required. Similar: 1870, includes detachable cold-weather boot and canopy with sun protection, $70. |
| **6-Speed OpenTop model 1484** | $70 | Six speeds. Four-position seat recline. Easy-entry, flip open tray. Plays 15 tunes. Two tray toys and mobile with three soft toys. Requires four D batteries. Similar six-speed models: 1488 has overhead mobile, no tray toys, $80; 1491 has coordinating blanket and a bead bar on toy tray, $90; 1490 has enhanced infant soft head support, no blanket, $100; 1494 has two electronic tray toys, infant head support, no blanket, $100; 1946 has blanket, two electronic tray toys that respond with sounds to baby's touch, soft infant head support, mobile with three soft toys, $110. |
| **J. MASON** | | |
| **Single Speed Swing** | $40 | Open top design. Flip-open tray. Three-position seat recline. Three-point restraint harness. Requires four D batteries. |
| **3-Speed Swing** | $60 | Open-top design. Flip open tray. Three speeds. Three-position seat recline. Three-point restraint harness. Requires four D batteries. |
| **6-Speed Open Aire** | $75 to $85 | Retractable canopy. Reclining seat back. Six speeds with music. Toy tray. Requires four D batteries. |
| **KOLCRAFT** | | |
| **Perfect Height Swing with Mini Maestro** | $60 to $95 | Height adjustable. Seat locks for feeding. Removable infant head support. Variable speed control. Seat reclines for napping. Removable snack tray. Musical toy bar. Folds for storage. Requires four D and three AA batteries. |

**CHAPTER**

# 34

# Toys

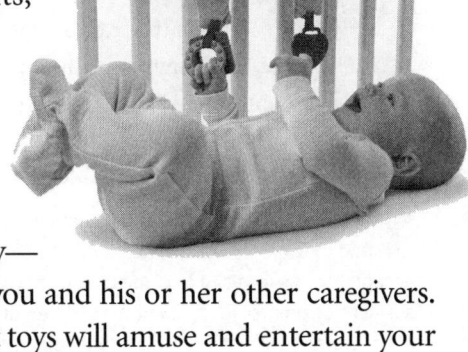

Toy manufacturers go all out to entice parents, grandparents, and gift-givers with new creations that promise to delight children and even turn them into budding prodigies. But the fact is that your child's favorite toy—and means of learning—will be you and his or her other caregivers. Of course, there's no denying that toys will amuse and entertain your child tremendously, adding to the fun. The trick is figuring out which toys will interest your baby for more than a few minutes.

Overall, a good toy should be safe for your child's age, well constructed, and durable. It should be appealing and interesting to your child and suited to his or her physical capabilities and mental and social development. The right toy can make key developmental stages more fun—for your child and for you. For ideas about what to buy, here's a closer look at your child's maturing play skills and a few general suggestions for age-appropriate toys.

## Birth to 3 Months

Babies at 3 months enjoy looking at the world around them—lights, shapes, patterns, and colors. They move their arms and legs, open and close their hands, begin to swipe at objects and try to reach for them. Their hearing is fully developed.

**SUGGESTED TOYS:** Rattles that make interesting noises, toys with high-contrast patterns, such as simple faces, and musical crib mobiles with objects or patterns. Keep toys out of the crib, however; mobiles can be suspended near or above the crib as long as they are safely mounted.

Babies experience much of their world through sucking, so expect that most toys will go straight to their mouths. For safe mouthing there should be no sharp edges or small parts that could detach.

## 4 to 8 Months

Babies can now reach for and grasp objects, move them from one hand to the other, and play with their feet. They'll search for the source of sounds.

**SUGGESTED TOYS:** Floor gyms, textured soft toys that can be safely mouthed, soft balls with sounds inside, musical toys and rattles, washable cloth baby books, and toys with flaps or lids that can be opened and closed. "From 2 to 7 months of age, my daughter really enjoyed her Gymini Baby Gym," says Jennifer Renton of Albany, Calif., referring to one brand of floor gym.

## CERTIFICATION

The Consumer Product Safety Commission (CPSC) regulates toys sold in the U.S., and toys must meet certain federal safety standards. For example, they must have acceptably low levels of lead in paint. If they're glass or metal, they must not have sharp surfaces or points. Toys meant for children under 3 years may not have small parts, such as small balls and marbles, that could pose a choking, ingestion, or inhalation hazard. Other items on the safety checklist: no pinching parts; no small wires that could poke through; no strings, cords, or necklaces that could capture a baby's neck.

Teethers and squeeze toys must be large enough not to pose choking hazards. The same goes for rattles, which also must be designed so they can't separate into small pieces. Labels on crib gyms and mobiles warn parents to remove them when baby can push up on his or her hands and knees (about 6 months).

In recent years the CPSC has recalled some models of rattles, mobiles, and toys that are parts of other products, such as walkers. If you've had a bad experience with a toy, call the CPSC at 800-638-2772 or log on to *www.cpsc.gov*. Your call may lead to a recall.

### 9 to 12 Months

Babies at this stage play by shaking, banging, throwing, and dropping toys. They enjoy searching for hidden objects, taking objects out of containers, and poking into holes with their fingers. They may be beginning to walk (typically around 12 months).

**SUGGESTED TOYS:** Stacking and building toys with rounded edges; bath and squeeze toys; soft dolls and puppets; lightweight balls; baby books; musical toys and toy telephones; and push-pull playthings, such as cars and trucks.

## Shopping Secrets

**Look for the manufacturer's recommended age range** on the front of the toy package—and take it seriously. A toy labeled for children over 3 is definitely not suitable for younger children. More than a friendly hint, this can alert you to a possible choking hazard, the presence of small parts, and other dangers. If you're buying a toy for a child over 3 who has a younger sibling, also be aware of small parts since it's likely that the younger child will find a way to get the toy.

**Cheap, poorly constructed toys are no bargain.** Flimsy plastic toys—the kind sometimes sold in drugstores, airports, and dollar stores—often have dangerous sharp edges or small parts that can break off easily.

**Used toys, especially solid, molded-plastic ones can be a great buy.** Thrift stores, consignment shops, and yard and garage sales often have toys in excellent condition. But carefully check every toy to see that it's well made and safe before giving it to your child.

## What's Available

When choosing toys, consider the classics, such as stackable plastic "doughnuts," shape sorters, building blocks, and interlocking plastic oversized beads—there's a reason they've been around so long. Browse stores, catalogs, and Web sites for other ideas. For more clues about what toys your child might like, take note of what toys he or she gravitates to on play dates and/or at day care. Also, ask other parents for suggestions.

Major brands of toys for newborns, infants, and toddlers include, in alphabetical order: Brio, Edushape, The First Years, Fisher-Price, Infantino, LeapFrog, Learning Curve (Lamaze), Little Tikes, Manhattan Toy, Munchkin, Neurosmith, Playskool, Sassy, Small World

- Keep toys intended for older children away from your baby.
- Check all toys from time to time for breakage and potential hazards. Repair them or throw them away.
- Keep uninflated and broken balloon pieces away from your baby; they're a major choking hazard.
- Keep toys out of your baby's crib, and when your baby can begin to push up on his or her hands and knees (at about 5 months), remove all toys that are strung across the crib or play yard.
- Keep all small round or oval objects, including coins, balls, and marbles, away from your baby.

Toys, and Tiny Love.

The list of toys that follows offers some ideas. These toys were chosen by the author as ones that should be fun as well as a good fit for your baby's skill level. Age recommendations are those of the manufacturers. Retail prices vary widely, so the prices listed here may not match what you'll encounter in stores. For information on plush or stuffed toys, see "Zebras and Other Stuffed Animals," starting on page 259.

**Crinkle & Chime Ball,** The First Years ($5, birth +). Babies delight in the sound of elephant's crinkly ears and body. Give him a shake, and your baby will be rewarded with a friendly chime.

**Dreamscapes Soother,** LeapFrog ($30, birth to 24 months). This crib attachment plays your choice of four selections—a poem, a song, a story, or lullabies—to help your baby get to sleep. Soft, colorful images scroll across the screen. The lights and music gradually fade after 10 minutes. Requires three C batteries.

**Fly-Away Ladybug and Discovery Farm Soft Book Set,** Lamaze ($23, birth +). It's never too early to read to your baby, who will love following Mama Ladybug on a journey through the forest and hearing you attempt different farm animal sounds.

**Jungle Pal Music Mirror,** Fisher-Price ($20, birth to 12 months). As if your baby's own image isn't entertaining enough, this playful crocodile mirror will spark baby's senses with music or giggles when he or she touches the mirror. Teethers dangle from the croc's feet and there's a hidden squeaker in his snout.

**IQ Baby Vroom Vroom Vehicles,** Small World Toys ($25, 1 to 30 months). This set of six soft vehicles with plastic rolling wheels will help enhance your little one's coordination and stimulate his or her senses with colors, textures, and mirrors. Comes with a handy vinyl bag for travel.

**Grip and Grab Rattle,** Lamaze ($10, 3 to 18 months). Small beads move through colorful textured plastic tubes—what could be simpler or more engaging? Perfect for shaking and teething—and keeping your baby occupied while you're trying to make dinner or change a diaper.

**Musical Activity Keys,** Fisher-Price ($8, 3 months and up). This colorful, chewable set of keys is loaded with activities to keep your baby busy: a key that rattles, one with a spinning window, beads, and a push button that plays music and sounds, such as a beeping car horn and a door bell.

**Baby Tap-A-Tune Piano,** Little Tikes ($14, 6 months and up). This charming piano with four easy-to-press keys will enchant your baby while it teaches basic colors, creative expression, and music appreciation. No batteries required.

**Musical Activity Walker,** Fisher-Price ($30, 6 months and up). Not-yet-mobile babies will enjoy the lively music, beads, gears, and colorful doors of this toy's activity center. Cruising babies will gain

## THE BUZZ ON HIGH-TECH TOYS

Step into any baby store and you'll see that a new generation of microchip-based toys is beeping, jingling, vibrating, flashing, and wailing its way into the nursery. Stimulating, tech-driven kid products aren't new, of course. What's noteworthy is the range of such offerings for babies—from an infant-sized "interactive play center" that entertains with microchip-powered songs, sounds, and flashing lights to stuffed animals that sing and vibrate when you press their paws.

High-tech baby products can stimulate and perhaps entertain the diaper crowd, but the chips inside aren't likely to add value for very little ones. As for those electronic toys that claim to stimulate infant development or creativity, researchers say there's no credible supporting evidence regarding their long-term effects. "If it's a new toy, then for an hour or so, they're a little more alert and involved," says Jerome Kagan, a child-development expert and research professor of psychology at Harvard University. "But you wouldn't want to make profound predictions."

In fact, says Kagan, the typical American household already provides enough sensory stimulation to make such toys unnecessary. "We should view the toys like an ice-cream cone," he says. "It's a brief source of pleasure that vanishes quickly."

Children will get far more meaningful stimulation from the sounds of the people, animals, and objects around them, notes Jane M. Healy, an educational psychologist in Vail, Colo., and author of *Your Child's Growing Mind*. There's also a role for quiet time, when the brain consolidates what it has learned. "If there's nothing that's entertaining, it gives the brain time and space to learn to manage itself," Healy says.

# WHICH BATTERIES ARE BEST?

You may not go through as many batteries as diapers during your baby's first couple of years, but sometimes it will seem pretty close. Because not every battery is right for every job, here's a rundown of what to consider before your next visit to the battery aisle:

## Disposables

**Alkalines.** Conventional alkalines sell best by far. Duracell and Energizer also offer high-drain Duracell Ultra and e2 versions for motorized toys, flash cameras, and other devices that draw short but intense bursts of energy.

In our past tests, high-drain alkaline cells outlasted conventional alkaline batteries in high-drain devices. But the price of a single high-drain alkaline battery will buy you two conventional alkalines, which, together, last longer than one high-drain cell.

With conventional alkalines, you can also save by buying the lowest-priced brand. In the case of AA batteries, the most common size, those from Duracell and Energizer cost about 90 cents each, while store brands go for about 60 cents and should do as well in most applications.

**Lithium batteries.** Even pricier than high-drain alkalines, lithium batteries are stronger still and, in our past tests, lasted nearly twice as long as regular alkalines in a flash camera. Lithium cells also last about 10 years on the shelf compared with five years for alkalines, but they can cost more than twice as much.

## Rechargeables

Rechargeable batteries cost the least over time, despite the high price you'll pay for the batteries and the charger (another $30 or so). Not all devices are designed for rechargeable cells, however; check the product literature. And some rechargeables aren't a stellar value.

**Nickel-metal hydride (NiMH) cells.** These batteries offer the best value. They may not power a toy, flash camera, or other high-drain gear for as long as disposable alkalines, but with 300 to 600 charge cycles, they cost the least overall and create the least waste, since they last the longest.

On the debit side, NiMH cells discharge when they aren't in use. That makes them the wrong choice for flashlights, remote controls, smoke detectors, and other devices that often sit idle. It also means you'll have to charge these cells before their first use.

## Recommendations

- Conventional disposable alkalines are a good choice for most uses.
- Rechargeable NiMH batteries are the most economical overall. Consider them for high-drain applications like digital cameras and other gear you use often. But first be sure the device can use NiMH cells.

walking confidence as they push their way across carpet or hardwood floors. Three AA batteries required.

**Silly Sounds Stackers,** Munchkin ($10, 6 to 15 months). These stacking toys of either a gator/duck or a cat/dog make silly sounds and characters when baby puts them together. They'll help your baby recognize new shapes, textures, colors, and sounds.

**Baby's First Wallet,** Sassy ($5, 9 to 36 months). Leave your wallet or purse on the ground for a second and, no doubt, your nearly year-old baby will be in there, searching for interesting things to play with. What's a parent to do? Get this baby version, which comes with baby's own keys, credit card, coins, business card, and stroller license. They're all tucked into pockets, which can help develop memory and dexterity.

**DiscoverSounds Workshop** or **Kitchen,** Little Tikes (both $35, 9 months and up). The workbench has 13 interactive accessories to entertain your budding carpenter as he or she learns about cause and effect. For example, your child can hammer shapes that make funny sounds and turn a crank to drop balls into a cup. The kitchen's stove-top makes cooking sounds, and its ice dispenser is a shape sorter.

**Poppin Pals,** Playskool ($13, 9 months and up). You'll enjoy this toy as much as your baby does as you watch him or her learn to open lids, turn dials, slide switches on and off, and grasp and manipulate objects (for the reward of seeing an animal pop up). No batteries are required.

## Recommendations

When toy shopping, follow the manufacturer's age recommendations displayed on the package. Although you may think that a more "advanced" toy will present a welcome challenge, in reality, it could be a source of frustration if it surpasses your baby's current stage of development. It may also be unsafe. A stuffed toy, for example, that says it's for a child over age 3 could have eyes that are potential choking hazards for a younger child.

Although the voluntary standard for toy safety says manufacturers should make squeeze toys and teethers large enough not to become lodged in an infant's throat, sometimes age recommendations can be difficult to find (or even nonexistent). You can test an item for safe size by slipping it through the tube of a toilet-paper roll (about 1¾ inches in diameter). If the toy passes through, it's too small for baby to play with. Also, look for anything that could be bitten or chewed off, such as hard, sewn-on parts like eyes, buttons, or wheels, and soft, small pieces, such as strings, ribbons, and stuffed animals' ears. All can be choking hazards.

Durability is another important factor. All baby toys should be unbreakable. Stuffed animals or any toys made of fabric should be washable and biteproof. Pull on fur to be sure it won't shed, and check that fabrics are heavy enough to keep the toy's stuffing inside. Dyes should be colorfast.

# Walkers

A traditional walker, consisting of either a molded plastic frame or a metal one, with a suspended seat in the center and wheels attached to the base, gives baby a quick way to get around before he or she is able to walk. The typical age range for using one is 4 to 18 months.

While walkers have their advantages, such as keeping a child away from certain dangers or letting him or her follow mommy around the house, they also raise concerns about safety and a child's normal development. Despite its name, a walker doesn't help a baby acquire walking skills—and that's only one of its problems. Walkers can strengthen lower leg muscles, but not the muscles in the upper legs and hips your baby will use most in walking. In fact, a number of studies have asserted that walkers can even delay the desire to walk unassisted because babies can scoot around in them too easily.

More important, some wheeled walkers pose a significant risk of injury. Old-style walkers can fall down stairways or steps between levels in your home. They can also turn over when their wheels get snagged, as well as roll up against hot stoves and

W-X-Y-Z

## CERTIFICATION

heaters. Outdoors, they can fall off decks and patios, over curbs, and into swimming pools. Safety gates can be helpful, but they aren't a guarantee of protection. Many accidents involving walkers occur despite the presence of safety gates—either because the gates were closed incorrectly or they didn't hold up against the impact of the walker.

For all of these reasons, a second-generation voluntary safety standard was issued for walkers in 1997. According to this standard, walkers must either be too wide to fit through a standard doorway or have features, such as a friction strip made of rubberized material on the bottom, that will stop the walker if its wheels drop away at the edge of a step. Walker-related incidents have declined substantially since the 1997 standard was introduced.

Even with these requirements in place, however, the American Academy of Pediatrics strongly urges parents not to use traditional baby walkers. Further, the Canadian government is currently working on a law that would prohibit the sale and importation of them. We agree that walkers can pose a safety hazard and believe there are plenty of safer alternatives.

## Shopping Secrets

To buy the safest walker possible:

**Select a model with a wheelbase** that's longer and wider than the frame of the walker to ensure stability.

**Look for the JPMA sticker.** Some brands are available that don't comply with the voluntary safety standards. Your safest bet is to buy a walker that's certified. (See the box above.)

**Take your baby with you** when you're shopping and make sure his or her feet can touch the ground on the seat's lowest setting.

**Examine attached toys for size** (they should be too large to fit through the tube of a toilet-paper roll, about 1¾ inches in diameter).

**Look for small parts** that can break off or screws that can loosen.

## What's Available

The major brands of traditional, wheeled baby walkers are, in alphabetical order: Baby Trend, Chicco USA, Delta Enterprise, Dorel Juvenile Group (the makers of Safety 1st), Graco, and Kolcraft.

Also called "mobile entertainers," walkers come in different shapes—circular, rectangular, square, and even styled like a small car. There are typically four to eight wheels on the base, and many have optional toy bars and toys. Walkers usually don't have safety belts, since belts can create problems on their own. Prices range from $30 to $80.

## Features to Consider

**Foldability.** Many models, especially larger ones, fold flat for easy storage.

**Friction strips.** They touch the floor when the wheels fall away on stairs or uneven pavement, making it difficult for a baby to push the walker farther. Gravity may still prevail at the top of the stairs, though. Most walkers that meet the voluntary safety standard have friction strips, but that's not a fail-safe design. Even a certified model may still pose a risk—although a much-reduced one.

**Parking stand.** This generally allows wheels to be lifted off the floor to limit baby's scooting. An alternative to look for is a walker with wheels that lock.

**Seat.** Some models have seats that swivel. Most can be removed and

## WALKER SAFETY

- Never leave your baby in a walker unattended or out of your sight.
- Make sure any springs and hinges on the walker have protective coverings.
- Use a walker only on flat floor surfaces, and clear all objects, such as dangling cords, that could cause it to tip over or that might pose a strangulation hazard.
- Keep stairways blocked with a gate or other enclosure.
- Keep your baby away from stoves, radiators, fireplaces, and swimming pools when he or she is in a walker.
- Don't carry a walker with your baby in it. It's too easy for you to trip.

are machine washable. Seat height can be raised or lowered, using either a locking mechanism located under the front tray, slots in the base of the walker, or adjusters on the seat.

**Toys.** Most walkers have rimmed trays, often with toys attached, some of which are equipped with lights and/or electronic sound effects. Toys are sometimes suspended from a removable U-shaped frame.

## Recommendations

Consider safer alternatives such as a stationary activity center. Or wait until around age 1, when your baby starts to "cruise" (walk from place to place by hanging onto the furniture), and get a push toy (also often called a walker). Both offer equal or greater play value compared with a traditional walker, plus greater safety. If you decide to buy a traditional walker, get one that's JPMA certified. Even if your walker has friction strips, consider using it only in a room that doesn't have access to stairs leading down. And keep the friction strips clean.

## PRODUCT GUIDE • WALKERS

Note: These products were not tested by Consumers Union. This alphabetical listing does not include all models available but rather is a selection of some widely distributed ones. Descriptions are derived from the manufacturers' claims. Prices are approximate retail. For manufacturer contact information, see the Brand Locator, starting on page 283.

| Line/model | Price | Details |
| --- | --- | --- |
| **BABY TREND** | | |
| **Walker model 3535T** | $30 | Bear-themed walker features wide base, high-back padded seat with three-position height adjustment, and removable toy bar. Not designed for use on carpet. |
| **Fire Truck Walker** | $80 to $100 | Fire-truck themed walker features wide base and high-back seat with three-position height adjustment, and caster wheels. Electronic, removable tray features songs, sounds, and flashing lights. Requires two AA batteries. |

# PRODUCT GUIDE • WALKERS

| Line/model | Price | Details |
|---|---|---|
| **DELTA ENTERPRISE** | | |
| **Playtime Walker with Toy Bar** | $35 | Basic walker with wide base on four wheels. Features washable seat cushion and bar with attached toys. |
| **Deluxe Safari Walker with Toys & Activities** | $40 | Jungle-themed walker with wide base on four wheels, washable seat cushion, and a variety of interactive toys on tray. |
| **Sound, Look, Listen & Learn Walker** | $45 | Basic walker with wide base on four wheels, washable seat cushion, and interactive toy tray that plays 24 different sounds. |
| **EVENFLO** | | |
| **Walk Around Rotating Walker** | $80 | Walker features "stay-put" gripper, which attaches to carpet, tile, or linoleum floors. Features rotating seat with seat lock, three-position seat-height adjustment, and surrounding interactive toys. Walker can be locked in a stationary position. |
| **GRACO** | | |
| **Little Tikes Sky Adventure** | $50 | Features three-position height adjustment, machine-washable cloth seat, and space-themed play tray with interactive toys. Friction strips around edge are designed to reduce motion against edges or uneven surfaces. |
| **Tot Wheels V Mobile Entertainer 4540 in Super Nova** | $60 | Spaced-theme traditional walker with three-position height adjustment. Can be made stationary with parking stand, which lifts oversize wheels off ground. Features 11 toys on tray with flashing lights and sounds. Similar models: Tot Wheels V Mobile Entertainer 4522 (no space theme, fewer toys on tray), $40; Tot Wheels V Mobile Entertainer 4512 (similar to 4522 but no parking stand), $30. |
| **KOLCRAFT** | | |
| **Tot Rider 2** | $15 to $25 | This traditional sit-down walker features three-position height adjustment, wipe-clean padded seat, and independent, front swivel wheels. Has two toys on tray with cup holder. Tiny Steps Walker with Mini Maestro |
| **Tiny Steps Walker with Mini Maestro** | $50 | This unit can be used as a sit-down walker or a walk-behind one. Features three-position height adjustment and stationary brake to limit mobility. Tray has toys with lights, sound, music, and cup holder. Requires three AA batteries. |

| Line/model | Price | Details |
| --- | --- | --- |
| **SAFETY 1ST** | | |
| **Safari Surprise Walker** | $30 | Jungle-themed traditional walker with three-position height adjustment, machine-washable padded seat, and grip strips along edge to reduce movement when encountering uneven surfaces. Features five interactive toys on front, removable tray. Folds for storage or travel. |
| **Nature's Friends Baby Steps Walker** | $50 | Features three-position height adjustment, machine-washable padded seat, and grip strips along edge to reduce movement when encountering uneven surfaces. Can be made stationary by engaging safety brake. Includes four interactive toys on front tray, which swings open in two sections. Folds for storage or travel. |
| **Grip 'n Go Folding Walker** | $55 | Features three-position height adjustment, machine-washable padded seat, and grip strips along edge to reduce movement when encountering uneven surfaces. Tray has two toys with sounds, lights, and window so baby can see his or her feet. Folds for storage or travel. |

CHAPTER

# 36

# Zebras
## & Other Stuffed Animals

**A**fter your baby's born—if not even before—your home is likely to resemble a zoo of stuffed animals. Although your baby probably won't show an interest in this popular gift item initially, a stuffed animal (or plush toy, as they're sometimes called) is likely to be his or her first friend in due time. And down the road, into the preschool years, a favorite stuffed toy can become an essential companion at bedtime.

Consider yourself warned: You're likely to spend what seems like hours in the toy store looking for just the right stuffed kitty, cow, alligator, or unicorn and gauging your child's reactions. You may also find yourself back at the store searching for the twin of some beloved stuffed animal that has become lost.

## Shopping Secrets

Stuffed toys are disarming because they're so squishy and cuddly. Yet, they can also pose safety hazards. When buying or introducing stuffed animals to your baby,

W · X · Y · Z

follow these guidelines.

**Make sure stuffed animals are washable and bite-proof.** The label on the product gives care and cleaning advice. Many are just surface washable. In our opinion, that's not good enough. Lightly pull on fur to be sure it won't shed, and see that fabrics are heavy enough to keep stuffing inside. Note that fur is exempt from federal small-parts regulations, but it can still cause choking. Dyes should be colorfast.

**Lean toward softer toys.** Purchase animals with the softest plush rather than those with scratchy fur. Nubby surfaces for teething are also a plus.

**Pick toys with contrasting or bright colors.** A stuffed zebra or dalmatian, for example, is likely to evoke more of a reaction from your baby than a cute pastel bunny. (Save that one for toddlerhood, when more subtle stuffed animals will get your child's attention.) Stuffed toys with securely embedded, unbreakable mirrors also tend to be a hit with the youngest set since children of that age are naturally enamored of their own image.

Noises are good, too. Squeaky, rattling, or jingly stuffed toys or those that reward baby with a song (or a "moo" or a "baa") if he or she pulls or pushes them will entertain more than those that are simply cuddly.

**Watch out for sharp edges or small parts that can detach.** Any stuffed toy you give your baby will likely end up in his or her mouth. To play it safe, follow the manufacturer's age recommendations on the label. Inspect the toy before and after washing to make sure any small parts, such as eyes, are securely attached.

**Make sure you have at least one take-along toy.** It should be small enough to "stuff" anywhere and bring to airports, doctor's waiting rooms, and supermarkets for emergency distractions and cuddlefests.

## What's Available

Major brands of plush toys for babies include, in alphabetical order: Baby Einstein, Carter's, The First Years, Funny Friends, Gund, Infantino, Manhattan Toy, The Right Start, Sassy, and Small Fry Design.

**REFERENCE**

# Money Matters
## Tips for New Parents

**W**e have a pretty good idea of how much sleep you're getting these days, so we'll try to make this as quick as possible. Even if you aren't sleep-deprived, money advice may not be your idea of lively leisure reading. But as a new parent, there are a few things you need to square away. They're covered here, in brief and in relative order of urgency.

### Your Will

Just about everybody needs a will, but only 44 percent of Americans have one, according to a recent survey. Both you and your spouse should have wills. If you are part of an unmarried couple with a child, having wills is all the more important in assuring that your estate is distributed the way you would want it to be if you happened to die.

You can buy software and write your own will, hire a lawyer to do it, or draft a will using that software and then take it to a lawyer to make sure you didn't miss something. If your estate is relatively simple, a lawyer may charge no more than a

## LITTLE BABY, BIG BUCKS

**H**ow much money are you likely to spend during baby's first year? How much have you got? Here, according to the U.S. Department of Agriculture, were the averages for families at three different income levels, as of 2002. These numbers represent a first child; subsequent children are a little cheaper. (But don't rush it on our account!)

Less than $39,700 .........................................................................$8,208.80

$39,700 to $66,900 ....................................................................11,445.20

More than $66,900 .....................................................................17,050.00

few hundred dollars or so. Don't hesitate to ask for an estimate, though, and don't hesitate to shop around since legal fees can vary widely from firm to firm.

A will is crucial for parents even if you don't have a lot of money or property to pass along. That's because it's where you designate a guardian for your child in case both you and the child's other parent die. If you die without a will naming a guardian, a court will appoint one, and he or she could be the last person you would ever have chosen. The guardian you pick may be a relative or a friend. You may want to name an alternate guardian too, just in case your first choice is unable to take on the job.

Your will may also give the guardian authority to manage whatever money you leave your child, until the child reaches the age of majority—18 in most states. However, if your estate is large or money management isn't one of your guardian's strong points, you may want to entrust another person or a financial institution, such as a bank, with that authority.

If your estate is large or complex, a lawyer can explain other options, including various forms of trusts. Your will may provide not only for your first child but also for any siblings that come along later. If your life changes in some major way, however, your lawyer should probably take another look at it just to be sure that it covers your current circumstances.

Whatever you decide, don't forget to sound out any prospective guardians before naming them in your will. Being a guardian can be a huge responsibility, financially and in every other possible way, and for a very long time. In other words, it's a lot like being a parent.

# Life Insurance

A new baby should be cause for celebrating life, not for contemplating your own demise. But there's one more thing you have to think about, just in case. That's making sure you have life insurance—and enough of it.

The basic job of life insurance is to provide money for your loved ones if you're not around to do it yourself. Both you and your spouse should have policies, even if one of you doesn't work outside the home. That's because the "nonworking" spouse performs services that you'd probably have to pay someone else to do if she or he were no longer there.

That leaves three major decisions to be made:

1. Which type of insurance do you need?
2. How much do you need?
3. Where do you buy it?

**Which type?** There are essentially two kinds of life insurance: term and whole life. Term, sometimes called "temporary" insurance, covers you for a specific term, such as one year. If you die during that period, the beneficiaries you've named on your policy collect the money. If you don't die, they don't get anything. On the other hand, you're still alive, which is good.

Whole life, also known as cash value, is sometimes called "permanent" insurance, especially by life insurance agents, who think that sounds a lot more solid. It is permanent in the sense that it can remain in effect for your entire lifetime (hence "whole life"), as long as you keep paying the premiums. However, it is considerably more costly than term insurance, both because it has a savings component (that's the "cash value") and because insurance agents tend to make greater commissions for selling it.

For example, a $300,000 term insurance policy for a 35-year-old nonsmoking male from one well-known insurance company would run between $262 and $427 a year, while a similar cash-value policy from the same company would cost about $3,524 a year. The annual

## INSURE YOUR BABY?

And now a word about some insurance you don't need, but that you will almost certainly receive offers in the mail for. That is baby life insurance. Unless your baby somehow supports the family (as a child model or TV star, say), insuring his or her life is a waste of money, pure and simple. Your money will be better spent—and your baby better protected—if you and your spouse are adequately insured.

premiums on the term policy used in this example would remain the same for the first 20 years, after which they would be subject to an increase, and probably a substantial one given that the policyholder would by then be 20 years older. In the case of the whole-life policy, premiums would remain unchanged until the policyholder reached age 95. While that predictability may appear to be a plus for a whole-life policy, it is a very costly plus. It could be comforting to have life insurance at age 85 or 90, but the time you most need it is when your kids are young and depend on your financial support.

Because you can buy far more coverage, dollar for dollar, with a term policy, CONSUMER REPORTS has long recommended it over cash-value insurance for most people. That's especially important for parents with young children, who may need a great deal of insurance and whose budgets are already being squeezed from many other directions.

Which brings us to the second question:

**How much?** With a new baby in the house and all the financial demands that go along with it, you don't want to buy more insurance than you need; at the same time, you don't want to risk leaving your family with less than they need should something happen to you.

You've probably heard rules of thumb about how much life insurance is the right amount. Some, for example, suggest you multiply your salary by this number or that. Those rules are better than nothing, but not much better. The box at right can help you get a closer estimate.

When you buy life insurance, your first goal should be to fill the gap between your family's expenses in future years and how much money they're likely to have available to meet those expenses. That means you also need to consider your other sources of income and any assets you have (such as stocks or rent-producing real estate) that may generate more income. If you're fortunate enough to have a substantial amount of money in mutual funds, say, you probably need less life insurance than you otherwise would.

**Where to buy?** When you're buying any type of insurance, look for a company that's likely to be around if and when you need to file a claim. While state-run guaranty associations are supposed to step in to protect policyholders if an insurer becomes insolvent, they may cover you only up to a certain limit. Besides, the last thing you want to leave your grieving heirs is another hassle.

# HOW MUCH INSURANCE DO YOU NEED?

**A**rriving at a precise number can be complicated. And even then it isn't that precise, since no one can predict things like future inflation rates with any accuracy. However, this five-step process, based on one CONSUMER REPORTS devised some years ago, should get you closer:

**1. Figure your family's current monthly living expenses.** Unless you are an incredible saver, your total monthly take-home pay is probably close enough.

**2. Estimate your family's future monthly expenses**—assuming you, for example, are out of the picture. For most families, multiplying the number in line 1 by 75 percent will produce a workable ballpark figure.

**3. Estimate your family's future monthly income.** Include the surviving spouse's pay plus any reliable investment income, such as stock dividends. You may also be eligible for Social Security survivor benefits; see *www.ssa.gov* for details.

**4. Subtract line 3 from line 2.** This is your monthly shortfall.

**5. Multiply the dollar figure on line 4** by the number of months your family will need the financial support that the life insurance provides. For example, if you wanted to provide that support until your newborn reached the age of 18, you'd multiply by 216 (that is, 12 months per year times 18 years).

The dollar figure you arrive at in line 5 is the amount of insurance your family would be likely to need simply to make up for the gap between their future expenses and future income. You may want to figure in some additional money to cover funeral expenses, the repayment of any debts (not including your mortgage, which is already accounted for under monthly expenses), and for your child's college education, which can be a big bill in its own right as we'll get to later.

If you already have some life insurance through your employer, you can subtract it from the total amount of insurance you need. However, in these times it's worth weighing how secure your job (and therefore that insurance) actually is.

Several ratings organizations regularly assess the financial health of life insurers. The best known are A.M. Best, Fitch, Moody's, Standard & Poor's, and Weiss. You can find their publications in many libraries, and some of their information is available online. Since some of these organizations are softer graders than others, you'd do well to compare several different ratings for any insurance company that you're considering.

All else being equal, buy by cost. You can obtain cost comparisons through an independent insurance agent (the kind who sells more than one brand of policy) or via the Web. While CONSUMER REPORTS hasn't evaluated insurance-oriented Web sites and can't vouch for their thoroughness, a few of the well-known ones are Accuquote.com, Insurance.com, and Insure.com. You may also have access to relatively low-cost life insurance through organizations you already have a financial relationship with, such as TIAA-CREF if you work in the nonprofit sector, USAA if you're a retired military officer or family member of one, or the Vanguard Group or Fidelity Investments if you own shares in their mutual funds.

## Your Baby's College Fund

"They grow up so quickly." How many times have you heard that phrase from some wistful parent, recalling when his or her own kids were little? Unfortunately, that also means you'll be facing college bills before you know it. Financial writers are fond of quoting big, scary numbers to impress upon readers just how expensive college is likely to be at some future date—so here goes:

### $306,136!

That's an estimate of the cost of four years of tuition, fees, and room and board at a private college for a baby born today. And that's a fairly conservative number, based on relatively modest price increases. In other words, it could be worse.

But few people ever have to pay that big scary number—at least right away. According to the College Board, in the 2002-2003 school year, some $105 billion of the nation's collective college bill was covered by a combination of grants and loans.

Still, you'd be smart to start saving what you can for college. As with any other kind of investing, the earlier you get going, the more your money is likely to grow.

Today's college investors have far more investment options than their own parents did. These are your key choices:

**529 college savings plans.** Though named for a section of the federal tax code, these plans are administered by the states. You can invest up to the limit set by your state (often about $250,000), and the earnings on your money grow federally tax-deferred. You can then withdraw money, tax-free, to pay for qualified college costs, although that attractive provision is scheduled to expire in 2010 unless Congress renews it. "Qualified costs" in this case typically means tuition and fees, books and other supplies, and room and board if the student attends at least half-time.

You don't have to invest in your own state's plan, although that's where you should look first, since it may also entitle you to a deduction on your state income taxes. You can compare your state's plan with competing ones at *www.collegesavings.org,* a Web site sponsored by a consortium of states. Another useful site is *www.savingforcollege.com,* run by Joseph Hurley, a 529 expert and certified public accountant.

As you compare plans, be sure to check out:

• Fees and expenses. These vary dramatically and can take a sizable bite out of your college savings. At this writing, management expenses range from less than 0.5 percent a year to more than 2 percent of the money you have invested. Also check out application and maintenance fees, which are other ways the companies that administer these plans may nibble away at your money. You can sign up for a 529 plan through a bank or a broker, but the most economical way is to invest directly and avoid commissions. That way you may also avoid being steered into an inappropriate out-of-state-plan simply because the broker stands to earn a higher commission. Plan phone numbers and Web addresses are available at the Web sites above.

• Investment options. In most states you'll have a choice of investments, though often only one company that provides them. These may range from conservative accounts with a guaranteed rate of return to more aggressive ones (typically investing in stocks), that offer no guarantees but may reward you more generously in the long run. The sooner you need to get your money out, the more conservatively you should usually invest it. With a new baby, you can probably afford to take some chances, but when your child reaches high-school age you may want to shift at least gradually into one of the less risky options. You can also diversify your 529 investments by spreading your money among several types of accounts.

Incidentally, if your child decides not to go to college, you can get the money back, although you will have to pay a penalty (currently 10 percent) on the account's earnings.

**Prepaid tuition plans.** Another variety of 529 plan, these arrangements let you buy credits to cover tuition at a particular college or group of colleges. Though less flexible than 529 savings plans, they offer the advantage of allowing you to lock in tomorrow's tuition at today's prices. However, unless you have a pretty good idea of where your brand-new baby will be going to college about 18 years from now, you may do better with a savings plan. More information about these plans is available at the Web sites listed earlier.

**Coverdell education savings accounts.** These are the latest spin on Education IRAs. As long as your income falls below certain limits (currently $110,000 in adjusted gross income for individuals, $220,000 for couples), you can invest up to $2,000 a year for a child under age 18. While you don't get any tax break for your contributions, the money in your account grows tax-deferred, much like a regular IRA. Money you withdraw to pay qualified educational expenses, including elementary and secondary school as well as college, is free from federal and sometimes state tax. You can open a Coverdell account at many mutual fund companies as well as banks and brokerage firms.

**Custodial accounts.** You (or any generous grandparents you happen to have handy) can also sock money away for your new baby in a custodial account. Often referred to as UGMAs (for Uniform Gifts to Minors Act) or UTMAs (for Uniform Transfers to Minors Act), these accounts allow you to invest up to $11,000 per year in your child's name, free of any gift taxes. As of this writing, the first $750 of income on the account each year is tax-free and the next $750 is taxed at your child's rate, which is likely to be lower than yours. Anything beyond $1,500 is taxed at your rate. Once your child reaches age 14, all income is taxed at his or her rate.

While these accounts can have their uses, they also come with a number of drawbacks. One is that they could have a negative effect on your child's eligibility for financial aid. Most financial aid formulas treat assets belonging to a child (as UGMAs and UTMAs are considered to be) less favorably than those of a parent (as is the case, for example, with 529 plans).

A potentially bigger problem is who controls the money. The trustee (presumably you) has control until your child reaches age 18 or 21, depending on the state. After that, however, it's the kid's cash to do with as he or she pleases. It may be hard to picture your little bundle of joy ever doing anything crazy or irresponsible with your hard-earned money, but it's been known to happen in even the finest of families.

If you have substantial assets to invest on your child's behalf and want to retain greater control over the money, a lawyer can acquaint you with other types of trusts.

**U.S. savings bonds.** Never the most glamorous of investments, but a reliable little performer in both good times and bad, U.S. savings bonds have been eligible since 1990 for special tax treatment if you

# WHAT COLLEGE COSTS TODAY

**T**hese numbers may seem downright nostalgic by the time your baby heads off to freshman orientation, but here's what tuition, room and board, and all the rest would set you back today, on average, at a public or private four-year college. Tuition increases have tended to outpace the general cost of living in recent times, so be warned.

|  | TUITION AND FEES | ROOM AND BOARD | TOTAL |
|---|---|---|---|
| **PUBLIC** | $ 4,694 | $5,942 | $10,636 |
| **PRIVATE** | $19,710 | $7,144 | $26,854 |

Source: The College Board, based on 2003-2004 school year

cash them in to pay for higher education. Series EE bonds issued in 1990 or later, as well as Series I bonds, qualify for the break. You don't have to indicate your intention to use the bonds for college when you buy them, so you can always change your mind. But they need to be registered in your name and/or your spouse's rather than your child's, and you must be at least 24 years old when you buy. Interest earned on the bonds is tax-free as long as your modified adjusted gross income is under certain limits. For example, in 2004 a married couple filing jointly was eligible for a full exclusion if their income was below $89,750. Between that figure and $119,750 they could claim a partial exclusion. For more details, visit this Web site: *www.publicdebt.treas.gov.*

**Investing in other ways.** You can, of course, simply invest on your own to cover your child's college costs. You'll miss out on some of the tax breaks mentioned above, although those breaks are no longer quite as attractive, given the reduction in the capital gains tax. You'll also have more flexibility in what you ultimately do with that money. This can be especially important if you're juggling other financial demands, such as saving for your retirement, at the same time.

Bear in mind that financial-aid formulas generally treat parents' assets more kindly than money they view as belonging to a child. That is, they expect the student to contribute a far greater percentage of his or her assets to pay the bill. If you expect financial aid to be a major consideration for you when the day finally comes, you may do well to have more money in your name and less in your child's.

## Special Tax Breaks for Parents

A generation ago, parents used to joke about their kids being "little deductions," good for a few bucks off their taxes every April 15. These days, parents are entitled to all kinds of tax breaks for their children, if they know to claim them.

If you use tax software to prepare your return, it should walk you through these tax breaks and make sure you receive them. A real live human accountant or other tax pro can do the same thing. Here's a quick overview:

First there's the dependency exemption, good in 2004 for $3,100 off your taxable income for every child in the family who qualifies as a dependent, as long as your adjusted gross income (on a joint return) doesn't exceed $214,050.

Then there's the child tax credit of $1,000 for every dependent child under the age of 17. Parents with three or more kids are entitled to an additional credit. A credit is even better than an exemption because it cuts your tax bill by that amount, rather than reducing the amount of your income that is subject to tax. Once more, there are income limits. In this case, couples filing jointly must have an adjusted gross income of $100,000 or less to qualify for the full credit.

Yet another credit, called the child and dependent care credit, helps parents with kids under the age of 13 cover some child-care expenses. Parents can claim a credit equal to 20 percent or more of amounts up to $3,000 per child. So, for example, a couple claiming $3,000 in child-care costs would be entitled to a credit of at least $600.

Parents can also use a flexible spending plan at work, if your employer offers one, to have up to $5,000 in pretax earnings deducted from your pay to spend on dependent care. The plan then reimburses your expenses, up to whatever amount you contributed, throughout the year. For parents in the 25 percent tax bracket (for 2003, that was joint filers with taxable income between $56,800 and $114,650), for example, this break would be worth $1,250.

There is also a one-time credit of up to $10,390 that's available to parents who adopt a child, called, as you might guess, the adoption credit. The credit is phased out if your modified adjusted gross income is over $150,000.

Finally, don't forget the charitable deduction you can receive when you donate your children's old clothes and toys to worthy organizations. Given how fast kids outgrow things, that's one deduction that you can count on year after year.

# Keeping Baby Safe

## Childproofing Your Home

**B**efore you know it, your baby will be highly mobile—and into everything. That's why it's a good idea to make your home a safety zone well before your baby starts crawling. You can do it yourself or hire a childproofing service, and you'll want to keep these preventive measures in place until they're no longer needed or effective. For instance, a safety gate's useful life ends when the child is about age 2 or big enough to climb over it. Other measures can be relaxed as your child shows some judgment, maybe by age 4.

Even a well childproofed home is no substitute for a watchful parent, of course. But the room-by-room guide that follows can make your home safer—both for your child and for you.

# BABY'S ROOM

### Broken parts
Check all baby equipment frequently for broken parts or malfunctioning hardware. Stop using anything, particularly a crib, if it has broken or missing parts.

### Crib
Remember that a crib is the safest place for baby to nap or sleep. But once your child attempts to climb out of the crib, consider using a bed with child railings or putting the mattress on the floor. Place the crib well away from wall hangings, toys, window blinds and curtains, and other furniture so that an adventurous baby can't reach anything dangerous.

### Crib bedding
Be sure that the crib mattress is firm, that there are no gaps between the mattress and the sides of the crib, and that the mattress cover and sheets fit snugly. Soft bedding—including pillows, quilts, and comforters—is a suffocation hazard for infants, so keep those items out of the crib. Instead, plan to dress baby warmly enough for comfort. If you use a lightweight blanket, it should be pulled up no farther than the baby's underarms.

### Floor and carpet
Position furniture and toys so you'll have a clear path when you enter the room at night. Any area rug or throw rug should have a nonskid backing or, better yet, be secured with double-faced tape, so no edges stick up.

### Furniture
Avoid high chests or tables. Bolt book cases and chests to the wall so they won't tip if a child climbs on them.

### Paint and other fumes
Allow time for fumes from new paint, wallpaper, drapes, and carpeting to subside before baby comes home. Paint the nursery at least a week before baby's arrival. When possible, use a paint that is low in volatile organic compounds, which may be irritating to a baby (and to some adults). To reduce fumes, air out new furniture and anything made of plastic or particleboard.

### Toy chests
Don't store toys in wooden chests with lids that can slam shut and hurt a child or cause suffocation. Chests designed specifically for holding toys have hinges or lid supports that will hold the lid open in any position to prevent such accidents. Open shelves or crates are safer alternatives and make it easier to find toys. Or look for a chest without a lid, one that has ventilation holes that won't be blocked if the chest is placed against the wall, or one that when closed, leaves a space between the lid and the sides of the chest to allow ventilation.

## Toys and mobiles

Keep soft toys out of the crib. They are a suffocation hazard for young babies and can be used as stepping stools for climbing out. If you buy a crib mobile, be sure to hang it out of baby's reach. A mobile should be taken down when babies are able to push up on their hands and knees, at about 6 months.

# BASEMENT, DRIVEWAY, AND GARAGE

## Door to house

Install a lock on the door leading outside or to the garage. Consider installing a self-locking "Dutch door" that allows you to pass groceries into the house without letting your toddler out.

## Garage-door openers

Test an electric garage-door opener's sensitivity by placing a 2-inch-high block of wood on the floor in the door's path. If the door doesn't stop, don't use the garage door opener. Instead, open and close the door manually, or replace the garage-door opener with a device equipped with optical sensors that prevent the garage door from closing if a child gets in the way.

## Hazardous substances

Store gasoline, oil, barbecue starter, insecticides, antifreeze, paint, car polish, and other hazardous substances behind locked cabinet doors.

## Laundry supplies

Stash detergent, bleach, and other laundry essentials in a locking cupboard. Keep all chemicals in their original containers; never transfer them to soda bottles or other beverage containers.

## Ride-on toys

Don't purchase a riding toy until you're certain your child is mature enough to use it safely. Attach a tall flag on the back of a tricycle so it's visible to motorists. The lower it is to the ground, the safer a wheeled toy is. Always supervise a child when riding. Be sure your child can ride without going into traffic, on steep hills, steps, or into driveways. If there's no safe place to ride, use a riding toy only for visits to the park. To keep children away from the garage, store tricycles and ride-on toys in the house instead.

## Stairs

To prevent falls down basement stairs, install a lock as high as you can reach on both sides of the basement door. Make sure stairs are well lit and keep all clutter and toys off steps.

## Water heater

Reduce the setting of your hot-water heater to 120° F. An infant's skin burns much more easily than an adult's.

## Workbench

Make your workbench off-limits, whether you're working there or not. Lock up power tools and all small or sharp objects.

# BATHROOM

## Bathroom doors

Keep bathroom doors securely closed or blocked off with a gate. You may also want to cover the inside door lock with duct tape to keep baby from locking you out. Install doorknobs that have a hole on the outside through which you can push a thin rod or screwdriver to disengage the lock in case baby gets locked inside the bathroom.

## Bathtub and water safety

When using a baby bathtub, always keep a hand on your baby. Never use a bath seat, or bath ring. There have been numerous reports of babies drowning when their parents turned their backs, even momentarily. Never leave your baby alone in water. When bathing a toddler, attach rubber strips to the surface of a regular bathtub to prevent slipping. Get a cover for the bathtub's spout to protect your child from its heat-conducting metal and hard edges.

## Diaper pail

If you use cloth diapers, make sure the pail has a tamper-proof lid with a solid locking device to eliminate a drowning hazard. Don't use deodorizing tablets, which can be ingested.

## Electrical devices

Store all electrical devices, such as curling irons and hair dryers, in a high cupboard outside the bathroom.

## Medicines

Keep medicines off of bedside tables and install a lock on the medicine cabinet. You might even store medications in a childproof locked box kept on a high shelf outside the bathroom. Put vitamin supplements out of reach, too—iron pills or vitamins containing iron are leading child poisoners. Choose child-resistant packaging for prescription and over-the-counter drugs and any vitamin supplements. Post the number of the poison-control center near your medicine cabinet and call before you administer any remedy.

## Toilet lid

Install a device to lock the lid of the adult toilet to keep baby out.

# DECKS, PORCHES, AND YARD

## Backyard play equipment

Don't assume play equipment is safe simply because it's made for children. Supervise constantly; toddlers don't understand heights, their own limitations, or the pendulum effect of swings. Don't allow toddlers to use a swing until their feet firmly touch the ground and you're sure they're mature and strong enough to hold on without losing their balance when leaning backward. Put infants and toddlers between the ages of 9 months and 3 years in specially designed swings with sides, backs, and crotch and waist belts to contain them. Look for smooth edges and surfaces with no ragged seams or corners, and no nooks or crannies that could trap a child's fingers.

### Doors leading outside

Install a latch high on the backyard door. Firmly lock sliding patio doors, and secure them with a bar in the door track.

### Lawn and garden equipment

Keep your tot indoors whenever you use a string trimmer, snow blower, power mower, hedge trimmer, or other outdoor equipment. Pour fuel into this equipment while outdoors, not in the garage, where fumes could become a hazard or possibly ignite.

### Pools

If you have a pool, surround it with a fence (required under most building codes, as well as by many insurance companies before they'll issue a policy) and a self-locking gate. Cover the pool during the off-season. Pool alarms for in-ground pools sound if a child falls in, but they are prone to false alarms.

### Porch or deck railing

The spaces between a porch or deck railing should be no more than 2⅜ inches. If they're wider than that, install a railing guard made of mesh or plastic.

### Water containers

Empty all outdoor containers of water, including buckets and wading pools, after use. Store them upside down, preferably in the garage.

## KITCHEN

### Fire extinguishers

Keep a box of baking soda near the stove to extinguish grease fires. Purchase a small fire extinguisher and mount it nearby. Familiarize yourself with its use.

### Harmful items

Anything that might be harmful to a child should be stashed away in drawers or cupboards equipped with child-resistant safety latches. The list includes all kitchen cleaners; plastic wrap, food storage bags, and food-wrap packages with a serrated edge; knives, scissors, and other sharp objects; refrigerator magnets or any small kitchen knickknacks; and any type of liquor.

### Kitchen access

When you cook, use a gate for the kitchen or keep baby in a play yard, swing, or high chair—in view but out of harm's way.

### Kitchen stepstool

Keep your kitchen stepstool in a closet when you're not using it to prevent your little one from climbing into trouble.

### Microwave ovens

Decide on an alternative to using a microwave oven to warm bottles of breast milk or formula or heat jars of baby food. In the cases of bottles, holding them under warm tap water should do the trick. A microwave can create hot spots in the milk or food that can burn a baby's mouth and throat. It may also cause jars, bottles, and nurser liners to explode.

### Small appliances

To prevent baby from tugging down small appliances—including coffee-makers, food processors, and toaster ovens—wrap up and fasten cords out of reach with twist ties or rubber bands. Or tape cords to the wall with masking tape. Irons are another hazard. Put baby safely in a safety seat or play yard whenever you iron, and don't leave an unattended baby and an iron in a room together.

### Stove

Pull off front stove knobs and store them safely until it's time to cook. You can also buy childproof knob covers. When possible, cook on the back burners, and always turn all pot handles toward the back of the cooktop.

- - - - - - - - - - - - - - - - - - - - - - - - - -

## LIVING ROOM OR DEN

### Fireplaces and wood-burning stoves

If you have a fireplace or wood-burning stove, teach your toddler to respect the warnings "Hot!" and "Don't touch!" Never leave a child in the room alone with a heat source, even if he or she seems safely enclosed in a play yard or seat. Consider installing a fireproof safety railing around the fireplace, and always use a fireplace screen. If your fireplace has a glass enclosure, keep your child from touching it, to prevent burns to his or her hands. Put fireproof padding around sharp brick edges on raised hearths.

### Glass doors and objects

Put large stickers on sliding glass doors to keep your child from crawling, walking, or running into them. Remove vases and other knickknacks your child could break, fall on, or swallow.

### Houseplants

Give away poisonous houseplants (poinsettias, dumbcane, dieffenbacia, philodendrons, calla lilies, mistletoe, and hyacinths, to name a few), or ask friends to take care of them until your child is older. Keep all remaining plants well trimmed, so a child can't reach them.

### TVs and VCRs

Childhood head injuries from falling television sets are a growing problem, according to Consumer Product Safety Commission statistics. The TV and VCR should be out of your child's reach. Secure them on a wall-mounted stand or on a shelf fastened to the wall.

## GENERAL SAFETY CONCERNS AROUND THE HOUSE AND BEYOND

### Area rugs

Secure all area rugs or throw rugs with foam carpet backing or double-sided tape. To protect children who are just learning to walk from stumbling, be sure no edges or corners curl up.

### Balloons

Don't let your child play with an inflated or deflated toy balloon. The material poses a choking hazard. Put packages of unused balloons safely out of reach.

### Buckets and sinks

To avoid a drowning hazard, never leave a bucket, such as a five-gallon paint bucket, or a sinkful of water or other liquid unattended when small children are around. It's possible for toddlers to fall in head first.

### Bug spray

Avoid using bug sprays in areas where baby spends a lot of time crawling around.

### Doorknob covers

Consider buying doorknob covers, which can be squeezed open only by an adult hand.

### Electrical outlets

Block unused electrical outlets with safety covers that screw into the outlet. (Small outlet plugs can be dangerous because exploring babies can remove them and put them in their mouths.) Check that all outlets in places where moisture may be present, such as bathrooms, basements, or outdoors have a ground fault interrupter, which senses imbalances in the current and immediately trips the circuit.

### Elevated spaces

Anything that raises your baby up off the ground—a changing table, a framed carrier, or a high chair, for example—has injury potential. Make sure these items have safety belts and use them. Avoid placing a car seat on a counter or table when your baby is in it.

### Emergency numbers

Gather emergency telephone numbers, including those of your baby's doctor-to-be and the toll-free poison-control center, as well as all contact numbers for family members. Post an easy-to-read copy next to each telephone, and be sure to go over emergency procedures with the baby sitter and other caregivers before you leave the house.

### Extension cords

Purchase extension cords equipped with locking plug covers. If your house is overloaded with extension cords, talk to an electrician about having additional outlets installed.

### Fire and carbon monoxide protection

Install a smoke alarm and a carbon monoxide detector in key locations on each floor of your home. Change the batteries when you set your clocks to standard time each October. Check the detectors every other week to make sure batteries are good. Place large street address numbers at the entrance to your driveway or on the front door for the fire department to see easily. Formulate an escape plan. Place all matches and lighters on a high surface or in a locking drawer or cabinet.

### Hazardous gaps

Beware of gaps in which babies can get stuck if they slip through, such as the leg openings of strollers or baby carriers, the space between the seat and tray of a high chair, the area between the slats of a crib or cradle, or that between a gate and the floor.

### Heavy furniture

Bolt or bracket bookcases and other heavy furniture, such as wall units or armoires, to the wall to prevent tipping if a toddler decides to climb on one of them.

### Helmets

When your baby gets to be toddler and preschool age, get him or her into the habit of wearing a helmet when riding a tricycle or bicycle. Choose a helmet that carries a certification sticker. Have your child try on different sizes to make sure you've got the right one. Your child should be able to see and hear well; the chin strap should be easy to fasten and release, and it should fit comfortably under the chin without chafing.

### Household cleaners and deodorizers

Assess household cleaning products. Cleaning ingredients such as ammonia can irritate a baby's nose and throat. Fragrances can irritate a baby's sensitive skin and respiratory passages and can even trigger allergic reactions. So you may want to skip floral or citrus scents once baby arrives. You'll probably want to avoid using plug-in or aerosol room deodorizers as well.

### Lead in tap water and furniture finishes

Have your home's tap water tested for lead and, if needed, purchase an effective water-purification system. Heirloom furniture, such as cribs and chests, may have been coated with lead-containing paints, lacquers, or varnishes. Old cribs, especially, besides having possibly malfunctioning parts, may have paint that contains high levels of lead, while all new cribs have very low and, therefore, safe levels. You can check antique finishes with a lead-testing kit. If you detect lead in a piece of furniture, put it in storage until your baby gets older.

## New clothes and bedding

Launder all new baby clothes and bedding in a fragrance-free detergent once or twice to remove chemicals. Don't use liquid fabric softener or dryer sheets. The fragrance may irritate baby's skin and respiratory system. Liquid softener may also reduce absorbency.

## Night-lights

Night-lights at floor level attract crawling babies and toddlers to sockets. Instead, place a night-light in a socket out of baby's reach, install a dimmer switch for the room's lighting fixture, or use a lamp with a low-wattage bulb.

## Old refrigerators

If you are discarding an old refrigerator, always remove the doors and store the unit facedown while awaiting trash pickup.

## Padded corners

Add safety padding to the sharp corners of coffee tables or consider storing them during baby's first few years.

## Parked cars

Never leave a little one alone in a parked car. Lock parked cars so children can't play in them. Kids who accidentally lock themselves in won't be able to unlock the doors.

## Pet safety

Consider obedience training for your pet to ensure safe, controlled behavior around baby. Talk to a trainer about easy ways to introduce your baby into a home with pets. Buy a tall gate or special pet gate to keep your dog in the kitchen or other safe area when appropriate. Move your cat's litter box to a spot that you know your toddler won't be able to reach.

## Plastic bags

Plastic bags pose suffocation hazards. Keep plastic garbage bags, laundry bags, food storage or grocery bags, and bags used in packaging everything from dry cleaning to electronics on a high shelf or in a locked cupboard. Tie a plastic bag in knots before throwing it out.

## Product registration

Mail in registration cards that come with baby products so you can be notified about recalls. Follow manufacturers' age or weight guidelines for use of products. Keep product instruction manuals in an easy-to-find location.

### Railings

If railings on staircases and balconies are spaced more than 2⅜ inches apart (the diameter of a soda can), install railing guards made of mesh or clear plastic to prevent your child from falling through or getting stuck.

### Small parts, edges, and hinges

Inspect your home for dangerously small objects. Check toys, pick up clutter, keep purses out of reach, and stash an older sibling's toys with small parts away from baby. Anything small enough to fit through the tube of a toilet-paper roll (about 1¾ inches in diameter) could pose a choking hazard. Keep small objects out of baby's reach. Also, thoroughly check toys, strollers, high chairs, play yards, gates, etc. to see that they're free of sharp edges or points and potentially dangerous hinges.

### Smoking

Ban smoking indoors or anywhere around an infant such as in the car. Secondhand smoke has been associated with Sudden Infant Death Syndrome (SIDS) and baby respiratory ailments.

### Stairways

Install a secure, hardware-mounted gate at the top of each staircase. For more information, see Gates chapter.

### Windows

Keep baby away from open windows. Window screens aren't strong enough to stop a child from falling out. Install window guards if you live in a high rise. Purchase window locks or guards from a hardware or home-supply store and install them according to the manufacturer's instructions. Also keep in mind that cords from draperies or blinds can entangle a baby. Cut looped cords in half to form two strings. You can also roll cords up and tie them with rubber bands or twist ties or mount a cleat (hook) high out of the child's reach to secure the excess cord. The ties of crib bumper guards should be no longer than 7 inches. Avoid small cord shorteners, which can be ingested.

# Brand Locator

| NAME | TELEPHONE | WEB ADDRESS |
| --- | --- | --- |
| Ameda | 877-992-6322 | www.ameda.com |
| Ansa Co. | 800-527-1096 | www.theansacompany.com |
| Aprica U.S.A. | 310-639-6387 | www.apricausa.com |
| Arm's Reach Concepts Inc. | 800-954-9353 | www.armsreach.com |
| Baby Bjorn/Regal Lager Inc. | 800-593-5522 | www.babybjorn.com |
| Baby Italia | 888-266-2848 | www.lajobi.com |
| Baby Jogger Co. | 800-241-1848 | www.babyjogger.com |
| Baby Luv | 718-385-1000 | www.deltaenterprise.com |
| Baby Trend | 800-328-7363 | www.babytrend.com |
| Baby's Dream Furniture Inc. | 800-835-2742 | www.babysdream.com |
| Beech-Nut Nutrition Corp. | 800-233-2468 | www.beech-nut.com |
| Bertini | 800-746-6463 | www.bertinistrollers.com |
| Britax Child Safety | 888-427-4829 | www.childseat.com |
| Canon | 800-828-4040 | www.usa.canon.com |
| Cardinal Gates | 800-318-3380 | www.cardinalgates.com |

| NAME | TELEPHONE | WEB ADDRESS |
|---|---|---|
| Carnation Good Start | 800-284-9488 | www.verybestbaby.com |
| Century Products | 800-837-4044 | www.gracobaby.com |
| Chicco USA | 877-424-4226 | www.chiccousa.com |
| Child Craft Industries Inc. | 812-883-3111 | www.childcraftind.com |
| COMBI International Corp. | 800-992-6624 | www.combi-intl.com |
| Cosco/Dorel Juvenile Group | 800-457-5276 | www.djgusa.com |
| Crown Crafts | 800-421-0526 | www.crowncraftsinfantproducts.com |
| Delta Enterprises | 718-385-1000 | www.deltaenterprise.com |
| Discovery Toys | 800-426-4777 | www.discoverytoysinc.com |
| Dr. Brown's | 800-778-9001 | www.handi-craft.com |
| Eddie Bauer | 800-544-1108 | www.djgusa.com |
| Enfamil | 800-222-9123 | www.enfamil.com |
| Evenflo Co. | 800-233-5921 | www.evenflo.com |
| The First Years | 800-225-0382 | www.thefirstyears.com |
| Fisher-Price | 800-432-5437 | www.fisher-price.com |
| Fujifilm | 800-800-3854 | www.fujifilm.com |
| Gerber Products Co. | 800-443-7237 | www.gerber.com |
| Graco Children's Products | 800-345-4109 | www.gracobaby.com |
| Handi-Craft Co. (Dr. Brown's) | 800-778-9001 | www.handi-craft.com |
| Hewlett-Packard | 800-752-0900 | www.hp.com |
| Hitachi | 800-448-2244 | www.hitachi.com |
| Huggies | 800-544-1847 | www.huggies.com |
| Infantino | 800-365-8182 | – |
| Inglesina USA | 877-486-5112 | www.inglesina.com |
| InSTEP LLC | 800-242-6110 | www.instep.net |
| International Playthings | 800-631-1272 | www.intplay.com |
| Johnson & Johnson | 800-526-3967 | www.jnj.com |
| J. Mason Products | 800-242-1922 | www.jmason.com |
| JVC | 800-252-5722 | www.jvc.com |
| Kelty K.I.D.S. | 800-535-3589 | www.kelty.com |
| KidCo | 800-553-5529 | www.kidcoinc.com |

| NAME | TELEPHONE | WEB ADDRESS |
| --- | --- | --- |
| Kids II | 800-230-8190 | www.kids11.com |
| KinderKraft | 800-822-6748 | www.kinderkraft.com |
| Kodak | 800-235-6325 | www.kodak.com |
| Kolcraft | 800-453-7673 | www.kolcraft.com |
| Kool-Stop International | 800-586-3332 | www.koolstop.com |
| Kyocera | 800-421-5735 | www.kyocera.com |
| Lego Baby/Lego Systems | 800-422-5346 | www.lego.com |
| Learning Curve Int. | 800-704-8697 | www.learningcurve.com |
| Little Tikes | 888-832-3203 | www.littletikes.com |
| Luvs | 800-285-6064 | www.luvs.com |
| Maclaren USA Inc. | 877-442-4622 | www.maclarenstrollers.com |
| Madden Mountaineering | 720-214-2194 | www.maddenusa.com |
| Minolta | 877-462-4464 | www.minoltausa.com |
| Nikon | 800-645-6689 | www.nikonusa.com |
| North States | 763-541-9101 | www.northstatesind.com |
| Olympus | 888-553-4448 | www.olympusamerica.com |
| Over the Shoulder Baby Holder | 800-637-9426 | www.babyholder.com |
| Pampers | 800-285-6064 | www.pampers.com |
| Panasonic | 800-211-7262 | www.panasonic.com |
| Peg Perego U.S.A. | 800-671-1701 | www.perego.com |
| Pentax | 800-877-0155 | www.pentaxusa.com |
| Prince Lionheart | 800-544-1132 | www.princelionheart.com |
| R.E.I. | 800-426-4840 | www.rei.com |
| Ross Products | 800-986-8510 | www.ross.com |
| Safeline Kids | 800-829-1625 | www.safelinekids.com |
| Safety 1st | 800-544-1108 | www.safety1st.com |
| Samsung | 800-726-7864 | www.samsungusa.com |
| Sassy | 616-243-0767 | www.sassybaby.com |
| Sharp | 800-237-4277 | www.sharpusa.com |
| Simmons Juvenile Products | 920-982-2140 | www.simmonsjp.com |
| Sony | 800-222-7669 | www.sonystyle.com |

| NAME | TELEPHONE | WEB ADDRESS |
| --- | --- | --- |
| The Step 2 Co. | 800-347-8372 | www.step2.com |
| Storkcraft Mfg. | 604-275-4242 | www.storkcraft.com |
| Summer Infant | 800-268-6237 | www.summerinfant.com |
| Theodore Bean Adventure Co. | 877-688-2326 | www.theodorebean.com |
| Tiny Love | 888-846-9568 | www.tinylove.com |
| Toshiba | 800-829-8318 | www.toshiba.com |
| Tot Tenders Inc. | 800-634-6870 | www.babycarriers.com |
| Tough Traveler | 800-468-6844 | www.toughtraveler.com |
| Unisar/Bebesounds | 800-430-0222 | www.bebesounds.com |
| Weego | 800-676-0352 | www.weego.com |
| Whisper Wear | 770-984-0905 | www.whisperwear.com |
| Zooper | 888-742-9899 | www.zooperbaby.com |

# Pediatric Drugs
## Common Prescriptions for Kids

T his section presents in one place key information parents need to know regarding medications commonly prescribed for babies and young children. Drugs are listed alphabetically.

Over-the-counter (OTC) medications, such as the pain and fever-reducing medications acetaminophen (Tylenol Children's Chewables, Tylenol Infants' Drops) or ibuprofen (Children's Advil, Children's Motrin) are also commonly used in young children. Even though these are "children's" medications, it's important to check with your pediatrician before using any OTC medication.

Dosage and manner of prescription drugs used by adults, of course, must be adjusted for small bodies. For prescription and nonprescription drugs, special care needs to be taken in measuring the dose. When using liquid formulations, use the dosing cup, spoon, or dropper included with the product. If one is not available, always use a measuring spoon, not a regular teaspoon, since such utensils can vary significantly in how much medicine they can hold. Read package labeling and insert information. Do not use any drug after the expiration date on the label, as it may no longer be effective. And remember, keep all medications, vitamins and minerals, and dietary supplements far out of the reach of young children.

*Portions of this material are copyright © 2003 Thomson MICROMEDEX Healthcare. All rights reserved.*

# Contents

............................................

# ALBUTEROL
**(nebulizer solution)**
**Sold under these brand names:**
Proventil
Salbutamol
Ventolin

## Description

Adrenergic bronchodilators are medicines that are breathed in through the mouth to open up the bronchial tubes (air passages) of the lungs. These medicines are used mostly for asthma and also for some cases of chronic bronchitis, emphysema, and other lung diseases.

These medicines are also breathed in through the mouth to prevent bronchospasm (wheezing or difficulty in breathing) caused by exercise.

## Before using this medicine

**Pregnancy.** These medicines are used to treat asthma in pregnant women. Although there are no studies on birth defects in humans, problems have not been reported. Some studies in animals have shown that they cause birth defects when given in doses many times higher than the human dose.

**Breast-feeding.** It is not known whether these medicines pass into the breast milk. Although most medicines pass into breast milk in small amounts, many of them may be used safely while breast-feeding. Mothers who are using these medicines and who wish to breast-feed should discuss this with their doctor.

## Proper use of this medicine

These medicines come with patient directions. Read them carefully before using the medicine. If you do not understand the directions or if you are not sure how to use the medicine, ask your health-care professional to show you how to use it.

## Dosing

*For inhalation aerosol dosage form:* Children up to 12 years of age: Dose must be determined by your doctor.

## Side effects of this medicine

*Check with your doctor immediately if any of the following side effects occur:* Severe dizziness; feeling of choking, irritation, or swelling in throat; flushing or redness of skin; hives; increased shortness of breath; skin rash; swelling of face, lips, or eyelids; tightness in chest or wheezing, trouble breathing, irregular heartbeat.

## Other side effects

**Common:** Fast heartbeat; headache; nervousness; trembling

**Less common:** Coughing or other bronchial irritation; dizziness or lightheadedness; dryness or irritation of mouth or throat.

**Rare:** Chest discomfort or pain; drowsiness or weakness; muscle cramps or twitching; nausea and/or vomiting; restlessness; trouble sleeping

## ALLEGRA
### (fexofenadine)

## Description

Fexofenadine (fex-oh-FEN-a-deen) is an antihistamine. It is used to relieve the symptoms of hay fever and hives.

## Before using this medicine

**Allergies.** Tell your doctor if your child has ever had any unusual or allergic reaction to fexofenadine. Also tell your health care professional if you are allergic to any other substances, such as foods, preservatives, or dyes.

**Pregnancy.** In animal studies, this medicine did not cause birth defects but did cause a decrease in birth weight of the infant. Discuss with your doctor whether or not you should continue to use this medicine if you become pregnant.

**Breast-feeding.** It is not known whether fexofenadine passes into breast milk. Although most medicines pass into breast milk in small amounts, many of them may be used safely while breast-feeding. Mothers who are taking this medicine and who wish to breast-feed should discuss this with their doctor.

**Children.** This medicine has been tested in children 6 years of age and older and, in effective doses, has not been shown to cause different side effects or problems than it does in adults. There is no specific information about the use of fexofenadine in children less than 6 years of age.

## Dosing

*For oral dosage form (capsules, tablets) for symptoms of hay fever:*

Children 6 to 11 years of age: 30 mg twice daily

Children younger than 6 years of age: Use and dose must be determined by your doctor.

*For symptoms of chronic hives:* Children 6 to 11 years of age: 30 mg twice daily.

Children less than 6 years of age: Use and dose must be determined by your doctor.

## Side effects of this medicine

Back pain; cough; dizziness; drowsiness; earache; fever; headache; nausea; pain or tenderness around eyes or cheekbones; painful menstrual bleeding; ringing or buzzing in ears; runny or stuffy nose; stomach upset; unusual feeling of tiredness; muscle aches and pains

# AMOXICILLIN

### Sold under these brand names:
Amoxil
Polymox
Trimox
Wymox

## Description

Penicillins are used to treat infections caused by bacteria. They work by killing the bacteria or preventing their growth. None of the penicillins will work for colds, flu, or other virus infections.

Penicillins are available only with your doctor's prescription, in the following dosage forms:

Capsules (U.S. and Canada)
Oral suspension (U.S. and Canada)
Tablets (U.S.)
Chewable tablets (U.S. and Canada)

## Before using this medicine

**Allergies.** Tell your doctor if your child has ever had any unusual or allergic reaction to any type of penicillin or to a similar class of antibiotics called cephalosporins.

**Pregnancy.** Penicillin has not been studied in pregnant women. However, it has been widely used in pregnant women and has not been shown to cause birth defects or other problems in animal studies.

**Breast-feeding.** Penicillin passes into the breast milk. Even though only small amounts may pass into breast milk, allergic reactions, diarrhea, fungus infections, and skin rash may occur in nursing babies.

**Children.** Many types of penicillins have been used in children and, in effective doses, are not expected to cause different side effects or problems in children than they do in adults.

Some strengths of the chewable tablets of amoxicillin contain aspartame, which is changed by the body to phenylalanine, a substance that is harmful to patients with phenylketonuria.

## Dosing

Newborns and infants up to 3 months of age: Dose is based on body weight and must be determined by your doctor. The usual dose is 15 mg per kg (6.8 mg per pound) or less every 12 hours.

Infants 3 months of age and older and children weighing up to 40 kg (88 pounds): Dose is based on body weight and must be determined by your doctor. The usual dose is 6.7 to 13.3 mg per kg (3 to 6 mg per pound) every eight hours or 12.5 to 22.5 mg per kg (5.7 to 10.2 mg per pound) every 12 hours.

## Precautions while using this medicine

Penicillins may cause diarrhea in some patients.

Check with your doctor if severe diarrhea occurs.

For mild diarrhea, diarrhea medicine containing kaolin or attapulgite (e.g., Kaopectate tablets, Diasorb) may be taken.

## Side effects of this medicine

*Stop taking this medicine and get emergency help immediately if any of the following side effects occur:* Fast or irregular breathing; fever; joint pain; lightheadedness or fainting; puffiness or swelling around the face; red, scaly skin; shortness of breath; skin rash, hives, itching

*Check with your doctor immediately if any of the following side effects occur:* Abdominal or stomach cramps and pain (severe); abdominal tenderness; convulsions (seizures); decreased amount of urine; diarrhea (watery and severe), which may also be bloody;

mental depression; nausea and vomiting; pain at place of injection; sore throat and fever; unusual bleeding or bruising; yellow eyes or skin

*NOTE:* Some of the above side effects (severe abdominal or stomach cramps and pain, and watery and severe diarrhea, which may also be bloody) may also occur up to several weeks after you stop taking any of these medicines.

# AUGMENTIN (amoxicillin plus clavulanate)

## Description

Penicillins and beta-lactamase inhibitors (clavulinic acid) are used to treat infections caused by bacteria. They work by killing the bacteria or preventing their growth. The beta-lactamase inhibitor is added to the penicillin to protect the penicillin from certain substances (enzymes made by the very bacteria you're treating) that can destroy the penicillin before it can kill the bacteria.

Oral suspension (U.S. and Canada)
Tablets (U.S. and Canada)
Chewable tablets (U.S.)

## Before using this medicine

**Allergies.** Tell your doctor if your child has ever had any unusual or allergic reaction to any of the penicillins, cephalosporins, or beta-lactamase inhibitors. Also tell your health-care professional if you are allergic to any other substances, such as foods, preservatives, or dyes.

**Pregnancy.** Penicillins and beta-lactamase inhibitors have not been studied in pregnant women. However, penicillins have not been shown to cause birth defects or other problems in animal studies.

**Breast-feeding.** Penicillins and sulbactam, a beta-lactamase inhibitor, pass into the breast milk. Even though only small amounts may pass into breast milk, allergic reactions, diarrhea, fungus infections, and skin rash may occur in nursing babies.

**Children.** Penicillins and beta-lactamase inhibitors have been used in children and, in effective doses, are not expected to cause different side effects or problems in children than they do in adults.

Some strengths of the chewable tablets and oral suspensions of amoxicillin and clavulanate combination contain aspartame, which is changed by the body to phenylalanine, a substance that is harmful to patients with phenylketonuria.

## Proper use of this medicine

Amoxicillin and clavulanate combination may be taken on a full or empty stomach. Taking amoxicillin and clavulanate combination with food may decrease the chance of diarrhea, nausea, and vomiting.

*For patients taking the oral liquid form of amoxicillin and clavulanate combination:* Use a specially marked measuring spoon or other device to measure each dose accurately. The average household teaspoon may not hold the right amount of liquid.

Do not use after the expiration date on the label. The medicine may not work properly after that date. If you have any questions about this, check with your pharmacist.

*For patients taking the chewable tablet form of amoxicillin and clavulanate combination:* Tablets should be chewed or crushed before they are swallowed.

## Dosing

*For oral dosage forms (chewable tablets and suspension):* Neonates and infants up to 12 weeks (3 months) of age: Dose is based on body weight and must be determined by your doctor. The usual dose is 15 mg of amoxicillin per kg (6.8 mg per pound) every 12 hours.

Infants 3 months of age and older and children weighing up to 40 kg (88 pounds): 6.7 to 22.5 mg of amoxicillin per kg (3 to 10.2 mg per pound), in combination with 1.7 to 3.2 mg of clavulanate per kg (0.8 to 1.5 mg per pound), every eight or 12 hours.

*For oral dosage form (tablets):* Infants and children weighing up to 40 kg (88 pounds): The amoxicillin and clauvulanate combination tablets are too strong for children weighing less than 40 kg (88 pounds). The chewable tablets or oral suspension are used in those children.

## Precautions while using this medicine

Check with your doctor if severe

diarrhea occurs.

For mild diarrhea, diarrhea medicine containing kaolin or attapulgite (e.g., Kaopectate tablets, Diasorb) may be taken.

### Side effects of this medicine

*Stop taking this medicine and get emergency help immediately if any of the following side effects occur:* Cough; fast or irregular breathing; fever; joint pain; lightheadedness or fainting; puffiness or swelling around the face; red, irritated eyes; shortness of breath or wheezing; skin rash, hives, itching; sore mouth or tongue; unusual tiredness or weakness; vaginal itching and discharge; white patches in mouth and/or on tongue

*Check with your doctor immediately if any of the following side effects occur:* Abdominal or stomach cramps and pain (severe); blistering, peeling, or loosening of skin and mucous membranes; chest pain; cloudy urine; convulsions (seizures); diarrhea (watery and severe), which may also be bloody; general feeling of illness or discomfort; nausea or vomiting; redness, soreness, or swelling of tongue; red skin lesions, often with a purple center; sore throat; swelling of face, fingers, lower legs, or feet; trouble in urinating; unusual bleeding or bruising; weight gain; yellow eyes or skin.

*NOTE:* Some of the above side effects (severe abdominal or stomach cramps and pain, and watery and severe diarrhea, which may also be bloody) may

also occur up to several weeks after you stop taking any of these medicines.

......................................

# BACTRIM, SEPTRA
## (sulfamethoxazole plus trimethoprim)

### Before using this medicine

**Allergies.** Tell your doctor if your child has ever had any unusual or allergic reaction to sulfa medicines, foods, preservatives (e.g., sulfites), or dyes.

**Pregnancy.** Sulfamethoxazole and trimethoprim combination has not been reported to cause birth defects or other problems in humans. However, studies in mice, rats, and rabbits have shown that some sulfonamides cause birth defects, including cleft palate and bone problems. Studies in rabbits have also shown that trimethoprim causes birth defects, as well as a decrease in the number of successful pregnancies. Sulfonamides are not recommended for use at the time of labor and delivery because these medicines may cause unwanted effects in the baby.

**Breast-feeding.** Sulfonamides and trimethoprim pass into the breast milk. These medicines are not recommended for use during breast-feeding. They may cause liver problems, anemia, and other unwanted effects in nursing babies, especially those with glucose-6-phosphate dehydrogenase (G6PD) deficiency.

**Children.** Sulfadiazine and trimethoprim combination should not be given to infants less than 3 months of age.

Sulfamethoxazole and trimethoprim combination should not be given to infants less than 2 months of age unless directed by the child's doctor.

## Proper use of this medicine

Sulfonamide and trimethoprim combinations are best taken with a full glass (8 ounces) of water. Several additional glasses of water should be taken every day, unless otherwise directed by your doctor. Drinking extra water will help to prevent some unwanted effects of sulfonamides.

For patients taking the oral liquid form of this medicine:

Use a specially marked measuring spoon or other device to measure each dose accurately. The average household teaspoon may not hold the right amount of liquid.

### Dosing

*For oral dosage forms (suspension, tablets):* Infants less than 2 months of age: Use is not recommended.

Infants 2 months of age and older and children up to 40 kg of weight (88 pounds): Dose is based on body weight. The usual dose is 20 to 30 mg of sulfamethoxazole and 4 to 6 mg of trimethoprim per kg (9.1 to 13.6 mg of sulfamethoxazole and 1.8 to 2.7 mg of trimethoprim per pound) every 12 hours.

## Precautions while using this medicine

Sulfonamide and trimethoprim combinations may cause skin to be more sensitive to sunlight than it is normally. Exposure to sunlight, even for brief periods of time, may cause skin itching, redness, rash, or a severe sunburn. When you begin taking this medicine:

Stay out of direct sunlight, especially between the hours of 10:00 a.m. and 3:00 p.m., if possible.

Wear protective clothing, including a hat and sunglasses.

Apply a sun-block product that has a skin protection factor (SPF) of at least 15. Some patients may require a product with a higher SPF number, especially if they have a fair complexion. If you have any questions about this, check with your health-care professional.

Apply a sun-block lipstick that has an SPF of at least 15 to protect lips.

## Side effects of this medicine

*Check with your doctor immediately if any of the following side effects occur:*

**More common:** Itching; skin rash

**Less common:** Aching of joints and muscles; difficulty in swallowing; pale skin; redness, blistering, peeling, or loosening of skin; sore throat and fever; unusual bleeding or bruising; unusual tiredness or weakness; yellow eyes or skin

**Rare:** Abdominal or stomach cramps and pain (severe); abdominal or stomach tenderness; anxiety; blood in urine; bluish fingernails, lips, or skin; confusion; diarrhea (watery and severe), which may also be bloody; difficult breathing; drowsiness; fever; general feeling of illness; greatly increased or decreased frequency of urination or amount of urine; hallucinations; headache, severe; increased thirst; lower back pain; mental depression; muscle pain or weakness; nausea; nervousness; pain at site of injection; pain or burning while urinating; seizures (convulsions); stiff neck and/or back; swelling of front part of neck

*NOTE:* Some of the above side effects (severe abdominal or stomach cramps and pain, and watery and severe diarrhea, which may also be bloody) may also occur up to several weeks after you stop using any of these medicines.

*Also, check with your doctor as soon as possible if the following side effect occurs:*

**More common:** Increased sensitivity of skin to sunlight

Other side effects may occur that usually do not need medical attention. These side effects may go away during treatment as your body adjusts to the medicine. However, check with your doctor if any of the following side effects continue or are bothersome:

**More common:** Diarrhea; dizziness; headache; loss of appetite; mouth sores or swelling of the tongue; nausea or vomiting; tiredness

Other side effects not listed above may also occur in some patients. If you notice any other effects, check with your doctor.

## BIAXIN
### (clarithromycin)

### Description

Clarithromycin (kla-RITH-roe-mye-sin) is used to treat bacterial infections in many different parts of the body. It works by killing bacteria or preventing their growth. However, this medicine will not work for colds, flu, or other virus infections.

### Before using this medicine

**Allergies.** Tell your doctor if your child has ever had any unusual or allergic reaction to clarithromycin or to any related medicines, such as erythromycin. Also tell your healthcare professional if you are allergic to any other substances, such as foods, preservatives, or dyes.

**Pregnancy.** Clarithromycin has not been studied in pregnant women. However, studies in animals have shown that clarithromycin causes birth defects and other problems. Before taking this medicine, make sure your doctor knows if you are pregnant or if you may become pregnant.

**Breast-feeding.** Clarithromycin passes into breast milk.

**Children.** Studies on this medicine have not been done in children up to 6 months of age. In effective doses, the medicine has not been shown to cause different side effects or problems in children over the age of 6 months than it does in adults.

## Proper use of this medicine
### Dosing

*For oral dosage forms (suspension and tablets):* Children 6 months of age and older: 7.5 mg per kilogram (kg) (3.4 mg per pound) of body weight every 12 hours for 10 days.

Infants up to 6 months of age: Use and dose must be determined by your doctor.

## Side effects of this medicine

**Rare:** Abdominal tenderness; fever; nausea and vomiting; severe abdominal or stomach cramps and pain; shortness of breath; skin rash and itching; unusual bleeding or bruising; watery and severe diarrhea, which may also be bloody; yellow eyes or skin

**Less common:** Change in sensation of taste; diarrhea (mild); headache.

. . . . . . . . . . . . . . . . . . . . . . . . . . . . . .

# CEFTIN
## (cefuroxime)

### Description

Cefuroxime is used in the treatment of infections caused by bacteria. It works by killing bacteria or preventing their growth. Cefuroxime will not work for colds, flu, or other virus infections.

### Before using this medicine

**Allergies.** Tell your doctor if your child has ever had any unusual or allergic reaction to any of the cephalosporins, penicillins, penicillin-like medicines, or penicillamine. Also tell your health-care professional if you are allergic to any other substances, such as foods, preservatives, or dyes.

**Pregnancy.** Studies have not been done in humans. However, most cephalosporins have not been reported to cause birth defects or other problems in animal studies.

**Breast-feeding.** Cefuroxime can pass into breast milk, usually in small amounts. However, it has not been reported to cause problems in nursing babies.

**Children.** Many drugs of this class have been tested in children and, in effective doses, have not been shown to cause different side effects or problems than they do in adults. However, there are some that have not been tested in children up to 1 year of age.

### Proper use of this medicine

Cefuroxime may be taken on a full or empty stomach. If this medicine upsets your stomach, it may help to take it with food.

### Dosing

*For oral suspension dosage form:* Infants and children 3 months to 12 years of age: 10 to 15 milligrams (mg) per kilogram (kg) (4.54 to 6.81 mg per pound) of body weight every 12 hours for 10 days.

### Missed dose

If you miss a dose of this medicine, take it as soon as possible. This will help to keep a constant amount of medicine in the blood or urine. However, if it is almost time for your next dose, skip the missed dose and go back to your regular dosing schedule. Do not double dose.

## Precautions while using this medicine

In some patients, cefuroxime may cause diarrhea:

Severe diarrhea may be a sign of a serious side effect.

## Side effects of this medicine

Along with its needed effects, a medicine may cause some unwanted effects. Although not all of these side effects may occur, if they do occur they may need medical attention.

*Check with your doctor immediately if any of the following side effects occur:*

**Less common or rare:** Abdominal or stomach cramps and pain (severe); abdominal tenderness; diarrhea (watery and severe, which may also be bloody); fever; unusual bleeding or bruising (more common for cefamandole, cefoperazone, and cefotetan)

NOTE: Some of these side effects may also occur up to several weeks after you stop taking this medicine.

**Rare:** Blistering, peeling, or loosening of skin; convulsions (seizures); decrease in urine output; hearing loss (more common with cefuroxime treatment for meningitis); joint pain; loss of appetite, nausea, or vomiting (more common with ceftriaxone); pain, redness, and swelling at place of injection; skin rash, itching, redness, or swelling; trouble in breathing; unusual tiredness or weakness; yellowing of the eyes or skin rash.

## CLARITIN
### (loratadine; also available OTC)

### Description

Antihistamines are used to relieve or prevent the symptoms of hay fever and other types of allergy. They work by preventing the effects of a substance called histamine, which is produced by the body. Histamine can cause itching, sneezing, runny nose, and watery eyes. Also, in some persons histamine can close up the bronchial tubes (air passages of the lungs) and make breathing difficult.

Some antihistamine preparations are available only with your doctor's prescription. Others are available without a prescription. However, your doctor may have special instructions on the proper dose of the medicine for your medical condition.

### Before using this medicine

**Allergies.** Tell your doctor if your child has ever had any unusual or allergic reaction to antihistamines. Also tell your health-care professional if you are allergic to any other substances, such as foods, preservatives, or dyes.

**Breast-feeding.** Small amounts of antihistamines pass into the breast milk. Use is not recommended since babies are more susceptible to the side effects of antihistamines, such as unusual excitement or irritability. Also, since these medicines tend to decrease the secretions of the body, it is possible that the flow of breast milk may be reduced in some patients. It is not known yet whether loratadine can cause these same side effects

**Children.** Serious side effects, such as convulsions (seizures), are more likely to occur in younger patients and would be of greater risk to infants than to older children or adults. In general, children are more sensitive to the effects of antihistamines. Also, nightmares or unusual excitement, nervousness, restlessness, or irritability may be more likely to occur in children.

## Proper use of this medicine

### Dosing

*For oral dosage forms (tablets or liquid):* Adults and children 6 years of age and older: 10 milligrams (mg) once a day.
Children 2 to 5 years of age: 5 mg once a day.

## Side effects of this medicine

**Less frequent or rare:** Fast or irregular heartbeat

**Less common or rare:** Sore throat; unusual bleeding or bruising; unusual tiredness or weakness

**Symptoms of overdose:** Clumsiness or unsteadiness; convulsions (seizures); drowsiness (severe); dryness of mouth, nose, or throat (severe); feeling faint; flushing or redness of face; hallucinations (seeing, hearing, or feeling things that are not there);

shortness of breath or troubled breathing; trouble in sleeping

## Other side effects

**More common:** Drowsiness; dry mouth, nose, or throat; gastrointestinal upset, stomach pain, or nausea; increased appetite and weight gain; thickening of mucus

**Less common or rare:** Blurred vision or any change in vision; confusion; drowsiness; dryness of mouth, nose, or throat; fast heartbeat; increased sensitivity of skin to sun; loss of appetite; skin rash; gastrointestinal upset; unusual excitement, nervousness, restlessness, or irritability; thickening of mucus

. . . . . . . . . . . . . . . . . . . . . . . . . . . . . . . . .

# CORTISPORIN
## (neomycin, polymyxin B, and hydrocortisone) Otic (ear) form

## Description

Neomycin, polymyxin B, and hydrocortisone (nee-oh-MYE-sin, pol-i-MIX-in bee, and hye-droe-KOR-ti-sone) is a combination antibiotic and cortisone-like medicine. It is used to treat infections of the ear canal and to help provide relief from redness, irritation, and discomfort of certain ear problems.

## Before using this medicine

**Allergies.** Tell your doctor if your child has ever had any unusual or allergic reaction to this medicine or to any related antibiotic, such as amikacin (e.g., Amikin), colistimethate (e.g., Coly-Mycin M), colistin (e.g., Coly-Mycin S), gentamicin (e.g., Garamycin), kanamycin (e.g., Kantrex), neomycin by mouth or by injection (e.g., Mycifradin), netilmicin (e.g., Netromycin), paromomycin (e.g., Humatin), polymyxin B by injection (e.g., Aerosporin), streptomycin, or tobramycin (e.g., Nebcin). Also tell your health-care professional if you are allergic to any other substances, such as preservatives or dyes.

**Pregnancy.** Neomycin, polymyxin B, and hydrocortisone otic preparations have not been studied in pregnant women. However, studies in animals have shown that topical corticosteroids (such as hydrocortisone) cause birth defects. Before using this medicine, make sure your doctor knows if you are pregnant or if you may become pregnant.

**Breast-feeding.** Neomycin, polymyxin B, and hydrocortisone otic preparations have not been reported to cause problems in nursing babies.

**Children.** Although there is no specific information comparing use of otic neomycin, polymyxin B, and hydrocortisone preparation in children with use in other age groups, this preparation is not expected to cause different side effects or problems in children than it does in adults.

## Proper use of this medicine

Lie down or tilt the head so that the infected ear faces up. Gently pull the earlobe up and back for adults (down and back for children) to straighten the ear canal. Drop the medicine into the ear canal. Keep the ear facing up for about 5 minutes to allow the medicine to coat the ear canal. (For young children and other patients who cannot stay still for 5 minutes, try to keep the ear facing up for at least 1 or 2 minutes.) Your doctor may have inserted a gauze or cotton wick into your ear and may want you to keep the wick moistened with this medicine. Your doctor also may have other directions for you, such as how long you should keep the wick in your ear or when you should return to your doctor to have the wick replaced. If you have any questions about this, check with your doctor.

To keep the medicine as germ-free as possible, do not touch the dropper to any surface (including the ear). Also, keep the container tightly closed.

## Dosing

*For otic (ear drops) dosage forms for ear-canal infection:* Children: Use three drops in the ear three or four times a day.

## Side effects of this medicine

**More common:** Itching, skin rash, redness, swelling, or other sign of irritation in or around the ear not present before use of this medicine

# DEXAMETHASONE

**Sold under these brand names**

Decadron

Decadron Elixir

Decadron-LA

Decadron Phosphate

## Description

Corticosteroids (kor-ti-koe-STER-oyds) such as dexamethasone (cortisone-like medicines) are used to provide relief for inflamed areas of the body. They lessen swelling, redness, itching, and allergic reactions. They are often used as part of the treatment for a number of different diseases, such as severe allergies or skin problems, asthma, or arthritis. Corticosteroids may also be used for other conditions as determined by your doctor.

Your body naturally produces certain cortisonelike hormones that are necessary to maintain good health. If your body does not produce enough, your doctor may have prescribed this medicine to help make up the difference.

Corticosteroids are very strong medicines. In addition to their helpful effects in treating your medical problem, they have side effects that can be very serious. If your adrenal glands are not producing enough cortisonelike hormones, taking this medicine is not likely to cause problems unless you take too much of it. If you are taking this medicine to treat another medical problem, be sure that you discuss the risks and benefits of this medicine with your doctor.

Elixir (U.S.)

Oral solution (U.S.)

Tablets (U.S. and Canada)

## Before using this medicine

**Allergies.** Tell your doctor if your child has ever had any unusual or allergic reaction to corticosteroids. Also tell your health-care professional if you are allergic to any other substances, such as foods, preservatives, or dyes.

**Diet.** If you will be using this medicine for a long time, your doctor may want you to:

Follow a low-salt diet and/or a potassium-rich diet.

Watch your calories to prevent weight gain.

Add extra protein to your diet.

Make certain your health-care professional knows if you are already on any special diet, such as a low-sodium or low-sugar diet.

**Pregnancy.** Studies on birth defects with corticosteroids have not been done in humans. However, studies in animals have shown that corticosteroids cause birth defects.

**Breast-feeding.** Corticosteroids pass into breast milk and may cause problems with growth or other unwanted effects in nursing babies. Depending on the amount of medicine you are taking every day, it may be necessary for you to take another medicine or to stop breast-feeding during treatment.

**Children.** Corticosteroids may cause

infections such as chickenpox or measles to be more serious in children who catch them. These medicines can also slow or stop growth in children and in growing teenagers, especially when they are used for a long time. Before this medicine is given to children or teenagers, you should discuss its use with your child's doctor and then carefully follow the doctor's instructions.

## Proper use of this medicine

Take this medicine with food to help prevent stomach upset. If stomach upset, burning, or pain continues, check with your doctor.

## Dosing

*For oral dosage forms (elixir, oral solution, tablets):* Children: Dose is based on body weight or size and must be determined by your doctor.

## Missed dose

*If you miss a dose of this medicine and your dosing schedule is:* One dose every other day: Take the missed dose as soon as possible if you remember it the same morning, then go back to your regular dosing schedule. If you do not remember the missed dose until later, wait and take it the following morning. Then skip a day and start your regular dosing schedule again.

One dose a day: Take the missed dose as soon as possible, then go back to your regular dosing schedule. If you do not remember until the next day, skip the missed dose and do not double the next one.

Several doses a day: Take the missed dose as soon as possible, then go back to your regular dosing schedule. If you do not remember until your next dose is due, double the next dose.

## Precautions while using this medicine

Do not stop using this medicine without first checking with your doctor. Your doctor may want you to gradually reduce the amount you are using before stopping the medicine completely.

Avoid close contact with anyone who has chickenpox or measles. This is especially important for children. Tell your doctor right away if you think you have been exposed to chickenpox or measles.

While you are being treated with this medicine, and after you stop taking it, do not have any immunizations without your doctor's approval. Also, other people living in your home should not receive the oral polio vaccine, since there is a chance they could pass the polio virus on to you. In addition, you should avoid close contact at school or work with other people who have recently taken the oral polio vaccine.

## Side effects of this medicine

Corticosteroids may lower your resistance to infections. Also, any infection you get may be harder to treat. Always check with your doctor as soon as possible if you notice any signs of a possible infection, such as sore throat, fever, sneezing, or coughing.

**Less common:** Decreased or blurred vision; frequent urination; increased thirst

**Rare:** Blindness (sudden, when injected in the head or neck area); burning, numbness, pain, or tingling at or near place of injection; confusion; excitement; false sense of well-being; hallucinations (seeing, hearing, or feeling things that are not there); mental depression; mistaken feelings of self-importance or being mistreated; mood swings (sudden and wide); redness, swelling, or other sign of allergy or infection at place of injection; restlessness; skin rash or hives

Additional side effects may occur if you take this medicine for a long time. Check with your doctor if any of the following side effects occur: Abdominal or stomach pain or burning (continuing); acne; bloody or black, tarry stools; changes in vision; eye pain; filling or rounding out of the face; headache; irregular heartbeat; menstrual problems; muscle cramps or pain; muscle weakness; nausea; pain in arms, back, hips, legs, ribs, or shoulders; pitting, scarring, or depression of skin at the place of injection; reddish purple lines on arms, face, groin, legs, or trunk; redness of eyes; sensitivity of eyes to light; stunting of growth; swelling of feet or lower legs; tearing of eyes; thin, shiny skin; trouble in sleeping; unusual bruising; unusual increase in hair growth; unusual tiredness or weakness; vomiting; weight gain (rapid); wounds that won't heal.

## Other side effects may occur

**More common:** Increased appetite; indigestion; loss of appetite (for triamcinolone only); nervousness or restlessness.

**Less common or rare:** Darkening or lightening of skin color; dizziness or lightheadedness; flushing of face or cheeks; hiccups; increased joint pain (after injection into a joint); increased sweating; nosebleeds (after injection into the nose); sensation of spinning

After you stop using this medicine, your body may need time to adjust.

# ELOCON, WESTCORT (mometasone/hydrocortisone valerate)

## Description

Topical corticosteroids (kor-ti-ko-STER-oyds) are used to help relieve redness, swelling, itching, and discomfort of many skin problems. These medicines are like cortisone. They belong to the general family of medicines called steroids.

## Before using this medicine

**Allergies.** Tell your doctor if your child has ever had any unusual or allergic reaction to corticosteroids. Also tell your health-care professional if you are allergic to any other substances, such as foods, preservatives, or dyes.

**Pregnancy.** When used properly, these medicines have not been shown to cause problems in humans. Studies on birth defects have not been done in humans. However, studies in animals have shown that topical corticosteroids, when applied to the skin in large amounts or used for a long time, could cause birth defects.

**Breast-feeding.** Topical corticosteroids have not been reported to cause problems in nursing babies when used properly. However, corticosteroids should not be applied to the breasts before nursing.

**Children.** Children and teenagers who must use this medicine should be checked often by their doctor since this medicine may be absorbed through the skin and can affect growth or cause other unwanted effects.

## Proper use of this medicine

Do not bandage or otherwise wrap the skin being treated unless directed to do so by your doctor.

*For patients using flurandrenolide tape:* This medicine usually comes with patient directions. Read them carefully before using this medicine.

Do not use this medicine more often or for a longer time than your doctor ordered.

Do not use this medicine for other skin problems without first checking with your doctor.

### Dosing

Follow your doctor's orders or directions on label.

## Precautions while using this medicine

Check with your doctor if your symptoms do not improve within one week or if your condition gets worse.

Avoid using tight-fitting diapers or plastic pants on a child if this medicine is being used on the child's diaper area. Plastic pants or tight-fitting diapers may increase the chance of absorption of the medicine through the skin and the chance of side effects.

## Side effects of this medicine

**Less frequent or rare:** Blood-containing blisters on skin; burning and itching of skin; increased skin sensitivity (for some brands of betamethasone lotion); lack of healing of skin condition; loss of top skin layer (for tape dosage forms); numbness in fingers; painful, red or itchy, pus-containing blisters in hair follicles; raised, dark red, wart-like spots on skin, especially when used on the face; skin infection; thinning of skin with easy bruising

**Less frequent or rare—usually mild and transient:** Burning, dryness, irritation, itching, or redness of skin; increased redness or scaling of skin sores; skin rash

. . . . . . . . . . . . . . . . . . . . . . . . . . . . . . .

# FLOVENT
## (fluticasone)

### Description

Fluticasone (floo-TIK-a-sone) belongs to the family of medicines known as corticosteroids (cortisone-like medicines). It is used to help prevent the symptoms of asthma. When used regularly every day, inhaled fluticasone decreases the number and severity of asthma attacks. However, it will not relieve an asthma attack that has already started.

Inhaled fluticasone works by preventing certain cells in the lungs and breathing passages from releasing substances that cause asthma symptoms.

This medicine may be used with other asthma medicines, such as bronchodilators (medicines that open up narrowed breathing passages) or other corticosteroids taken by mouth.

This medicine is available only with your doctor's prescription, in the following dosage form(s):

Aerosol (U.S. and Canada)

Powder for inhalation (U.S. and Canada)

## Before using this medicine

**Allergies.** Tell your doctor if your child has ever had any unusual or allergic reaction to fluticasone. Also tell your health-care professional if you're allergic to any other substances, such as foods, especially milk, preservatives, or dyes.

**Pregnancy.** Inhaled fluticasone has not been studied in pregnant women. However, in animal studies, fluticasone given by injection was shown to cause birth defects. Also, too much use of corticosteroids during pregnancy may cause other unwanted effects in the infant, such as slower growth and reduced adrenal gland function.

**Breast-feeding.** It is not known whether inhaled fluticasone passes into breast milk. However, in animals given fluticasone by injection, the medicine did pass into breast milk. Although most medicines pass into breast milk in small amounts, many of them may be used safely while breast-feeding. Mothers who are taking this medicine and who wish to breast-feed should discuss this with their doctor.

**Children.** Corticosteroids taken by mouth or injection have been shown to slow or stop growth in children and cause reduced adrenal gland function. If enough fluticasone is absorbed following inhalation, it is possible it also could cause these effects. Your doctor will want you to use the lowest possible dose of fluticasone that controls asthma. This will lessen the chance of an effect on growth or adrenal gland function. It is also important that children taking fluticasone visit their doctors regularly so that their growth rates may be monitored. Children who are taking this medicine may be more susceptible to infections, such as chickenpox or measles. Care should be taken to avoid exposure to chickenpox or measles. If the child is exposed or the disease develops, the doctor should be contacted and his or her directions should be followed carefully. Before this medicine is given to a child, you and your child's doctor should talk about the good this medicine will do as well as the risks of using it.

## Proper use of this medicine

Inhaled fluticasone is used to prevent asthma attacks. It is not used to relieve an attack that has already started. For relief of an asthma attack that has already begun, you should use another medicine. If you don't have another medicine to use for an attack or if you have any questions about this, check with your health-care professional. In order for this medicine to help prevent asthma attacks, it must be used every day in regularly spaced doses, as ordered by your doctor.

Inhaled fluticasone is used with a special inhaler and usually comes with patient directions. Read the directions carefully before using this medicine. If you do not understand the directions or you are not sure how to use the inhaler, ask your health-care professional to show you what to do.

## Dosing

*For bronchial asthma, for inhalation aerosol:* Children younger than 12 years of age: Use and dose must be determined by your doctor. Canadian labeling recommends: For children 4 to 16 years of age: 50 to 100 mcg two times a day. For children up to 4 years of age: Use and dose must be determined by your doctor.

*For powder for inhalation:* Children 4 to 11 years of age: 50 to 100 mcg two times a day.

Children younger than 4 years of age: Use and dose must be determined by your doctor.

## Side effects of this medicine

**More common:** White patches in mouth and throat

**Less common:** Diarrhea; earache; fever; lower abdominal pain; nausea; pain on passing urine; redness or discharge of the eye, eyelid, or lining of the eye; shortness of breath; sore throat; trouble in swallowing; vaginal discharge (creamy white) and itching; vomiting

Other side effects that may occur include: Cough; general aches and pains or general feeling of illness; greenish-yellow mucus in nose; headache; hoarseness or other voice changes; loss of appetite; runny, sore, or stuffy nose; unusual tiredness; weakness.

# KEFLEX
## (cephalexin)

### Description

Cephalexin is used in the treatment of infections caused by bacteria. They work by killing bacteria or preventing their growth. It will not work for colds, flu, or other virus infections.

### Before using this medicine

**Allergies.** Tell your doctor if your child has ever had any unusual or allergic reaction to any of the cephalosporins, penicillins, penicillin-like medicines, or penicillamine. Also tell your health-care professional if you are allergic to any other substances, such as foods, preservatives, or dyes.

**Pregnancy.** Studies have not been done in humans. However, cephalexin has not been reported to cause birth defects or other problems in animal studies.

**Breast-feeding.** Most drugs of this class pass into breast milk, usually in small amounts. However, they have not been reported to cause problems in nursing babies.

**Children.** Cephalexin has been tested in children and, in effective doses, have not been shown to cause different side effects or problems than they do in adults.

## Proper use of this medicine

Cephalexin may be taken on a full or empty stomach. If this medicine upsets your stomach, it may help to take it with food.

## Dosing

*For oral dosage forms (capsules, oral suspension, or tablets):* Children 40 kg (88 pounds) of body weight and over: 250 mg to 1 gram every six to 12 hours.

Children 1 year of age and older and up to 40 kg (88 pounds) of body weight: 6.25 to 25 mg per kilogram (kg) (2.84 to 11.36 mg per pound) of body weight every six hours, or 12.5 to 50 mg per kg (5.68 to 22.72 mg per pound) of body weight every 12 hours.

Infants and children 1 month to 1 year of age: 6.25 to 12.5 mg per kg (2.84 to 5.68 mg per pound) of body weight every six hours.

## Missed dose

If you miss a dose of this medicine, take it as soon as possible. This will help to keep a constant amount of medicine in the blood or urine. However, if it is almost time for your next dose, skip the missed dose and go back to your regular dosing schedule. Do not double doses.

## Precautions while using this medicine

*In some patients, cephalexin may cause diarrhea:* Severe diarrhea may be a sign of a serious side effect.

## Side effects of this medicine

Along with its needed effects, a medicine may cause some unwanted effects. Although not all of these side effects may occur, if they do occur they may need medical attention.

*Check with your doctor immediately if any of the following side effects occur:*

**Less common or rare:** Abdominal or stomach cramps and pain (severe); abdominal tenderness; diarrhea (watery and severe, which may also be bloody); fever; unusual bleeding or bruising

NOTE: Some of these side effects may also occur up to several weeks after you stop taking this medicine.

**Rare:** Blistering, peeling, or loosening of skin; convulsions (seizures); decrease in urine output; hearing loss; joint pain; loss of appetite, nausea, or vomiting; pain, redness, and swelling at place of injection; skin rash, itching, redness, or swelling; trouble in breathing; unusual tiredness or weakness; yellowing of the eyes or skin

# LURIDE
## (sodium fluoride)

## Description

Fluoride (FLURE-ide) has been found to be helpful in reducing the number of cavities in the teeth. It is usually present naturally in drinking water. However, some areas of the country do not have a high enough level in the water to prevent cavities. To make up for this, extra fluorides may be added to the diet. Some children may require both dietary fluorides and topical fluoride treatments by the dentist. Use of a fluoride toothpaste or rinse may be helpful as well.

Taking fluorides does not replace good dental habits. These include eating a good diet, brushing and flossing teeth often, and having regular dental checkups.

The daily amount of fluoride needed has been defined in different ways.

U.S. Recommended Dietary Allowances (RDAs) are the amount of vitamins and minerals needed to provide for adequate nutrition in most healthy persons. RDAs for a given nutrient may vary depending on a person's age, sex, and physical condition (e.g., pregnancy).

Daily Values (DVs) are used on food and dietary supplement labels to indicate the percent of the recommended daily amount of each nutrient that a serving provides. DV replaces the previous designation of U.S. Recommended Daily Allowances.

There is no RDA for fluoride. Daily recommended intakes for fluoride are generally defined as follows:

Infants and children birth to 3 years of age: 0.1 to 1.5 milligrams (mg).

Children 4 to 6 years of age: 1 to 2.5 mg.

Children 7 to 10 years of age: 1.5 to 2.5 mg.

## Before using this medicine

**Allergies.** Tell your health-care professional if your child is allergic to any other substances, such as foods, preservatives, or dyes.

**Pregnancy.** It is especially important that you are receiving enough vitamins and minerals when you become pregnant and that you continue to receive the right amount of vitamins and minerals throughout your pregnancy. The healthy growth and development of the fetus depend on a steady supply of nutrients from the mother. However, taking large amounts of a dietary supplement in pregnancy may be harmful to the mother and/or fetus and should be avoided. Sodium fluoride occurs naturally in water and has not been shown to cause problems in infants of mothers who drank fluoridated water or took appropriate doses of supplements.

**Breast-feeding.** It is especially important that you receive the right amounts of vitamins and minerals so that your baby will also get the vitamins and minerals needed to grow properly. However, taking large amounts of a dietary supplement while breast-feeding may be harmful to the mother and/or baby and should be avoided. Small amounts of sodium fluoride pass into breast milk.

**Children.** Problems in children have not been reported with intake of normal daily recommended amounts. Doses of sodium fluoride that are too large or are taken for a long time may cause bone problems and teeth discoloration in children.

## Proper use of this medicine

Take this medicine only as directed by your health-care professional. Do not take more of it and do not take it more often than ordered. Taking too much fluoride over a period of time may cause unwanted effects.

## Dosing

*For oral dosage form (lozenges, solution, tablets, or chewable tablets) to prevent cavities in the teeth (where there is not enough fluoride in the water):* Children: Dose is based on the amount of fluoride in drinking water in your area. Dose is also based on the child's age and must be determined by your health-care professional.

## Precautions while using this medicine

Do not take calcium supplements or aluminum hydroxide-containing products and sodium fluoride at the same time. It is best to space doses of these two products 2 hours apart, to get the full benefit from each medicine.

Inform your health-care professional as soon as possible if you notice white, brown, or black spots on the teeth. These are signs of too much fluoride in children when it is given during periods of tooth development.

## Side effects of this medicine

Sores in mouth and on lips (rare).

Sodium fluoride in drinking water or taken as a supplement does not usually cause any side effects. However, taking an overdose of fluoride may cause serious problems.

Black, tarry stools; bloody vomit; diarrhea; drowsiness; faintness; increased watering of mouth; nausea or vomiting; shallow breathing; stomach cramps or pain; tremors; unusual excitement; watery eyes; weakness

Pain and aching of bones; stiffness; white, brown, or black discoloration of teeth occur only during periods of tooth development in children

. . . . . . . . . . . . . . . . . . . . . . . . . . . . . . . . .

# MYCOSTATIN
## (nystatin) Oral form

## Description

Nystatin (nye-STAT-in) belongs to the group of medicines called antifungals. The dry powder, lozenge (pastille), and liquid forms of this medicine are used to treat fungus infections in the mouth.

## Before using this medicine

**Allergies.** Tell your doctor if your child has ever had any unusual or allergic reaction to nystatin. Also tell your health-care professional if you are allergic to any other substances, such as foods, preservatives, or dyes.

**Pregnancy.** Studies in humans have not shown that oral nystatin causes birth defects or other problems.

**Breast-feeding.** Oral nystatin has not been reported to cause problems in nursing babies.

**Children.** This medicine has been tested in children and has not been reported to cause different side effects or problems in children than it does in adults. However, since children up to 5 years of age may be too young to use the lozenges (pastilles) or tablets safely, the oral suspension dosage form is best for this age group.

## Proper use of this medicine

### Dosing

*For the lozenge (pastille) and tablet dosage forms:* Adults and children 5 years of age and older: 1 or 2 lozenges or tablets three to five times a day for up to 14 days.

Children up to 5 years of age: Children this young may not be able to use the lozenges or tablets safely. The oral suspension is better for this age group.

*For the suspension dosage form:* Adults and children 5 years of age and older: 4 to 6 milliliters (mL) (about 1 teaspoonful) four times a day.

For older infants: 2 mL four times a day.

For premature and low-birth-weight infants: 1 mL four times a day.

## Side effects of this medicine

Diarrhea; nausea or vomiting; stomach pain

......................................

# MYCOSTATIN
## (nystatin) Topical form

### Description

Nystatin (nye-STAT-in) belongs to the group of medicines called antifungals. Topical nystatin is used to treat some types of fungus infections of the skin.

Nystatin is available in the U.S. only with your doctor's prescription. It is available in Canada without a prescription; however, your doctor may have special instructions on the proper use of this medicine for your medical problem.

### Before using this medicine

**Allergies.** Tell your doctor if your child has ever had any unusual or allergic reaction to nystatin. Also tell your health-care professional if you are allergic to any other substances, such as preservatives or dyes.

**Pregnancy.** Nystatin topical preparations have not been shown to cause birth defects or other problems in humans.

**Breast-feeding.** It is not known whether nystatin passes into breast milk. Although most medicines pass into breast milk in small amounts, many of them may be used safely while breast-feeding. Mothers who are using this medicine and who wish to breast-feed should discuss this with their doctor.

**Children.** Although there is no specific information comparing use of topical nystatin in children with use in other age groups, this medicine is not expected to cause different side effects or problems in children than it does in adults.

## Proper use of this medicine

Topical nystatin should not be used in the eyes.

Apply enough nystatin to cover the affected area.

Sprinkle the powder between the toes, on the feet, and in socks and shoes.

To help clear up your infection completely, keep using this medicine for the full time of treatment, even if your condition has improved. Do not miss any doses.

## Dosing

*For topical dosage forms (cream or ointment):* Adults and children: Apply to the affected area(s) of the skin two times a day.

*For topical dosage form (powder):* Adults and children: Apply to the affected area(s) of the skin two or three times a day.

## Side effects of this medicine

Skin irritation not present before use of this medicine.

# PATANOL
## (olopatadine)
## Opthalmic (eye) form

## Description

Olopatadine (oh-loe-pa-TA-deen) ophthalmic (eye) solution is used to temporarily prevent itching of the eye caused by a condition known as allergic conjunctivitis. It works by acting on certain cells, called mast cells, to prevent them from releasing substances that cause the allergic reaction.

## Before using this medicine

**Allergies.** Tell your doctor if your child has ever had any unusual or allergic reaction to olopatadine. Also tell your health-care professional if you are allergic to any other substances, such as certain preservatives.

**Pregnancy.** Olopatadine has not been studied in pregnant women. However, studies in animals have found that this medicine given in extremely high doses results in a decreased number of live births; it has not been found to cause birth defects. Before using this medicine, make sure your doctor knows if you are pregnant or if you may become pregnant.

**Breast-feeding.** It is not known whether olopatadine passes into human breast milk. However, it does pass into the milk of animals with nursing young. Discuss with your doctor whether or not to breast-feed while using this medicine.

**Children.** Studies on this medicine have been done only in adult patients, and there is no specific information comparing use of olopatadine in children up to 3 years of age with use in other age groups.

## Proper use of this medicine

### Dosing

*For ophthalmic dosage form (eye drops):* Adults and children 3 years of age and older: Use one drop in each affected eye two times a day, with each dose being at least six to eight hours apart.

Children up to 3 years of age: Use and dose must be determined by your doctor.

## Side effects of this medicine

**More common:** Headache

**Less common:** Burning, dryness, itching, or stinging of the eye; change in taste; eye irritation or pain; feeling of something in the eye; redness of eye or inside of eyelid; runny or stuffy nose; sore throat; swelling of eyelid; unusual tiredness or weakness

. . . . . . . . . . . . . . . . . . . . . . . . . . . . . . . .

# PREDNISOLONE, PREDNISONE

**Sold under these brand names:**
Prednisone Intensol
Pred-Pak 79

## Description

Corticosteroids (kor-ti-koe-STER-oyds) (cortisone-like medicines) are used to provide relief for inflamed areas of the body. They lessen swelling, redness, itching, and allergic reactions. They are often used as part of the treatment for a number of different diseases, such as severe allergies or skin problems, asthma, or arthritis. Corticosteroids may also be used for other conditions as determined by your doctor.

Your body naturally produces certain cortisone-like hormones that are necessary to maintain good health. If your body does not produce enough, your doctor may have prescribed this medicine to help make up the difference.

Corticosteroids are very strong medicines. In addition to their helpful effects in treating your medical problem, they have side effects that can be very serious. If your adrenal glands are not producing enough cortisone-like hormones, taking this medicine is not likely to cause problems unless you take too much of it. If you are taking this medicine to treat another medical problem, be sure that you discuss the risks and benefits of this medicine with your doctor.

Oral solution (U.S. and Canada for prednisolone; U.S. for prednisone)

Syrup (U.S.)

Tablets (U.S. for prednisolone; U.S. and Canada for prednisone)

## Before using this medicine

**Allergies.** Tell your doctor if your child has ever had any unusual or allergic reaction to corticosteroids. Also tell your health-care professional if you are allergic to any other substances, such as foods, preservatives, or dyes.

**Diet.** If you will be using this medicine for a long time, your doctor may want you to:

Follow a low-salt diet and/or a potassium-rich diet.

Watch your calories to prevent weight gain.

Add extra protein to your diet.

Make certain your health-care professional knows if you are already on any special diet, such as a low-sodium or low-sugar diet.

**Pregnancy.** Studies on birth defects with corticosteroids have not been done in humans. However, studies in animals have shown that corticosteroids cause birth defects.

**Breast-feeding.** Corticosteroids pass into breast milk and may cause problems with growth or other unwanted effects in nursing babies. Depending on the amount of medicine you are taking every day, it may be necessary for you to take another medicine or to stop breast-feeding during treatment.

**Children.** Corticosteroids may cause infections such as chickenpox or measles to be more serious in children who catch them. These medicines can also slow or stop growth in children and in growing teenagers, especially when they are used for a long time. Before this medicine is given to children or teenagers, you should discuss its use with your child's doctor and then carefully follow the doctor's instructions.

## Proper use of this medicine

Take this medicine with food to help prevent stomach upset. If stomach upset, burning, or pain continues, check with your doctor.

## Dosing

*For oral dosage forms (oral solution, syrup, tablets):* Children: Dose is based on body weight or size and must be determined by your doctor.

## Missed dose

*If you miss a dose of this medicine and your dosing schedule is:* One dose every other day: Take the missed dose as soon as possible if you remember it the same morning, then go back to your regular dosing schedule. If you do not remember the missed dose until later, wait and take it the following morning. Then skip a day and start your regular dosing schedule again.

One dose a day: Take the missed dose as soon as possible, then go back to your regular dosing schedule. If you do not remember until the next day, skip the missed dose and do not double the next one.

Several doses a day: Take the missed dose as soon as possible, then go back to your regular dosing schedule. If you do not remember until your next dose is due, double the next dose.

## Precautions while using this medicine

Do not stop using this medicine without first checking with your doctor. Your doctor may want you to reduce gradually the amount you are using before stopping the medicine completely.

Avoid close contact with anyone who has chickenpox or measles. This is especially important for children. Tell your doctor right away if you think you have been exposed to chickenpox or measles.

While you are being treated with this medicine, and after you stop taking it, do not have any immunizations without your doctor's approval. Also, other people living in your home should not receive the oral polio vaccine, since there is a chance they could pass the polio virus on to you. In addition, you should avoid close contact with other people at school or work who have recently taken the oral polio vaccine.

## Side effects of this medicine

Corticosteroids may lower your resistance to infections. Also, any infection you get may be harder to treat. Always check with your doctor as soon as possible if you notice any signs of a possible infection, such as sore throat, fever, sneezing, or coughing.

**Less common:** Decreased or blurred vision; frequent urination; increased thirst

**Rare:** Blindness (sudden, when injected in the head or neck area); burning, numbness, pain, or tingling at or near place of injection; confusion; excitement; false sense of well-being; hallucinations (seeing, hearing, or feeling things that are not there); mental

depression; mistaken feelings of self-importance or being mistreated; mood swings (sudden and wide); redness, swelling, or other sign of allergy or infection at place of injection; restlessness; skin rash or hives

Abdominal or stomach pain or burning (continuing); acne; bloody or black, tarry stools; changes in vision; eye pain; filling or rounding out of the face; headache; irregular heartbeat; menstrual problems; muscle cramps or pain; muscle weakness; nausea; pain in arms, back, hips, legs, ribs, or shoulders; pitting, scarring, or depression of skin at place of injection; reddish purple lines on arms, face, groin, legs, or trunk; redness of eyes; sensitivity of eyes to light; stunting of growth (in children); swelling of feet or lower legs; tearing of eyes; thin, shiny skin; trouble in sleeping; unusual bruising; unusual increase in hair growth; unusual tiredness or weakness; vomiting; weight gain (rapid); wounds that will not heal

**More common:** Increased appetite; indigestion; loss of appetite (for triamcinolone only); nervousness or restlessness

**Less common or rare:** Darkening or lightening of skin color; dizziness or lightheadedness; flushing of face or cheeks; hiccups; increased joint pain (after injection into a joint); increased sweating; nosebleeds (after injection into the nose); sensation of spinning

After you stop using this medicine, your body may need time to adjust. The length of time this takes depends on the amount of medicine you were using and how long you used it.

......................................

# PULMICORT
## (budesonide) respules for nebulizer

### Before using this medicine

**Allergies.** Tell your doctor if your child has ever had any unusual or allergic reaction to corticosteroids. Also tell your health-care professional if you are allergic to any other substances, such as foods, preservatives, or dyes.

**Pregnancy.** Although studies in animals have shown that inhaled corticosteroids cause birth defects and other problems, in humans these medicines, when used in regular daily doses during pregnancy to keep the mother's asthma under control, have not been reported to cause breathing problems or birth defects in the newborn. Also, corticosteroids may prevent the effects of poorly controlled asthma, which are known to be harmful to the baby. Before taking an inhaled corticosteroid, make sure your doctor knows if you are pregnant or if you may become pregnant.

**Breast-feeding.** It is not known whether inhaled corticosteroids pass into breast milk. Although most medicines pass into breast milk in small amounts, many of them may be used safely while breast-feeding. Mothers who are using this medicine and who wish to breast-feed should discuss this with their doctor.

**Children.** Inhalation corticosteroids

have been tested in children and, except for the possibility of slowed growth, in low effective doses, have not been shown to cause different side effects or problems than they do in adults.

Studies have shown that slowed growth or reduced adrenal gland function may occur in some children using inhaled corticosteroids in recommended doses. However, poorly controlled asthma may cause slowed growth, especially when corticosteroids taken by mouth are needed often. Your doctor will want you to use the lowest possible dose of an inhaled corticosteroid that controls asthma. This will lessen the chance of an effect on growth or adrenal gland function. It is also important that children taking inhaled corticosteroids visit their doctors regularly so that their growth rates may be monitored.

Regular use of inhaled corticosteroids may allow some children to stop using or decrease the amount of corticosteroids taken by mouth. This also will reduce the risk of slowed growth or reduced adrenal function.

Children who are using inhaled corticosteroids in large doses should avoid exposure to chickenpox or measles. When a child is exposed or the disease develops, the doctor should be contacted and his or her directions should be followed carefully.

Before this medicine is given to a child, you and your child's doctor should talk about the good this medicine will do as well as the risks of using it. Follow the doctor's directions very carefully to lessen the chance that unwanted effects will occur.

## Proper use of this medicine

Inhaled corticosteroids will not relieve an asthma attack that has already started. However, your doctor may want you to continue taking this medicine at the usual time, even if you use another medicine to relieve the asthma attack.

Use this medicine only as directed. Do not use more of it and do not use it more often than your doctor ordered. To do so may increase the chance of side effects. Do not stop taking this medicine abruptly. This medicine should be discontinued only under the supervision of your doctor.

In order for this medicine to help prevent asthma attacks, it must be used every day in regularly spaced doses, as ordered by your doctor.

Gargling and rinsing your mouth with water after each dose may help prevent hoarseness, throat irritation, and infection in the mouth. However, do not swallow the water after rinsing. Your doctor may also want you to use a spacer device to lessen these problems.

*For patients using budesonide powder for inhalation:*

**To prime the inhaler:** Unscrew the cover of the inhaler and lift it off.

Hold the inhaler upright with the brown piece pointing downward. Turn the brown piece of the inhaler in one direction as far as it will go. Then twist it back until it clicks. Repeat this step one more time and the inhaler will be primed.

Prime each new inhaler before using it the first time. After it has been primed, it is not necessary to prime it again, even if you put it aside for a long period of time.

**To load the inhaler:** Unscrew the cover of the inhaler and lift it off.

Hold the inhaler upright with the brown piece pointing downward. Turn the brown piece of the inhaler in one direction as far as it will go. Then twist it back until it clicks.

**To use the inhaler:** Hold the inhaler away from your mouth and breathe out slowly to the end of a normal breath.

Place the mouthpiece in your mouth and close your lips around it. Tilt your head slightly back. Do not block the mouthpiece with your teeth or tongue.

Breathe in quickly and evenly through your mouth until you have taken a full deep breath.

Hold your breath and remove the inhaler from your mouth. Continue holding your breath as long as you can up to 10 seconds before breathing out. This gives the medicine time to settle in your airways and lungs.

Hold the inhaler well away from your mouth and breathe out to the end of a normal breath.

Replace the cover on the mouthpiece to keep it clean.

This inhaler delivers the medicine as a very fine powder. You may not taste, smell, or feel this medicine.

This inhaler should not be used with a spacer.

When the indicator window begins to show a red mark, there are about 20 doses left. When the red mark covers the window, the inhaler is empty.

*For patients using budesonide suspension for inhalation:* This medicine is to be used in a power-operated nebulizer equipped with a face mask or mouthpiece. Your doctor will advise you on which nebulizer to use. Make sure you understand how to use the nebulizer. If you have any questions about this, check with your doctor.

Any opened ampul should be protected from light. The medicine in an open ampul must be used promptly after the ampul is opened. Ampuls should be used within 2 weeks after the envelope containing them is opened.

**To prepare the medicine for use in the nebulizer:** Remove one ampul from the sheet of five units and shake it gently.

Hold the ampul upright. Open it by twisting off the wing.

Squeeze the contents of the ampul into the cup of the nebulizer. If you use only half of the contents of an ampul, add enough of the sodium chloride solution provided to dilute the solution.

Gently shake the nebulizer. Then attach the face mask to the nebulizer and connect the nebulizer to the air pump.

**To use the medicine in the nebulizer:** This medicine should be inhaled over a period of 10 to 15 minutes.

Breathe slowly and evenly, in and out, until no more mist is left in the nebulizer cup.

Rinse your mouth when you are finished with the treatment. Wash your face if you used a face mask.

**To clean the nebulizer:** After each treatment, wash the cup of the nebulizer and the mask or mouthpiece in warm water with a mild detergent.

Allow the nebulizer parts to dry before putting them back together again.

## Dosing

*For powder for inhalation: for bronchial asthma:* Children 6 years of age and older: At first, 200 mcg two times a day. Then your doctor may increase the dose to 400 mcg two times a day, depending on your condition. A lower dose of 200 mcg or 400 mcg once daily, either in the morning or in the evening, may sometimes be used for mild to moderate asthma when the symptoms are well controlled.

Children up to 6 years of age: Use and dose must be determined by the doctor.

*For suspension for inhalation: for bronchial asthma:* Children 12 months to 8 years of age: 250 to 500 mcg mixed with enough sterile sodium chloride solution for inhalation, if necessary, to make 2 to 4 mL. This solution is used in a nebulizer for a period of 10 to 15 minutes. The medicine should be used two times a day.

Children up to 12 months of age: Use

and dose must be determined by the doctor.

## Precautions while using this medicine

Check with your doctor if:

You go through a period of unusual stress to your body, such as surgery, injury, or infection .

You have an asthma attack that does not improve after you take a bronchodilator medicine.

You are exposed to viral infections, such as chickenpox or measles.

Signs of infection occur, especially in your mouth, throat, or lung.

Your symptoms do not improve or if your condition gets worse.

Your doctor may want you to carry a medical identification card stating that you are using this medicine and that you may need additional medicine during times of emergency, a severe asthma attack or other illness, or unusual stress.

Before you have any kind of surgery (including dental surgery) or emergency treatment, let the medical doctor or dentist in charge know that you are using this medicine.

Do not stop taking the corticosteroid taken by mouth without your doctor's advice, even if your asthma seems better.

## Side effects of this medicine

**Rare:** Shortness of breath, troubled breathing, tightness in chest, or wheezing; signs of hypersensitivity reactions, such as swelling of face, lips, or eyelids

**Less common:** Bruising; burning or pain while urinating, blood in urine, or frequent urge to urinate; chest pain; creamy white, curd-like patches in the mouth or throat and/or pain when eating or swallowing; dizziness or sense of constant movement or surroundings; general feeling of discomfort or illness; irregular or fast heartbeat; itching, rash, or hives; sinus problems; stomach or abdominal pain; swelling of fingers, ankles, feet, or lower legs; unusual tiredness or weakness; weight gain

## RITALIN
### (methylphenidate)

## Description

Methylphenidate (meth-il-FEN-i-date) belongs to the group of medicines called central nervous system (CNS) stimulants. It is used to treat attention-deficit hyperactivity disorder (ADHD), narcolepsy (uncontrollable desire for sleep or sudden attacks of deep sleep), and other conditions as determined by the doctor.

Methylphenidate works in the treatment of ADHD by increasing attention and decreasing restlessness in children and adults who are overactive, cannot concentrate for very long or are easily distracted, and are impulsive. This medicine is used as part of a total treatment program that also includes social, educational, and psychological treatment.

## Before using this medicine

**Allergies.** Tell your doctor if you

have ever had any unusual or allergic reaction to methylphenidate. Also tell your health-care professional if you are allergic to any other substances, such as foods, preservatives, or dyes.

**Pregnancy.** Studies on effects in pregnancy have not been done in either humans or animals.

**Breast-feeding.** It is not known whether methylphenidate passes into breast milk. Although most medicines pass into breast milk in small amounts, many of them may be used safely while breast-feeding. Mothers who are taking this medicine and who wish to breast-feed should discuss this with the doctor.

**Children.** Loss of appetite, trouble in sleeping, stomach pain, fast heartbeat, and weight loss may be especially likely to occur in children, who are usually more sensitive than adults to the effects of methylphenidate. Some children who used medicines like methylphenidate for a long time grew more slowly than expected. It is not known whether long-term use of methylphenidate causes slowed growth. The doctor should regularly measure the height and weight of children who are taking methylphenidate. Some doctors recommend stopping treatment with methylphenidate during times when the child is not under stress, such as on weekends.

### Proper use of this medicine

Take this medicine with or after a meal or a snack.

To help prevent trouble in sleeping, take the last dose of the short-acting tablets before 6 p.m., unless otherwise directed by your doctor.

### Dosing

*For attention-deficit hyperactivity disorder:* Children up to 6 years of age: The dose must be determined by the doctor.

### Precautions while using this medicine

Your doctor should check your progress at regular visits and make sure that this medicine does not cause unwanted effects, such as high blood pressure.

Methylphenidate may cause dizziness, drowsiness, or changes in vision.

### Side effects of this medicine

**More common:** Fast heartbeat; increased blood pressure

**Less common:** Chest pain; fever; joint pain; skin rash or hives; uncontrolled movements of the body

**Rare:** Black, tarry stools; blood in urine or stools; blurred vision or other changes in vision; convulsions (seizures); muscle cramps; pinpoint red spots on skin; uncontrolled vocal outbursts and/or tics (uncontrolled and repeated body movements); unusual bleeding or bruising

### Symptoms of overdose

Agitation; confusion (severe); convulsions (seizures); dryness of mouth or mucous membranes; false sense of well-being; fast, pounding, or irregular heartbeat; fever; hallucinations (seeing, hearing, or feeling things that are not there); headache (severe); increased blood pressure; increased sweating; large pupils; muscle twitching; overactive reflexes; trembling or shaking; vomiting

. . . . . . . . . . . . . . . . . . . . . . . . . . . . . .

# TOBREX
## (tobramycin)
## Opthalmic form

### Description

Ophthalmic tobramycin (toe-bra-MYE-sin) is used in the eye to treat bacterial infections of the eye. Tobramycin works by killing bacteria.

Either the drops or the ointment form of this medicine may be used alone during the day. In addition, both forms may be used together, with the drops being used during the day and the ointment at night.

### Before using this medicine

**Allergies.** Tell your doctor if your child has ever had any unusual or allergic reaction to ophthalmic tobramycin or to any related medicines, such as amikacin (e.g., Amikin), gentamicin (e.g., Garamycin), kanamycin (e.g., Kantrex), neomycin (e.g., Mycifradin), netilmicin (e.g., Netromycin), streptomycin, or tobramycin by injection (e.g., Nebcin). Also tell your health-care professional if you are allergic to any other substances, such as preservatives.

**Pregnancy.** Studies have not been done in humans. However, tobramycin ophthalmic preparations have not been shown to cause birth defects or other problems in animals even when given at high doses.

**Breast-feeding.** Tobramycin ophthalmic preparations may be absorbed into the eye. However, tobramycin is unlikely to pass into the breast milk in large amounts and little would be absorbed by the infant. Therefore, this medicine is unlikely to cause serious problems in nursing babies.

**Children.** This medicine has been tested in children and, in effective doses, has not been shown to cause different side effects or problems than it does in adults.

### Proper use of this medicine

*For patients using tobramycin ophthalmic solution (eye drops):* First, wash your hands. Tilt the head back and with the index finger of one hand, press gently on the skin just beneath the lower eyelid and pull the lower eyelid away from the eye to make a space. Drop the medicine into this space. Let go of the eyelid and gently close the eyes. Do not blink. Keep the eyes closed for 1 or 2 minutes, to allow the medicine to come into contact with the infection.

If you think you did not get the drop of medicine into your eye properly, use another drop.

To keep the medicine as germ-free as possible, do not touch the applicator tip to any surface (including the eye). Also, keep the container tightly closed.

If your doctor ordered two different

ophthalmic solutions to be used together, wait at least 5 minutes between the times you apply the medicines. This will help to keep the second medicine from "washing out" the first one.

*For patients using tobramycin ophthalmic ointment (eye ointment):* First, wash your hands. Tilt the head back and with the index finger of one hand, press gently on the skin just beneath the lower eyelid and pull the lower eyelid away from the eye to make a space. Squeeze a thin strip of ointment into this space. A 1.25-cm (approximately ½-inch) strip of ointment usually is enough, unless you have been told by your doctor to use a different amount. Let go of the eyelid and gently close the eyes and keep them closed for 1 or 2 minutes, to allow the medicine to come into contact with the infection.

To keep the medicine as germ-free as possible, do not touch the applicator tip to any surface (including the eye). After using tobramycin eye ointment, wipe the tip of the ointment tube with a clean tissue and keep the tube tightly closed.

To help clear up your eye infection completely, keep using tobramycin for the full time of treatment, even if your symptoms have disappeared. Do not miss any doses.

## Dosing

*For ophthalmic ointment dosage forms for mild to moderate infections:* Adults and children: Use every eight to twelve hours.

*For severe infections:* Adults and children: Use every three to four hours until improvement occurs.

*For ophthalmic solution (eye drops) dosage forms for mild to moderate infections:* Adults and children: One drop every four hours.

*For severe infections:* Adults and children: One drop every hour until improvement occurs.

## Side effects of this medicine

**Less common:** Itching, redness, swelling, or other sign of eye or eyelid irritation not present before use of this medicine.

**Symptoms of overdose:** Increased watering of the eyes; itching, redness, or swelling of the eyes or eyelids; painful irritation of the clear front part of the eye.

**Less common:** Burning or stinging of the eyes

. . . . . . . . . . . . . . . . . . . . . . . . . . . . . . . .

# ZANTAC, ZANTAC 75, ZANTAC 150 GELDOSE, ZANTAC 300 GELDOSE (ranitidine)

## Description

Histamine H 2 -receptor antagonists, also known as H 2 -blockers, are used to treat duodenal ulcers and prevent their return. They are also used to treat gastric ulcers and for some conditions, such as Zollinger-Ellison disease, in which the stomach produces too much acid. In over-the-counter (OTC) strengths, these medicines are used to relieve and/or prevent heartburn, acid indigestion, and sour stomach. H 2 -blockers may also be used for other conditions as determined by your doctor.

H 2 -blockers work by decreasing the amount of acid produced by the stomach.

Capsules (U.S.)
Effervescent granules (U.S.)
Syrup (U.S. and Canada)
Tablets (U.S. and Canada)
Effervescent tablets (U.S.)

## Before using this medicine

**Allergies.** Tell your doctor if your child has ever had any unusual or allergic reaction to cimetidine, famotidine, nizatidine, or ranitidine.

**Pregnancy.** H 2 -blockers have not been studied in pregnant women. In animal studies, famotidine and ranitidine have not been shown to cause birth defects or other problems. Make sure your doctor knows if you are pregnant or if you may become pregnant before taking H 2 -blockers.

**Breast-feeding.** Ranitidine passes into the breast milk and may cause unwanted effects, such as decreased amount of stomach acid and increased excitement, in the nursing baby. It may be necessary for you to take another medicine or to stop breast-feeding during treatment. Be sure you have discussed the risks and benefits of the medicine with your doctor.

**Children.** This medicine has been tested in children and, in effective doses, has not been shown to cause different side effects or problems than it does in adults when used for short periods of time.

## Proper use of this medicine

For patients taking the nonprescription strengths of these medicines for heartburn, acid indigestion, and sour stomach:

Do not take the maximum daily dosage continuously for more than 2 weeks, unless directed to do so by your doctor.

If you have trouble in swallowing, or persistent abdominal pain, see your doctor promptly. These may be signs of a serious condition that may need different treatment.

## Dosing

The dose of histamine H 2 -receptor antagonists (also called H 2 -blockers) will be different for different patients. Follow your doctor's orders or the directions on the label. The following information includes only the average doses of these medicines. If your dose is different, do not change it unless your doctor tells you to do so.

*For oral dosage forms (capsules, effervescent granules, syrup, tablets, effervescent tablets) to treat duodenal ulcers:* Children: 2 to 4 mg per kilogram (kg) (1 to 2 mg per pound) of body weight two times a day. However, your dose will not be more than 300 mg a day.

*To prevent duodenal ulcers:* Children:

PEDIATRIC DRUGS

Dose must be determined by your doctor.

*To treat gastric ulcers:* Children: 2 to 4 mg per kg (1 to 2 mg per pound) of body weight two times a day. However, your dose will not be more than 300 mg a day.

*To treat heartburn, acid indigestion, and sour stomach:* Children: Dose must be determined by your doctor.

*To prevent heartburn, acid indigestion, and sour stomach:* Children: Dose must be determined by your doctor.

*To treat some conditions in which the stomach produces too much acid:* Children: Dose must be determined by your doctor.

*To treat gastroesophageal reflux disease:* Children: 2 to 8 mg per kg (1 to 3.6 mg per pound) of body weight three times a day. However, most children usually will not take more than 300 mg a day.

*For injectable dosage form to treat duodenal or gastric ulcers:* Children: 2 to 4 mg per kg (1 to 2 mg per pound) of body weight a day, injected slowly into a vein.

### Precautions while using this medicine

Remember that certain medicines, such as aspirin, and certain foods and drinks (e.g., citrus products, carbonated drinks, etc.) irritate the stomach and may make your problem worse.

### Side effects of this medicine

**Rare:** Abdominal pain; back, leg, or stomach pain; bleeding or crusting sores on lips; blistering, burning, redness, scaling, or tenderness of skin; blisters on palms of hands and soles of feet; changes in vision or blurred vision; confusion; coughing or difficulty in swallowing; dark-colored urine; dizziness; fainting; fast, pounding, or irregular heartbeat; fever and/or chills; flu-like symptoms; general feeling of discomfort or illness; hives; anxiety, agitation, nervousness, shortness of breath; slow heartbeat; swelling of face, lips, mouth, tongue, or eyelids; unusual bleeding or bruising; wheezing; yellow eyes or skin

**Less common or rare:** Constipation; trouble in sleeping

## ZITHROMAX
### (azithromycin)

### Description

Azithromycin (az-ith-roe-MYE-sin) is used to treat bacterial infections in many different parts of the body. It works by killing bacteria or preventing their growth. However, this medicine will not work for colds, flu, or other viral infections.

### Before using this medicine

**Allergies.** Tell your doctor if your child has ever had any unusual or allergic reaction to azithromycin or to any related medicines such as erythromycin.

Also tell your health-care professional if you are allergic to any other substances, such as foods, preservatives, or dyes.

**Pregnancy.** Azithromycin has not been studied in pregnant women. However, azithromycin has not been shown to cause birth defects or other problems in animal studies.

**Breast-feeding.** It is not known whether azithromycin passes into breast milk. Although most medicines pass into breast milk in small amounts, many of them may be used safely while breast-feeding. Mothers who are taking this medicine and who wish to breast-feed should discuss this with their doctor.

**Children.** This medicine has been tested in a limited number of children up to the age of 16. In effective doses, the medicine has not been shown to cause different side effects or problems than it does in adults.

## Proper use of this medicine

Azithromycin capsules and pediatric oral suspension should be taken at least 1 hour before or at least 2 hours after meals. Azithromycin tablets and adult single dose oral suspension may be taken with or without food.

## Dosing

*For the capsule dosage form for bronchitis, strep throat, pneumonia, and skin infections:* Children up to 16 years of age: Use and dose must be determined by your doctor.

Children 6 months to 12 years of age: Use and dose must be determined by your doctor.

*For otitis media and pneumonia:* Children 6 months to 12 years of age: 10 milligrams (mg) per kilogram (kg) (4.5 mg per pound) of body weight once a day on the first day, then 5 mg per kg (2.2 mg per pound) of body weight once a day on days two through five.

*For strep throat:* Children 2 to 12 years of age: 12 mg per kg (5.4 mg per pound) of body weight once a day for five days.

Children up to 2 years of age: Use and dose must be determined by your doctor.

*For the tablet dosage form for bronchitis, strep throat, pneumonia, and skin infections:* Children up to 16 years of age: Use and dose must be determined by your doctor.

Children up to 16 years of age: Use and dose must be determined by your doctor.

## Missed dose

If you miss a dose of this medicine, take it as soon as possible. However, if it is almost time for your next dose, skip the missed dose and go back to your regular dosing schedule. Do not double doses.

## Side effects of this medicine

*Stop taking this medicine and get emergency help immediately if any of the following side effects occur:*

**Rare:** Abdominal or stomach cramps or pain (severe); abdominal tenderness; diarrhea (watery and severe, which may be bloody); difficulty in breathing; fever; joint pain; skin rash; swelling of face, mouth, neck, hands, and feet

## Other side effects:

**Less common:** Diarrhea (mild); nausea; stomach pain or discomfort; vomiting

**Rare:** Dizziness; headache

....................................

# ZOVIRAX
## (acyclovir)

## Description

Acyclovir (ay-SYE-kloe-veer) belongs to the family of medicines called antivirals, which are used to treat infections caused by viruses. Usually these medicines work for only one kind or group of virus infections.

Acyclovir is used to treat chickenpox, shingles, herpes virus infections of the genitals (sex organs), the skin, the brain, and mucous membranes (lips and mouth), and widespread herpes virus infections in newborns.

## Before using this medicine

**Allergies.** Tell your doctor if your child has ever had any unusual or allergic reaction to acyclovir, ganciclovir, or valacyclovir. Also tell your health-care professional if you are allergic to any other substances, such as foods, sulfites or other preservatives, or dyes.

**Pregnancy.** Acyclovir has been used in pregnant women and has not been reported to cause birth defects or other problems. However, studies have not been done in humans. Studies in rabbits have shown that acyclovir given by injection may keep the fetus from becoming attached to the lining of the uterus (womb). However, acyclovir has not been shown to cause birth defects or other problems in mice given many times the usual human dose, or in rats or rabbits given several times the usual human dose.

**Breast-feeding.** Acyclovir passes into breast milk. However, it has not been reported to cause problems in nursing babies.

**Children.** A limited number of studies have been done using oral acyclovir in children, and it has not caused different effects or problems in children than it does in adults.

## Proper use of this medicine

If you are taking acyclovir for the treatment of chickenpox, it is best to start taking acyclovir as soon as possible after the first sign of the chickenpox rash, usually within one day.

Acyclovir capsules, tablets, and oral suspension may be taken with meals or on an empty stomach.

If you are using acyclovir oral suspension , use a specially marked measuring spoon or other device to measure each dose accurately. The average household teaspoon may not hold the right amount of liquid.

Acyclovir is best taken with a full glass (8 ounces) of water.

## Dosing

*For oral dosage forms:* Children up to 12 years of age: Use and dose must be determined by the doctor.

*For treatment of chickenpox:* Children 2 years of age and older and weighing 88 pounds (40 kilograms) or less: Dose is based on body weight and must be determined by the doctor. The usual dose is 20 mg per kilogram (kg) of body weight, up to 800 mg, four times a day for five days.

Children up to 2 years of age: Use and dose must be determined by the doctor.

## Precautions while using this medicine

If your symptoms do not improve within a few days, or if they become worse, check with your doctor.

The areas affected by herpes, chickenpox, or shingles should be kept as clean and dry as possible. Also, wear loose-fitting clothing to avoid irritating the sores (blisters).

It is important to remember that acyclovir will not keep you from spreading herpes to others .

## Side effects of this medicine

For both oral acyclovir and acyclovir injection blistering, peeling, or loosening of skin; changes in facial skin color; changes in vision; confusion; convulsions (seizures); coughing; difficulty in breathing or swallowing; dizziness or feeling faint, severe; fast heartbeat; muscle cramps, pain, or weakness; nausea or vomiting; red or irritated eyes;

seeing, hearing, or feeling things that are not there; sense of agitation or uneasiness; skin rash, itching, or hives; sore throat, fever, or chills; sores, ulcers, or white spots in mouth or on lips; swelling of eyelids, face, feet, hands, lower legs or lips; swollen, painful, or tender lymph nodes (glands) in neck, armpit, or groin

**More common:** General feeling of discomfort or illness

**Less common:** Diarrhea; headache

**Frequency not determined:** Agitation; loss of hair; burning, prickling, or tingling sensations; drowsiness

## ZYRTEC
### (cetirizine)

## Description

Antihistamines are used to relieve or prevent the symptoms of hay fever and other types of allergy. They work by preventing the effects of a substance called histamine, which is produced by the body. Histamine can cause itching, sneezing, runny nose, and watery eyes. Also, in some persons histamine can close up the bronchial tubes (air passages of the lungs) and make breathing difficult.

Some antihistamine preparations are available only with your doctor's prescription. Others are available without a prescription. However, your doctor may have special instructions on the proper dose of the medicine for your medical condition.

## Before using this medicine

**Allergies.** Tell your doctor if your child has ever had any unusual or allergic reaction to antihistamines. Also tell your health-care professional if you are allergic to any other substances, such as foods, preservatives, or dyes.

**Breast-feeding.** Small amounts of antihistamines pass into the breast milk. Use is not recommended since babies are more susceptible to the side effects of antihistamines, such as unusual excitement or irritability. Also, since these medicines tend to decrease the secretions of the body, it is possible that the flow of breast milk may be reduced in some patients. It is not known yet whether astemizole, cetirizine, loratadine, or terfenadine cause these same side effects.

**Children.** Serious side effects, such as convulsions (seizures), are more likely to occur in younger patients and would be of greater risk to infants than to older children or adults. In general, children are more sensitive to the effects of antihistamines. Also, nightmares or unusual excitement, nervousness, restlessness, or irritability may be more likely to occur in children.

## Proper use of this medicine

*For oral dosage forms (syrup and tablets):* Children younger than 2 years of age: Use and dose must be determined by your doctor.

Children 2 to 6 years of age: 2.5 mg once a day, up to a maximum of 5 mg once a day or 2.5 mg twice a day.

Children 6 years of age and older: 5 to 10 mg once a day.

## Side effects of this medicine

**Less frequent or rare:** Fast or irregular heartbeat.

Also, check with your doctor as soon as possible if any of the following side effects occur:

**Less common or rare:** Sore throat; unusual bleeding or bruising; unusual tiredness or weakness

**Symptoms of overdose:** Clumsiness or unsteadiness; convulsions (seizures); drowsiness (severe); dryness of mouth, nose, or throat (severe); feeling faint; flushing or redness of face; hallucinations (seeing, hearing, or feeling things that are not there); shortness of breath or troubled breathing; trouble in sleeping

## Other side effects

**More common:** Drowsiness; dry mouth, nose, or throat; gastrointestinal upset, stomach pain, or nausea; increased appetite and weight gain; thickening of mucus

**Less common or rare:** Blurred vision or any change in vision; confusion; drowsiness; dryness of mouth, nose, or throat; fast heartbeat; increased sensitivity of skin to sun; loss of appetite; skin rash; gastrointestinal upset; unusual excitement, nervousness, restlessness, or irritability; thickening of mucus

# Product Recalls

The majority of baby products are regulated by two federal agencies. The National Highway Traffic Safety Administration oversees child car-seat safety, and the Consumer Product Safety Commission administers mandatory federal standards for cribs, seats, pacifiers, rattles, and toys. There are also general regulations, applicable to all products, that cover small parts that a baby could ingest, sharp edges and sharp points that can cut, and lead in paint. The regulations require manufacturers of baby products to report consumer complaints about injuries or deaths.

The agencies monitor consumer complaints and injuries, and issue a recall when there's a safety problem. Sometimes manufacturers will recall products voluntarily. You may never hear about a recall unless you stay informed. Mail in all product-registration cards for car seats so the manufacturer can contact you. (If you lose your car-seat registration card, call the NHTSA hotline at 800-424-9393 for a new one.) And check product-safety information sources yourself.

This book includes a category-by-category list of products recalled since early 1998. We go over the typical things that go wrong with each type of product, as well as applicable standards and safety advice. You'll find company contact information within each listing. If you discover an item you've purchased or received as a gift has been recalled, follow the advice for remedial action.

You can find additional product-recall listings monthly in CONSUMER REPORTS and on its online service at *www.ConsumerReports.org.* These sources list the most far-reaching recalls.

If you have questions about a specific car-seat model, you can call the NHTSA auto safety hotline, 888-327-4236, or check its Web site *(www.nhtsa.dot.gov)* for recalls. To report an unsafe product or get recall information, call the CPSC hotline, 800-638-2772. Consult the Web site *(www.recalls.gov)* for up-to-date recall data.

Should your child have an accident that's clearly a product's fault, such as hardware that fails or parts that cause harm or entrap, check the manufacturer's Web site for the address, then report the problem in writing to the manufacturer (with a copy to the CPSC or NHTSA), giving the model number and all the details you can supply about the model (usually on a manufacturer's sticker or label somewhere on the product). It's possible that a company will try to put the responsibility for the injury on you. By law, manufacturers must report injury data to the CPSC or face being sued and fined. You might want to follow up with the appropriate federal agencies to make sure this occurred, and, if needed, to help get satisfaction from the manufacturer.

## Product Certification

The Juvenile Products Manufacturers Association (JPMA) sponsors and administers a voluntary certification program for juvenile products. Programs are currently in effect for full- and non-full-sized cribs, toddler beds, high chairs, portable hook-on chairs, play yards, strollers, gates, and walkers. A voluntary standard for soft carriers is being developed with Consumers Union's participation.

The JPMA retains an independent laboratory to periodically perform or witness tests of sample units. Products are certified if they meet the minimum safety performance standards developed by the American Society for Testing and Materials (ASTM). They may then carry a sticker reading "CERTIFIED: This model tested by an independent laboratory for compliance with ASTM safety standard." But certification isn't fail-safe, so don't view the sticker as a safety guarantee. Voluntary standards cover only major hazards and require only minimum safe-performance levels. Standards vary in strictness from one product category to another. Plus, tests are conducted on brand-new products, not those that have sustained the daily wear and tear of baby use. For specifics on test standards, see the separate product categories throughout the book and in the following recalls.

In this book we note the certification status of each product category. Or you can obtain the most recent directory of certified products by contacting JPMA.

# BASSINETS

## Kids Line Inc.
## Le Cradle bassinet

**Problem:** Infant could become trapped in the opening between the bassinet's side and mattress platform, posing suffocation risk. Also, infant could suffer scrapes or get caught in metal frame if fabric comes off.

**Products:** 46,000 bassinets sold 1/89-5/00 nationwide at juvenile product stores for $100 to $200. Bassinet is oval and has white metal base with wheels and removable canopy. It consists of a metal wire frame and wooden base-board that rests on metal base. Fabric-covered foam mattress covers wooden board. Matching fabric covers bassinet frame and comes in various colors and designs. Sticker on mattress platform gives instructions for use and says: "Le Cradle, Kids Line, Los Angeles California."

**What to do:** Call Kids Line toll-free at 866-532-7235 for free repair kit.

# BATHING ACCESSORIES

## First Years 2-In-1 Fold-Away tub and step stool

**Problem:** When used as tub, body parts could be pinched if footrest is not extended so that it clicks into place.

**Products:** 120,000 products, model number 3141, sold 1/99-2/02 at mass-merchandise stores nationwide for about $17. Model number appears on underside of base. Product is a folding baby bathtub that can be used as a step stool for an older child. In step-stool mode, top of turquoise lid has raised lettering that reads, "the first years." Near bottom of lid appears the following: "MAXIMUM LOAD/POIDS MAXIMUM: 200lbs/90kg" and "USE ONLY ON A LEVEL SURFACE." In bathtub position, seatback has purple pad. Base and footrest are white. On underside of base is tiny raised clock showing year of manufacture (for example, "9/9") surrounded by the numbers of the clock. Only products bearing date codes 1999 and 2000 ("9/9" or "0/0") are subject to recall. There have been 20 reports of babies being pinched while using tubs.

**What to do:** Stop using this tub until you receive new instructions on proper use to prevent pinch hazard. Call The First Years at 800-533-6708 or go to *www.thefirstyears.com.*

## Graco and Children on the Go activity trays and bath sets with suction cups

**Problem:** Suction cups could detach and pose choking hazard to small child.

**Products:** 100,000 devices sold 1/98-8/99 at discount, department, and juvenile-product stores nationwide, including Toys "R" Us and Sears, for

$10 to $15. Recall involves the Graco and Children on the Go brand Stroller Snack and Activity Tray, Bathtime Activity Tray, and Bathtime Toy Netting products. Activity trays attach with suction cups to tiled or smooth surfaces, and four toys are affixed to each tray.

Toys are removable and interchangeable with other Mix 'N Move toys, which can be bought separately. Stroller Snack and Activity Tray toys include toucan, rolling ball, star, and dog. Bathtime Activity Tray's toys include octopus, U-tube, spinning ball, and paddle wheel. "Graco" or "Children On The Go" appears on underside of tray. Bathtime Toy Netting consists of clam soap holder and fish washcloth holder that attaches with suction cups to various surfaces. A net, used to store toys, hangs between clam and fish.

**What to do:** Call Graco at 800-446-1366 or access company's Web site at *www.gracobaby.com* to receive free repair kit. Consumers can also write to Graco Children's Products, Attn.: Consumer Affairs, P.O. Box 100, Elverson, PA 19520.

### Sassy Scoop Pour 'N Squirt and Bath Time Pals bath sets

**Problem:** The fish's size, texture, shape, and easy compressibility make it possible for an infant to compress the toy and place it in his or her mouth. If the toy reaches the back of the mouth and expands, it may block the child's airway.

**Products:** 370,000 squirting fish found in the Scoop Pour 'N Squirt and Bath Time Pals bath toy set sold in mass-merchandise stores and toy stores 02/99-12/00 for about $5. The Scoop Pour 'N Squirt bath toy set has a large plastic fish-shaped scoop with a green textured handle and a spout for pouring water and two small plastic squirting fish. The Bath Time Pals bath toy set comes with one squirting frog, two squirting pearls, and two squirting fish.

**What to do:** Remove the squirting fish from young children and throw them away. For additional information or to receive replacement squirt toys, contact Sassy, toll-free, at 800-764-8323 or visit its Web site at *www.sassybaby.com*.

## BOOSTER SEATS

### Safety 1st Fold-up booster seat

**Problem:** Child could fall from seat and suffer serious injury.

**Products:** 1.5 million seats, model numbers 173, 173A, and 173B, sold 1/94-8/99 at toy, hardware, and department stores for about $18. Model number appears on back of seat, inside left arm panel. Seat is intended for use by children who can sit unassisted.

It's made of blue plastic with green and red arms and includes yellow feeding tray. Device also has a restraint system made of a two-piece waist strap and a crotch strap. "SAFETY 1ST" is molded into top and bottom of seat insert.

**What to do:** Call Safety 1st toll-free at 888-579-1730 for free repair kit.

........................................

## BOUNCER SEATS

### KIDS II bouncer seats

**Problem:** The removable toy bar that attaches to the seat can suddenly release and cause injuries to babies. (You can continue to use the bouncer seat for the baby to sit in as long as the toy bar is removed.)

**Products:** 99,000 bouncer seats sold in mass-merchandise and juvenile-specialty stores nationwide 10/97-4/00 for about $25 to $35. Only models with semicircular (not rectangular) toy bars holding three toys were recalled. The seats were sold under the names "Soft Toy Bouncer Seat" or "Comfort Me Bouncer." The Kids II logo is embroidered on each seat's crotch strap. The bouncer seats have a ruffled seat pad in three patterns: a black, white, and red cow print; a teddy bear, rocking horse, and toy box print; and a nursery rhyme print. Each pattern has certain model and lot numbers, which are found on a tag attached to the seat. The Comfort Me Bouncers feature vibration and soothing sounds, including music, waves, and heartbeat. Some of the recalled seats came with white toy-bar tethers.

**What to do:** Remove the semicircular toy bar immediately and contact Kids II

toll-free at 877-325-7056 between 7:30 a.m. and 4:30 p.m. EST Monday through Friday for a free in-home repair kit. You can continue to use the bouncer seat as long as the toy bar is removed.

........................................

## CAR SEATS

### Britax Roundabout convertible child safety seat

**Problem:** Might not provide adequate head protection in crash.

**Products:** 9,922 Model No. 161 safety seats made 1/13/99-3/14/99. Manufacturing date appears on black-and-white label on back or arm of seat shell.

**What to do:** Call Britax toll-free at 800-683-2045 for free repair kit, which includes a shoulder pad that would prevent excessive head movement during sudden stop. Consumers can also write to Britax Child Safety Inc., 460-R Greenway Industrial Dr., Fort Mill, SC 29708.

### Britax model E9022 convertible child safety seat

**Problem:** Might not provide adequate protection in crash.

**Models:** 4,959 safety seats made 3/5/01-7/26/01. Model number and date of manufacture are located on label on side of seat.

**What to do:** Call Britax at 888-427-4829 for free repair kit.

## Britax Super Elite child car seats

**Problem:** Might not adequately restrain child in a crash.

**Products:** 2,689 car seats made 4/25/01-2/15/02. Manufacturing date appears on a label on the seat. Super Elite car seats made as of 2/19/02 are not affected by the recall.

**What to do:** All Super Elite owners who returned the product registration card should have received a free harness replacement kit. If you didn't register the seat or haven't received the kit, call 888-427-4829 for free replacement parts.

## Cosco Arriva and Turnabout infant carrier/safety seats

**Problem:** When used as carrier, plastic handle locks may break or release, allowing baby to fall to the ground and suffer injuries.

**Products:** 1.2 million safety seats made through 1/31/00. This recall is an expansion of a 7/99 recall involving 670,000 of these same seats. Juvenile product, mass merchandise, department and major discount chains nationwide sold the seat/carriers from 9/97-12/00 for $30 to $60, and for $90 to $140 packaged with a stroller. The recall involves the following Arriva models: 02-665, 02-727, 02-728, 02-729, 02-731, 02-732, 02-733, 02-750, 02-751, 02-755, 02-757, 02-774.

It also involves the following Turnabout models: 02-753, 02-756, 02-758, 02-759, 02-760, 02-761, 02-762, 02-763, 02-764, 02-765, 02-770, 02-771, 02-772. The model number and date of manufacture appear on label on the side of the seat. Dorel Juvenile Group, the manufacturer, has received 416 reports of the handle locks on newly recalled seats breaking or unlatching, resulting in nine injuries.

**What to do:** Call Dorel Juvenile Group at 800-880-9435 or go to *www.djgusa.com* for free repair kit. Parents can continue to use the Arriva and Turnabout as a safety seat but should stop using the unit as a carrier.

## Evenflo Joyride child safety seat/ infant carrier

**Problem:** When used as carrier, handle could release and allow infant to fall to ground.

**Products:** 3.4 million seats sold 1/88-12/98 nationwide at juvenile-product, mass-merchandise, and major discount stores for about $30 alone, $48 with detachable base (marketed as "Travel Tandem"), and $89 with matching stroller. Recall involves all Joyride seats, which are gray or white plastic with various color pads. Seats also bear model numbers beginning with 203, 205, 210, 435, or 493, located on label beneath seat or on side of seat or carrier. "Evenflo Joyride Seat/Carrier" is written on outside of handle locks. There have been 240 reports of handles unexpectedly releasing, resulting in 97 injuries, according to the Consumer

Product Safety Commission (CPSC).

**What to do:** Call Evenflo at 800-557-3178 or visit *www.joyridecarseat.com* for free repair kit. Note: Consumers should not carry seat by handle until repair is made. However, the CPSC says seat can still be used as safety restraint in vehicle.

## Evenflo On My Way Position Right child safety seat

**Problem:** Over time, infant carrier might not latch securely to its base, resulting in inadequate protection in crash.

**Products:** 164,144 carriers/bases made 1/26/99-2/10/00. Date of manufacture appears on white label on underside of base. Base bears words "Position Right" and has large red knob in front. Base was sold individually, with On My Way Position Right safety seat, or as part of Easy Comfort Premier or Trendsetter Advantage travel system (with safety seat and matching stroller). Hazard exists because alignment posts in base could bend. If so, consumer could encounter difficulty installing carrier onto base or in latching components together. According to Evenflo, consumers may still use carrier as a safety seat without the base, using the built-in safety-belt guides.

**What to do:** Call Evenflo at 800-316-4779 or visit its Web site, *www.evenflo.com,* for free repair kit, consisting of metal clip, which is designed to keep posts in base from bending.

## Evenflo Two-In-One booster car seats

**Problem:** Seatback could separate from base in crash, increasing likelihood of injury to child.

**Products:** 32,000 plastic child seats with cloth pad, designed for children weighing 22 to 65 pounds. Recalled seats were made 1/7/98-3/20/98 and have six-digit model number starting with 636 or 637. Date of manufacture and model number are on label on backrest.

**What to do:** Call 800-985-7328 for free replacement seat.

## Fisher-Price Safe Embrace convertible child safety seat

**Problem:** Might not provide adequate protection in crash.

**Products:** 54,500 safety seats, model 79700, made 5/97-3/98. Model number and manufacture date are on seat shell.

**What to do:** Call 800-355-8882 for replacement harness adjuster.

## Fisher-Price Safe Embrace safety seats

**Problem:** Shoulder-harness locking mechanism may malfunction, compromising protection in a crash.

**Products:** 55,000 "Safe Embrace" convertible child safety seats, manufactured 5/97-3/98. Product comes with a tether that secures the top of the seat to the car's rear shelf or cargo area.

**What to do:** Call Fisher-Price at 800-355-8882 for a free replacement harness-adjuster (consumers who had registered the seat with Fisher-Price will automatically receive one). It's OK to continue using the seat until the new adjuster arrives, but inspect the seat each time it's used to be sure the harness belts stay locked in place.

## Graco SnugRide infant car seat and carrier

**Problem:** Might not provide adequate protection in a crash.

**Products:** 53,926 car seats made in the U.S. 3/7/03-3/8/03, including the following model numbers: 8402L03, 840301, 840302, 840303, 8442GMP, 8442LBLW, 8442LCYP, 8442LMAD, 8444LHAB, 8444LHIG, 8446LFKB, 8446LVIN, 8447LHAV, 8448LSAR, 8463AMB, 8463GMP, 8463JUN, 8463YL, 8464MAC, 8464MEL, 8602AMB, 8602JUN, 8602MAN, 8603MIC, 8603MLL, 8605HIG, 8605KER, 8605PLT, 8607LAG, 8607NGS, 8608DIA, and 8609FOF. Model number and manufacturing date appear on a label on the base or seat. Hazard exists because of missing hooks and pins that could prevent the seat from securely attaching to the base. SnugRide infant car seats sold as part of a travel system (stroller/infant carrier/car-seat base combination) and stand-alone units made in China are not affected. This recall is an extension of an earlier corrective action involving 650,000 of the following SnugRide models made 3/1/02-3/6/03: 8402, 8412, 8442, 8442L, 8443, 8443L, 8444, 8444L, 8446, 8446L, 8447, 8447L, 8448, 8448L, 8457, 8458, 8459, 8601, 8463, 8464, 8470, 8471, 8478, and C844342.

**What to do:** Inspect car seat. If hooks or pins are missing, stop using the base. Then call Graco at 800-345-4109 to determine whether seat or base should be returned for free replacement. Until new base arrives, seat can still be used alone. Instructions appear at *www.gracobaby.com*. Go to that Web site or write to Graco Children's Products at 150 Oaklands Blvd., Exton, PA 19341 for help identifying suspect units.

## Graco SnugRide infant carrier/child safety seat

**Problem:** When used with base as a child safety seat, carrier could detach from base in crash, subjecting child to serious injury.

**Products:** 918,930 safety seats made 8/31/99-2/28/02, including the following models (model number may be preceded by the letter A): 7493G9, 7493RS, 7497HL, 7497SY, 7499LK, 7499N2, 841101, 841102, 841103, 841203, 8412T02, 8457D5, 8457DVB, 8457F3, 8457GP, 8457IND, 8457MA, 8457MV, 8457RG, 8457TMJ, 8457TMP, 8457YL, 8458A5, 8458AE, 8458B7, 8458D8, 8458FKB, 8458HE, 8458HH, 8458KY, 8458N5, 8459VL, 8460LV, 8462HAV, 8462JAM, 8471UVB, 8472BLW, 8473BRN, 8472CYP, 8472GMP, 8472MAD, 8472YL, 8474HAB, 8474MEL, 8476VIN, 8477HAV, 8477JAM, 8477NGS, and 8478SAR. Model name and number, as well as date of manufacture, appear on label on seat or base. Hazard exists because of missing hardware (metal hooks and U-shaped bars) used to secure seat to base. Base was also sold separately through Graco Customer Service. If base was purchased that way, model number may not be evident; you will need to contact the company to determine if the device is subject to recall. The seat portion of the unit can still be used as an infant carrier or safety seat when strapped to vehicle without the base, according to Graco.

**What to do:** Call Graco at 800-345-4109 for free replacement seat or base. Company will also help consumers identify suspect models.

## Graco SnugRide infant car seats equipped with base

**Problem:** Seat may be missing hardware to attach carrier to base. In a sudden stop or crash, the carrier may detach from the base, possibly resulting in serious injury or death.

**Products:** 50,000 SnugRide infant car seats manufactured in the U.S. 3/1/02-3/6/03. Affected models carry the following model numbers: 8402, 8412, 8442, 8442L, 8443, 8443L, 8444, 8444L, 8446, 8446L, 8447, 8447L, 8448, 8448L, 8457, 8458, 8459, 8601, 8463, 8464, 8470, 8471, 8478, and C844342. The model number and date of manufacture are located on a label attached to the car seat or base. No injuries have been reported or associated with the safety problem.

SnugRide infant car seats sold as part of a travel system of stroller/carrier/car seat base and and stand-alone and safety seats made in China are not subject to the recall.

**What to do:** You can continue to use the infant carrier without its base as a car seat. Instructions for installing the carrier without the base are in the original instruction manual or online at *www.gracobaby.com*. Parents who own one of the affected seats can call Graco at 866-473-0163 or visit the Web site for guidance on how to inspect the seat. Graco will provide a new base or a new seat if hardware is missing or improperly assembled.

## Peg Perego Primo Viaggio infant safety seats

**Problem:** Seat may not latch securely to base, increasing risk of injury or death in sudden stop or crash.

**Products:** 14,087 safety seats made 2/01-6/01. Seats were sold separately with base as Primo Viaggio infant seat or bundled with stroller and sold as Pliko Travel System or Primo Viaggio Travel System. Date of manufacture appears on seat. Latch mechanism on left side of seat does not completely engage latching rod on base because of manufacturing mistake.

**What to do:** Call Peg Perego toll-free at 877-737-3468 or visit *www.perego.com* for easy-to-follow repair instructions. Consumers can also write to company at 3625 Independence Dr., Fort Wayne, IN 46808.

### Safety 1st and Beatrix Potter Designer 22 infant safety seats/carriers

**Problem:** When seat is used as carrier, handle could unexpectedly release, allowing unrestrained infant to fall to the ground and suffer serious injury.

**Products:** 26,000 safety seats made 1/3/02 and 2/13/02 and sold from 1/02-4/02 at mass-merchandise and department stores for $40 to $70. Suspect units bear the following model numbers/color codes: 02-621-SAL, 02-620-AZY, and 02-620-BEA. Model information and date of manufacture appear on label on side of seat/carrier. Note: None of suspect seats/carriers were sold in Canada.

**What to do:** Stop using seat as carrier (but continue to use it as safety restraint in vehicle) and call manufacturer, Dorel Juvenile Group, at 800-536-1090, for free repair kit. You can also visit *www.djgusa.com* for information.

· · · · · · · · · · · · · · · · · · · · · · · · · · · · · ·

# CARRIERS

### Evenflo Hike 'N Roll child carrier

**Problem:** Child could slip through leg openings and strangle.

**Products:** 22,000 child carriers, models 522101 and 522102, made 6/1/96-10/31/97 and sold 6/96-6/98 for about $65. Model number and date of manufacture are on white tag on bottom of carrier. Device, used as backpack carrier or stroller, is green and blue,

or blue and beige, with "Evenflo" on front and back.

**What to do:** Call 800-649-0071 for free seat insert to reduce size of leg openings.

### Evenflo Snugli Front & Back Pack soft infant carriers

**Problem:** Small infants can slip through the leg openings of these carriers and fall, especially infants under 2 months of age.

**Products:** 327,000 models were sold in retail stores nationwide from 1/96-05/99 for about $40. Affected model numbers begin with 075 and 080 and can be found on a tag inside that reads, "SOFT CARRIER" followed by the model number. The brand name, "Snugli'®" is located on the outside of the carrier. These carriers were designed for use as both a front carrier and a backpack and feature a unique vertical strap for adjusting seat height. Color combinations include royal blue with magenta trim, teal with navy blue trim, and navy blue with purple trim.

**What to do:** Immediately stop using it and call Evenflo at 800-398-8636 anytime to receive instructions on how to exchange the carrier for a free, new version with smaller leg openings.

### Hufco-Delaware Gerry Trailtech backpack baby carriers

**Problem:** Small infants can slip through the leg openings and fall.

**Products:** 111,000 backpack baby carriers sold from 1/96-7/00 in department and baby-products stores nationwide for about $65. Affected models have black, plastic, contoured frames in color combinations of slate blue with teal trim, green with black trim, navy blue and purple with green trim, and blue and purple with silver trim. A tag on the outside of the carrier reads "GERRY®." A long tag, originally inside the carrier when sold, reads, "GERRY TRAIL TECH/TRAIL TECH HP." Writing imprinted on the plastic frame reads, "GERRY."

**What to do:** Stop using immediately and call Hufco-Delaware at 800-881-9176 anytime for a free repair kit that replaces the seat of the carrier with one that has smaller leg openings.

## Kelty K.I.D.S. Backpack child carriers

**Problem:** Child could fall out of carrier and suffer serious injury.

**Products:** 26,000 backpack child carriers sold 3/99-12/99 at specialty and sporting goods retailers such as L.L. Bean, REI, and Eastern Mountain Sports for $100 to $250. Affected models bear the following names: Expedition, Trek, Explorer, Country, and Elite and Town. Model name appears on side of carrier. Carriers are blue and have Kelty K.I.D.S. logo on backrest of seat. Kelty is also recalling carrier that L.L. Bean sold under its "L.L. KIDS" label; it bears Kelty logo on black frame hinge that connects kickstand to main frame. Kelty and L.L.

KIDS carriers bought before 3/99 have different type of seat adjustment strap and are not subject to corrective action. Seat-height adjustment strap could slip out of buckle and allow child to slide downward and fall out of carrier.

**What to do:** Call Kelty at 800-423-2320 or go to *www.kelty.com* for free repair kit.

## L.L. Bean backpack child carrier

**Problem:** Child could become entangled in harness and strangle or wriggle out of harness and fall out.

**Products:** 10,000 child carriers, model AC25, sold 1/97-10/98 for about $100 through catalog and Web site and at company's retail stores in Delaware, Maine, New Hampshire, and Oregon. Carriers are forest green with gray harness; kickstand holds device upright. Model number AC25 is on tag on upper left side of rear storage compartment. L.L. Bean label is on back of carrier.

**What to do:** Call 800-555-9717 for instructions on returning carrier for refund.

# CLOTHING

## Gap and Old Navy children's pajamas

**Problem:** Garments may be neither flame-resistant nor self-extinguishing if fabric ignites, in violation of federal flammability standards.

**Products:** 231,000 garments sold

8/99-12/99 at GapKids, babyGap, Gap Outlet, and Old Navy stores for about $20 to $40. Six pajama styles are subject to recall, including the following:

**Style 353558:** two-piece flannel pajama sets with long sleeves and pants, and buttons in front. Sets came in yellow with penguin print or navy with bear print. Labeled "Gap" and "100% polyester." Sold in sizes 2 through 14.

**Style 353554:** Like 353558, but in fleece material. Came in white, blue, and pink with snowflake print.

**Style 466291:** One-piece fleece footed pajama with zipper front and long sleeves. Came in navy with white star print. Labeled "babyGap" and "100% polyester." Sold in infant and toddler sizes XS through 3XL.

**Style 674060:** Two-piece button-front top with long sleeves and long pants. Came in lavender or blue with white piping around pant cuff; shirt has piping around collar, front placket, and cuff. Labeled "Old Navy" and "100% polyester." Sold in infant sizes 6 to 12 months through toddler sizes 2T to 3T.

**Style 733002:** One-piece fleece footed pajama with zipper front and long sleeves. Came in blue with white snowflake print. Labeled "babyGap" and "100% polyester." Sold in infant and toddler sizes XS through 4XL.

**Style 733032:** Like 733002, but in black-and-white pony print and cheetah print. Labeled "babyGap" and "100% polyester." Sold in infant and toddler sizes XS through 3XL.

**What to do:** Return garment to any Gap or Old Navy store for refund plus $10 gift certificate. For information, call Gap at 800-427-7895 or 800-653-6289, or visit *www.gap.com* or *www.oldnavy.com.*

## Gymboree Baby Boy bodysuits

**Problem:** Zipper pull could twist off and create choking hazard.

**Products:** 5,500 one-piece, short-sleeve outfits, for toddlers sizes 0 to 3T, sold 3/01-5/01 at Gymboree stores and via the company's Web site for about $17. Outfits come in green and red and have wheel-shaped zipper pull. On left arm is patch that reads "1st Place Soap Box Derby." White care label inside outfit reads "Made in Thailand" and "2000 Gymboree."

**What to do:** Return outfit to any Gymboree store for refund. For information, call 800-222-7758 or visit *ww.gymboree.com.*

## Gymboree fleece pants with elastic waistband and drawstring

**Problem:** Plastic cord lock on drawstring could come off and pose choking hazard to small child.

**Products:** 125,000 pairs of pants, sizes 0 to 3T, sold nationwide 9/00-2/01 at Gymboree stores and via the company's Web site for about $15. Pants have blue, gray, red, or green legs with stitching around the knees; gray elastic waistband; and black elastic drawstring with plastic cord lock at either end. Label on back pocket says "Gymboree"; care label says "Made in Indonesia" and "2000 Gymboree."

**What to do:** Return pants to store for refund. For information, call 800-222-7758 or visit *www.gymboree.com.*

## Infant and toddler acrylic knit hats

**Problem:** One-piece chin strap could strangle child if it snags playground equipment or other catch point.

**Products:** 150,000 hats sold 1985-1998 at mass-merchandise and discount stores for $2 to $4. Hats, which aren't identified by brand, came in various colors and styles. Inside tag reads, in part: "100 percent Acrylic . . . Made in U.S.A. . . . RN 36299" or "RN 82864."

**What to do:** Cut one-piece chin strap in half. (Consumer Product Safety Commission urges consumers not to put any type of cord around child's neck. CPSC also recommends removing drawstring from hood and neck of any children's clothing and buying children's outerwear with other types of closures such as snaps, buttons, Velcro, or elastic.)

## Nike Little Air Jordan XIV infants' and children's sneakers

**Problem:** Paint in red trim contains lead, toxic if ingested.

**Products:** 110,000 pairs of white sneakers, in sizes 2C to 10C, sold 1/99-3/99 for about $40. "JORDAN" appears on outside of tongue. Model number 132549 102 is on label on inside of tongue, above UPC code.

**What to do:** Return sneakers to store for replacement or store credit.

## OshKosh B'Gosh newborn girls' garments

**Problem:** Heat-sealed flowers on the front of the garments can detach after washing, posing a choking hazard to young children.

**Products:** 21,800 newborn girls' garments sold nationwide 8/01-12/01 for about $38. The recall includes two separate garments sold as sets. One garment is a lavender-colored velour jumpsuit with a floral printed rib knit top. The other garment is a lavender-colored French terry and velour top with printed rib knit bottom. Only jumpsuits with style numbers 516-8240 and 516-8340 and top and bottom sets with style numbers 516-8241 and 516-8341 are included in the recall. Both garments have felt fabric flowers on the front bodice. The jumpsuit has one large purple flower and two teal colored leaves on the front. The top has one large purple flower and two small blue flowers on each side. A label sewn on the inside neck of the garments reads in part "Baby OshKosh B'Gosh®," and "Made in Malaysia." Both garments were sold in sizes 0-3, 3-6, and 6-9 months.

**What to do:** Stop using these garments immediately and return them to OshKosh B'Gosh for a refund.

Contact OshKosh B'Gosh at 800-282-4674 for return instructions or go to *www.oshkoshbgosh.com.*

### Spiegel Navy blue stretch-knit velvetlike baby garments

**Problem:** Metal snaps could come off and choke child.

**Products:** 4,200 garments sold 11/98-2/99 including the following: cardigan with snap front, item number 82-5609, sold for about $15; coveralls with long sleeves and snaps at shoulder, legs, and crotch, item number 82-5604, sold for about $20; and long-sleeve T-shirt with snaps at shoulder, item number 82-5610, sold for about $13. Collar tag on garments says "elements baby… exclusively spiegel." Clothes were sold through various Spiegel catalogs and at Spiegel Ultimate Outlet stores.

**What to do:** Return garment to Spiegel Ultimate outlet store for refund.

### Tommy Hilfiger Infant cardigans

**Problem:** Snaps could come off and pose choking hazard.

**Products:** 3,800 long-sleeve fleece sweaters, in sizes 3 months to 24 months, sold 8/98-10/98 at department stores for about $36. Sweater came in red or navy and has four plastic snaps and two pockets on front.

**What to do:** Call Tommy Hilfiger Consumer Relations Dept. toll-free at 877-866-6922 for refund or exchange.

### Tommy Hilfiger white socks for infants and children

**Problem:** Heat-sealed Tommy Hilfiger flag logo could come off and pose choking hazard to small child.

**Products:** 360,000 pairs of socks sold 1/99-1/00 in two-pair packages at department and specialty stores for about $10. Recalled socks came in sizes "S/M" for 6-12 months; "L/XL" for 12-24 months; and toddler shoe sizes 7-11½. Each sock has a red, white, and blue Tommy Hilfiger flag logo applique on its side. Writing on sock reads "TOMMY HILFIGER."

**What to do:** Call distributor, Mountain High Hosiery Ltd., at 877-729-4916 or visit *www.mtnhighinc.com* to learn how to get refund or replacement socks.

## CRIBS

### Gerry and Evenflo portable wood cribs

**Problem:** If assembly hardware isn't installed tightly, mattress could fall through bottom of crib onto floor, causing child to be injured.

**Products:** 364,000 cribs, most of which were marketed under the Gerry name, sold 1/91-12/02 at department and baby-products stores for about $100. Recall involves the following models (number is located on label on mattress platform): 8212, 8222, 8232, 8242, 8252, 8282, 8301, 8302, 8311,

8312, 8321, 8322, 8331, 8332, 8341, 8342, 8351, 8352, 8381, 8382, 8512, 8522, 8532, 8542, 8552, 8582, 8712, and 8752. There have been 41 reports of mattresses falling through cribs, according to the Consumer Product Safety Commission; 17 children have reportedly suffered bumps, bruises, or scratches.

**What to do:** Stop using crib and call 800-582-9359 for free upgrade kit, which includes additional support for mattress platform. For more information, go to *www.portablewoodcrib.com.*

## Next Generation Pisces crib

**Problem:** Slats on endboards could come loose and create space wide enough to trap infant's head, possibly resulting in strangulation.

**Products:** 6,600 cribs, model 67-8100, made 3/4/97-3/10/98 and sold through 12/98 for about $200. Model No. and date of manufacture appear on sticker on bottom of headboard. Crib comes in natural-wood finish and has high-arched headboard and footboard with middle slats joined in small arch underneath top rails. Drop siderail bears "NEXT GENERATION" stamped in gold-colored letters. Fully assembled, crib measures around 30 inches wide, 54 inches long, and 50 inches high. Model 67-8102 Pisces cribs are not involved in recall.

**What to do:** Call manufacturer at 800-736-1140, Ext. 224, for replacement endboards.

## Simmons Little Folks cribs

**Problem:** Mattress could collapse and trap baby, possibly causing suffocation.

**Products:** 68,600 ash or maple cribs sold 1/98-12/00 at mass-merchandise, juvenile- product, and department stores for $200 to $600. Most cribs were made in 1998. Those sold at Sears were made from 1998-2000. "Simmons" and two-digit year of manufacture appear on label attached to headboard. "Little Folks" is written on a second label on headboard. Cribs come in more than a dozen colors, including natural, golden, and white. "Simmons" name appears on top rail. Bracket hooks used to position mattress height could break. In the past four months, Simmons has received more than 800 reports of broken bracket hooks.

**What to do:** Call Simmons at 800-421-2951 or visit *www.simmonsjp.com* for free replacement brackets.

## Tiffany and Josephine wooden cribs sold at Babies 'R' Us stores

**Problem:** Slats on drop-side rails could loosen or detach and allow child's head to be caught in the gap. Child could also fall through slat opening.

**Products:** About 2,000 cribs sold at Babies "R" Us stores from 7/01-1/03 for about $500. The cribs are made of solid wood, natural in color, and have chest of drawers attached to footboard. Many cribs can be converted into a toddler bed or adult bed. Tiffany cribs were made 6/01-10/01; Josephine model was made 1/01-10/01. Manufacture date code appears on inside bottom of headboard. The four middle numbers inside the eight-digit production number indicate month and year of manufacture. Tiffany cribs with production date codes (four middle numbers) 0601, 0701, 0801, 0901 and 1001, and Josephine cribs with codes (four middle numbers) 0101, 0201, 0301, 0401, 0501, 0601, 0701, 0801, 0901, and 1001 are subject to recall. The Consumer Product Safety Commission and manufacturer Babi Italia/LaJobi Industries have received 41 reports of slats separating from rails of the crib. No serious injuries have been reported.

**What to do:** Stop using crib and call company at 877-440-2224 for free replacement drop-side rails. Parents can also go to *www.babiitalia.com.*

· · · · · · · · · · · · · · · · · · · · · · · · · · · · · ·

# FURNITURE

### Children's furniture sold at Target stores

**Problem:** Paint contains excess lead, which is toxic if ingested.

**Products:** 8,300 pieces of furniture, decorated in circus or princess theme, sold 4/98-7/98 for about $15 to $80. Pieces include: Seal Wall Mirror (purple seal with yellow-framed mirror balanced on nose); Circus Rover (purple box/cart on yellow wheels with circus pictures on side); Circus Table and Chair Set (yellow table with red legs

and two yellow and red chairs); Clown Coat Hook (wall coat rack with clown face and red hooks); Circus Wall Shelf (with large red and yellow clown face); Clown Stepping Stool (aqua two-step stool with clown face on top step and arms and clown body on sides); Clown Tot Stool (with red top, yellow sides, and circus pictures); Banana Coat Tree (with yellow star at top, pictures of monkey, and banana-shaped coat hooks); Rocking Elephant (red, with yellow seat and aqua rockers); Princess Step Stool (two-step stool with pictures of castle on sides and rose on top step); Princess Rocker (pink, with "PRINCESS" printed on back); Crown Wall Hooks (pink crown-shaped rack with red clothes pegs); Princess Table and Chair Set (with picture of crown on each corner of tabletop and on each chair back); Crown Mirror (rectangular; pink, white, and yellow-green); Crown Wall Shelf (white, with picture of pink crown on back); Crown Tot Stool (white, with pink top and picture of crown on each end); and Crown Coat Tree (pink, with picture of crown on top).

**What to do:** Return furniture to any Target store for refund or call 800-935-5060.

### Little Ones decorative children's lamps sold at Kmart

**Problem:** Could short-circuit and catch fire.

**Products:** 280,000 wooden accent

lamps sold 1/93-3/00 for $13 to $15 in the following six styles: airplane, alphabet (ABC) letters, numbers (123), baseball bat, train, and sailboat. Products are about 15 inches high with wood base. Price label on bottom of base reads, "Made in China for Kmart Corporation." "Little Ones fun accent lamps for kids" is written on paper insert on shade.

**What to do:** Return lamp to Kmart for refund. For information, contact company at 800-635-6278.

## GATES AND LATCHES

### Evenflo Home Décor Swing™ wooden baby gates

**Problem:** The plastic mounting hardware that attaches to the wall can crack or break, allowing the wooden gate to unlatch. Children can then gain access to restricted areas, such as stairs. Also, the plastic hardware attached to the side of the gate can break, creating small parts that pose a choking hazard to young children.

**Products:** 20,500 baby gates sold nationwide from 6/99-9/01 for about $100. These Home Décor Swing™ gates have turned wooden spindles and were sold in oak or cherry finishes. Only model numbers 1555/6 with manufacture dates before September 2001 are included in this recall. Model numbers and date codes appear on the label located on the bottom of the gate.

No other Evenflo gates are affected by this recall.

**What to do:** Stop using these gates immediately, and call Evenflo at 800-576-0507 or go to *www.swinggate.com* to receive free replacement hardware.

### First Alert True Fit child safety gate

**Problem:** Plastic parts such as bumpers and hinges could break into small pieces and choke child or make gate insecure.

**Products:** 36,800 white plastic gates with gray handle, model CSSG1, sold since 10/96 for about $35. Label on gate lists brand and model. Expandable gate is pressure-mounted, but can also be installed with screw-mounted hinges so it swings open like a door. One version fits 28-inch to 47-inch openings; other version, 29½-inch to 46-inch openings.

**What to do:** Call 888-777-5599 for refund. Note: In 9/97 company recalled same model, offering free replacement gate. This recall extends to all First Alert True Fit safety gates, including those replaced during previous recall. Company no longer makes safety gates.

### Safety 1st cabinet and drawer child-lockout latches

**Problem:** Latch could break and release spring, posing choking hazard to small child. Also, child could gain access to cabinet or drawer that may contain hazardous items.

**Products:** 1.7 million packages, each containing three or four latches, sold 1/93-12/99 nationwide at toy, hardware, and department stores for about $7. Latches are white plastic with spring that keeps device closed. "SAFETY 1st" is written on top of items. Packaging reads, in part: "SAFETY 1ST" and "CABINET & DRAWER SPRING LATCHES." Straight end of metal spring is exposed on suspect latches; replacements have plastic tab over short, straight end of spring.

**What to do:** Call Safety 1st at 800-366-1282 for free replacement latches. For information, visit *www.safety1st.com.*

. . . . . . . . . . . . . . . . . . . . . . . . . . . . . .

# HIGH CHAIRS

### Cosco Options 5 high chair

**Problem:** Seat could collapse and allow child to tumble to ground, possibly resulting in serious head and facial injuries. Also, some chairs have faulty metal restraint anchors that might allow child to slip through and fall out.

**Products:** 1 million high chairs, model No. 03-286, made 12/1/97-8/11/00 and sold at mass merchandise, juvenile products, and major discount department stores for $40 to $50. Model number and date of manufacture appear on bottom of seat. High chair has five options for use: high chair, infant feeding, youth chair, play chair, and booster seat. Seat can be used in reclined infant position or adjusted to accommodate seven upright height positions for toddlers. It has four tray positions, vinyl seat pad, and removable footrest. "Cosco" appears on leg support bar, tray, and on sticker on bottom of seat. Restraint system consists of waist/crotch belt and plastic T-bar attached to tray. The Consumer Product Safety Commission and Cosco have received 168 reports of incidents involving the seats or restraints, including 57 injury reports, mostly to the head and face. Collapsing seat hazard exists with seat in either upright or recline positions.

**What to do:** Call Cosco at 800-221-6736 or visit *www.coscoinc.com* for free repair kit. The company is offering two separate kits, depending on date of manufacture. Before calling, be sure to note the four-digit date code and double check the model number.

### Graco high chairs (various models)

**Problem:** Legs could come out, causing chair to collapse and child to suffer serious injuries.

**Products:** 860,000 high chairs with white plastic seat and white metal legs, sold 1/95-6/98 at mass-merchandise, juvenile-product, and discount department stores for $30 to $35. To determine whether unit is subject to recall, check the sticker beneath seat, which bears the model and serial numbers. Model number contains 3170, 36051, or 74001 within it. The first six numbers indicate the date of manufacture. Recalled high chairs were made 1/1/95-

12/8/97 (code: 010195 through 120897). "Graco" is printed on front of tray. Company has received reports of 105 injuries, including a concussion, broken noses, cuts, black eyes, bumps, and bruises associated with high chair collapsing.

**What to do:** Call Graco at 800-617-7447 for free repair kit. (You'll need to have the high chair nearby.) For more information, visit *www.gracobaby.com* or write to the company at Box 100, Elverson, PA 19520.

## Peg Perego Prima Pappa, Roller, and Martinelli Pappa and Nanna high chairs

**Problem:** When the seat is reclined, the high chairs have a space between the armrest and backrest in which a child's head or arm can become entrapped. This can pose a risk of suffocation or injury to the heads or arms of young children.

**Products:** 325,000 high chairs sold nationwide from June 1996 through October 1999 for about $180. The recalled high chairs have seats that can be raised or lowered, and a lever on the back of the chair that allows the seat to be tilted back. The model names are located on the footrest or the seat back. A sticker on the brace connecting the front leg to the back leg reads in part, "Peg-Perego" and "Italy." High chairs with 9-inch armrests are not included in this recall.

**What to do:** Stop using the high chairs immediately. Call Peg Perego at 877-

737-3464 or go to *www.perego.com* to receive free replacement armrests that will eliminate the entrapment hazard. Consumers should not return the high chair to the store where purchased.

. . . . . . . . . . . . . . . . . . . . . . . . . . . . . . .

# JUMPERS

## Cosco Bungee Baby jumpers

**Problem:** Metal clasps can detach from the bungee cord that suspends the seat, causing the unit to fall to the floor and babies to suffer bumps, bruises, and scratches, primarily to the head.

**Products:** Recalled were 171,000 jumpers sold in juvenile-product, mass-merchandise, discount department, and specialty stores nationwide, 05/96-03/01, for about $40 to $50. The model number 04-461 or 04-468 is located on the bottom of the tray. Model number 04-461 is the Bungee Jumper and model 04-468 is the Bungee Combo Pack, which consists of the Bungee Jumper and parts to convert the Bungee Jumper to a stationary exerciser. (The stationary exerciser, called the Bungee Bouncer Exerciser, is not part of this recall.) Both bungee baby jumper models have a multicolored fabric seat with a white plastic frame with a red foam trim. Three yellow cords connect the seat to a blue plastic strap holder, which says "Cosco." Above the blue plastic strap holder is a thick yellow strap, which connects to a green bungee cord. The bungee cord attaches to a blue door hook.

**What to do:** Stop using the jumper immediately and contact Cosco at 800-314-9327 between 8 a.m. and 4:30 p.m. EST Monday through Friday or through the Web site *www.coscoinc.com* to receive a free repair kit.

. . . . . . . . . . . . . . . . . . . . . . . . . . . . . . .

# MISCELLANEOUS

## Playskool spillproof plastic drinking cups

**Problem:** Flexible spout could tear apart and pose small part choking hazard to young child.

**Products:** 273,000 two-handled cups, for children ages 6 months and older, sold nationwide 1/98-7/99 for $3 to $6. Cup includes twist-on lid with flexible yellow spout. Lid comes in various colors and bears word "Playskool." Bottom of cup reads "MADE IN CHINA" and "HASBRO." The following models are subject to recall: the Spillproof (in 6- and 8-oz. sizes); Spillproof Trainer (6 oz.); Easy Grip Spillproof (7 and 10 oz.); and Spillproof Trainer (8 oz.) and Spillproof (6 oz.) with Teletubby character decals imprinted on them. Cups came in packages of one or two.

**What to do:** Call Playskool toll-free at 888-690-6166 of visit company's Web site at *www.hasbro.com* for free replacement lid and additional information.

## Playtex Classic Patterns Cherubs and Soft Comfort latex pacifiers

**Problem:** Nipple could detach from shield and choke baby.

**Products:** 1.8 million pacifiers sold nationwide before 6/00 for $2 to $4. Classic Patterns pacifiers bear word "Cherubs" embossed in block letters on colored knob of shield. Soft Comfort model has soft, butterfly-shaped shield (with or without swivel handle). "Playtex" is embossed on swivel handle. Pacifiers came in a variety of colors and designs, and were packaged individually or in sets of two as follows:

• Soft Comfort Pacifier (1-pack), UPC code 078300-05448-1; 2-pack, UPC code 078300-05528-0

• Soft Comfort Angled Orthodontic Pacifier (1-pack), UPC code 078300-05442-9; 2-pack, UPC code 078300-05529-7

• Classic Patterns/Cherubs Oval Pacifier (1-pack), UPC code 078300-01023-4; 2- pack, UPC code 078300-01024-1

• Classic Patterns/Cherubs Angled Orthodontic Pacifier (1-pack), UPC code 078300-01118-7; 2-pack, UPC code 078300-01128-6

• Classic Patterns/Cherubs Pacifier & Holder Set, UPC code 078300-01041-8

**What to do:** Return pacifier to Playtex for free replacement or $3 coupon toward purchase of another Playtex infant feeding or soothing product. Mail to: Playtex Pacifiers, Playtex Products Inc., 20 Troy Road, Whippany, NJ 07981. Company will reimburse postage expense. For information, call 800-522-8230.

## Prince Lionheart electric baby-wipe warmer

**Problem:** Poses shock hazard.

**Products:** 152,000 warmers, style number 0224, sold 2/98-12/99 at toy, department, baby specialty stores (including Toys "R" Us and Burlington Coat Factory), and by catalog for about $25. Warmers are white plastic boxes, about 9 inches long, 6 inches wide, and 4¾ inches high. Suspect devices bear date codes 9803 through 9901. Style number and date code appear on bottom of unit. "PRINCE LIONHEART" is written on lid, and orange light is located on front to indicate when unit is on. Affected warmers might have cracks in interior tub, which allows water to contact electrical components.

**What to do:** Unplug warmer, remove wipes, and check interior. If it appears cracked, call distributor, Advance Thermo Control, at 888-843-8718, for free replacement. If tub is not cracked, unit is not subject to recall, and consumers can continue to use product, according to Consumer Product Safety Commission.

## Sassy rattles

**Problem:** The sewn-on, spherical shaped fabric eyes on the rattles can detach, posing a choking hazard to small children.

**Products:** 455,000 soft rattles sold nationwide from 8/99-10/01 for about $5. The rattles involved in the recall include:

"Lily Pad Rattle"—a green frog with four plastic legs and a multicolored belly. "Bitty Kitty Rattle"—a clear, plastic tube filled with beads connects a purple, catlike face to a purple ball. Three plastic pieces encircle the plastic tube and make a rattle sound when shaken. "This Little Piggy Rattle"—a pink piglike face is connected to a green ball by a yellow and pink arm and a blue arm. Beads inside the green ball make a rattle sound when shaken. "Goo Goo Goldfish"—A multicolored fish with pink lips, an orange fin, and a clear, plastic tube that connects the head to the tail. Beads inside the tube make a rattle sound when shaken. "Smoochie Poochie Rattle"—a blue, puppylike face with green spotted ears is connected to a blue and green spotted body. Five plastic pieces encircle the body and make a rattle sound when shaken. "Crinkly Crown Dragon Rattle"—a green dragon with a scaled, curved tail. Three blue ridges protrude from the dragon's back. A caretag attached to the head of each rattle reads in part, "Sassy" and "1999 Made in China." Rattles with the same appearance but embroidered eyes are not involved in this recall.

**What to do:** Take these toys away from young children and return them to Sassy to receive a free replacement toy. Contact Sassy at 800-781-1080 for information on how to receive the replacement toy.

### Wiggly Giggler baby rattles

**Problem:** Can break and expose noise-maker in handle, which poses choking hazard to small child.

**Products:** 100,000 rattles, a 3-inch long tube with mushroom caps on either end, sold 5/00-9/01 at specialty toy stores nationwide for $2 or $3. Rattle can be shaken, stacked, and rolled. It came in three color combinations: green with purple caps, orange with pink caps, and purple with orange caps. "Wiggly Giggler" is written on tube. Rattles with small number "3" imprinted in painted circle on base of mushroom cap end are not subject to recall.

**What to do:** Call distributor, HandsOn Toys, at 888-442-6376 for free replacement toy.

. . . . . . . . . . . . . . . . . . . . . . . . . . . . .

## PLAY YARDS

### Century Fold-N-Go care centers

**Problem**: Infant could become trapped in loose fabric in bassinet and suffocate.

**Products:** 50,000 devices, models 10-750 and 10-760, sold 3/98-8/98 for $100 to $130. Care Center is multifunction portable device on wheels that serves as play yard, bassinet, and changing table with side storage compartment. Model 10-760 has canopy. Model number and date of manufacture are on tube supporting underside of play yard. "Century" is imprinted on side of play yard. Only Fold-N-Go Care Centers with bassinet are being recalled. If bassinet has yellow inspection sticker on bottom tubing or was made 9/98 or later, it is not subject to recall.

**What to do:** Stop using the bassinet immediately and destroy the product.

### Various brands of foldable mesh-sided play yards/playpens

**Problem:** Child could strangle if clothing or loose strings catch on protruding rivets.

**Products:** More than 9.6 million play yards/play pens sold since 1960. Only models with protruding rivets are subject to recall; rivets stick out ¼-inch to ½-inch from the outside top rails. Rivets are similar to nut-and-bolt fasteners but can't be removed. Except for the Evenflo Houdini, all models are drop-sided mesh playpens that fold in half for storage. The Houdini is also mesh-sided but folds up compactly for storage or travel. The affected brands:

• 2 million Graco products made '76-11/90 and sold for $35 to $55. Word "Graco" is written on floorboard or side rail. Company is offering $20 refund with proof of destruction.

• 409,000 Bilt-Rite products made through 1989 and sold for $35 to $55. "Bilt-Rite" is written on floorboard. Company is offering $20 refund with proof of destruction.

• 2.6 million Kolcraft and Playskool

products made 1/86-5/98 and sold for $40 to $70. "Kolcraft" or "Playskool" appears on floorboard or side rail. Company is offering free repair kit.

• More than 4 million Pride-Trimble products made '90-9/91 and sold for $35 to $55. "Pride-Trimble Corp." appears on floorboard. Company is offering $15 refund with proof of destruction.

• 100,000 Pride-Trimble products—with words Pride-Trimble Inc. on floorboard—made 10/91-10/93 and sold for $35 to $55. Company is out of business; destroy and discard play yard.

• 205,000 Evenflo "Houdini" play yards made '94-96 and sold for $45. "'Evenflo" is written on plastic hinge covers. Company is providing free repair kit. Note: Models are subject to recall even if they have plastic covers over rivets. Covers can crack, break, or come off.

• 100,000 Gerry products made '86-92 and sold for $35 to $45. "Gerry" appears on floorboard. Company is offering free repair kit.

• 200,000 Strolee products made through '83 and sold for $35 to $55. "Strolee" is on side rail. Company is out of business; destroy and discard play yard.

**What to do:** Call the Consumer Product Safety Commission at 800-794-4115 for the appropriate manufacturer's telephone number. If you own a suspect play yard from a company not mentioned above, call the CPSC's hotline at 800-638-2772 to report it.

························

# STATIONARY ENTERTAINERS

## Graco Stationary Entertainer children's activity toys

**Problem:** Screw securing clicker toy to tray can come out and choke or scratch child.

**Products:** 19,000 toys, model numbers 4118C, 4118RA, and 34429, made 4/24/98-8/6/98 and sold for $59 to $69. Device resembles baby walker without wheels and has plastic tray supported by three adjustable legs. Chair in center swivels so child can play with toys attached to tray. Model and serial numbers are on label under tray; first six digits of serial number are date of manufacture. Clicker toy, made of yellow plastic, has three knobs. Yellow "Graco" label is on front of tray.

**What to do:** Remove clicker toy and call 800-281-3676 for redesigned attachment screw and instructions.

## Graco Tot Wheels Entertainer Activity Center infant walker

**Problem:** Could collapse in use and injure child.

**Products:** 31,000 walkers, model numbers 4032LN and 4032BLA, sold 9/99-2/00 at stores nationwide, including Wal-Mart and Toys "R" Us, for about $50. Model number appears underneath tray. Multicolored walker has animal-print fabric seat, five-position height adjustment, and removable green play tray. It includes 12 activities, such as a steering wheel, ball spinner, and flashing lights. "Graco Lights & Sounds" is written on label on tray. "Tot Wheels Entertainer Activity Center with Bounce" is written on label on base. According to the Consumer Product Safety Commission, Graco has received 27 reports of collapsing walkers, resulting in cuts, bruises, and sprains.

**What to do:** Call Graco at 800-345-4109 or visit *www.gracobaby.com* for free repair kit. Consumers can also write to Customer Affairs, Graco Children's Products Inc., Box 100, Elverson, PA 19520. Note: Similar Graco products also have green play tray and print seat. Only walkers with model numbers specified above are subject to corrective action.

. . . . . . . . . . . . . . . . . . . . . . . . . . . . . .

# STROLLERS

### Baby Trend Road Runner jogging strollers

**Problem:** Strollers were shipped without straps attached to the frame to secure the seat. Unless the frame straps are attached, a child in the seat of the stroller can lean forward and fall out.

**Products:** About 1,500 aluminum, three-wheeled strollers with hand brakes sold in Baby's "R" Us stores 01/99-04/99 for about $200. The affected strollers have a seat and seatback made from a blue canvas-type fabric.

The stroller has a three-strap harness that secures the child in the seat. Two additional straps snap together and secure the back corners of the seat to the stroller frame. "Baby Trend" is written on the aluminum frame. The recalled stroller is model number 9592T. The model number is written on a label located in the center of the rear axle.

**What to do:** Stop using these strollers immediately and examine the stroller to determine if the seat is strapped to the stroller frame. For more information, consumers should call Baby Trend toll-free at 800-328-7363 between 8:30 a.m. and 4:30 p.m. PST Monday through Friday, or write to Baby Trend., 2019 S. Business Pkwy., Ontario, CA 91761. Consumers also can visit the company's Web site at *www.babytrend.com.*

### BOB Trailers Inc. Sport Utility Stroller and Sport Utility Stroller D'lux

**Problem:** The stroller's front-wheel connector can crack during use, causing the wheel to separate from the frame. A jogger could lose control of the stroller or the stroller could suddenly collapse, resulting in injury to a child.

**Products:** About 3,700 jogging strollers sold through bike, baby, and outdoor-product stores and Web sites from 11/98-03/00 for about $280 to $370. The involved strollers have three wheels and are Pacific blue and black, or hunter green and black. Each stroller has a canopy. The "BOB" logo is on the stroller's frame, canopy, and seat back.

**What to do:** Stop using the stroller immediately, and return it to the store where purchased for repair. Consumers also can return the strollers to BOB Trailers for repair. For more information, call the company's toll-free number, 800-893-2447, between 9 a.m. ST Monday through Friday or access the company's Web site at *www.bobtrailers.com.*

## Century Take 2, Travel Solutions, Pioneer, Travelite, and Pro Sport 4-in-1 strollers

**Problem:** The strollers can unexpectedly collapse or the car seat/carrier adapter can unexpectedly detach. When this happens, an infant or young child inside the stroller or an attached car seat/carrier can fall to the ground and suffer serious injuries.

**Products:** 650,000 Take 2, Travel Solutions, Pioneer, Travelite, and Pro Sport 4-in-1 strollers sold in mass merchandise, juvenile-products, and discount department stores nationwide from 12/96-3/01 for between $100 and $200.

The recalled strollers are for toddlers when used alone and for infants when a car seat/carrier is connected to the stroller. The model names for the recalled strollers can be found on the footrest, the seat pad, the legs of the frame or on a white label on the side locks. The Take 2 was manufactured in 2000; Travel Solutions 1999-2000; Pioneer 1998-2000; Travelite 1997-1998; Pro Sport 1996-1999.

**What to do:** Consumers should stop using these strollers and call Graco, which now owns the Century brand name, toll-free at 800-345-4109 any time to order a free repair kit. Consumers should have their strollers available, as Graco will help them determine if they have one of the recalled models. Consumers can also log on to the company's Web site at *www.gracobaby.com.* Parents should continue to use these carriers as car seats.

## Cosco Geoby Two Ways tandem strollers

**Problem:** Plastic locks on folding mechanism could break, allowing stroller to collapse. Besides suffering injuries from fall, child could cut arm or hand on locking mechanism.

**Products:** 57,000 strollers, model numbers 01-644 and 01-645 (which includes car seat), made 2/97-2/98 and sold for about $110 and $170 at mass-merchandise and juvenile-product stores. Model number and manufacturing date (representing week and year product was made) are stamped on label on back of leg frame, just above wheel. Those made between 0697 and 0698 are subject to recall. Stroller is designed so two babies can sit one behind the other or face-to-face. Back seat reclines. Stroller has dual quilted canopies, market basket, and utility bag. "Cosco by Geoby" is written on plastic side-lock covers, and "Two Ways" is embroidered on front-seat crotch support.

**What to do:** Call 800-221-6736 for free repair kit.

## InStep and Healthrider single and double jogging strollers

**Problem:** Brake could fail and allow stroller to roll, resulting in possible injury to child.

**Products:** 44,000 strollers, model numbers ZS100, ZD200, ZS100WS, ZD200WS, ZS100HR, ZD200HR, PR100 or PR200, made 12/98-7/99 and sold at Burlington Coat Factory, J.C. Penney, Healthrider, The Sports Authority, and Target stores, among others, for about $100 for (single jogger) and $250 (double). Date of manufacture, written as T "month" R "'year" I, is located on a sticker on the lower cross tube (for example, T01R99I is January 1999). "InStep" and model number also appear on sticker. InStep model numbers ZS100, ZD200, ZS100WS, ZD200WS, PR100 and PR200 have blue and green seat, and green canopy. "ZII" is on the top and "InStep" is on the front of the stroller. Healthrider model numbers ZS100HR and ZD200HR have a blue and gray seat, and blue canopy. "Healthrider" is on the top and front of stroller.

Note: The InStep Z 11 ZS100, tested for a January 2000 Consumer Reports article, passed industry standards and

CR's own tougher standards for brakes. Our samples were manufactured outside of the manufacturing period that is subject to the recall.

**What to do:** Call InStep LLC at 800-242-6110 or visit *www.instep.net* for free, easy-to-install repair kit.

## Kolcraft LiteSport Stroller

**Problem:** Could collapse suddenly, allowing baby to fall out.

**Products:** 115,000 strollers, model 36122, sold 12/97-12/00 at department and juvenile-products stores nationwide for about $30. Label with word "LiteSport" appears on front of footrest. Model number is located on another label on back leg frame. "Kolcraft" is written on front of stroller. Kolcraft has received 124 reports of the lock mechanisms breaking, including 31 reports of the stroller collapsing.

**What to do:** Call Kolcraft at 800-922-2130 for more information and free repair kit.

## Kolcraft Ranger and Ranger Quattro strollers

**Problem:** Lock mechanisms, found on both sides of the stroller, can break and create a pinch-point hazard. Young children can be injured when their fingers, arms, or hands are pinched between parts of the locking mechanism.

**Products:** About 25,500 strollers manufactured from 12/99-06/00 and sold by mass-merchandise and juvenile-products stores nationwide 01/00-11/00 for about $80. The model number can be found on a sticker on the back-leg frame of the stroller with the manufacture date below it. Models include the Kolcraft Ranger and Ranger Quattro with model numbers 46720 and 46721. The strollers have a sticker with "Ranger" or "Ranger Quattro" on the front of the footrest, and "Kolcraft" sewn into the safety-belt harness material in the stroller's seat. The strollers also have a reversible handle that allows consumers to push the stroller while either facing the child or from behind the child. (Ranger and Ranger Quattro strollers manufactured after 06/00 have different side-lock mechanisms, and are not included in this recall.)

**What to do:** Stop using the stroller immediately and call Kolcraft's toll-free number anytime, 800-757-4770, to receive a free repair kit.

## SWINGS

### Baby Trend 'Trend Swing' infant swings sold at Toys 'R' Us stores

**Problem:** Seat could come apart, causing baby to fall out.

**Products:** 15,000 swings, models 8711 and 8722, sold 11/01-9/02 for $60 to $90. Model number appears on label on bottom of seat. Swings came in khaki/gingham and navy/white plaid, and feature a toy bar, song player, and timer. "Baby Trend" is printed on front of seat's tray; "Trend Swing" appears on swing support arm. "Baby Trend" and "Made in China" are also printed on label on bottom of seat.

**What to do:** Call Baby Trend at 800-328-7363 or visit *www.babytrend.com* or free repair kit.

### Fisher-Price 3-in-1 Cradle Swing with detachable carrier

**Problem:** When swing is used as carrier, handle locks could suddenly release, causing seat to flip forward and infant to tumble onto ground.

**Products:** 105,000 cradle swings, models 79321 and 79322, sold 3/97-1/99 nationwide at mass-merchandise, juvenile-products, and major discount stores for about $100. Model number appears on underside of motor housing and on bottom of seat. "Fisher-Price" appears on front of motor housing and on bottom of seat. Only swings with detachable carrier are subject to recall.

**What to do:** Stop using seat as infant carrier and call company at 800-505-0600 for free repair kit, or visit *www.fisherprice.com/us/help/cradle.asp* for information.

### Fisher-Price Lift & Lock Swing

**Problem:** Child could wiggle out of T-shaped restraint and fall out, resulting in serious injury.

**Products:** 2.5 million swings, model

numbers 2092, 75960, 75970, 75973, and 75980, sold 1/91-8/00 at mass-merchandise, juvenile-product, and discount department stores for about $20. Swings have red or purple seat, yellow T-shaped restraint, and blue ropes. "Fisher-Price" appears on front of shield. Model number is molded into back of seat. Fisher-Price has received 110 reports of children falling out of swing, eight of whom have suffered skull and other fractures, concussions, or severe cuts.

**What to do:** Call Fisher-Price at 800-343-1502 for free repair kit. For more information, visit *www.fisher-price.com.*

## Fisher-Price Smart Response infant swing

**Problem:** Seat could flip forward and allow baby's head to strike floor.

**Products:** 42,000 swings, product numbers 79644, 79645, and 79647, sold 12/01-3/02 at discount and juvenile-products stores for about $70. Product number is molded onto back of seat. Device is for use by infants until they are able to sit up unassisted. Swing operates in response to a sound sensor and plays music. Metal legs are blue or beige; seat, beige or white. Fisher-Price logo appears on tray. Seat can be assembled in a way that gives false impression of being securely attached.

**What to do:** Stop using swing. Call Fisher-Price at 800-942-5912 to determine whether seat is secure. If not, company will provide free replacement seat and installation instructions. For more information, visit *www.fisher-price.com.*

## Graco infant swings (various models)

**Problem:** Under certain conditions, child could fall out or slip down into seat, become tangled in safety belts and strangle.

**Products:** 7 million swings made before 11/97 and sold through 1/98 at mass merchandise, juvenile products, and major discount department stores for about $70 to $120. Swings are battery-powered or windup and are either in the traditional A-frame or open-top designs. Date of manufacture appears on label on housing on top of swing. Label bears various information, including model and serial numbers. Date is first six digits of serial number (for instance, 110197, which translates into Nov. 1, 1997). Restraint system on suspect swings consists of waist belt only; a hinged or removable tray on the products also helps restrain baby. Hazard exists if parts are missing, the restraints aren't used, or if tray pops off. There have been six deaths, according to the Consumer Product Safety Commission, and 181 reports of infants falling from swing.

**What to do:** Call company at 800-934-9082 to learn is swing is subject to corrective action and to obtain free replacement safety restraint. Consumers can also visit *www.gracoba by.com,* or write to Graco Children's Products Inc., Att: Consumer Affairs,

P.O. Box 100, Elverson, PA 19520.

## Little Tikes
## Snug 'n Secure swings

**Problem:** The buckles on the swing can break and the shoulder restraint straps can pull out of the back of the seat, causing young children to fall.

**Products:** 250,000 2-in-1 Snug 'n Secure swings sold nationwide from 12/00-9/01 for about $20. The swings are made of molded plastic and have a blue seat with a red T-shaped restraint front. The model number 4117-00 is molded underneath the seat. The "Little Tikes" logo is written on the T-shaped restraint bar on the front of the swing. The swings were sold for children ages 9 months through 4 years old. The swing is suspended with four yellow ropes. Only swings with blue or white buckles are included in this recall.

**What to do:** Stop using the swings immediately and contact Little Tikes at *www.littletikes.com* or call 800-815-4820 to receive a repair kit.

. . . . . . . . . . . . . . . . . . . . . . . . . . . . . .

# TOYS

## Baby Buzz'r
## interactive infant toy

**Problem:** Red, green, and blue button covers can come off and pose choking hazard to small child.

**Products:** 8,800 toys sold 6/01-9/01 at juvenile specialty stores, by catalog, and via the Internet for about $13. Baby Buzz'r is round plastic toy with face on front, red and blue "teethable" ear on each side, and yellow circular mirror on back. Device has red, blue, and green buttons on top. When they are pressed, toy vibrates, sounds music, or eyes light up. Consumers can identify suspect toys by squeezing button covers on top of toy with pliers. Button covers on recalled toys are rubbery and can be squeezed out of shape. Recall does not pertain to any Baby Buzz'r toys currently available.

**What to do:** Call Baby Buzz'r International at 866-222-9289 or visit *www.babybuzzr.com* to arrange free replacement.

## The Betesh Group
## John Lennon
## musical crib mobiles

**Problem:** The screws that connect the mobile's arm assembly and crib clamp can become loose if overtightened. The arms can detach and fall into the crib, injuring the baby inside.

**Products:** 47,000 mobiles sold in department and specialty stores from 06/99-08/00 for about $39. John Lennon Musical Mobiles hang from white wooden dowels that attach to cribs with white clamps. "John LennonTM" and "MADE IN CHINA" is written on the windup music box that turns the mobile. The music box plays the song "Imagine." The mobile has colorful wooden cutouts of a rhinoceros, two elephants, a giraffe, and a bird hanging from yellow ribbons. Below each animal is a round disk with a drawing of the animal it hangs from on the bottom.

**What to do:** Immediately stop using the mobile and contact The Betesh Group toll-free, 877-810-4264, or write to: The Betesh Group, One East 33rd St., New York, NY 10016, to receive a free replacement plastic mobile with stuffed animals.

## Brio Curious George monkey plush toy

**Problem:** Fabric-filled mobile phone poses choking hazard to small child.

**Products:** 3,100 toys sold 7/01-11/01 nationwide at specialty toy stores, by catalog, or via the Internet for about $25. Curious George is dressed in yellow plastic space suit with matching gloves. Toy comes with gray mesh detachable backpack that also contains red, fabric-filled mobile phone. Phone measures 1¼ inches by 1½ inches, and is tethered to backpack with 4¾-inch string. Label in collar of space suit reads: "Curious George by BRIO." "Activity George" appears on packaging. Toy is labeled for children 18 months of age and older. Back of box reads "Removable backpack with mobile phone!" Model number 32900 appears on front of box.

**What to do:** Call Brio at 888-274-6869 for refund or free replacement toy. For information, visit *www.briotoy.com*. To return toy to company, write to: Brio Corp., Safety Recall, N120 W18485 Freistadt Road, Germantown, WI 53022.

## Electronic Light 'N' Learn activity gym

**Problem:** Toy features detachable rattles with pegs that could break off and present choking hazard to small child.

**Products:** 115,000 toys sold 9/00-1/01 nationwide at KB Toys stores, KB Toy Works, KB Toy Outlet, Big Lots, Odd Lots, Pic N Save, and MacFrugals for $20 to $30. Activity gym is multicolored toy that converts into three different toys, including a crib toy, floor gym, and musical keyboard. Gym's main console has five buttons with numbers that make music when pressed and that can automatically light up. Five detachable rattles shaped like bear, snail, star, half moon, and horse hang from bottom of console. Label under handle on main console reads, in part: "'ELECTRONIC LIGHT N' LEARN ACTIVITY GYM MODEL: 8735, MADE IN CHINA."

**What to do:** Return toy to store for refund. Consumers who bought toy online should return it to nearest KB Toys store. For information, call KB Toys at 800-279-5066.

## Fisher-Price Bounce 'n Play Activity Dome

**Problem:** Nylon bands that keep play area level could detach and cause surface to tilt. That could cause infant to slide into one end, become trapped, and possibly suffocate.

**Products:** 235,000 activity domes, model 79534, sold since 12/98. Dome is portable play and nap space for infants.

To determine if product is subject to recall, check the model number and six-character code on tag on bottom of unit. All codes that end with 8 are subject to recall, as are those with codes ending in 9 and beginning with numbers 001 through 286. "Fisher-Price" appears on canopy. Note: Activity domes with a green dot on bottom (and a "quality approved" label on sticker on box) have been repaired and are not subject to corrective action.

**What to do:** Call Fisher-Price at 800-505-0600 to obtain free repair kit and installation instructions or visit *www.fisherprice.com/us/help/cradle.asp #BounceNPlay* for information.

## Fisher-Price Intelli-Table toys

**Problem:** Two red knobs on the toy can break off, creating small parts that can pose a choking hazard for young children.

**Products:** About 20,000 of the toy tables sold in mass-merchandise and discount stores nationwide 10/00-03/01 for about $70. The recalled model is a round, plastic activity table with a blue, removable top with a Fisher-Price logo on the top and a date code from 269(0) through 281(0) molded into the underside. The base of the unit is red with three legs that are blue, yellow, and teal green. Model number 77148 and the words "Mattel, Inc." and "China" are molded into the bottom of the red base. Only models manufactured from 09/25/00-10/07/00

are being recalled. The red knobs that break off are located on the yellow and white interchangeable play rings.

**What to do:** Remove the toy from young children and contact Fisher-Price's toll-free Recall Hotline, 800-220-7137, anytime, to order a free repair kit with two replacement knobs and new screws. Consumers can also visit the Fisher-Price Web site at *www.fisher -price.com* for more information.

## Fisher-Price Sparkling Symphony battery-powered spinning crib mobiles

**Problem:** Liquid from corroded batteries could drip onto the infant, possibly causing chemical burns.

**Products:** About 233,000 mobiles, model number 71985, sold 12/99-12/01 at toy and discount department stores for about $25. The Fisher-Price logo appears at the top of the upper arm, over the silver decoration. The model number appears on the lower arm. The suspect units were made between 10/99 and 11/00. A six-character date code is on the upper arm. A remote control carries both model number and date code. The company has received 30 reports of leaking batteries, six of which resulted in minor burns.

**What to do:** Stop using the mobile. Call Fisher-Price at 800-357-9460 or go to *www.service.mattel.com.* If the mobile is subject to recall, the manufacturer will mail you a free repair kit to seal the battery compartment and prevent leakage.

## KB Toys Electronic Light N' Learn Activity Gym

**Problem:** Five detachable hanging rattle toys have small round pegs at the top of the toys that can break off, posing a choking hazard to young children.

**Products:** 115,000 activity gyms sold in KB Toy stores, KB Toy Works, KB Toy Outlet, Big Lots, Odd Lots, Pic N Save, and MacFrugals from 9/00-1/01 for $20 to $30. The Electronic Light N' Learn activity gym is a multicolored toy that converts into three different toys, including a crib toy, a floor gym, and a musical keyboard. The gyms' main console has five buttons with numbers that make music when pressed and automatically light up when the continuous song play option is selected. Five detachable rattles in the shape of a bear, snail, star, half-moon and horse hang from the bottom of the console. A label under the handle on the gyms' main console reads in part "ELECTRONIC LIGHT N' LEARN ACTIVITY GYM MODEL: 8735, MADE IN CHINA."

**What to do:** Remove the toy from children immediately and return it to the store where purchased for a refund. Consumers who purchased the toy online should return the toy to the closest KB Toy store or contact KB Toys for return information. For additional information, contact KB Toys at 800-279-5066 between 8 a.m. and 1 a.m. ET Monday through Saturday and between 10 a.m. and 10 p.m. ET Sunday. Consumers also can visit the firm's Web site at *www.kbkids.com.*

## Mula stacking toy sold at Ikea stores

**Problem:** Red ball could choke small child.

**Products:** 28,000 toys, 8½ inches high, sold 10/91-4/99 for about $6. Toy consists of eight brightly colored wooden rings, red ball on top, and pedestal base with stacking rod. Sticker under base reads "Design and Quality" and "IKEA of SWEDEN." Toy came in white cardboard box with "MULA" printed in orange, or was shrink-wrapped with "MULA" and "Stacking rings" printed on plastic.

**What to do:** For replacement top piece, bring red ball to store or mail it to Ikea, 496 W. Germantown Pike, Plymouth Meeting, PA 19462 (postage will be reimbursed). Or bring entire toy to store for refund.

## Playskool Busy Poppin' Pals toys

**Problem:** Small springs inside these toys can break loose, posing a choking and laceration hazard to young children.

**Products:** 590,000 Busy Poppin' Pals toys and Sesame Street Busy Poppin' Pals toys recalled in two different actions. Busy Poppin' Pals were sold in mass-merchandise stores and toy stores 1/96-8/00. Sesame Street Busy Poppin' Pals were sold 11/94-12/96 in merchandise and toy stores, including Toys "R" Us. Both toys sold for about $10. Busy Poppin' Pals is a 13-inch-long white plastic toy with blue, yellow, and red buttons, levers, and knobs of various shapes that, when activated, make animal characters pop up from under the toy's base. The animals are hidden under blue, yellow, or red lids that have the numbers 1 through 5 on top. The lid colors match the color of the buttons, levers, and knobs that activate them. The pop-up animals are a giraffe, elephant, panda bear, lion, and monkey. The toy has a white carry handle and has the Playskool logo on the front. The model number 5415 and "MADE IN CHINA" are imprinted on the bottom of the toy. Sesame Street Busy Poppin' Pals toy is similar toy, but with a green button instead of red. Sesame Street characters pop up from under the toy's base. The characters-Elmo, Ernie, Big Bird, Bert, and Cookie Monster are hidden under corresponding blue, yellow, or green lids that have the numbers 1 through 5 imprinted on top. The model number, "5446," "MADE IN CHINA," and "C-023B" are imprinted on the bottom of the toy. (Busy Poppin' Pals with model number 6205 have different springs, and are not part of the recalls.)

**What to do:** Remove from children immediately and contact Playskool, toll-free, at 877-518-9743 anytime or visit its Web site at *www.hasbro.com* to receive a free, redesigned replacement toy.

## Playskool Weebles toy tractor

**Problem:** Plunger on top could break off and choke child.

**Products:** 116,000 toys sold since 1/96 for $13. Plastic tractor is mostly yellow with blue wheels and red plunger. Trailer is mostly red with blue wheels. Farm girl spins when you press plunger. Item number 5242 is on bottom of tractor.

**What to do:** Call 888-377-3335 for free replacement.

## Precious Moments Tender Tails plush toys

**Problem:** Pom-poms could come off and pose choking hazard to small child.

**Products:** 472,000 stuffed toys sold 5/98-8/99 nationwide at gift, card, and collectible stores for about $7. Recalled toys include Lady Bug (item number 476080), Bee (464295), Butterfly (482234), and Reindeer (381969). Item number appears on purple "adoption registration" attached to toy. Toys are about 6 inches long and bear label that reads, in part: "TENDER TAILS, by ENESCO," and "MADE IN CHINA." Pom-poms are antennae on head of ladybug, bee, and butterfly. On reindeer, they appear as holiday ornaments on antlers.

**What to do:** Cut off pom-poms and return them, with your name, address, and phone number, to Enesco for free Tender Tails Hippo toy (another Tender Tails toy will be substituted when hippo supply is exhausted).

Write to Enesco, P.O. Box 499, Itasca, IL 60143-0499. For information, call 800-632-7968, visit *www.enesco.com*, or e-mail the company at ttpompoms @enesco.com.

## Safari Ltd. Shapes or Peek Inside wooden toy puzzle

**Problem:** Small parts could choke child.

**Products:** 10,200 puzzles sold 4/98-1/99 for about $5. Puzzle has 10 different-shaped pieces with colorful laminated paper veneer and plastic knob handles. Lifting piece reveals name of shape underneath. Oval and rhombus pose choking hazard. Puzzle is labeled "SHAPES… SAFARI… No.9536-12 … 1997 SAFARI LTD." Card insert in plastic packaging says "SAFARI LTD … PEEK INSIDE PUZZLE, Made in Taiwan, NO. 9536-12 SHAPES."

**What to do:** Call 800-615-3111 for refund or replacement. (Redesigned puzzle, model 9549-12, isn't being recalled.)

## Snuggle Bear plush toy distributed as a premium with Snuggle fabric softener

**Problem:** Eyes and nose could come off and pose choking hazard to small child.

**Products:** 4 million 5-, 8-, and 10-inch cream-colored stuffed bears given away with Snuggle fabric softener. The 5-inch bears come in four styles: Pajama Bear wears blue pajamas with yellow moon and star design; Nightcap Bear wears blue nightcap with yellow moon and star design; Purple Blanket Bear holds purple blanket; Pink Blanket Bear holds pink blanket. The 8-inch-long bear is made of terry or plush fabric. The 5-inch and 8-inch bears were included with Snuggle that was sold 5/99-7/01 at grocery and discount department stores. The Pajama and Nightcap 5-inch bears also were given away to consumers who mailed in proofs of purchase for Snuggle 11/01-12/01. The 10-inch plain stuffed bear is in a sitting position and has tan paws and ears. The 10-inch bears were distributed 5/97-5/98 to consumers who sent in a proof of purchase for Snuggle plus additional money. All bears have tags that read "Snuggle®" and "Made in China." Unilever Home and Personal Care USA, the maker of Snuggle, has received 32 reports of the eyes and noses coming off. No injuries have been reported.

**What to do:** Be sure children can't reach the toy. Contact Unilever at 800-896-9479 or visit *www.snuggletime.com* for information on how to receive a coupon for free Snuggle fabric softener. No other Snuggle Bears are involved in this recall. In May 2001, the Nightcap Bears were recalled because the yellow pom-pom on the nightcap could detach, also posing a choking hazard.

## 'Sulley and Boo' plush dolls sold at The Disney Store

**Problem:** Boo doll's ponytail holder could detach and pose choking hazard to small child.

**Products:** 14,500 dolls, from the 2001 animated movie Monsters, Inc., sold 7/02-10/02 at The Disney Store nationwide for about $20. Recalled "Sulley" doll is a 12-inch blue monster with purple spots, a tail, and horn. Character is holding in its right arm a 6-inch doll named "Boo," a little girl with dark hair and small pink ball ponytail holders and rubber bands. Labels on Sulley doll reads, "Disney Store, SULLEY W/BOO 12," and "Made in China." Recall involves only the 12-inch "Sulley and Boo" dolls sold exclusively at The Disney Store, not those sold through the Disney catalog or any other retail outlet. Also, the battery-operated talking version of this toy is not subject to recall.

**What to do:** Remove and discard ponytail holders and rubber bands from Boo doll's hair or return toy to any Disney Store for refund. For information, call 800-566-3161 or visit *www.disneystore.com.*

### Tiger Electronics Pooh Poppin' Pianos

**Problem:** Green top of carrot-shaped microphone could break off and pose choking hazard to small child.

**Products:** 202,000 toys sold 8/97-8/99 at toy and discount department stores for about $20. Piano is mostly lime green with eight characters from "Winnie the Pooh" series that move up and down when corresponding keys are pressed. Orange and green microphone attaches to piano with short cord. Toy announces eight color names and plays piano sounds and children's songs. Only pianos with serial number starting with "CO15D" or "WT" are subject to recall. Serial number appears on label inside battery compartment and on bottom of packaging.

**What to do:** Call Tiger Electronics toll-free at 888-748-2860 or go to *www.tigertoys.com* for instructions on returning toy for free replacement.

### VeggieTales' Dave and the Giant Pickle play set

**Problem:** Figures pose choking hazard for young children.

**Products:** 44,000 play sets with 10 figures, including asparagus, grape, gourds, French peas, pickle, sheep, and tents, sold 9/98-2/99 at Christian bookstores and by catalog for about $20. Six figures have plastic plug in base that could come out, and French peas figure poses choking hazard because of size and shape. Toys came in mostly blue box showing scenes from animated video. Product number SPCN 9834 501 358 appears under UPC code on back of box.

**What to do:** Call 800-743-2514 for replacement figures.

. . . . . . . . . . . . . . . . . . . . . . . . . . . . .

# WALKERS

### Bikepro and Oriental International Trading baby walkers

**Problem:** Fail to meet voluntary safety

standard to reduce the risk of baby tumbling down stairs.

**Products:** 50,000 Bikepro walkers sold 1/00-8/01 at independent discount stores in Arizona, California, Colorado, Michigan, Missouri, New York, and Texas for $18 to $22. Walkers are blue, green, yellow, and pink, with musical tray and thick foam-padded seat; some have "stoppers" on the side. Suspect units bear the following model numbers on product packaging: 305, 308RK, 309STP, 384, 386, 388, 388STP, 389STP, 392STP, 393STP, 395, or 399STP. Warning label affixed to walker reads, in part: "WARNING: NOTE: NEVER LEAVE CHILD UNATTENDED" or "NEVER LEAVE YOUR BABY ALONE IN THIS BABY WALKER" or "USE ONLY FOR CHILDREN WHO CAN SIT UNASSISTED." Walker may also bear label with the word "BEBELOVE." Also, 3,500 Oriental International Trading "Honey" walkers sold 5/01- 6/02 in Arizona, California, Illinois, North Carolina, New York, and Texas for $18 to $22. Suspect units bear model numbers 802, 820, 860, or 862 on seatback.

**What to do:** Stop using walker and return it to store for refund. For Bikepro walker, call 800-261-2559 between 9 a.m. and 5 p.m. Pacific time, or send e-mail to bikeproinc@aol.com. For Honey walker, call Oriental Trading Co. at 866-666-9868 between 9 a.m. and 5 p.m. Pacific time, or go to *www.bike-stroller.com.*

## Fisher-Price Get Up & Go walker

**Problem:** Car-shaped toy, designed for children to lean on as they're learning to stand and walk, could tip over. Also, some toys have windshield wipers that stick out. Both conditions could lead to injuries.

**Products:** 246,000 three-sided push toys, sold 7/97-8/00 at toy, mass-merchandise, and discount stores for about $30. Device is white with blue sides and has activities such as rotating mirror/phone, windshield wiper, and steering wheel with yellow horn. Back wheels can be locked into place to prevent rolling. Fisher-Price logo appears between headlight decorations. Models with front bar for babies to grasp and/or green windshield wipers are subject to recall. Fisher-Price, which has received 330 reports of children falling while using or standing near toy and suffering bumps, bruises, and cuts, will help consumers determine whether they have suspect product.

**What to do:** Call company at 800-343-1502 for free repair kit that will eliminate front bar and windshield wiper. For information, visit *www.fisher-price.com.*

## Kolcraft Tot Rider walkers

**Problem:** Cover on walker's removable music center could break off and pose choking hazard to small child.

**Products:** 3,356 walkers, model 14302, sold 2/00-1/01 at mass-merchandise and juvenile-product stores for $40 to $50. Model number and date of manufacture appear on base of walker. "Tot Rider," "Music Center," and "Kolcraft" appear on front of device. Music center tray has steering wheel, gear shift, buttons, and speaker that plays music.

**What to do:** Remove music center and call Kolcraft at 800-453-7673 for free replacement tray. Note: Kolcraft Tot Rider, model 14303, is not subject to recall.

## Kolcraft toy attachments on walkers sold under Tot Rider and Carter's names

**Problem:** Flower toy on walker tray could detach and expose sharp edges, which could cut the child.

**Products:** 410,000 baby walkers sold 12/00-10/02 at department, discount, and juvenile product stores for $20 to $40, including the following: "Tot Rider" models 14303-AC, 14303-CC, and 14401-OT. Model number is printed on sticker on inside wall of base. "Tot Rider" and "Kolcraft" are printed on sticker on front of walker. "Carter's" models 14303-LB, 14303-UE, and 14304-LJ. Model number is printed on sticker on inside wall of base. "Carter's" and "Music Center" are printed on sticker on front of walker. Models 14303 and 14304 were made 12/00-8/02; model 14401 was made 1/00-7/02. Date of manufacture appears on sticker bearing model number. Some walkers were made in the U.S.; others were made in China.

**What to do:** Remove detachable toy bar or music-center toy tray and call Kolcraft at 888-695-9988 for free replacement bar or tray. Or go to *www.kolcraft.com.*

## Safety 1st Mobile 4 Wheelin Walker

**Problem:** Three-spoke steering wheels pose a hazard to children's lower teeth, and telephone could break apart, posing a choking hazard.

**Products:** 170,000 walkers, model numbers 45701, 45701A or 45701B only, sold 4/98-4/99 for about $50 at mass-merchandise, juvenile-product, and major discount department stores. Model numbers are stamped underneath the walker tray. Walker has a green body and includes a three-spoke steering wheel with squeaking horn, clicking keys, two rearview mirrors, and a phone with electronic ring. Other writing under the body includes "Made in the U.S.A., 1997," and "Safety 1st, Inc."

**What to do:** Call 800-964-8489, or write to Consumer Relations Dept., Safety 1st Inc., 45 Dan Road, Canton, MA, 02021, Attn: Repair Kit, for free repair kit.

# Index